FALL OF EAST PAKISTAN:
THE FORGOTTEN WAR
FORGOTTEN YET NEVER FORGIVEN

The most comprehensive and incisive
account of the 1971 War between
India and Pakistan which resulted in

THE CREATION OF BANGLADESH
and
THE SURRENDER AT DACCA

W0010594

Brigadier (Retired) Karrar Ali Agha

ISBN: 978 – 969 – 23257 – 0 – 7

ABOUT THE AUTHOR

Brigadier Karrar Ali Agha was born in 1941 and educated at Cadet College, Hasan Abdal (1954-56) and Government College, Lahore (1956-60).

He was commissioned in the Pakistan Army in April 1962. Participated in the Rann of Kutch Operation in April 1965, and thereafter in the 1965 Indo-Pak War in the Chawinda Sector as a Captain.

In March 1969, he was posted to the elite Corps of East Pakistan Rifles (EPR), where he served in several key appointments: Adjutant Chittagong Sector; Commander 11 Wing EPR Chittagong; GSO-2 in HQ EPR, Dacca; Commander 1 Wing EPR Comilla; and, second-in- command Dacca Sector. In these assignments, he came across events and personalities, which normally fall to the experience of far more senior officers in normal Army duty. He thus gained an invaluable insight into the political landscape of East Pakistan.

He witnessed the cataclysmic events of 25th March 1971 and its aftermath while in Comilla. For a brief period, April to June 1971, he also functioned as the Administrator of Comilla city. He reverted to the Army in late August 1971 and then participated in the 1971 Indo-Pak War in the Shakargarh Sector.

He attended the Command & Staff College, Quetta in 1973 and the same year was selected to attend the Technical Staff Course in Royal Military College of Science, UK (1973-74). On return, he was posted as the Brigade major of an infantry brigade.

He was promoted Lt Col in 1976 and was soon to serve on the faculty of Command & Staff College Quetta, 1978-79. He attended the Armed Forces War Course in the National Defence College Rawalpindi in 1980. Promoted a Colonel in 1981, He was posted as the Colonel Staff of an infantry division. In 1983, he was promoted a Brigadier. Later, he served as Director Operations & Intelligence in Joint Staff Headquarters, Rawalpindi 1986-89.

He retired in 1990.

The Author

**This book is a humble homage
to
The officers and men
Of
The Pakistan Army
and
The East Pakistan Rifles
and
their families
who sacrificed their lives during this war.**

"There is much for Pakistan to come to terms with what happened in 1971. But the answers don't lie in unthinking vilification of the fighting men who performed so well in the war against heavy odds in defence of national policy. Rather in failing to honour them, the nation dishonours itself."

Sarmilla Bose, *"Dead Reckoning"*

(Sarmilla Bose is a niece of "Netaji" Subhash Chander Bose, Assistant Editor, Anand Bazaar Patrika, Calcutta, Visiting Scholar at George Washington University, USA.)

TABLE OF CONTENTS

PREFACE

This book is essentially a continuation of and a sequel to my earlier book WITNESS TO CARNAGE 1971. In that book, the saga of the separation of East Pakistan was described from its earliest stages, eventually leading up to the events that took place in Operation SEARCHLIGHT till the end of May 1971. This book, THE FORGOTTEN WAR, then takes up the narrative thereafter right till the cataclysmic day of 16th December 1971 and the surrender of Dacca (now Dhaka).

16th December always evokes painful, bitter and melancholy memories in the heart of every Pakistani as the secession of East Pakistan and the emergence of Bangladesh as an independent, sovereign state became a tangible reality on this date in 1971. The real story of how and why this national catastrophe precipitated, a defeat in detail as far as Pakistan was concerned in all its dimensions, political, military and social, has been described in these two books 'WITNESS TO CARNAGE 1971' and the current volume 'THE FORGOTTEN WAR', an honest, unbiased and accurate rendition and analysis of facts as they really occurred.

My personal association with this horrendous human and national tragedy commenced in March 1969, when I was posted to the East Pakistan Rifles (EPR), an elite paramilitary force of East Pakistan. Coincidently, I reported for my new assignment in Dacca just one day after the declaration of Martial Law in Pakistan on 25th March 1969 by General Agha Muhammad Yahya Khan, the Army C-in-C.

After a brief sojourn in Dacca, I was posted to Chittagong as the Adjutant of the Sector Headquarters of EPR, in which appointment I continued till October 1969. I was then appointed, on promotion to the rank of major, to command the prestigious 11 EPR Wing, also located in Chittagong. In that capacity, I was responsible for border protection and anti-smuggling duties over much of Chittagong Hill Tracts (bordering India) and Cox's Bazar area along River Naaf, bordering Burma. At the same time, I was also responsible for law and order and internal security duties in the civil districts of Chittagong and Chittagong Hill Tracts, as and when required by the civil authorities.

Consequently, I was a regular participant of periodic conferences held by Sub Martial Law Administrator (SMLA) Chittagong, Commissioner Chittagong Division, and Deputy Commissioners of Chittagong and Chittagong Hill Tracts districts. These meetings as well as frequent official and social interaction with these key officials and the civil society in general provided me with an understanding of the political, economic and social problems as well as complexities of that troubled province at a relatively early stage of my career.

I was not destined to stay for long in Chittagong and in April 1970 I was posted to the critical appointment of General Staff Officer-2 (GSO- 2) in Headquarters (HQ) of East Pakistan Rifles in Dacca. In that key appointment, I was the principal staff officer of Director General EPR, dealing with Operations and Intelligence. As part of my duties, I routinely dealt with senior functionaries of Headquarters Eastern Command, 14 Infantry Division as well as the Government of East Pakistan. I attended nearly all important conferences dealing with law and order, internal security and political affairs, and thus formed an understanding of the multifarious problems and their inherent complexities then facing East Pakistan.

In February 1971, I was posted to command 1 Independent Wing EPR at Comilla. I had barely settled down in my new job when the cataclysmic events of March 1971 overtook us all and I was caught right in the middle of it. After the situation somewhat stabilized there, I was recalled to Dacca in June 1971 to help reorganize and transform a truncated, demoralized and non-functional EPR into East Pakistan Civil Armed Forces (EPCAF).

I was posted back to West Pakistan in September 1971. Even after my return, I continued to maintain an active interest in the affairs and developments taking place in East Pakistan, leading up to the war and then the inevitable ignominy of surrender. Though I did not actually participate in the Indo-Pakistan War 1971 in the Eastern Theatre, I learnt its detailed accounts from several friends and colleagues on their eventual repatriation from India. This book THE FORGOTTEN WAR is indeed based upon this critical, factual input, supplemented by a vast research into most of the available source material and books by authors from Pakistan, India and Bangladesh, including many by actual participants at various level.

As can be expected, much has already been written about the Indo-Pakistan War of 1971, but it is not without surprise and disappointment that I noted two very glaring incongruities in most of these accounts:

a. In almost every account of this war, both the Pakistani and Indian authors have generally preferred to narrate the events from their own side only and simply glossed over the actions and reactions on the other side. Moreover, many of these accounts have remained restricted in their scopes to events relating to their own unit or formation only. Thus, hardly any holistic, multidimensional and comprehensive account of what really happened in that war in real time is currently available.

b. Most of these accounts, particularly by senior officers who actually participated in these events one way or another, have engaged in self-justification as well as character assassination of other participants; some honourable exceptions notwithstanding.

This author, in all humility, has made a conscious effort to avoid these pitfalls. It is for the esteemed reader to judge how far he has succeeded in this endeavour.

We certainly owe it to the future generations of Pakistan and Bangladesh to apprise them of the undisguised and unvarnished TRUTH as only we, who lived through that horrible period, know it. After our generation is gone, this truth will be lost forever in the sands of time and leave behind deep, permanent scars on the collective psyche of the two nations, that were once one country.

In a way, thus, these two books are a message to the peoples of both these nations to learn, understand and rationalize the real and essential truth behind the traumatic events of that tragic period. This is an appeal to develop the emotional maturity to confront reality, since that is the only way we shall be able to put this tragedy finally behind us. It is no doubt a plea to forgive and forget, but only from an altar of truth and reality, and not from chauvinistic rhetoric.

This narrative will, perhaps, make it obvious that these tragic events were matrixed in a psychology of arrogance, ambition, demagoguery and relentless lust for power. Despite that, it is our contention that there were neither permanent heroes nor enduring villains amongst the main characters of this saga; no angels and no demons. Perhaps they were all *honourable men* who, in words of Bhagvad Geeta, were only performing their perceived *Karma*, without paying any heed to the consequences.

Brigadier (Retired) Karrar Ali Agha

ACKNOWLEDGMENTS

I gratefully acknowledge the liberal use that I have made of the published works of a large number of authors and commentators from Pakistan, India and Bangladesh in order to develop and present a holistic, comprehensive, and multidimensional account of this war. I have made a conscious effort to acknowledge this debt, wherever applicable. I humbly offer my apologies where, due to oversight, I failed to do so; the omission is in no way intentional.

I would also like to bring on record that the views expressed in this book are entirely my own or those of the quoted sources. These do not reflect any Government or official opinion *per se;* neither have I taken recourse to any unpublished classified official records or protected documents.

I am also grateful to my friends Lt General Javed Ashraf Qazi and Nasim Ahmed Khan and my son Dr Irfan Ali Agha for reviewing my manuscript and making useful suggestions. I would be failing in my duty if I did not bring on record the efforts put in by Qudrat Ullah, a draftsman of my old unit, 25 Signals Battalion, in drawing up the operational maps. Last but not the least, I must acknowledge the technical expertise and hard work put in by my young grandson Hasan Syed in converting my manuscript to book format. I also thank my young grandchildren Shahnawaz Syed in improving these maps further and Zoha Raza who helped me a lot in typing.

One word of explanation. I have consciously chosen to designate various places in this narrative by the names as applicable at the time of the specific occurrence. Thus, Dhaka has been called Dacca till the time it was changed by the Government of Bangladesh. Thus, it was East Bengal till 23rd March 1956 and East Pakistan, till the fall of Dacca. Similarly, Kolkutta remains Calcutta in this narrative. No other implication is implied or intended.

Karrar Ali Agha

1

THE AFTERMATH OF THE ARMY OPERATION

Niazi Takes Command

Within about a week of the commencement of Operation SEARCHLIGHT on 25th March 1971, it had become fairly clear to the military planners in Pakistan, that what had been originally conceived as essentially a law and order situation had now developed into a full scale civil war. The Eastern Command was then facing stiff and determined resistance by the revolting Bengali troops and had also become vulnerable to the possibility of Indian intervention. On 28th March, 1971 a review of the overall situation in East Pakistan was submitted to HQ CMLA by Major General Farman Ali Khan wherein the situation was succinctly summarized as follows:

"The Army in complete control of Dacca Airport, cantonments of Comilla, Sylhet, Rangpur, Saidpur, Khulna and Jessore. They are all isolated. No road communication exists between them. Chittagong under rebel control." [1]

According to General Farman, the writ of the Pakistan Army was then confined to just a few cantonments, and even these were under heavy pressure from the revolting troops. The rebels were in complete control of the countryside as well as the entire railway system. They had set up parallel administrations in every district and ruthless atrocities were being perpetrated against West Pakistanis, Biharis, and pro-Pakistan Bengalis. Anyone loyal to Pakistan was labelled as a collaborator, and subjected to the severest punishment, often summary executions.

The logistic situation in the Eastern Theatre at that point in time was summed up by Major General Mitha, in a message to the GHQ as follows:

---

[1] Maj Gen Farman Ali Khan, How Pakistan Got Divided, page 88.

1

"This operation has now developed into a civil war. No long distance moves possible. No ferries or boats available. In fact, the movement has become the chief obstacle for conducting operations or restoring economy and will remain so for some time. It is therefore essential that Armed Forces develop own independent capabilities in all fields...." [2]

In view of this serious situation, a complete review of the command set-up in East Pakistan was deemed necessary by the GHQ. A change in the critical appointment of Commander Eastern Command, held by General Tikka Khan in addition to the gubernatorial functions, was logically the first one to be reviewed.

A cruel fate thus smiled on Major General Amir Abdullah Khan Niazi, who was then enjoying the command of an infantry division in the city of Lahore. On 3rd April 1971, he was summoned to the GHQ in Rawalpindi to meet with General Abdul Hameed Khan, the Army Chief of Staff (COS). Niazi was conferred his third star in an out of turn promotion and directed to take over the Eastern Command with immediate effect. At that time, he was twelfth in the seniority list of the Pakistan Army; a couple of senior generals had already declined to accept the third senior-most post of the Army and wriggled out of it on one pretext or another. On this occasion, General Hamid was pleased to describe Niazi as "the highest decorated officer of our Army, and one of our best field commanders". Yet there were many others who openly disagreed with this hyperbolic description. Lt General Gul Hasan Khan in his memoirs has described him as, *"one of the weaker divisional commanders prior to his promotion to Lt General and his appointment to Eastern Command"*. At another point he candidly opines, *"His professional ceiling was no more that of a company commander".* [3]

The newly promoted Lt General Niazi arrived in Dacca the next day but formally took over the command only on 10th April. Just a day later, the GHQ ordered a comprehensive reorganization of the Martial Law as well the Eastern Command hierarchy, as follows:

• General Tikka Khan's portfolio of responsibilities was simplified; he was relieved of his military command and tasked to focus on his duties as the full- time Governor/Martial Law Administrator of the province. Henceforth, his sole purview would be the civil as well as martial law administration of the troubled province.
• Major General Farman Ali Khan appointed the Advisor to the

---

[2] Lt Gen A A Khan Niazi, The Betrayal of East Pakistan, OUP, 1998, page 48.
[3] Lt Gen Gul Hasan Khan, *Memoirs,* page 82.

Governor.

• Brigadier Ghulam Jilani Khan appointed Chief of Staff Eastern Command, replacing Brigadier Ali el Edroos.

• Major General Rahim Khan appointed GOC 14 Division, relieving Major General Khadim Raja.

• Major General Muhammad Jamshed, SJ & Bar, MC appointed DG EPR, now EPCAF (East Pakistan Civil Armed Forces) replacing Brigadier Nisar Ahmed Khan, SJ.

• Majors General Shaukat Riza and Nazar Hussain Shah continued as GOCs 9 and 16 Divisions respectively.

• Rear Admiral Muhammad Sharif and Air Commodore Inamul Haq continued as commanders of Naval and Air Force components of the Eastern Command respectively.

• Major General A. O. Mitha, who had been unofficially functioning as Deputy Commander Eastern Command, reverted to the GHQ.

General Niazi had thus assumed overall command on 10th April 1971. Before him, Major General Khadim Raja was in charge of all the operations under Operation SEARCHLIGHT. It was therefore incumbent upon him to brief all the newly arrived general officers on the operational environment in East Pakistan. First of all, he briefed Major General Rahim Khan regarding the operational responsibilities and other relevant matters relating to 14 Division. Next, he was scheduled to brief General Niazi *"about the overall military situation in the province and give him suggestions on the conduct of operations in the foreseeable future on 11 March."[4]*

On the morning of 11th April, General Raja went over to HQ Eastern Command to meet General Niazi with a view to briefing him. He had already requested Niazi to have a map of East Pakistan available in his office. As Khadim entered Niazi's office a rather astonishing situation accosted him; no map but Niazi in a nonchalant mood. In a very jovial bonhomie, he put his hand on General Khadim's shoulder, and said, *"Yar, larai ki fikr nahin karo, who to hum kar lain gey. Abhi to mujhey Bengali girlfriends' kay phone number dey do."[5]* (Don't worry about the war, my friend, we will manage that. For now, just give me the phone numbers of your girlfriends.

For General Khadim Raja, renowned in the Army for being straitlaced and upright in his personal conduct, these words must have come like a thunderbolt. In disgust, he just left General Niazi's office, saying *"General,*

---

[4] Maj Gen Khadim Hussain Raja, *"A Stranger in my Own Country"*, OUP, page 96.
[5] Ibid, page 99.

3

you should have known me better." After that, he walked across to the office of the Chief of Staff, Brig Ghulam Jilani Khan (later Lt General) and left some notes on his table. Reproduced as **Annexure A.**[6]

As General Niazi assumed command, the situation on the ground was extremely precarious. He hardly had any choice but to continue with the deployment as well as ground operations generally in accordance with the notes left by General Khadim; this pattern was to continue till 31st May. These operations prioritized relief of the besieged garrisons in various cantonments. By middle of April, gradually, some semblance of order began to emerge. 9 and 16 Divisions, recently airlifted from West Pakistan, were so far being employed only reactively; to douse random fires rather than as a structured, coherent force. The primary challenge of properly articulating the command of his forces in a meaningful and combat-effective manner could hardly be implemented by General Niazi in the face of very fluid ground situation. This constrained him to continue with essentially the same pattern of deployment as inherited from General Tikka Khan. Nevertheless, he did attempt to assert his command, in the middle of April, by formally confirming the areas of responsibility already held by his formations as follows:

 a. 14 Division. Responsible for Dacca-Mymensingh as well as Jessore-Khulna Sectors with its Headquarters at Dacca. Brigades were placed as follows:

(1) 27 Brigade, with its Headquarters at Mymensingh.
(2) 57 Brigade, with its Headquarters at Dacca.
(3) 107 Brigade, with its Headquarters at Jessore.

b. 9 Division. Responsible for the entire area East of River Meghna, comprising civil districts of Sylhet, Comilla, Chittagong and Chittagong Hill Tracts, with its Headquarters at Comilla. Brigades were placed as follows:

(1) 53 Brigade, with its Headquarters at Chittagong.
(2) 117 Brigade, with its Headquarters at Comilla.
(3) 313 Brigade, with its Headquarters at Sylhet.

c. 16 Division. Responsible for the North Bengal Sector, comprising civil districts of Rangpur, Dinajpur, Rajshahi and Bogra, with its Headquarters at Natore, near Bogra. Its Brigades were located as follows:
(1) 23 Brigade, with its Headquarters at Rangpur.

---

[6] Ibid.

4

(2) <u>34 Brigade</u>, with its Headquarters at Bogra.

At the same time, the Eastern Command issued an Operational Directive tasking these formations to launch relentless, multiple thrusts right up to the border without caring for own flank or rear protection, so as to seal the routes of reinforcement and withdrawal of the rebel forces. Niazi correctly identified speed as the most vital feature of these sallies. He visualized the completion of operation in four phases by 15th May:[7]

• <u>Phase I.</u> Clearing of all major border towns and sealing of the routes of infiltration, exfiltration, and smuggling. Clearing Chittagong base and keeping it safe from artillery and mortar fire.

• <u>Phase II.</u> Opening of essential river, road, and rail communications.

• <u>Phase III.</u> Clearing of all towns in the interior and coastal areas of Mukti Bahini.

• <u>Phase IV.</u> Combing of the whole of the province and eliminating rebels/infiltrators.

Even at this early stage, evidence of infiltration and direct involvement of Indian military elements in support of the Bengali rebel troops had become fairly obvious. No doubt a cause for alarm, this was hardly unexpected or unanticipated. Nevertheless, its myriad effects on the entire operational cycle in East Pakistan had to be taken into serious consideration by the planners at Eastern Command as well as the GHQ. This Indian involvement has been verified by some credible Indian sources too:

"Exploiting the minimum Pakistani presence in inaccessible areas, and the undue time Pakistani troops took to react in others, the sector commanders organized some bold forays deep inside Pakistani-held territory. Some enterprising local commanders of the Border Security Force, who had learnt of Pakistani atrocities from the refugees and revolting Bengali elements, often joined in the raids, especially in the Jessore and Sylhet regions."[8]

General Niazi was fully conscious of the multidimensional problems staring him in his new command. He was also aware of his critical deficiencies in weapons, equipment and manpower. In his own words:

---

[7] *Ibid,* page 59.
[8] Maj Gen Sukhwant Singh, *The Liberation of Bangladesh, Volume I,* Lancer Publications, New Delhi, 1980, page 12.

"I had only three under-strength and ill-equipped divisions. As two divisions had moved by air, they could not bring their tanks, artillery, engineering stores and bridging equipment, transport, or other defence stores such as mines and barbed wires. The total fighting strength available to me was forty-five thousand----34000 from the army, plus 11000 from CAF and West Pakistan civilian police and armed non-combatants. Out of 34000 regular troops, 11000 were from armour, artillery, engineers, signals, and ancillary units and only 23000 were infantry, to man the trenches on FDLs and go into attack........."9

A veritable perfect storm was thus brewing against the Eastern Command: the Bengali resistance was tenacious, numerically superior and intimately familiar with the terrain; their allied Indian military elements were becoming increasingly active in providing them aid and succour, directly and indirectly. On the other hand, the outnumbered and spread out West Pakistani troops were operating in hostile territory in unfamiliar ground and weather conditions.

Despite these multi-dimensional problems, the Eastern Command did succeed in achieving appreciable success. By the end of April, most all border towns had been gradually brought under control and almost all the old BOPs (Border Outposts) had been activated. This, in effect, signified the re-establishment of the East Pakistan borders. Most of the routes of infiltration/exfiltration had also been denied to the rebel troops. By early May, the sea and river routes serving Chittagong, Khulna and Chalna had been cleared and the ports pressed into service, including the nodal riverport of Chandpur in Comilla district. Rail communication was restored and began to operate in the province. The rebels, having been defeated in towns, had retreated into inaccessible areas in the interior or had crossed over into India. The detailed accounts of these operations have been covered in the relevant chapters of my earlier book, Witness to Carnage 1971.

The phenomenal success of Pakistan Army operations at this time has been acknowledged by some Indian authors too:

"By the end of April, the Army had reoccupied most BOPs, recaptured the rebel stronghold of the Belonia bulge, covering approximately 57.9 square kilometers, cleared the rivers and sea routes to the ports of Chalna, Khulna and Chittagong, restored all rail communications in most areas. Except for a few small pockets in outlying and inaccessible peripheral areas, the rebellion had outwardly been suppressed by end of May."10

---

9 Lt Gen A A K Niazi, *Op Cito,* page 52.

Buoyed by the success in these pacification operations, General Niazi now felt confident to execute a pivot towards an operational posture. He sent a detailed signal to the GHQ on 13th May highlighting the ambient situation, current pattern of rebel activities and the extent of the Indian involvement. He proposed major changes in the boundaries and the operational responsibility of his formations. This was duly accorded approval by the GHQ.[11]

Accordingly, on 30th May, the areas of responsibility of 9, 14, and 16 Divisions were reorganized as under:

• 9 Division comprising two brigades under Major General M H Ansari to be responsible for area Jessore, Kushtia, Faridpur, Barisal, Bhola Island, and Khulna; Paksey Bridge on River Jamuna was also included in their area. Its Brigades were deployed as under:
  (1) 57 Brigade. Jhenida
  (2) 107 Brigade. Jessore

• 14 Division comprising three brigades under Major General Rahim Khan to be responsible for Dacca, Mymensingh, Sylhet, Comilla up to and including River Feni, and also included Bhairab Bazar Bridge on River Meghna. The Brigades were placed as follows:
  (1) 27 Brigade. Mymensingh
  (2) 117 Brigade. Comilla
  (3) 313 Brigade. Sylhet

• 16 Division comprising two brigades and an armoured regiment under Major General Nazar Hussain Shah in North Bengal area. Its Brigades remained deployed as before as under:
  (1) 23 Brigade. Rangpur
  (2) 34 Brigade. Bogra

• 53 Independent Brigade. Responsible for Chittagong and Chittagong Hill Tracts, with most of the commando elements placed under its command.

Thus, by the end of May, the rebel forces had been denied territory and dispensed heavy punishment in men and material. Along with a high number of casualties suffered by them, some forty thousand rifles, sixty-five machine guns, thirty-one mortars, twelve recoilless rifles and huge quantities of ammunition were captured from the rebel troops.[12]

---

[10] Maj Gen Sukhwant Singh, *Op Cit* page 14.
[11] Lt Gen A A Khan Niazi, *Op Cit*, page 61.

7

Demoralized by these heavy reverses, the rebel elements had retreated mainly into sanctuary sites in India. The writ of the Federal Government had been restored in almost all the towns. The political leadership of the Awami League either went underground or slipped away into India. Bengali civil servants and most of police personnel gradually began to report back for duty.

Hardly a fan of General Niazi, Major General Shaukat Riza has also recounted these successes of the Eastern Command offensive and has described it as the highest point of success that the Pakistan Army would ever attain in East Pakistan:

"Summing Up: In eight weeks the Pakistan Army, in spite of many handicaps, had re-established government authority in almost all the towns. The insurrection had been apparently crushed. The rebels were in a sorry state......."[13]

This was hardly an easy success for Pakistan Army too. Due to the dispersed nature of these operations, the formations and units had become overstretched. Most infantry battalions were deployed over great distances, sometimes over hundreds of miles. There were critical deficiencies in arms, equipment, ammunition as well as support services. The formation headquarters were operating without effective communications as their Signals units lacked heavy hardware. Having flown in emergently, the units of the Corps of Engineers and EME had also moved without major equipment. Hospitals were short of staff, medicines and even basic first aid equipment like bandages.

At the same time, the very speed and success of the Pakistani operations precipitated some unintended consequences as well. Firstly, alarmed by the rapid collapse of the insurgency, the Indian Government was constrained to prematurely enhance its level of involvement to keep it propped up. It thus had to adopt several measures at the peril of overtly obvious involvement. The numerical strength of the Mukti Bahini had to be increased by extending the recruitment to a large number of Bengali civilians. The quality of weapons and equipment being supplied to them had also to be upgraded. This increasingly overt involvement could not be kept under wraps indefinitely. The international press was thus alerted and India's image did take a hit to some extent.

Secondly and more importantly, the dramatic success greatly inflated

---

[12] *Ibid,* page 63.
[13] Maj Gen Shaukat Riza, *The Pakistan Army 1966-71*, Services Book Club, 1990, pages 100-101.

Niazi's hubris. Already known for his arrogance and self-approval, he now became full of unfounded bravado. Instead of building on his success and consolidating his operations, he started dreaming up operational fantasies centered around offensive action inside the Indian territory. This reflected very adversely upon his lack of insight into the international scenario as well as the nuances of higher strategy. Unfortunately, he was destined to repeat the display of such ignorance time and again in the ensuing months.

Yahya's Political Blunders Continue

Let us recapitulate the situation as at the end of May 1971. By then, the Army had succeeded in restoring some measure of control over East Pakistan and the writ of the Federal Government had been re-established over most of the cities and towns. The insurrection had been crushed at least on the surface; the Bengali rebels still in the field were facing a serious crisis of confidence and demoralization. The Mukti Bahini had yet to develop into an effective organization. Most of the Bengali political and military leadership was, at that point of time, amenable to a reasonable and rational political settlement. By all considerations, the time then was ripe for a magnanimous political gesture by President Yahya Khan.

By this time, it had become manifest even to the President that a political dialogue was absolutely necessary to resolve the situation amicably; typically, however, he blundered yet again. Instead of taking the rational and reasonable course of engaging the exiled Awami League leadership, he decided to ignore them and instead to contrive an alternative leadership from the other, relatively minor, political parties in East Pakistan. In pursuit of this objective, he arranged a meeting with the veteran Bengali politician Nurul Amin in June 1971 and succeeded in convincing him of his own sincerity in seeking a political solution. Then on, Nurul Amin was to become an enthusiastic supporter of the regime to the bitter end and beyond. Having arrived at a modicum of understanding with Nurul Amin, President Yahya launched a fresh political initiative on 28th June 1971. The main features of his new plan were:

• The Awami League members of the National and East Pakistan Provincial Assemblies *"who have taken part in anti-state activities, or have committed criminal acts, or have indulged in anti-social activities"* will be disqualified from membership.

• The vacancies so caused shall be filled through bye-elections to complete the membership of the assemblies.

• A committee comprising constitutional experts would draft a new Constitution, subject however to amendment by the new National Assembly.

• As soon as the Constitution was drafted and the bye-elections completed, the President would summon the National and Provincial Assemblies, and form the governments at the Federal as well as provincial levels.

• HOWEVER, the initiation of this plan would be subject to the attainment of a reasonable level of normalcy in the country.[14]

In July 1971, Yahya held another detailed meeting with Nurul Amin in Rawalpindi. They reviewed the current situation and came to the conclusion that the situation in East Pakistan had stabilized sufficiently for the initiation of the preceding Presidential Plan. It was also decided in this meeting that General Tikka Khan would now be replaced by a civilian governor to bestow a softer, more humane face to the provincial government. The person selected as the new governor was Dr. Abdul Malik, a senior respected Bengali politician, who had held numerous political portfolios in the past, including a ministerial slot during the Ayub period. He, accordingly, assumed his new appointment on 1st September 1971.

The President's initial impulse was to retain General Tikka in East Pakistan as Commander Eastern Command and to recall General Niazi, who even during this short stay had earned an unenviable reputation for his foul language, nocturnal visits to houses of ill-repute, and involvement in betel leaf trade. This is where fate intervened! The Governor-elect Dr. Malik expressed strong reservations on Tikka's continued stay in East Pakistan because of the unfortunate epithet "Butcher of Bengal" attributed to him by the man in the street. The President was left with no option but to let General Niazi continue in command. General Tikka Khan was a professional soldier, obedient, loyal, straight-forward and honest. As a person, he was a very soft-hearted gentleman and I am personally a witness to many acts of humanity by him. Determined as a commander, he was never upset by reverses. In the informed opinion of General Farman Ali Khan and many other contemporaries, had he been placed in command at this time, he would have given a better account of himself and his command in the looming War.

---

[14] Hasan Zaheer, *The Separation of East Pakistan*, pages 328-329.

By this time, only about 70 of the original 160 Awami League MNAs were still known to be present in East Pakistan, the rest having gone across to India. Consequently, the immediate priority of the President was to evolve a mechanism for filling up these vacancies. In order to decide the intricate modalities of this complex process, a Committee comprising General Farman, General Akbar Khan (Director General Inter- Services Intelligence), and N A Rizvi (Director Intelligence Bureau), was constituted by the President, which held several meetings during July and August. General Farman is on record as having proposed a very sound and practical suggestion on this issue. His proposal was that a session of the National Assembly, as elected in December 1971, be convened forthwith; those who failed to attend it be disqualified under the prescribed procedure. In his opinion, this procedure was entirely in accordance with established parliamentary practice and no constitutional expert, at home or abroad, could take exception to it. Unfortunately, intelligence organizations everywhere have their own agendas, interests and favourites to take care of. So, this eminently reasonable suggestion was summarily ignored by the other participants, who then proceeded to draw up their own lists of the parliamentarians to be disqualified. Eventually, some 78 originally elected Awami League MNAs were identified to be disqualified.

However, another suggestion made by General Farman was accepted. This aimed at completion of this entire process and installation of a political government in East Pakistan latest by October 1971. In Farman's astute assessment, India was most likely to commence open hostilities any time after November and that it would be diplomatically more awkward for it to resort to military means if a constitutionally-elected political government was functional in the province by then. Fate intervened yet again and the Federal Government, without taking Governor Malik or General Farman into confidence, arbitrarily changed this date to November on rather flimsy grounds.[15]

However, as the events transpired, this ambitious Plan began to run into complications almost immediately. Firstly, an essential component of the Plan was the President's decision to install Nurul Amin as the Prime Minister of Pakistan at the end of this electoral exercise. This decision was indeed being supported by political parties like Jamaat-i-Islami, PDP, three factions of Muslim League and Nizam Islam Party. These, however, were all small parties with hardly any electoral strength on the ground, particularly in the ambient situation. The Awami League MNAs still in the

---

[15] Hasan Zaheer, Ibid, page 337; and Maj Gen Farman Ali Khan, *Op Cit,* pages 96-97.

11

province were in any case not on board with this plan till then.

Another complication arose when it became manifest that it would be entirely impracticable to hold the bye-elections because of Mukti Bahini operations, which had registered a marked increase June onwards. As a working compromise, it was decided that instead of holding bye-elections under the present conditions, the vacancies in the national assembly should be divided among the parties supporting Nurul Amin in accordance with the ratios achieved by them in the General Elections of 1970. This proposal too hit a snag when it was realized that even this methodology would not enable Nurul Amin to be elected prime minister, as these parties had not fared so well electorally.

Thus, the plan had to be heavily re-modified and it was instead decided that out of the 78 anticipated seats, the maximum number will be allotted to the PDP, Nurul Amin's own party. Furthermore, through the good offices of Begum Akhtar Suleman, the daughter of former Prime Minister Husain Shaheed Suhrawardi, General Farman met some 62 Awami League MNAs still in East Pakistan and managed to convince them to support Nurul Amin's candidature as the Prime Minister in the National Assembly.

While all this was going on in East Pakistan, a different drama was unfolding in West Pakistan, where the PPP was engaged in the process of finalizing their own future political strategy. Bhutto, with his uncanny faculties, had come to realize that the Yahya era was rapidly drawing to a logical close. And, this was perhaps one instance when Bhutto's ambitions to become the prime minister came vividly to the fore; he simply could not reconcile with the situation where Nurul Amin became the Prime Minister while he was relegated to the wings yet again. He prevailed upon President Yahya to direct General Farman to allocate 24 bye-election seats to the PPP, which would ensure a PPP majority in the National Assembly, as and when it met.

For General Farman, this was a totally unexpected development, one which was likely to compromise his entire plan. He reacted rather sharply and told the President bluntly that East Pakistan would be lost to us unless the next prime minister hailed from that wing. However, the President continued to persist and prevailed upon Farman to lobby with the East Pakistan leaders to achieve this objective. In the event, General Farman could persuade them to surrender only twelve seats to the PPP.

A delegation of the PPP comprising Abdul Hafeez Peerzada, Mahmud Ali Kasuri, Kamal Azfar and Khursheed Hasan Meer reached Dacca soon thereafter. Initially, and rather surprisingly, they chose to ignore General Farman, and instead preferred to meet General Niazi and Governor Malik to 'demand their pound of flesh' in the form of the promised 24 seats. However, both Niazi and the Governor were hardly in a position to re-assure them in this respect. Left with no other option, Mahmud Ali Kasuri and Khursheed Hasan Meer then perforce had to call on Farman.

They were due for a great disappointment as General Farman apprised them that, even after great persuasion, the East Pakistan leaders had agreed to give them only twelve seats and that too in two packages of six each. The delegation thereupon flew back to Rawalpindi and made their report to Bhutto. He, in turn, met the President and averred that he, and consequently West Pakistan, had yet again been betrayed by a great conspiracy to keep him out of power. Yahya summoned Farman yet again but ironically did not appear too perturbed by this situation; in fact, he was rather apologetic about the whole affair. In the end, the PPP had to be content with an allocation of six seats in all.[16]

On 12th October, the President announced his timetable for the transfer of power. This was followed by a Martial Law Regulation on 14th October permitting political activities in the country, albeit within well-defined limits. The salient features of the timetable were:[17]

- The National Assembly was scheduled to be summoned to meet on 27th December on the premise that by then the bye-electoral process would have been completed.
- Following the inaugural session of the National Assembly, the Federal Government would be formed.
- The provincial assemblies of West Pakistan would be summoned to meet at short notice thereafter.
- The East Pakistan Assembly would meet later, sometimes after 7th January 1972, by which date the bye-elections on its 193 vacant seats would have been completed.

Changing Operational Environment

While all this was going on in Pakistan, the Indian Government was watching these political developments with a growing disquiet. They evidently considered it entirely against their interests to allow the East Pakistan crisis to be politically defused, one way or the other. Any such

---

[16] Maj Gen Farman Ali Khan, Ibid, pages 101-103.
[17] Hasan Zaheer, *Op Cit*, page 339.

development would certainly have shattered their visions of a *"chance of a century"* to dismember Pakistan. By this time, General Manekshaw, the Indian Army Chief, had already issued his Operational Instruction in August 1971, and the Indian war machine was all set for a war at a time of their determination. Indira Gandhi, the Indian Prime Minister, was already on record as having stated that even if the whole world disapproved of her action, she was going to force her solution on Pakistan. As such, she could hardly accept any peaceful political compromise in East Pakistan with equanimity. India was thus fully resolute to foment and encourage conditions in East Pakistan aimed at ensuring the failure of any such political initiative by Pakistan.

While the Indian Army was making hectic preparations for the looming war, their political planners were already planning for the day after. They were, even at this point in time, engaged in conceiving long term plans aimed at facilitating pro-India environment in a *post-independence* Bangladesh. They envisioned the Mukti Bahini as a possible eventual antagonist to Indian hegemonic designs. They were particularly apprehensive of its hard-core leadership, comprising former armed forces officers of Pakistan. The Indian planners, led by the formidable D P Dhar, the Political Adviser to Prime Minister Indira Gandhi, had developed a very effective strategy, a double-edged sword, to deal with the situation. It was designed, on one hand, to ensure enfeeblement of the Mukti Bahini through maximum attrition, and on the other, keep the Pakistan Army embroiled in futile tactical operations, thus losing their strategic focus on the looming war.

According to this plan, the Mukti Bahini, with full support of Indian forces, where required, was to be launched in multiple, short offensive operations all along the border and within the province too. According to the succinct description of General Farman, it was to kill two birds with one stone----- both being Muslims. In their estimation, the Indians hoped that these operations would eventually accrue the following advantages to them:

- The real combat potential of Mukti Bahini would become considerably reduced by suffering heavy casualties in these operations and thus less likely to be a post-independence hazard to the Indian hegemonic designs.

- The combat potential of the Pakistan Army in East Pakistan would also be gradually compromised as Niazi was most likely to make it a prestige point to counter-attack every such intrusion by the Mukti Bahini. Consequently, the Army perforce would become strung out all along the border in an exaggerated forward posture.

- By the time the war actually commenced, the Pakistan Army would be fully exhausted due to lack of relief and constant engagement.

At this time, both the GHQ as well as General Niazi had become obsessed with the apprehension that any chunk of territory seized by the Mukti Bahini would be readily recognized by India as Bangladesh, which in turn would furnish the Indians with the fig leaf of de jure justification for an armed intervention on the invitation of a 'sovereign state'. Thus, Niazi became prone to acting and reacting on the slightest provocation and further aggravated the problems faced by the units on the ground by stretching them more and more. These debilitating 'search & destroy' missions were to become the order of the day. On their part, the Indians continued to play upon these fears and apprehensions through their broadcasts and rumour-mongering, evoking more and more reaction by the Pakistan Army; it truly entered a vicious circle at this stage!

Falling a blind prey to this Indian strategy, the Mukti Bahini too resumed their activities in the beginning of July. This phase of the Mukti Bahini operations in effect heralded the commencement of their much publicized 'Monsoon Offensive'. The impact of training imparted by the Indians as well as improvement in their weapons and leadership now manifested itself through a marked upgradation in their tactical handling and battle techniques. Indeed, many of their attacks were company and battalion level affairs, often supported by Indian artillery and mortar fire. Now, they appeared to be operating under a coordinated plan, with clear and well defined objectives. Their basic policy at this stage was to avoid close combat with the regular Pakistani troops; it was, indeed, a true war of attrition based on classic hit and run tactics. The raids were aimed at drawing the Pakistan Army troops more and more towards the border as they launched futile attacks on an elusive enemy. It was a transparent ruse but a belligerent and over-confident Niazi readily fell for it, in the process exhausting his troops without accruing much tactical advantage.

That was not all. A large number of Mukti guerillas infiltrated into the countryside and caused widespread damage to the provincial infrastructure. They attacked isolated police stations, blew up bridges and road culverts, and killed loyal citizens, Bengali as well as non-Bengali. Power stations, electric pylons, and gas stations were also attacked relentlessly. The lines of communications were their prime targets, aimed at impeding the movement of the Army as well as damaging the industrial potential of the Province.

In time, they succeeded in notching up some notable successes. In early July, Lt Colonel Mazhar ul Qayyum SJ, CO 33 Baluch Battalion, while leading a search and destroy mission, was ambushed in Salda Nadi in Comilla Sector and killed along with two of his officers and the subedar major of the unit. On 21st July, Brigadiers Salimullah, and Atta Malik, who had just arrived from West Pakistan, narrowly escaped with their lives in a well- planned ambush. By the end of August, there was hardly a day when one incident or the other did not occur in Dacca, Chittagong, Rajshahi or other large cities/towns. In September, the Mukti Bahini grew so bold as to begin attacking the BOPs directly. Daring attempts were also made on ships in Chittagong and Chalna harbours by trained frogmen. At Chalna, in three night attacks launched between 18th and 22nd September, they damaged or destroyed four merchant ships, one oil tanker and one barge. These activities continued to gather momentum with time.

The Army, under General Niazi's orders, reacted sharply everywhere and so was stretched more and more towards the border. Thus, the implicit Indian strategy managed to tie down Pakistani troops along the border and, at the same time, compromised their capacity to undertake strategic or operational manoeuvres by damaging the requisite communication infrastructure. In the process, the Army suffered heavy casualties. During the period April to October, the number of casualties suffered by the Eastern Command due to these activities was as follows:[18]

- Officers.   237.
- JCOs.   136
- Other Ranks.   3559.

The Mukti Bahini operations began to take their toll on the performance of the local police as well. Many of them simply deserted from their posts while some found safety in collaborating with the rebels. To meet this growing menace, the Eastern Command had to carry out a massive reorganization of the second line forces in the province. After the disbandment of East Pakistan Rifles (EPR), it was replaced by East Pakistan Civil Armed Forces (EPCAF) in May, recruiting half the strength from West Pakistan and the other half locally in East Pakistan. A large contingent of Frontier Corps (FC), West Pakistan Rangers (WPR) and police was also inducted from West Pakistan.

---

[18] Maj Gen Shaukat Riza, Op Cit, page 109.

However, in view of the mounting pressure of the Mukti Bahini operations, even this strength was considered inadequate. To meet the enhanced requirement, a Razakar (Volunteer) Force was raised from amongst the loyal Bengalis as well as the Biharis in July and August. They were merely imparted some essential basic training, armed with antique .303 rifles, and hastily deployed in the interior, generally near their own villages. The main drawback of this force was the total absence of any command structure. Yet, they accomplished a fairly useful function in guarding vulnerable points like bridges, culverts, electric infrastructure. More notably, however, they were an important morale boosting factor for the rural population by providing them with a measure of protection. Even their limited effectiveness resulted in a marked decrease in guerilla activities during August and September.

Despite severe limitations and heavy casualties, the Razakars generally performed well against the rebels, which forced the Mukti Bahini to change their strategy late September onwards. Their new objective was to demoralize this force. They took to attacking solitary positions held by the Razakars and inflicted heavy casualties on them. In many cases, the families of Razakars were identified and executed. Generous monetary rewards were also offered to the defecting Razakars. Despite these problems, the Razakars' performance generally remained satisfactory till the end. After the fall of East Pakistan, they paid the highest price for their loyalty to Pakistan and most of them were killed in cold blood by the Mukti Bahini or other rebel groups. Their deeds of valour and loyalty have generally remained shrouded in oblivion!

Owing to the combined efforts of the Army, civil armed forces and the Razakars, some semblance of normalcy was attained in early September and the much- heralded Monsoon Offensive of the Mukti Bahini was perceived as having been thwarted. The respite was, however, only temporary and proved to be a mere change of strategy by their Indian handlers. In October, Mukti Bahini went on the offensive again. This time, company and battalion sized operations at several places along the border were launched, fully supported by the Indian Army as well as their Border Security Force under effective artillery cover. Sizeable chunks of territory considered to be of eventual operational value to the Indian Army began to be lost as part of a coordinated strategy. Time was running out fast for the beleaguered Pakistan Army.

The End Game

By early November, the effects of the foregoing Indian strategy had become tangibly manifest on the ground. General Farman made his last trip to the GHQ on 4th November and took this opportunity to brief the President in detail about the deteriorating situation in East Pakistan. On a map of East Pakistan, he briefed General Yahya on the magnitude of Mukti Bahini activity; he also showed him the areas which had already fallen into their control. He warned the President bluntly that General Niazi, quite contrary to the actual situation, was deliberately painting a misleading picture merely to bolster his reputation as a fighting general. In reality, a very large area along the borders and 'substantial areas within the province' were already under the Mukti/rebel control. Farman also advised the President that a General War with India was not in Pakistan's strategic interest. He literally begged the President not to initiate the war in the Western Theatre in any case as that would provide India with a genuine excuse to use its full combat potential against East Pakistan. In such a situation, the Eastern Garrison would be extremely hard pressed to counter both the external as well as internal threats. Yahya categorically assured him that he had no intention of starting the war in the west and that he was not going to commit the same mistake as Ayub. General Farman returned to Dacca a reasonably satisfied and reassured person.[19]

During the month of November, the situation in East Pakistan continued deteriorating almost by the day. Reports kept pouring in of Razakars, including the members of Al-Badr and Al-Shams cadres, going over to the Mukti Bahini and surrendering to them the police stations entrusted to their charge. Attacks on religious scholars and madrassas also became very frequent. Destruction of power lines and communication infra-structure became intensified to create pressure on the already shattered economy; the movement of troops became progressively more difficult. In November, East Pakistan was practically in a state of undeclared war.

Too late in the day, and rather reluctantly, Yahya finally realized the necessity of inducting some kind of a representative government. On 30th November, he called Bhutto to Rawalpindi and had two meetings with him, at one of which Nurul Amin was also present. They both agreed to be part of a coalition government, subject to certain conditions, mainly proposed by Bhutto. However, no follow up steps were actually initiated by Yahya to induct the civilian government until 7th December, when war had already broken out.

On that date, the President expressed his desire to send Bhutto to New

---

[19] Maj Gen Farman *Ali Khan*, Op Cit, page 102.

York to represent Pakistan at the UNO. Bhutto rightly pointed out that it would prejudice Pakistan's position if he were perceived addressing the UN Security Council as the representative of an unpopular military regime. Yahya had no choice then but to acquiesce with Bhutto's suggestion. So, on 8th December, he announced the formation of a coalition government with Nurul Amin as the Prime Minister and Bhutto as the Vice Prime Minister as well as the Foreign Minister. However, neither of them was formally inducted into office and Bhutto had to depart for New York the same day, merely as Vice Prime Minister and Foreign Minister-designate.[20]

On 1st December, Dr. Malik, the Governor of East Pakistan, returned from West Pakistan after meeting the President. He apprised Farman that though he had talked to the President on the subject of war, he had received no categorical assurance from him that the war in the west would not be initiated. However, the President had assured the Governor that General Abdul Hamid Khan, the Army COS, would visit Dacca on 2nd December to review the military situation personally.

The promised visit, however, never materialized. Instead, on that day, the Governor was intimated that General Hamid would not be coming in view of his pressing commitments elsewhere. On being informed of this development, an astute General Farman immediately concluded that the war was imminent. He had a standing permission from the President to visit Rawalpindi whenever he deemed necessary. For a fleeting moment, he was tempted to do just that, if only to escape the coming war and its obvious aftermath. But his conscience did not permit him to desert his colleagues and comrades at such a critical time!

On 3rd December, Farman was still working in his office to finalize the details of making the East Pakistan MNAs attend the National Assembly session to be held in Rawalpindi on 16th December. At precisely that time, President General Yahya Khan finally decided to start the general war against India.

The fateful day of 16th December 1971 did eventually dawn but was destined to witness an entirely different drama in Dacca!

---

[20] Hasan Zaheer, *Op Cit*, page 344.

EAST PAKISTAN AT A GLANCE

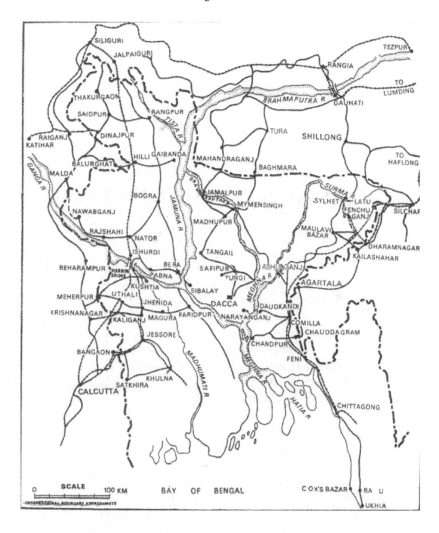

2

OPERATIONAL PLANNING IN EAST PAKISTAN

Purely from a military viewpoint, the defence of East Pakistan suffered from several inherent problems. It was separated by over 1200 miles of hostile Indian Territory from West Pakistan. The resource constraint, to which a developing country like Pakistan always remained exposed, had effectively precluded the option of garrisoning both its wings with adequately strong and effective defence forces. It was also obvious to its defence planners that the positioning of the available forces equally between the two wings would weaken both, and thus compromise the defence of the country as a whole.

Keeping in view the geo-strategic and geopolitical location of West Pakistan, it was consciously decided to place the major weight of defence resources there. This decision almost certainly was influenced by issues such as the Kashmir dispute and the endemic water problems with India. The evolution of the doctrine *'The defence of East Pakistan would lay in West Pakistan'* was the logical inference of this decision. In simple terms, it meant that in case of any potent military threat generated by India against East Pakistan, a massive counter-offensive from West Pakistan must be launched to force her to recoil. Another critical assumption underlying this doctrine was that the planners in Pakistan never conceived of a situation where a massive Indian offensive would be launched against East Pakistan and the garrison there would have to fight on their own. Yet, this was precisely the major dilemma which would face the Pakistan High Command during the 1971 crisis.

Critical Topographical Factors

East Pakistan was surrounded on three sides by Indian Territory; only a small portion in the south-east lay along the Burma border (now Myanmar). In the south, East Pakistan was bounded by the Bay of Bengal. The border with India, measuring almost 2000 kilometers was hardly a well-defined line, interspersed as it was with hundreds of enclaves of varying sizes on both sides.

Topographically, it is a low- lying land mass, essentially comprising the deltaic region of three major river systems, originating from India or beyond: Meghna, Brahmaputra (Yamuna), and Ganges (Padma). Innumerable large and small tributaries of these three rivers further fragmented the land, forming effective barriers to land movement. The Ganges and the Brahmaputra (Yamuna) made a junction at Goaludo Ghat, some 60 kilometres northwest of Dacca and thereafter it was called the Padma. This huge river was in turn joined by the Meghna, some 50 kilometres south of Dacca, and then was known as the Meghna till it fell into the Bay of Bengal in the south. There were only two major bridges over this entire riverine system in the province: Coronation Bridge over River Meghna at Ashuganj, and Paksey or Hardinge Bridge over River Ganges near Pabna. Due to lack of roads and bridges, ferries were used extensively for movement across and along the rivers. Two major ferry sites, at Daudkundi over the Meghna and Goalundu Ghat over the Ganges, were militarily quite significant.

Waterways were thus the main means of communications, but it would be misleading to conclude that major fighting would remain confined to riverine operations only. In fact, since population centres in the province were the main political and operational objectives, the land communications linking them essentially determined the actual strategic pattern of operations there. Nevertheless, the waterways could not be entirely neglected and no sane commander would willingly surrender this advantage to the enemy.

The alignment of roads in East Pakistan further complicated the pattern of operations. Dacca, the obvious political and strategic objective of any major offensive, was linked by roads with all the important cities in the province, yet it could not be reached from any direction without ferrying across at least one major river. The alignment of the road network was such that most major roads converged from the borders towards Dacca, but there were hardly any lateral roads. As such, the road network facilitated movement directly on to Dacca, but only after negotiating a major river obstacle; Dacca was naturally protected on three sides by major rivers. Conversely, Dacca could effectively be defended by concentrating major forces around the natural zone created by these rivers, often designated as "Dacca Bowl".

Chittagong was the main port in East Pakistan. However, all rail/road traffic to the hinterland had to pass through the bottleneck of Feni, which lay within mortar range from the Indian border. The destruction of the rail and road bridges at Feni could effectively sever all movement from/to Chittagong. Khulna was the second important port but had severe marine limitations; it could not berth large sea-going vessels and so all ships had to be loaded/unloaded at Chalna, some 45 kilometers down river. Chandpur, near Comilla, was a nodal inland river port.

Important cities like Rajshahi, Dinajpur, Rangpur, Jessore, Khulna, Pabna, Comilla, Brahmanbaria, and Mymensingh all lay very close to the border, while most river obstacles lay much to the rear of these cities. This essentially dictated a forward posture on the defender; conversely, basing the defences behind these rivers meant withdrawal from large swathes of territory. This decision had to be weighed against the political risk it entailed; thus, it was essentially a political rather than a military decision.

Strategic Compartmentation of East Pakistan

The river system of East Pakistan divided the province into four well-defined, natural zones or sectors. This compartmentation tended to impose severe strategic compulsions on the pattern of operations in the theatre since separate operational cycles for each Sector had to be conceived. These Sectors, identified as such by both Pakistan and Indian armies were: Northwestern Sector; Southwestern Sector; Central Sector; and, Eastern Sector. A brief description of these Sectors follows; however, they have also been analyzed in greater detail in the relevant chapters.

- **Northwestern Sector**. This Sector was bounded on the west and north by the border with India, on the east by River Brahmaputra (Yamuna) and on the south by River Ganges. The Brahmaputra had no bridge over it as it was about ten miles wide; the Ganges in the south only had the Paksey (Hardinge) Bridge near Pabna. A prominent Indian salient abuts in this Sector just south of Dinajpur usually denoted as Hilli-Gaibanda axis; any Indian thrust here could effectively bisect this Sector laterally, making this a critical and sensitive axis. Bogra was the obvious strategic objective in this Sector for any offensive towards Dacca. For India, this Sector assumed critical strategic significance because even a minor northwards offensive action emanating from this Sector could effectively sever the Siliguri

24

corridor, thus, cutting off all the eastern states of India.

- **Southwestern Sector**. This Sector was defined by River Ganges in the north, River Padma in the east, the border with India on the west and the Bay of Bengal in the south. It was vertically bisected by River Madhumati, which branched off from the Ganges near Kushtia. Strategically, this Sector offered a broad front to an invader from the west, who could advance along two major roads as well as several subsidiary axes. In the absence of any worthwhile obstacles at the border, River Madhumati was the first major obstacle to be encountered. However, major cities like Jessore, Khulna, Magura and Kushtia all lay to the west of this river; this in effect negated the utility of this obstacle to the defender. Khulna and Chalna ports were important objectives in this Sector.

- **Central Sector**. This sector was shaped somewhat like an inverted triangle, with its apex at Dacca, the base along the border in the north, and its two sides resting along River Meghna in the east and River Padma in the west; both its flanks thus rested on major obstacles. From the north, it provided the most direct and obvious approach to Dacca, with only one water obstacle en route, a relatively minor river locally called the Old Brahmaputra. After crossing it, several good roads emanated onwards to Dacca.

- **Eastern Sector.** This Sector stretched from Sylhet in the north, through Comilla in the middle, and down to Chittagong in the south; from there on, a narrow strip led to Cox's Bazar and Teknaf along the Burmese border. On the western side, this sector was bounded by the River Meghna from Sylhet to Chandpur. Geographically, this was the most vulnerable sector, comprising some 700 miles of exposed border with India. Moreover, it also offered the shortest approach to Dacca, the distance from the border to the line of River Meghna hardly exceeding 60-70 miles. Agartala Salient from the Indian state of Tripura provided a direct access to River Meghna. There was a major rail bridge over the Meghna near Ashuganj. Chittagong is the main port in the area. Comilla is an important communication centre, served by an all-weather airfield as well. Chandpur, Daudkundi and Ashuganj are important river ports.

Main Conclusions

A detailed analytical study of the terrain, weather, and communications infrastructure lead to the following broad conclusions from the defence point of view:

- The political and strategic position of Dacca as the main objective of any major invasion of East Pakistan was fairly obvious and well established. Thus, the relative operational significance of various Sectors and important communication centres had to be related to this cardinal factor.

- The Hilli-Gaibanda axis emerged as the most critical approach in the

26

Northwestern Sector. A major thrust along this axis would bifurcate the defensive system of this Sector into two lateral segments. Bogra was the most likely prime objective in this Sector as it dominates the ferry sites providing access to Dacca.

- Jessore and Magura stand out as critical nodal points in the Southwestern Sector. Jessore owed its primacy to being a major city and an important cantonment. Magura was located astride approaches to the ferry sites over River Madhumati as well as Goalundo Ghat and Faridpur over the Padma; its capture would be vital for any thrust towards Dacca. The seaports of Khulna and Chalna were important strategic objectives.

- The Eastern Sector provided the most obvious and the shortest approach to Dacca. Chandpur, Daudkundi and Bhairab Bazar were important river ports along the Meghna, linked with Dacca by rail/road as well as by rivercraft. Control over the area between Chandpur and Daudkundi was necessary to develop operations against Dacca. Lalmai Hills and Maynamati complex offered good defensible positions to the defender but could be bypassed from either flank. The most critical thrust line in the area was the Akhaura-Brahmanbaria-Ashuganj axis which offered the shortest route between the border to a crossing site over the Meghna. Chittagong and Sylhet were important cities but conferred no immediate strategic advantages on the invader.

- The Central Sector possessed the least water obstacles en route to Dacca; any advance from the north through this Sector would thus lie along the grain of the country. River Old Brahmaputra in this Sector, a minor tributary of the Yamuna, was hardly a formidable obstacle compared to the major rivers in other sectors and could be ferried across easily at multiple points. Tangail was an important communication centre in the area, providing a direct road approach to Dacca.

The geographical situation of East Pakistan, the shape of its border, and the orientation of its strategic communications made it extremely vulnerable to attack and infiltration from India. Even a casual look on the map would reveal that it was a prominent salient brazenly protruding into Eastern India, almost severing the mainland India from its eastern most states like Assam, Mizoram, Tripura etc. Theoretically, a salient of this size possesses two main strategic characteristics:

- The forces within the salient enjoy the inherent advantage of operating along interior lines while the other side is constrained to operate along exterior lines. However, to gain maximum advantage, the forces within must have recourse to good lines of communication and the liberty of action to use them during the operations. In retrospect, both these facilities were denied to Pakistan in the then ambient operational environment.

• If the forces within the salient are numerically strong as well as qualitatively superior, they possess the flexibility of launching multiple offensives in diverse directions. But if these forces are weak or ill-equipped, the advantage passes on to the enemy who then has the liberty to launch multi-directional operations at will. This is precisely what befell the Pakistan forces in 1971.

The Strategic Concept of War with India

Application of force in war is primarily guided by some fundamental principles of war. A cardinal principle is to concentrate maximum combat strength at the point of main decision by exercising economy of effort in less important areas. Since the creation of Pakistan, the basic strategy, the *grund norm*, of defense planning had always been the dictum *"The defense of East Pakistan lies in West Pakistan."* Thus, the major bias of Pakistan's defence effort had always tilted heavily towards the Western Theatre. In the specific context of the operational environment prevalent in the latter half of 1971, this concept could be translated in more tangible terms as follows:

• The major operations with India would be fought and decided in the Western Theatre.
• The Eastern Garrison, while defending East Pakistan, would keep maximum Indian Forces involved and tied down for *a given period;* the accent here was on a stipulated timeframe and not indefinitely.

• During this stipulated period, a major strategic advantage in the Western Theatre must be secured by the Pakistan Forces there.

This concept remained the basis of all strategic and operational planning in Pakistan till 1971 and the planning carried out by the Eastern Command was thus defined and limited by this basic constraint. Accordingly, the War Directive issued by the Government of Pakistan in early 1969 and which remained unchanged through 1971 prescribed the following mission for the Pakistan Army:[21]

28

"To defend the territorial integrity of Pakistan, in the process destroying the maximum number of enemy and capturing as much enemy territory as possible."

Its salient features were as follows:.
- The main battles would be fought in the west (the Punjab).
- The fate of East Pakistan would hinge upon whatever operations were undertaken in the west.

Keeping in view the topographical compulsions in the operational environment of 1971, it was an obvious conclusion that every inch of East Pakistan could not be defended with the available forces. Pakistan could at best hope that its Eastern Garrison would *"remain in being"* till a political solution could be arrived at through the good offices of the United Nations. The obvious strategy then was to adopt a defensive posture as far forward as the water obstacles in the sectors permitted; fighting successive delaying actions; and, gradually falling back on the final defence line of the Dacca Bowl. This however was easier said than done. A strategic withdrawal, while in contact with the enemy, is one of the most difficult operations of war and requires meticulous planning and preparation at all levels. Thus, to adopt and implement this strategy, it was essential to fulfill the following vital pre-requisites:

- All the successive defensive positions conceived for occupation by the withdrawing troops must be identified and prepared for occupation beforehand. Moreover, the logistic resources for each such position must be placed *in situ* even before the first bullet is fired.
- The plans for this intricate operation must be known to commanders at various levels and they must be mentally prepared to execute it while operating under intense enemy pressure. At the same time, however, this must not inculcate in them a tendency to look over their shoulders and withdraw from their positions after merely a half-hearted effort at defending them.

- The routes of withdrawal from one position to the next must be identified and kept open. Critical defiles like bridges and ferry sites must be guarded by para-military forces, police and armed volunteers to ensure smooth passage of the withdrawing troops.

---

[21] Lt Gen Gul Hasan Khan, *Memoirs,* OUP, page 290.

29

Evolution of War Plans for East Pakistan

According to Major General Farman Ali Khan, who as a colonel was posted as DDMO (Deputy Director Military Operations) in the GHQ in 1967, the plan then held in the Military Operations Directorate for defence of East Pakistan was nothing more than a collation of divisional level plans submitted by brigades of 14 Division. *"What in military terms is called operational strategy with Hypotheses and Concept of Operations had not been thought out."* Farman set to work and in due course evolved the first consolidated plan for *"Defensive Operations under the Hypothesis of enemy's main attack against West Pakistan while India remains on the defensive in East Pakistan."* The plan was approved by the then C-in-C General Yahya as well as the President Field Martial Ayub Khan. With that, Farman was also promoted and posted to East Pakistan as Commander Artillery 14 Division. [22] Thus, began the tryst with history of this extra-ordinary man!

Soon after reporting for duty in East Pakistan, he was asked to conduct an operational planning war game, Exercise SUNDER BAN I, as its director. At the conclusion of the exercise, some significant points related to the defence of East Pakistan were succinctly brought on record by him in the presence of the then CGS Major General Sahibzada Yaqub Khan and the GOC 14 Division, Major General Muzaffaruddin, as follows:

"1. East Pakistan is like Poland was in World War II. It is surrounded by the enemy. Its major cities like those of Poland are on the border, thereby attracting our forces outwards, creating a vacuum in the middle, and thereby exposing Dacca to the enemy.

*2. Defence of every inch of the territory is not possible. The mission of Pakistan Army should be changed from 'Defence of East Pakistan' to '**Remaining in Being**'. (This terminology was used perhaps for the first time in Pakistan.)*

3. The final attack on Dacca will come from the north in the same manner as delivered by Guderian in Poland. Therefore, adequate measures be taken to defend Dacca at all costs."[23]

These were very pertinent and poignant points made by an astute military mind and were accepted by the then CGS. These were of great help to the GHQ in finalizing the concept of operations for defence of East Pakistan, which formed the basis of the GHQ Operational Directive dated

---

[22] Maj Gen Farman Ali Khan, Op Cit, page 18.
[23] Ibid, pages 18-20.

9th August 1967. It visualized the following mission for the East Pakistan garrison:

"In the East, contain and neutralize as many enemy troops as possible inflicting maximum casualties without running the risk of annihilation."[24]

The salient features of this Directive, which remained the essential component of the defence plan of East Pakistan till General Niazi appeared on the scene, were as follows:[25]

• Defence of territory was not possible. It was more important for the forces to **remain in being.**

• Defence was to utilize the maximum river obstacles to enhance the defence capabilities.

• Dacca was to be defended at all costs.

On 12th November 1969, GHQ issued another Operational Directive, specific to Eastern Command (called 3 Corps till then), which assigned it a mission in just five simple words:

"3 Corps will defend East Pakistan."

Based on this rather vague directive, and keeping in view the developing political situation, Lt General Yaqub Khan, Commander Eastern Command, formulated two broad contingencies and based his defence plans accordingly:[26]

- **Contingency A.** A local uprising, with India providing moral and material support but not carrying out a physical attack.

- **Contingency B.** A major insurgency, accompanied by India invading East Pakistan.

- In case Contingency A materialized, Eastern Command would adopt a forward posture. Troops would be deployed all along the border to deal with uprisings anywhere in East Pakistan and

---

[24] Lt Gen Kamal Matinuddin, *Tragedy of Errors*, Services Book Club, 1994, page 339.
[25] Maj Gen Farman Ali Khan, Op Cit, page 114.
[26] Lt Gen Kamal Matinuddin, Op Cit, page 339.

would prevent the capture of any significant chunk of territory by the rebels.

- In case Contingency B materialized, the main defensive position would be taken around the Dacca Bowl, which would be strongly defended at all costs, making full use of the major water obstacles; only light and mobile elements would be deployed ahead of the main defences to inflict maximum casualties and delay on the enemy.

- An essential assumption inherent in the plan was that sufficient time and warning would be available for transition from Contingency A to Contingency B.

(**Note:** This, incidentally, was the only occasion where the terms 'Contingency A' and 'Contingency B' were used in the operational planning process of East Pakistan. In particular, the use of 'Contingency B' to denote the location of the main defensive position around the Dacca Bowl was never used again, nor was there ever afterwards any such plan in existence. Yet, later on, these terms did serve to create some confusion in this respect in uninitiated minds.)

Based on the above Directive of the Eastern Command, HQ 14 Division, then the only division in East Pakistan, issued its own Operational Instruction on 17th September 1970. Based upon the then current Army hypotheses, it visualized a threat perception of three divisions against East Pakistan. The Mission stipulated in this operational instruction was as follows:

• Defend East Pakistan while inflicting maximum attrition on the enemy, but avoiding the destruction of own forces and;

• Ensure defence of Dacca at all costs.

Based upon the conclusions of this war game, the GHQ too, soon thereafter, issued another Operational Instruction, in which the defence of Dacca at all costs was the predominant consideration.[27]

Incidentally, the Eastern Command plan had been tested and formulated after lengthy and intense discussions during the war game TITU MIR I in August 1970. I also had the opportunity to attend this war game as

---

[27] Lt Gen Gul Hasan Khan, Op Cit, page 298.

a staff officer to DG EPR. There was a lot of discussion on the concept of mobile defence and how it could be applied in the likely operational environment of East Pakistan. At the end of the exercise, General Sahibzada Yaqub Khan gave an illuminating talk to the participants on the concepts and modalities of mobile defence. For about twenty minutes, he only spoke on the difference between 'mobile defence' and 'defence which is mobile'. And what a learned discourse it was! He brought out relevant examples from military history to make his point; elaborated the fine differences in the teachings of institutions like Imperial Defence College UK, Ecole Superieur de Guerre France, US War College as well as the War Course at Pakistan's National Defence College. All those who were there would never forget his command of language and his professional insight into such an obtuse subject. And then, what a change from Sahibzada to Niazi!

Yes, the operational thinking changed abruptly when General Niazi took over as the Commander Eastern Command. He had seen active service as a junior officer in Burma, Malaya and Java during the Second World War. As such, the basic technique of fighting in the sub-tropical climate and riverine/deltaic terrain of East Pakistan could hardly be new to him. But what affected his professional judgment adversely in East Pakistan were his rigid and fixed ideas and his false sense of pride in never falling back in the face of the enemy; yet another carryover from his World War experience. Perhaps his limited academic background and his aversion to further learning may have been major factors in his restricted and narrow military outlook. I myself heard him boasting that he had sited each and every machine gun in East Pakistan personally. I recall thinking even then that if he was performing the duties of a platoon commander, who would do his job as a theatre commander. His arrogance and misplaced over-confidence, unfortunately, conspired to make him a victim of his own reputation. He was also prone to exercising excessive control over his sub-ordinate commanders, even in minor operational details.

After taking over as Commander Eastern Command in April, General Niazi hardly had any time to carry out any operational planning for his command. It was only after the situation in the province stabilized to some extent in May that this subject began to nebulously loom somewhere on his professional horizon. In June 1971, General Abdul Hamid Khan, the Army COS, paid a visit to East Pakistan and General Niazi took this opportunity to present his somewhat half-baked views on the subject. In his own words, his operational perspective underlying these proposals was as following:

"Our spirits were high and that of Bengalis low. They were on the run, the Indians

33

were in a spin, and the Russians were wonderstruck. My troops had had their battle inoculation, while the Indians still had to go through their teething troubles. I argued that we should strike while the iron was hot." [28]

Leading from this, he outlined three basic options for offensive action *on the Indian soil:*

1. **Hot Pursuit.** Niazi's basic premise was, that at the moment the Indian Army was not prepared to withstand a surprise assault from an unexpected direction. He advocated chasing the rebels to their Indian sanctuaries and thus rendering them ineffective as a fighting force. He argued that by the time the Indians would be ready to react in strength, the Eastern Command would have achieved their primary object.

2. **Limited Offensive Action.** Niazi's second option was relatively more audacious. He proposed limited ground offensives to capture Agartala and sizeable chunks of Assam, as well as several other thrusts into Indian Bengal. His only requirement for this was the replenishment of the Eastern Command in men and material, especially in armour and artillery. He also requested an additional brigade group and one squadron of modern aircraft to execute his plan.

3. **Full Scale Offensive Action.** Niazi's third option was an extremely ambitious plan. It envisaged a full- scale war with India in the East. In his own words: *"Fight not only the battle of East Pakistan but of Pakistan in the east and on the Indian soil".* It called for the induction of two more infantry divisions as well as some air force and air defence elements in the Eastern Theatre. It also stipulated replenishment of existing deficiencies. Thinking quite hyperbolically, Niazi envisaged that the Indians would need to induct at least fifteen divisions to check his proposed offensive. In addition, they would require several formations for internal security duties as well as the defence of the Chinese border. Thus, he visualized a massive imbalance in the Western Theatre, giving Pakistan a decisive strategic advantage there, perhaps even allowing the liberation of Kashmir in the process.

After listening patiently to Niazi, a virtue for which General Hamid was famed in the Army, he said that though the suggestions made by Niazi were sound, any of these options would result in an open war with India, for which the Government of Pakistan was not prepared at the present time. Instead, he directed General Niazi as follows:

---

[28] Lt Gen A A Khan Niazi, Op Cit, page 65.

"Your task is not to allow the Indians to establish a Government of Bangladesh on the soil of East Pakistan, and if you can accomplish that we will be happy and satisfied with your work, with you and your troops. To sum it up, you will neither enter Indian Territory nor send raiding parties into India, and you will not fire into Indian Territory either. You should evict any hostile element entering East Pakistan."[29]

With that directive, apparently, the chapter of East Pakistan was closed once for all by the Pakistan High Command!

At least one Indian general, Major General Sukhwant Singh, found merit in Niazi's options:

"Yahya had valid reasons for crossing international borders in the eastern wing in pursuit of guerrillas as well as to overrun their bases in India about the end of May 71 and of the opportunity to enlarge conflict into a full-fledged war by hitting India also in the West. That was India's worst hour, its reserve formations were in the hinterland, it had serious shortfalls of war material, and soldiers and civilians were not mentally attuned to immediate war. If Yahya had struck at that time, he could have gained profitable objectives both in the Western and Eastern theatres before the onset of monsoons."[30]

Generals Niazi as well as Sukhwant Singh were perhaps basing their opinions on narrow lines of operational strategy but were certainly ignoring the geopolitical and grand strategic scenarios then in ambiance in the sub-continent as well as in the international community. The choice of strategy for a war is heavily dependent on several other factors besides purely military considerations. The foreign support, the financial situation, the logistical constraints, and the psycho-social factors too bear heavily on purely military considerations.

Indian leadership, particularly Prime Minister Indira Gandhi, had launched a very potent and effective exterior manoeuvre aimed at highlighting India's cause and isolating Pakistan and its leadership for its perceived "atrocities and genocide". Had Pakistan chosen to launch an offensive, even a minor one, at that point in time, it would have immediately been castigated as an aggressor victimizing a hapless India. Pakistan would have almost certainly lost the sympathy of even the very few friends it still had at that time. Pakistan could hardly afford such a risky course of action!

---

[29] Ibid, pages 66-67.
[30] Maj Gen Sukhwant Singh, Op Cit, page 65.

35

Even on purely military considerations, Niazi's offensive plans could hardly be considered sound. They were, apparently, based on the assumption that all the forces in the Eastern Theatre would be available to him for offensive tasks. His operational thinking was the reflection of hubris and over-confidence over his earlier tactical successes in pacifying the province. He failed to take into account that he would still need to keep a substantial number of his troops in an internal security posture just for maintaining law and order in the province. Thus, the actual number of troops available to him for offensive tasks would be substantially less than his expectations.

Furthermore, the move of any significant number of reinforcements from West to East Pakistan would certainly have been detected by the Indians as all such movement had to transit via Sri Lanka. This would have alerted the Indians in time to move some of their own reserve formations to the Eastern Theatre; Niazi's proposed offensive may well have stalled in its tracks. This, unfortunately, was not the only occasion where Niazi was to betray his utter lack of strategic acumen. On all these considerations, General Hamid was certainly correct to dissuade General Niazi from such foolhardy manoeuvres.

General Niazi at that time had only the following strategic courses open to him for the defence of East Pakistan:

- Defend the frontier in strength and deploy as close to the borders as tactically feasible in order to deny ingress to the Indians along the communication routes. Then gradually withdraw behind the line of the major rivers to defend the Dacca Bowl. Inherent in this option was the risk of piecemeal dispersion of his forces as well as their exposure to the IAF by day and guerrilla attacks by night. In any such defensive deployment, the enemy would always possess the inherent advantage of concentrating at a point of his choosing and forcing a breakthrough. There was thus a clear possibility of a defeat in detail.

- Concentrate *ab initio* on the defence of Dacca Bowl and thus impose maximum delay on the Indian Army, particularly if their main objective was the capture of Dacca. The political disadvantages of losing major chunks of territory without any serious resistance had to be considered very seriously as this would practically provide a carte blanche to the Mukti Bahini to declare a viable state of Bangladesh on the captured soil.

- Organize positional defence along the likely routes of ingress.

36

Occupy nodal points along the main axes of advance open to the Indian forces and turn them into Fortresses; stock them adequately to withstand long siege. Organize Strong Points on important communication centres. Each operational sector to have adequate reserves to harass, delay and defeat enemy forces using strong points as anvils.

- Adopt a combination of positional and mobile defence and fight along successive, pre-designated and pre-prepared delaying positions. This strategy, if employed judiciously, would impose maximum delay and inflict maximum casualties on the enemy. The line of major rivers around the Dacca Bowl would be the last defensive position to be held in strength, beyond which there would be no withdrawal. The time so gained would be used on the western front to achieve a measure of success by the strategic reserves of the Pakistan Army, which would somewhat off-set the losses incurred on the Eastern Front.

Operational strategy in its simplest manifestation is an interaction and trade-off between three primary factors: TIME, SPACE, AND RELATIVE STRENGTH. In the scenario then confronting General Niazi, the Indians enjoyed a definite superiority in the numbers game and thus the advantage of Relative Strength certainly lay with them. That left Niazi with only one option: trade off space to gain maximum time in which the Pakistan forces in the Western Theatre would be able to make substantial gains on the Indian territory; or, by which time the United Nations would impose a cease fire to bring the war to an end, thus offering a fig leaf of honour to a beleaguered Niazi. This essentially pointed to a strategy of mobile defence rather than a rigid positional defence. Thus, the best course for General Niazi under these circumstances would have been to adopt a strategy which could gain him maximum time and thus delay the fall of Dacca for as long as possible. Ironically, he, instead, opted to adopt a course of action which was entirely based upon political considerations; quite predictably, it eventually proved to be militarily disastrous.

The Political Directive issued by the CMLA Headquarters to the Eastern Command, which remained applicable throughout this period, was NOT to permit the Mukti Bahini or other militant forces to occupy any sizeable chunk of territory, where they could establish Bangladesh. This, unfortunately, became Niazi's over-riding obsession; he made it a point of honour as a soldier not to concede even a small portion of East Pakistan and, with time, this became his sole objective. Apparently, the possibility that India might launch a full- scale offensive against East Pakistan remained a very remote possibility for him. Consequently, the Eastern Command became entirely pre-occupied with "search and destroy" missions, aimed at the recapture of any gains made by the Mukti Bahini. In operational terms, this degenerated into adoption of an extreme forward posture, at places even ahead of the line of the BOPs.

By his temperament and lack of training in operational handling of large formations, General Niazi was simply not suited for the most problematic and delicate independent command in the Pakistan Army at that juncture. He was primarily at home in simple unit and sub-unit level tactical operations and perhaps totally out of his league as a theatre commander. He simply failed to analyze the complex situation facing him in East Pakistan in its historical, sociological and political perspectives and instead ended up over-simplifying the problem. His weaknesses, personal as well as professional, rapidly became obvious to the entire Army fairly soon, not the least to the officers serving in his Command. Since many Indian generals had served with him before the Partition, his professional weaknesses were well known to them too and they were to exploit and capitalize on this fore-knowledge again and again during the December War.

Despite this, it might be rather unfair to lay the entire blame on the shoulders of Niazi alone. The situation at that time had become totally confused by conflicting orders and instructions issued to the Eastern Command by the CMLA Headquarters and the GHQ. Even after two and a half years, no clear division of responsibility had ever evolved between these two centers of national power. The inherent limitations of this ad hoc system were to become fatally obvious as the East Pakistan situation progressively deteriorated over time. While the CMLA HQ ought to have confined itself to purely political and policy guidance, it had an obsessive compulsion to brazenly intrude even into purely technical military matters at times, and that too without taking the GHQ into the loop.

To some extent, this situation was an inherent feature of the martial law system where the CMLA was also the Army Chief and the Supreme Commander of the Armed Forces. He was thus prone to passing direct instructions and orders to Commander Eastern Command either on phone or by signal messages, the information of which was rarely conveyed to the GHQ. General Abdul Hamid Khan, the Army COS, was usually taken on board but he rarely condescended to sharing his knowledge with the Chief of the General Staff (CGS) at the GHQ. The result was a highly disgruntled CGS, Lt General Gul Hasan Khan, who was usually ignorant of what was actually happening on the ground in East Pakistan. To further aggravate the problem, his own personal relations with other principal staff officers

(PSOs) were also far from cordial and an environment of tension and uncertainty prevailed within the entire GHQ.

The Myth of Fortresses and Strong Points

The plan that General Niazi did adopt in the end was, albeit only in his own assessment, designed to impose maximum delay upon the enemy. It envisaged blocking all the major routes of entry from India by occupying strong defensive positions along all road approaches. Raised in the tradition of the British Indian Army, his expectation of the Indian design of battle in the impending war remained confined to set-piece attacks, well- defined phase lines and resumption of advance only after extensive grouping/regrouping. As he struggled to balance his formations on this specific design of battle, he ended up basing his plan on the concept of fortresses and strong points.

Theoretically, these Fortresses were to be stocked with 45 days' rations and 60 days' ammunition. In addition, selected nodal points and communication centres along the roads leading to fortresses and from there on towards Dacca were to be developed as Strong Points. Conceptually speaking, the enemy penetration and ingress was to be fixed between these well-sited positions, using which as pivots, operational reserves were to be launched to defeat the enemy in detail. The Dacca Bowl had to be defended to the last; till the United Nations finally intervened to enforce a ceasefire.

In theory, it was perhaps a fine concept but was totally compromised by an enormous deviation between theory and practice on the ground. By the time the war started in real earnest, General Niazi had spread out his forces along the line of BOPs to such an extent that he was left with troops neither for properly manning the fortresses/ strong points nor for creating any operational reserves.

By instinctively reacting to Indian provocations during October-November 1971, he had entirely denuded himself of operational reserves as well as totally compromised his own strategic reaction capability. In the end, he was hardly left with any combat troops even for defence of Dacca. Thus, these so-called fortresses and strong points eventually proved to be a mere myth and only served to decorate the operational maps in Dacca and Rawalpindi with nice looking symbols. It was clearly a recipe for a defeat in detail. This is what had constrained the Hamoodur Rahman Commission to make the following scathing comments on this situation:

"The planning, if any, was hopelessly defective and there was no plan at all for defence of Dacca."[31]

Niazi's Operational Plan – July 1971

It was in this frame of mind that Niazi issued his Operational Instruction No. 3 on 15th July 1971.[32] According to the general concept of operation conceived by General Niazi in this plan, the defence of East Pakistan was to be conducted in three broad layers:

- Before the commencement of open hostilities with India, the border to be secured by defending Border Out Posts (BOPs) with the civil armed forces and Razakars, beefed up with regular troops, where necessary.

- Rebel concentrations and any areas captured by them in the interior of the Province were to be dealt with reserve Army troops located in the vicinity.

- In case open hostilities broke out with India, the defence of the area would be conducted from pre-determined and well stocked strong points.

The salient features of this Plan were as follows:

1. <u>Mission.</u> Defend East Pakistan while:

   a. Taking offensive in the direction of Tripura, Calcutta and Siliguri.
   b. Capturing maximum Indian Territory.
   c. Ensuring defence of Dacca at all costs.

2. East Pakistan was divided into five sectors; their operational responsibility and tasks assigned them were as follows.

3. <u>Jessore Sector</u>

   a. <u>Responsibility</u>: 9 Division (less Brigade).

---

[31] *Hamoodur Rahman Commission Report*, Vanguard Books, Lahore, page 402/34.
[32] Maj Gen Shaukat Riza, Op Cit, pages 119-121.

b. Tasks

(1) Develop Khulna, Jessore, Jhenida, and Kushtia as Fortress Defences.

(2) Develop Darsana and Goalundu Ghat as strong points.

(3) Keep corridor between the Kumar River and Ganges clear for operations by the Command Reserve.

(4) Plan capture of Chuagacha salient up to River Khamati, Basir Hat, Krishan Nagar, and Rana Ghat upto River Jhalangi.

4. Bogra Sector

a. Responsibility. 16 Division

b. Tasks

(1) Develop Dinajpur, Saidpur, Rangpur, Gaibanda, Bogra, Naogaon and Rajshahi into Fortress Defences.

(2) Develop Hilli, Sirajganj Ghat, and Nagarbari Ghat as strong points.

(3) Hold Paksey (Hardinge) and Tista Bridges at all costs.

(4) Be prepared to eliminate Hilli Salient.

5. Dacca Sector

a. Responsibility. 14 Division

b. Tasks

(1) Develop Dacca, Jamalpur, Mymensingh, Brahmanbaria, Comilla, Feni, Chandpur, Daudkundi into Fortress Defences.

(2) Develop Bahadurabad Ghat, Jagannathganj Ghat and Aricha into strong points.

(3) Deny Dacca at all costs.

(4) Defend Bhairab Bazar Bridge at all costs.

(5) At the outbreak of hostilities, launch the following offensives:

(a) Against Tripura with 313 Brigade (less battalion) from direction of Maulvi Bazar or Belonia.

(b) Occupy approaches leading into the area Jamalpur and Mymensingh with 27 Brigade less battalion.

4. **Sylhet Sub Sector**

a. Troops. Battalion ex 313 Brigade.

3 x Wings Frontier Corps
b. Tasks

(1) Develop Sylhet into Fortress Defence.

(2) Develop Sherpur Ferry into strong point.

5. **Chittagong Sub Sector**

a. Troops. 3 x Wings EPCAF
1 x Wing WPR

b. Tasks
(1) Develop Chittagong as a Fortress Defence.
(2) Develop Ramgarh, Karer Hat, Sitakund, Kaptai, and Rangamati as strong points.

6. **27 Brigade Task Force.** Will capture general areas Madhupur, Jamalpur and defiles of Mahendraganj, Barengapara and Baghmora at

the outbreak of hostilities.

7. **313 Brigade Task Force.** Will perform the following tasks:

a.   Detach a battalion for defence of Maulvi Bazar.
b.
b. Launch offensive against Tripura salient at the outbreak of hostilities.

8. **COMMAND RESERVE.**   53 Brigade, located at Aricha (on River Padma).

9. **SSG UNITS.** Under command HQ Eastern Command.

Plan Ends

The most glaring weakness of this plan was Niazi's obsession with launching offensive strikes against India in three different sectors. Considering the ambient geopolitical and operational environment and the limited forces available to him, such thinking was nothing less than foolhardiness on his part. It was indeed a clear manifestation of his limited professional acumen and reflected adversely on his ability to be placed in command of an active theatre of operations. Predictably, therefore, when the above Plan was submitted to the GHQ for approval in early August, it was accorded approval in early September with the following modifications:

• Counter offensive plans be biased towards the west, posing threat to Calcutta area.
• Strong offensive for capture of English Bazar and Farakha Barrage be planned.
• SSG targets to be selected and integrated in the plan.
• Regular troops for the defence of Chittagong be positioned.

The basic concept underlying this Plan was perhaps still reflective of General Niazi's obsession with not losing an inch of territory, and to check the militants as close to the border as possible. It was seemingly based on the assumption that in order to discourage the militants from attempting to infiltrate and thus bringing the rebel activity to the minimum, it was essential to create two conditions: firstly, the militant infiltration must be effectively checked right on the border; secondly, any militants, who did regardless succeed in infiltrating, must be quickly and effectively eliminated by immediate action by tactical or operational reserves.

What was neglected in the process was the age-old principle of strategy that trying to be strong everywhere results in weakness all over. The quantum of forces available to General Niazi were simply insufficient to effectively defend the entire border with India. As pressure by the Indian Army increased with the passage of time, the quest to be strong everywhere became the self-defeating sole objective of the Eastern Command. In due course, this policy resulted in compromising even the basic principles of military organization as units/sub-units were attached and detached indiscriminately for employment on the BOPs. The efficiency and effectiveness of cohesive command and control at unit level was thus sacrificed at the altar of expediency. Thus, by end of November, the Pakistan forces had been committed to a rigid form of linear defence. In the process and with his obsession with holding maximum territory, General Niazi had allowed his forces to be drawn out to the border, with hardly any reserves.

There is, however, no doubt that Niazi was facing a very complex situation, to which there were hardly any easy solutions. Some of the complex problems he was then facing were:

The initiative of declaring open hostilities lay entirely with India, which it would exercise at the time of its own convenience. India, obviously, also possessed the option to execute a scheme of manoeuvre, which would maximize its chances of early success and Niazi could only play a waiting game.

The forces under Niazi's Command had been under continuous employment since April, primarily for internal security duties. By the late autumn, the factor of battle fatigue had assumed serious dimensions.

- The vast border to be defended had forced an extended deployment on the Pakistani units and formations; the consequent troops to space ratio had become so diluted as to be tactically unsound. On the other hand, even if Niazi had opted for compact brigade/ divisional positions, they would essentially be fighting isolated, independent battles with the inherent risk of being bypassed and dealt with later.

- In the prevalent situation, Niazi could hardly concentrate his command to defend just Dacca and some other major cities. The Indian Army and the Mukti Bahini would have simply enjoyed a walk over in the rest of the province and set up a functioning Bangladesh there. They could then have imposed a continuous war of attrition on the formations still holding out and it would be only a matter of time when they ran out of their logistic support. Counting on the United Nations to salvage the situation for Pakistan was perhaps an unrealistic option in view of the total support being given to India by the entire Soviet bloc.

Despite these operational constraints, had the formations been deployed in compact positions to defend not urban but major communication centres, it would have given them the opportunity to put up a much better performance and an opportunity to employ their maximum combat potential, such as it was after a long spell of internal security duties and employment on usually futile search and destroy missions. Even HQ Eastern Command would have been able to conduct the war in a more coherent and coordinated manner.

In the end, Niazi was forced to take resort to the creation of fortresses and strong points, which further diluted his deployment. The endless groupings and regroupings of units and formations further compromised the whole fabric of his command. His ability to influence the operations at critical moments was also totally compromised in the absence of a viable Command Reserve. Within a day or two of the war, he was reduced to a mere spectator.

In the meantime, the Indians had been methodically concentrating their forces around East Pakistan. By now, according to the GHQ assessment, they could muster some seven to eight infantry divisions, five to six armoured regiments, thirty- two BSF battalions, and some 100000 Mukti Bahini troops. It was also quite obvious that India, with its superior naval strength, would be able to effectively blockade East Pakistan. According to the assessment carried out by the Pakistan Air Staff, India could employ up to eleven combat squadrons, including a bomber squadron, against only one, depleted squadron of the PAF.

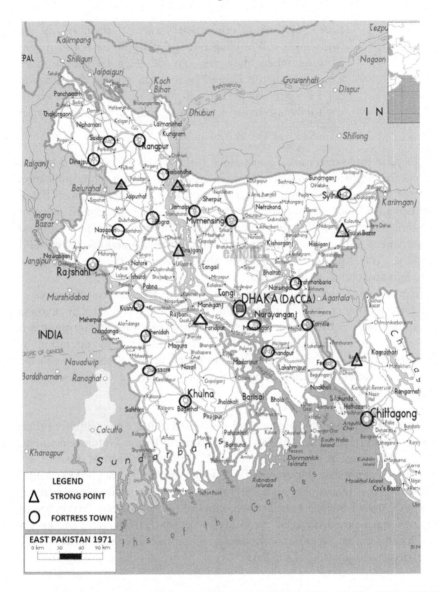

LOCATION OF PROPOSED FORTRESSES AND STRONG POINTS

As the strength and pattern of this menacing deployment became manifest, the GHQ eventually came to realize that the current plans of the Eastern Command needed major changes. An Operational Directive was consequently issued by the GHQ in September 1971, which directed the Eastern Command as follows:[33]

- The Eastern Command was to be kept in being under all circumstances.

- No offensive plans for operations into the Indian Territory to be made.

- East Pakistan to be defended by a mobile defence which envisaged the employment of only light, mobile forces on the borders to guard it; strategically important areas in each sector, including the Dacca Bowl, were to be strongly defended.

Despite this clear Directive, General Niazi remained convinced in his heart that India would not launch any large- scale military operation in East Pakistan. His entire operational policy as well as pattern of deployment was, therefore, based on dealing with the Mukti Bahini operating with only limited support provided by the Indian Army, mainly from their side of the border. He obdurately refused to even consider the possibility of India launching a major offensive against East Pakistan. Thus, he consciously elected to disregard even this GHQ Directive.

General Gul Hasan Khan, the CGS, paid his last visit to East Pakistan in October 1971. By that time, the intelligence agencies were already receiving clear indications that the war with India was imminent in East Pakistan. Gul Hasan raised this issue with General Niazi and advised him to thin out from the BOPs and even some of the strong points but was informed that HQ CMLA had made it plain that not one inch of territory would be abandoned to the rebels.

In words of General Gul Hasan,

"Thus, the political and military aims were to remain in conflict with no solution in sight. We were to pay dearly for the double set of directives that had been issued to the Eastern Command".[34]

---

[33] Lt Gen Kamal Matinuddin, Op Cit, pages 344-345.
[34] Lt Gen Gul Hasan Khan, *Op Cit*, pages 314-315.

The Hoax of Ad Hoc Formations

As mentioned previously, the Eastern Command was beset with several major operational disadvantages: the glaring numerical disparity against the likely Indian deployment; no likelihood of meaningful reinforcement from West Pakistan; the deteriorating security situation, almost by the day; relentless attacks along the border by the Mukti Bahini as well as the Indian Army, resulting in loss of critical areas; and, the adoption of an unsound extreme forward posture.

The only remedy which General Niazi and his staff could envision under these constraints, some of their own creation, was to conceive a rather transparent form of strategic deception. He resorted to raising of several ad hoc formation headquarters within his Command by juggling around with his existing resources in order to convey a false impression to the enemy. He had obtained permission for this deception directly from the COS Army during his last visit to East Pakistan in October without making any reference to the GHQ. [35]

In the end, he simply could not achieve his objective as hardly anyone in the Indian hierarchy was deceived by the ruse. They were closely monitoring the entire process of reinforcement from West to East Pakistan and obviously did not observe any such activity. The only advantage Niazi possibly accrued from the entire exercise was to improve the articulation of command within the Eastern Command by utilizing the large number of senior officers present in East Pakistan on non-operational assignments. In an oblique way, it did act as a morale booster for the troops who could see more senior officers in the operational area.

Under this policy, one divisional headquarters and five brigade headquarters were raised in October, followed by one divisional and one brigade headquarters just before the commencement of the war in the east. The following ad hoc formations, hereafter denoted by the letter 'A', were raised as a part of this policy:

- HQ 36 (A) Division. Major General Muhammad Jamshed
- HQ 39 (A) Division. Major General Rahim Khan
- HQ 91 (A) Brigade. Brigadier Taskin-ud-din.
- HQ 93 (A) Brigade. Brigadier Abdul Qadir Niazi
- HQ 97 (A) Brigade. Brigade Atta Malik
- HQ 202 (A) Brigade. Brigadier Saleemullah

---

[35] Ibid, page 318.

• HQ 314 (A)Brigade. Colonel Fazal Hameed

It would, however, be entirely misleading to compare the combat effectiveness of these ad hoc headquarters with regular formations. They were short of everything except the commanders. There were no staff trained officers, and hardly any transport. Their communication resources mainly comprised what the Command or divisional signals could spare for them out of their own rather meagre resources. Consequently, they had to rely extensively on civilian communication systems.

Growing Concerns at the GHQ

During all this time, several senior officers from the GHQ had visited East Pakistan off and on and the precarious situation on the ground could hardly escape their professional eye. They became very concerned at the deteriorating situation in the province as well as the glaring weaknesses in Eastern Command's pattern of deployment. On their return to West Pakistan, most of them recorded their impressions in their After-Visit Reports and, in due course, some of these reports did find their way to the office of the COS Army. In addition, a number of senior officers, having direct access to him, apprised him of their misgivings verbally as well. The COS was advised almost unanimously that the Eastern Command must be immediately ordered to fall back from the forward line of BOPs and to occupy their main defensive positions in compliance with their operational plans. However, no action seems to have been taken by General Hamid neither were any orders or instructions issued by the GHQ on the subject.

In early October, the DMI, Brigadier (later General) Muhammad Iqbal, visited East Pakistan and he too was highly perturbed to see the troops deployed in penny packets. While still there, he discussed the problem with Brigadier Baqir Siddiqui, COS Eastern Command, and advised him to concentrate the troops in battle positions to avoid a defeat in detail. On his return on 12th October, he advised the CGS General Gul Hasan that the BOP concept of defense, as being followed by the Eastern Command, should be abandoned and troops deployed according to defense plans. The CGS took the DMI and DMO with him to see the COS Army and after highlighting the prevalent situation, recommended that it was high time a firm directive was issued to the Eastern Command to adopt the proper posture to fight tactical battles. The reaction of the COS was characteristic of the man as he said, *"The decision should be left to the man on the spot. Let him fight his battles as he deems fit."* And there the matter rested till early November when Major General Anwar Ahmed Qureshi, the VCGS, returned from a visit to East Pakistan after forming similar impressions. Another effort was then made, this time more forcefully, to convince the COS to take some

49

action. In the end, he agreed to send the DMO to East Pakistan but when the DMO laconically asked, with what instructions, the COS gave no answer and the idea was dropped. As a last resort, it was decided to summon COS Eastern Command for briefing and discussion.

Presentation of the Final Plans at GHQ

Consequently, in November 1971, General Niazi detailed Major General Muhammad Jamshed, DG EPCAF, Commander 36 (A) Division, and for all intents and purposes his second-in-command, to accompany his COS Brigadier Baqir Siddiqui to the GHQ to make a detailed presentation of his Appreciation of the Situation and his Operational Plan. General Hamid, the COS Army, presided over the Conference held on 15th November where the GHQ staff was represented by CGS, QMG, VCGS, DMO and DMI. Admiral Muzaffar Hasan, C-in-C Navy, also dropped in for some time.

Brigadier Baqir Siddiqui presented the plan over the next two days, including the follow up discussion. He explained the BOP concept of defense in detail and justified its utility under the present situation. He also asserted that in case of Indian invasion, the Eastern Command did have the detailed plans to fall back on the fortresses and strong points in the rear.

A query was raised by the VCGS at this stage as to why the EPCAF and Mujahids were not being entrusted with the defence of the BOPs, thus relieving the Army troops to be withdrawn to their defensive positions. In reply, the COS Eastern Command argued that the para-military forces were not yet ready to take over the BOPs and in any case, could not operate without the backing of the Army in the prevalent environment. The next was a query from the DMO about the arrangements had been made to construct defence works around Dacca and their progress so far. Brig Baqir Siddiqui assured him that the needful was being done.

At this stage, the Conference came to an abrupt end as General Hamid was urgently called by the President and he immediately left along with the Naval Chief. The way this conference ended displayed an entirely unprofessional and cavalier approach of the Army hierarchy towards the issues relating to the defence of East Pakistan. Perhaps, that was one reason why rumours became rife that in their minds the High Command had already abandoned the province to its fate.

After this inconclusive conference, the DMI took General Jamshed to the MI Operations Room and there briefed him on the latest known Indian deployment along the East Pakistan borders. He entreated that the situation being very serious, *'Let us not destroy ourselves by distributing our troops in penny packets.'* General Jamshed became pensive on seeing the Indian build-up and remarked that under the situation, the Eastern Command should be issued with operational instructions or a directive by the GHQ. And there the matter rested.

Eastern Command Plan- 15th November

The following is the gist of the Plan presented by COS Eastern Command at the GHQ Conference on 15th November:[36]

Enemy Hypotheses

General Niazi was still convinced that the most likely Indian option would be to employ Mukti Bahini forces in an offensive role with full support of the Indian Army and the BSF, essentially from their own side of the border. However, in case India opted for a full-scale invasion, Niazi expected an invasion by a force comprising up to eleven divisions, four independent brigades, one independent armoured brigade, and about thirty-nine BSF battalions. Depending upon the time of war, this number could also increase to twelve divisions as the passes on Sino-Indian Border would become snow-bound in December. Keeping all these likely scenarios in view, he had conceived the following hypotheses of action:

1. **Hypothesis 1**

    a. Intensification of subversive activities all along the border as well as in the interior of East Pakistan, to include:

    (1) Disruption of lines of communication.

    (2) Concurrent wide-spread non-cooperation and civil disobedience movement by the civilian population.

    (3) Frustrating the current re-election efforts as well as transfer of powers to the elected civilians.

    b. Mukti Bahini to take the following actions on the border:

    (1) All-out attacks, supported by Indian infantry and artillery in

---

[36] Lt Gen A A K Niazi, Op cito, pages 103-106.

all sectors.

(2) Nibbling at the borders and capture of own BOPs one by one with full Indian support.

(3) Exploit weak spots and creep forward wherever possible in order to cut line of communications along Chittagong-Comilla-Sylhet border.

c. Establish the writ of Bangladesh in the captured chunks of territory; in due course, Bangladesh will be accorded recognition by the Indians.

2. Hypothesis 2 (Most Dangerous)

a. Full-scale Indian invasion of East Pakistan.

b. H-1, to be in progress simultaneously in order to provide full support to the invasion.

3. Hypothesis 3

a. H-1 launched for about a month or so.

b. If no tangible results, go for H-2.

Courses Open to Own Forces

It was submitted to the GHQ that, in the context of the overall internal and external environment, there were now only three courses open to the Eastern Command to meet the threat and to successfully prosecute the war against India:

1. **Course A.** Pull back the bulk of troops to fortress areas and strong points:

This would leave the actual borders and some of the adjacent areas undefended or lightly held, which could then be easily over run by the rebels with direct support from the Indian Army. Areas thus occupied could well be declared by them as Bangladesh. The enemy would thus achieve their mission without much fighting and bloodshed. All the hard work, hard fighting and sacrifices would go waste and the disintegration of Pakistan would become a certainty.

2. **Course B.** Hold the Border Strongly.

This would give cohesion to Eastern Command and, if successful, no land will be lost. However, this course was considered unsound due to the vastness of the area to be held and the lack of troops, firepower and mobility. As such, this would result in little depth with no reserves, no flexibility or maneuverability, and limited freedom of action. There was the possibility and risk of defeat in detail. This would also result in unnecessary casualties. A war of attrition would suit the enemy objectives. On the other hand, the Eastern Command would be in a position to carry out raids into Indian territory as well as subject them to artillery fire, forcing them to employ troops to protect their gun areas, tank harbours etc.

2. **Course C.** Induct Sufficient Additional Troops in the Eastern Theatre.

Make up deficiencies so as to be effective on the front line as well as in the interior; thus, continue to fight profitably the undeclared war against the Indian Army; and deal with and eliminate the rebels in the interior. This was the course of action recommended for adoption by the Eastern Command.

The only major change in the pattern of his defensive deployment, as envisaged in his Plan of 15th July 1971, was to entrust specific areas of responsibility to the two newly raised ad hoc divisional headquarters. The consequent changes in the articulation of his command were as follows:

- No change in the areas of responsibility of 9 Division in the Southwestern Sector (Jessore-Khulna) and 16 Division in the Northwestern Sector (North Bengal).
- The operational responsibility for Dacca as well as the Central Sector was divested from 14 Division and handed over to 36 (A)Division under the command of Major General Muhammad Jamshed SJ.
- 14 Division was allocated the responsibility for Sylhet, Maulvi Bazar and Brahmanbaria areas, designated Northeastern Sector.
- 39 (A) Division under the command of Maj Gen Rahim Khan was allocated the responsibility of Comilla, Chandpur and Feni areas, designated Southeastern Sector.
- Chittagong and Chittagong Hill Tracts, though nominally under 39 (A) Division, were to operate as an independent sub-sector.

<u>Plan Ends.</u>

The ORBAT of Eastern Command and its deployment on the eve of the war is given at Annexure "B".

There has been some controversy relating to what decisions, if any, were given by the GHQ at the conclusion of this critical Planning Conference. According to General Niazi, the GHQ had agreed with Course C, since in the case of the first two courses, the enemy would be in a better position to achieve its mission, creating an unacceptable situation for Pakistan. Course C was also in keeping with the mission of not losing any areas of importance and tying down maximum Indian troops in this theatre, which would likely create a favourable relative strength situation in the Western Theatre as well. However, the Eastern Command Team strongly emphasized that additional troops and making up of existing deficiencies were essential for adopting this course of action.[37]

However, no participant of this Conference from the GHQ has verified or corroborated this assertion made by General Niazi. According to all of them, it was an inconclusive conference, an exercise in futility, in which no firm decisions were taken.

Niazi has also claimed that his Team had indeed managed to have a subsequent, exclusive meeting with General Hamid, and, on their return to Dacca, Major General Jamshed and Brigadier Baqir Siddiqui brought him the following verbal directive from the COS Army:[38]

- The Political Mission of the Eastern Command would remain unchanged.

- According to very reliable intelligence reports, India was likely to attack East Pakistan on the Eid day, i.e. 21st November 1971.

- The Eastern Command must continue fighting in the forward defensive posture, as well as against the insurgents in the interior.

- The Eastern Command request for meeting the existing

---

[37] Lt Gen A A Khan Niazi, *Op Cit*, pages 103-109.
[38] *Ibid*, page 108.

54

imbalances, i.e. additional artillery and more troops, was partially agreed to. GHQ promised to immediately dispatch eight infantry battalions and one engineer battalion.

The abrupt and inconclusive GHQ Conference on 15th November thus failed to give much meaningful guidance to the Eastern Command at that critical moment. This could only mean that the COS Army as well as the President were quite satisfied with the pattern of defence and the conduct of operations in East Pakistan at that time. As a result of this equanimity, the troops in East Pakistan, on the eve of the major Indian invasion, were placed in a position of such immense disadvantage as no other present day army of this size has ever been placed. All this while, the time for the withdrawal of troops from forward positions on the border and their concentration in their designated battle locations was fast running out. The troops were heavily committed in battles on the BOPs, thus playing into the hands of the Indian planners. The strategic and operational mobility of the Eastern Command had been reduced drastically due to extensive guerrilla activities in the rear as well as sabotage of numerous road bridges, ferries and river craft. Thus, the movement of troops from one place to another or across major river obstacles became well-nigh impossible.

The GHQ pledge of sending eight additional infantry battalions to Eastern Command remained only partially fulfilled. In the end, only three battalions were moved to East Pakistan, but without their heavy weapons and equipment. Niazi in the meantime, relying on this pledge, had already moved his Command Reserve, 53 Brigade, to form part of the newly raised 39 (A) Division. The battalions he did receive from West Pakistan were also moved to 9 Division to make up their existing deficiencies. Niazi was planning to utilize the remaining five battalions for defence of Dacca on arrival; these, however, never arrived. Consequently, Dacca was completely denuded of regular infantry units. This was to have serious repercussions in the end.

Thus, the Eastern Command, under an over-confident commander, continued to operate on the original strategy of not ceding any territory to the Mukti Bahini lest they should establish a Bangladesh Government on the soil of East Pakistan. He appeared blissfully unaware that he had already lost some 7700 kilometers of territory to the Mukti Bahini in the shape of several salients and enclaves, which were enough to declare Bangladesh if that were the sole Indian objective. In his heart, he was still convinced that the Indians would not launch any major offensive in East Pakistan but restrict their operations merely to provide maximum support to the Mukti Bahini as visualized in his Hypothesis 1.

Surprisingly, however, he had no variant planned for the contingency in which the second, his most dangerous, hypothesis materialized. This is a cardinal sin in terms of operational strategy. Although he was certainly conscious of the critical importance of Dacca, he left the capital city virtually undefended in the wane hope that some formation or the other would be able to fall back on Dacca in time to defend it.

The last straw in all this dismal scenario was his Directive to the troops that there would be no withdrawal from any position till 75 % casualties had been suffered. This by itself denied the necessary mental mobility to his subordinate commanders. Such desperate orders are never given to the first line of defence in any case as it negates the very concept of mobile defence and fighting on successive lines of defence.

By 20th November India had succeeded in capturing almost all the BOPs, without evoking any serious response from the hard- pressed defenders. At several places, they had established forward bases and jump off points well inside the Pakistan territory to facilitate their future offensive plans. As a result of this constant pressure, the Pakistan forces had been denied the time and the opportunity to regroup and consolidate into the planned fortresses and strong points. In fact, because of their pre-occupation with the defence of BOPs, they hardly had the time to even properly prepare these fortresses and strong points. Thus, as the Indian invasion of East Pakistan started in earnest on 21st November, most of the Pakistan troops were caught totally unbalanced.

3

INDIA PLANS FOR WAR

Indian Policy on East Pakistan

"Undoubtedly India's national interest lay in having a friendly regime in neighbouring East Pakistan as the economic and cultural affinities of the two Bengals were linked indivisibly. Part of the same province in undivided India, the correlation of industries and sources of raw materials had not foreseen the effect of **the artificial territorial partition in 1947.**"[39] (Emphasis added.)

Indeed, India had never even attempted to conceal this obvious objective of its foreign and defence policies and never lost any opportunity to underscore it, as became particularly evident during the 1965 Indo-Pakistan War. While India launched a full-scale offensive against West Pakistan with all its might, it did not undertake any major offensive operation against East Pakistan, because it did not possess the quantum of troops required to generate any meaningful operations there. Despite that, the Indian Government adopted the narrative that this differential treatment to the two wings of Pakistan was a deliberate policy. To further reinforce this deceptive posture, the Indian leadership made several official statements; for instance, Yashwant Rao Chavan, the Defence Minister of India, made this policy statement in the Indian Parliament on 8th September 1965:

"Pakistan has attempted to escalate the war in the Eastern Sector. **We have no quarrel with East Pakistan** *while our troops have taken up positions within our territory in order to meet any threat of aggression by Pakistan."* (Emphasis added.)

---

[39] Maj Gen Sukhwant Singh, Op Cit, page 16.

Again, on 23rd September 1965, the Indian Prime Minister Lal Bahadur Shastri in a broadcast to the nation stated that in pursuance of the Indian policy of friendship towards East Pakistan, he *'did not permit the extension of hostilities to this region in the conflict despite the temptation of an easy victory'*.[40]

This policy unfortunately gave rise to the misperception that East Pakistan had remained safe from aggression in this war only because of Chinese threats or Indian munificence. This erroneous misperception came to be believed not only in East Pakistan but was believed in West Pakistan as well. In due course, this was to affect the Bengal street adversely. In retrospect, perhaps this was the point at which many political minds in East Pakistan seriously began to think in terms of independence. India on its part left no stone unturned to further accentuate this line of thinking. It was in this environment that the leading Indian intelligence agency Research & Analysis Wing (RAW) conceived the Agartala Conspiracy in collaboration with the top leadership of the Awami League as well as some recalcitrant elements in the armed forces and bureaucracy; its full details have been covered at length in my earlier book, WITNESS TO CARNAGE 1971. This Conspiracy however was detected by the intelligence agencies of Pakistan at a rather early stage and so died while still at the conception stage.

Despite this setback, RAW abandoned neither its ambitions nor the useful inroads it had made within the inner sanctums of Awami League. Indeed, it continued to set its goals progressively higher with time. The subsequent events in Pakistan leading to imposition of martial law in 1969, followed by the general elections in December 1970, served to provide the RAW with further opportunities. In cahoots with some top Awami League leaders, it drew up a multi-dimensional strategy to ensure the secession of East Pakistan from its mother country. The broad outlines of this ambitious strategy have been spelt out by an important former RAW official Asoka Raina as follows:

1. Should the Awami League be successful in attaining political power in Pakistan as a result of the elections; it should adopt a strategy aimed at removing economic disparity between the two wings as soon as possible, and then declare unilateral independence.

2. In case the transfer of power to the Awami League is denied by the military government, the Party should foment an insurgency aimed at the creation of Bangladesh, to be spearheaded by Bengali youth

---

[40] *Ibid*, page 17.

and the rebel elements from within the armed forces. These recalcitrant elements would be actively helped by Indian agents in key positions within East Pakistan, and fully backed by the physical participation of selected personnel of BSF and the regular army.

3. Once the insurgency had been successfully inflamed, the Indian Army would create a credible threat so as to draw Pakistan troops towards the border and keep them pegged down. Simultaneously, elements of East Bengal Regiment and East Pakistan Rifles, supported by rebellious groups as well as Indian agents in the garb of insurgents would spread into the countryside and attempt to seize the control of the government.

In words of Asoka Raina himself:

"The Bangladesh Operation possibly began a year before actual operation was underway. Even when the World got whiff of it in the shape of Mukti Bahini, many remained unaware of RAW's involvement. By then Phase I of the operation was already complete. Phase II saw the Indian forces poised for the independence of Bangladesh.

"In order to bring a clear synopsis of the events that brought RAW into Bangladesh Operation, one must review the intelligence activities that started soon after its formation in 1968. But by then the Indian operatives had already been in contact with the 'pro-Mujib faction'. A meeting convened in Agartala in 1962-63 between Intelligence Bureau Foreign Desk operatives and the Mujib faction gave some clear indications of what was to follow."[41]

This abiding interest had naturally necessitated development and maintenance of potent intelligence assets by India in East Pakistan. Thus, the Indian establishment had been keeping a close and watchful eye on the developments in East Pakistan since the last days of President Ayub Khan and then during the turbulent regime of President Yahya Khan. All this time, Indian agents and operatives were providing help and advice to the Awami League leadership, as borne out by several Bengali and Indian writers. The plan for a massive revolt by Awami League cadres, spearheaded by the battalions of East Bengal Regiment and the rifle wings of the East Pakistan Rifles in the wee hours of 26th March 1971 is now a well-documented fact. In retrospect, it is also pertinent to mention the important episode of the hi-jacking of the Indian aircraft GANGA on 30th January 1971. This provided a convenient pretext to the Indians to ban overflights over the Indian airspace. This alone more than any other factor

---

[41] Asoka Raina, *Inside RAW: The Story of India's Secret Service*, pages 48-50.

served to underline the physical and psychological barriers separating the two wings of Pakistan.

However, by the end of the monsoon season of 1971, the Indians had come to realize that the Mukti Bahini did not possess the capability of seizing power on their own and if the Indians continued to persist with the policy of placing primary reliance on the Mukti Bahini to produce strategic effects, they would meet with an eventual failure. Perhaps this was the point at which the Government of India finally decided to launch a full scale offensive action against East Pakistan. The chain of events leading to this critical decision, however, commenced much earlier; in fact, right since March 1971.

India Decides on War

As mentioned, India had always maintained an extensive and effective intelligence network in East Pakistan. The Indians, thus, usually remained fairly well informed of the events following the general elections in December 1970, but after the third week of March, the flow of information was somehow overtaken by the fast moving political and military developments. Thus, the swift crackdown by the Pakistan Army, the clampdown on the radio and television channels, and the expulsion of foreign correspondents, caught the Indians by surprise. Ironically, the Indians received the earliest information of the Army crackdown through their overt channels rather than any covert intelligence links.

It was at about midday on 26th March, when the Vice Chief of the Indian Army was telephonically informed that a Bengali non-commissioned officer (NCO) of the EPR along with about thirty soldiers had sought asylum at an Indian BOP in the Belonia Salient (near Comilla). The NCO had informed the BSF personnel about the military action and the revolt of the East Bengal battalions and EPR wings; he also intimated that fierce clashes were taking place between the two sides in several cities. This was the first inkling that India received about the situation in East Pakistan.[42] Soon enough, this was further confirmed when a heavy exodus of refugees began to pour into the India all around the border.

The Indian media, think tanks, several retired generals, and intellectuals like K. Subrahmanyam had vocally and vociferously advocated that this indeed was *"opportunity of the millennium"* to settle scores with Pakistan once for all. Even at that early stage, most of them were advocating that war with

---

[42] Maj Gen Sukhwant Singh, *Op Cit*, page 7.

Pakistan over this issue would eventually be inevitable, and that any delay in initiating the eventual war would make it proportionately costlier for India in men and resources. This concerted drumbeat advocating early recourse to military means was to grow exponentially as time passed. On its part, the Indian Government too hardly lost any time in unmasking its ambitions to exploit this opportunity to the fullest extent.

As early as 27th March, the Indian External Affairs Minister, Sardar Swaran Singh, in a statement before Rajya Sabha, the Upper House of the Indian Parliament, expressed concern over the events in East Pakistan.[43]

On the same day, Indira Gandhi, the Indian Prime Minister, made the statement, *'Something new had happened in East Pakistan'* which was of *'historic importance'* and to which *'we are fully alive'*. She assured the members that *'we shall keep constantly in touch with what is happening and what we need to do'*.[44]

Only four day later, on 31st March, a resolution was moved by Indira Gandhi in the Indian Parliament and unanimously passed by it, which stated, inter alia, that the Parliament:

Expressed *'deep anguish and grave concern at the recent developments in East Bengal'*;

Conveyed *'its profound sympathy for and solidarity with the people of East Bengal in their struggle for a democratic way of life'* and,

Recorded *'its profound conviction that the historical upsurge of the 75 million people of East Bengal will triumph'*.
(Note the change from East Pakistan to East Bengal. Author.)

During the month of April, while the Indian hawks, including many cabinet ministers, were openly advocating to strike, Pakistan's rulers were still in panic and disarray. Indira Gandhi too was also feeling tremendous public pressure, particularly from right wing parties like the Jan Sangh. By the end of April, she had apparently given in to this vociferous lobby and took the crucial decision.

Accordingly, on 28th April 1971, she called the Indian Army Chief General Sam Manekshaw before the Cabinet Committee of Political Affairs comprising Sardar Swaran Singh, the Foreign Minister, Jagjivan Ram, the

---

[43] *Bangladesh Documents*, page 651.
[44] *Ibid*, page 669.

Defence Minister, Fakhruddin Ali Ahmed, the Agriculture Minister, and Yashwant Rao Chavan, the Finance Minister. According to General Manekshaw, a *"very angry"* Prime Minister read out reports from the Chief Ministers of West Bengal, Assam and Tripura on the situation created by the heavy influx of refugees. Then she turned towards him and told her that she wanted him to *"enter East Pakistan"*.

A person of lesser mettle and self-confidence would perhaps have wilted under this angry demand by a very powerful and determined prime minister, but Manekshaw was no ordinary general. He stood his ground and patiently explained to her why an immediate resort to war was not a feasible option at that time. Some of the points made by him were as follows:[45]

- With the summer being around the corner, the mountain passes in NEFA were due to open any day and India might get involved in a three-front war situation in case the Chinese decided to support Pakistan openly.

- Two infantry divisions stationed in West Bengal were currently deployed in penny packets on internal security duties since the previous year to guard against the Communist threat and it would take at least one month to concentrate them in their normal organization.

- The armoured division was still located in its peace station, Jhansi, and it would take about a month to move it to its battle location opposite West Pakistan. Moreover, at the moment it just had thirteen tanks in running condition due to financial constraints.

- By the time these constraints were overcome, monsoons would commence in East Pakistan, which would make any offensive movement almost impossible.

Based upon these very pertinent points, General Manekshaw convinced the Prime Minister to delay the war to late November or early December in order to give time to the armed forces to make full preparations in the intervening period so as to ensure eventual success. Soon after this meeting, General Manekshaw is on record as having told General William Westmoreland, the US Army Chief of Staff, that the Indian military had sobered its hawkish civilian politicians, who were eager to strike in East

---

[45] Field Marshal Manekshaw, *Lecture at Indian Defence Services Staff College, Wellington*, 11th November 1988.

Pakistan.[46] Perhaps, this may have been the earliest indication of Indian designs received by the United States. This reprieve in the projected time of war was to be utilized by the Indian leadership very productively. Then onwards, the Indian Army, under its dynamic Chief, embarked upon a methodical programme of development, upgradation and consolidation to prepare it to ensure victory in the impending war with Pakistan.

The Indian leadership, headed by Indira Gandhi, also made a fruitful use of the intervening period. They launched a very powerful and effective exterior manoeuvre in the world at large, mainly based on the plight of the hapless Bengali populace as well as the immense problems caused by the heavy influx of refugees into the contiguous Indian provinces.

At the diplomatic level, the Indo-Soviet Treaty of Friendship was formalized in August 1971. This Treaty assured India of full support from the entire Soviet bloc. The Treaty, in effect, served notice on China not to interfere in the ensuing war in any meaningful manner. In any case, the timeframe of the operations visualized by General Manekshaw practically ruled out any large-scale operations by the Chinese against India. Moreover, the rivers in East Pakistan became free of floods during winter months and their flow became smooth. The smaller rivers became fordable at many points while the span of the major rivers became reduced appreciably, thus requiring considerably less engineering effort.

By the end of April 1971, the Indian Government had succeeded in formulating a clear policy and a tentative time table on the East Pakistan situation. For the implementation of this policy, the Government of India had also taken the following critical decisions, which eventually ensured a successful and seamless conduct of the ensuing war at the highest level:

- The overall direction and crisis management was delegated to the Prime Minister and the Cabinet Committee of Political Affairs.
- General Manekshaw, the Chief of the Army Staff, who at that time was also the Chairman of the Chiefs of Staff Committee, was granted direct access to the Prime Minister, without any bureaucratic impediments.
- A Policy Planning Committee was established in the Ministry of External Affairs under P N Haksar, Prime Minister's Principal Secretary and her closest confidante, to oversee day to day crisis management. D P Dhar, a Kashmiri political advisor to Mrs. Gandhi and then the Indian Ambassador to Moscow was a

---

[46] Gary J. Bass, Op Cit, page 93.

frequent participant too.

- The following coordination committees were also set up to facilitate the smooth implementation of the policy:

  - Joint Intelligence Committee under the Vice Chief of the Army Staff, comprising representatives of civil and military intelligence agencies.
  - Joint Planning Committee to coordinate inter-services operational plans.
  - A Combined Services Operational Headquarters for overseeing joint operations.
  - A Secretaries Committee comprising secretaries of Ministries of Defence, Home, Finance, and External Affairs to coordinate Government responses to the emerging crises.

Planning at Army Headquarters

At the strategic level, General Manekshaw entrusted the Military Operations Directorate in the Indian Army Headquarters with conceiving, developing and then implementing the plan for this war. This Directorate was then headed by Major General K K Singh, with Brigadier Sukhwant Singh as his Deputy Director. In late August, K K Singh was promoted to command I Corps, deployed opposite West Pakistan; Major General Inderjeet Gill then took over as the DMO and carried the ball thereafter.

The strategic plan conceived by General Manekshaw was strikingly reminiscent of the Battle of Tannenberg during the Great War in which the Hindenburg - Ludendorff combine inflicted a decisive defeat on two numerically superior Russian armies. On the same pattern, Manekshaw decided to initially concentrate his maximum effort for offensive operations against East Pakistan, while exercising economy of effort by adopting defensive posture against West Pakistan. After the perceived capture of East Pakistan, he planned to switch most of his formations to the Western Theatre for delivering a decisive coup de grace to the Pakistan Army. He made optimum use of the intervening time to thoroughly prepare for both these phases of his strategic plan. In the implementation of his plan, he could count upon the support of two critical strategic assets: an overall naval superiority against Pakistan, which could ensure total blockade of East Pakistan; and, complete air supremacy over East Pakistan and the flexibility to quickly switch over their air power to the Western Theatre, as and when required.

In warfare, time has always been a critical factor. In the Indian planning against Pakistan in 1971, this factor assumed paramount significance because of two primary geo-political considerations. Firstly, in order to concentrate the requisite force quantum against East Pakistan, the Indian Army had no option but to employ some of its mountain divisions, normally earmarked for the Chinese Front. In case the war was not brought to a quick conclusion within a specific timeframe, the Chinese threat was likely to re-emerge as a potent threat. In such a scenario, the reversion of these formations to their primary role in the north would become inevitable, which would obviously reduce the Indian combat power while the offensive was still in progress. Secondly, in case the war did not conclude within an optimum timeframe, the intervention of the United Nations and the Super Powers to enforce a ceasefire could not be entirely ruled out despite total diplomatic support of the Soviet Union; a premature ceasefire would totally compromise the basic Indian war aim, the dismemberment of Pakistan.

Consequently, in order to conclude their offensive at the earliest, as well as to fully exploit the strategic disadvantage of a weak and over-extended enemy bottled up within a salient, the Indian planners came to the obvious conclusion that they needed to launch simultaneous broad front thrusts against East Pakistan from multiple directions. Here, they were challenged by yet another consideration: to prevent the withdrawal of major Pakistan forces to the "Dacca Bowl".

In simple terms, they not only had to conceive several offensive manoeuvres along multiple axes leading into the heart of East Pakistan; but, to execute these manoeuvres with such speed that the Pakistani forces were given no opportunity to withdraw behind the major rivers to form a very strong line of concentrated defence. In case the Pakistan forces did manage to fall back in tact to defend the "Dacca Bowl" in strength, it could take the Indians a fairly long time to penetrate it. This was hardly acceptable to the Indians in view of the geo-political constraints identified above. To prevent the materialization of this scenario thus became the scarlet thread of the Indian planning.

Perception of Force Levels

According to the Indian intelligence estimates, Pakistan was likely to deploy the following quantum of forces in the Western Theatre: Ten infantry divisions, two armoured divisions, two independent armoured brigades, two artillery brigades, two independent infantry brigades and some additional armoured regiments. (These infantry divisions included the two which had only very recently been raised to make up the deficiency caused by the move of 9 and 16 Divisions to East Pakistan.)

Against this force in the Western Theatre, India could deploy twelve infantry divisions, one armoured division, two independent armoured brigades, two independent infantry brigades, two infantry brigades, three artillery brigades, and one para brigade. On paper, thus, India had a marginal advantage in infantry but this was offset by Pakistan's advantage in armour.

In the Eastern Theatre, according to the Indian perception, Pakistan had built up almost four infantry divisions, comprising some thirty-five infantry battalions, seven wings of para-military forces inducted from West Pakistan, seventeen wings of locally raised EPCAF, and a large number of non-regular second line forces like Razakars and Mujahids. Its main limitation was extreme shortage of artillery; it possessed only six field regiments and some mortar batteries. Armour consisted mainly of one regiment of Chaffee tanks, one independent Chaffee squadron, and one ad hoc squadron of Chaffee and PT-76 tanks.

Against these Pakistan forces in East Pakistan, India could readily muster up to seven infantry divisions, made up as follows:

- One division in situ, normally earmarked for operations against East Pakistan.
- Two divisions, to be relieved from counter-insurgency operations in Nagaland and Mizoram.
- Three divisions, located in Siliguri Corridor forming strategic reserves earmarked for China.
- One division pulled back from UP-Tibet border, accepting some risk in that sector.
- Three armoured regiments, two independent armoured squadrons and one APC borne battalion.

The Indian Air Force (IAF) at that time could boast of a total of forty-five combat and transport squadrons against Pakistan's thirteen squadrons. By then, the IAF had replaced almost all its vintage aircraft with latest SU-7 and MiG-21 aircraft of Soviet origin. PAF, on the other hand, was mainly relying on Chinese origin MiG-19, much inferior in performance to the Indian fleet. It had, however, recently acquired twenty-four Mirage aircraft, which were superior to anything held by the Indians, but these were all deployed in West Pakistan. Only one fighter squadron was deployed in East

Pakistan, equipped with some 20-25 vintage F-86 sabre jets.

Indian Perception of Pakistan's Strategy

In the Indian perception, Pakistan could take recourse to very limited strategic options in the Eastern Theatre. Being well aware of Pakistan's strategic paradigm that *'the defence of East Pakistan lay in West Pakistan'*, the Indian planners had based their planning on the fairly reasonable assumption that Pakistan would not increase the current force level in the Eastern Theatre. Pakistan was constrained to maintain an adequate and credible force level in West Pakistan so as to be capable of launching a strong counter-offensive from there in order to ensure that any gains made by India in East Pakistan would be off-set by the gains made by Pakistan in the west. Quite obviously, this placed constraint on the Indian High Command as well by limiting the maximum quantum of forces that could be fielded against East Pakistan without exceeding the acceptable level of risk in the west.

While the Indian High Command had no option but to plan for a two-front war scenario against Pakistan, they were really loath to even conceive a situation in which they had to open a third front against China. Thus, in their view, the most dangerous policy Pakistan could adopt was to somehow induce Chinese participation in the conflict, which would effectively impose a three- front war scenario on India. Such a contingency would obviously necessitate the dispersion and dissipation of Indian forces. This anxiety loomed very large on their minds till 9th August 1971, the date on which The Indo-Soviet Treaty of Peace, Friendship and Cooperation was signed between India and the Soviet Union. In particular, Article IX of this Treaty was a source of great satisfaction and solace to the Indian planners, besides sounding ominous warning bells in Islamabad and Beijing; it read as follows:

"Each High Contracting Party undertakes to abstain from providing any assistance to any third country that engages in armed conflict with the other Party. **In the event of either being subjected to an attack or a threat thereof, the High Contracting Parties shall immediately enter into mutual consultations in order to remove such threat and to take appropriate effective measures to ensure peace and security of their countries."**[47] (Emphasis added.)

After the signing of this Treaty, the apprehension of Chinese

---

[47] *Survival*, XIII, October 1971, pages 351-353.

intervention was effectively minimized, while the Chinese role perceptibly became confined to merely extending diplomatic support to Pakistan. However, during the period when the planning process was in progress, the possibility of meaningful Chinese intervention could not be wholly ignored by the Indian planners and did serve to impose some caution on them while deciding to transfer forces from the Northern (Chinese) Front to the East Pakistan theatre. Indeed, General Manekshaw remained acutely apprehensive of this possibility throughout the war, as we shall later see.

In the Indian perception, Pakistan did possess a fleeting option around the middle of May to cross the East Pakistan border with India in hot pursuit of the Mukti Bahini rebels or even to destroy their camps and bases established on the Indian soil. They were also apprehensive of the possibility of Pakistan opting to broaden this conflict into a full-fledged war at that time by launching an offensive in the Western Theatre too. Indian planners openly admit that militarily this was India's weakest hour; her reserve formations were still in their peace locations in the hinterland; her armed forces still suffered from severe shortages of ammunition and other war material; and, her civilian population was still not conditioned for an immediate, open war on this issue. This contingency loomed large on their minds till such time as the monsoons had commenced, making large scale offensive highly problematic.

President Yahya Khan, in any case, did not elect to exercise this option, probably because at that time he felt fairly certain that the Pakistan Army would be able to pacify East Pakistan, thus removing the *casus belli* for India. It is also possible that in his opinion, the quick move of two of his reserve divisions to East Pakistan had unbalanced his strategic reserves at that time, notwithstanding the immediate raising of two new formations as replacements.

In the Indian assessment, Pakistan's Eastern Command had two main strategic options for its deployment: it could either choose to defend every inch of East Pakistan; or, it could make effective use of river obstacles and abandon large swathes of indefensible terrain. However, as brought out in the preceding chapter, General Niazi strongly felt that India would be content with limited gains of territory, aimed at establishing the provisional Bangladesh Government on East Pakistan soil. Pakistan was to pay heavily for his obsession.

Development of the Embryonic Plan

The methodology for planning operations at this level usually

68

commences with identification of the main aim and objectives of the entire operation. It then proceeds to assessing the quantum of troops required for each main objective. This then leads to the total quantum of troops and other resources required for the operation as a whole. Confronted as they were by an over-riding compulsion to maintain an optimal strategic balance against West Pakistan and China, the Indian planners were constrained to reverse this paradigm.

So, first they proceeded to determine the minimum quantum of troops required to maintain strategic balance on the Western Theatre as well as along the Chinese border. The residual force then dictated the total force level and resources which could be made available for the offensive operation against East Pakistan. This force level would in turn define the Aim and Objectives of the offensive and thus govern the actual scope of the military operations. Working on this reversed paradigm and without compromising the constraints of strategic balance against West Pakistan and China, the maximum force that India could field against East Pakistan worked out to some eight infantry/mountain divisions.

Through an active and penetrative Mukti Bahini network as well as their own intelligence sources in East Pakistan, the Indian planners were fairly well informed of the Pakistan Eastern Command Order of Battle (ORBAT), as well as their locations down to each infantry battalion. This enabled them to carry out an accurate analysis of the relative strength of the two sides in each sector of the Eastern Theatre. The picture that emerged before them could hardly be termed very satisfactory from their viewpoint. The Indian planners thus came to the conclusion that they did not possess such a preponderance of numerical superiority as to opt for stereotyped, step by step, attrition- oriented offensive operations. To achieve quick success in a relatively short war scenario, as dictated by their geo-political and geo-strategic constraints, they had to conceive an audacious plan relying essentially on the criticality of manoeuvre as well as psychological ascendency.

Keeping all the above limitations in mind, Major General K K Singh conceived the following initial, strategic guidelines for an offensive against East Pakistan, which were duly approved by General Manekshaw as the basis for further planning:

1. The early capture of Chittagong and Khulna ports with a view to creating a psychology of isolation in the East Pakistan Garrison, accentuating their fears of being cut off from their base in West Pakistan. This would also prevent any third- party evacuation of the

retreating Pakistan troops by sea.

2. The early capture of such objectives as would prevent any inter-sector movement of Pakistan forces, such as the bridges at Feni, which would cut off Chittagong from the rest of the province; and the Hardinge (Paksey) Bridge, which would prevent movement between Northwestern and Southwestern Sectors.

3. Early capture or incapacitation of such major ferry sites as would facilitate trans-sector movement of the Indian forces along the major waterways.

4. Airfields to be secured or rendered unserviceable at an early stage to ensure uninterrupted movement of Indian troops and equipment.

5. Early capture of such Communication Centres within the sector areas as would paralyze the enemy's capability to fight in an organized manner.

6. Operations to be conducted in such a manner as to ensure that the enemy formations deployed forward be unable to withdraw to depth positions.

7. Utmost speed would be of vital importance and, in this context, bypassing the opposition en route was to be the accepted strategy.

Next the Indian planners proceeded to identify the main objectives in each sector of East Pakistan as well as assess the resources required for them:

- **Northwestern Sector.** In this Sector, Bogra was selected as the objective, the capture of which would unbalance and unhinge the Pakistan forces operating in the Sector. The shortest way to reach Bogra was identified as a thrust along Hilli-Gaibanda axis, which would also isolate Pakistan forces operating north of this thrust line from the rest of East Pakistan. Other main cities were intended to be dealt with later by secondary thrusts. It was assessed that one division would be required to develop the main effort towards Bogra while up to two additional brigades would be required to fix the Pakistan troops deployed in Dinajpur-Rangpur area. It was also decided to entrust the overall command of this Sector to a corps headquarters.

- **Southwestern Sector.** The main objective here was Khulna, the shortest approach to which lay along Barisal-Satkhira-Khulna axis. However, this approach lay against the grain of the ground and involved several river-crossing operations. It was therefore decided to capture Jessore first, which was the main communications centre in the area and could also lead direct to Dacca along Jhenida-Magura-Faridpur axis. Thereafter, using Jessore as a pivot for further operations, the capture of Khulna would be undertaken. Another thrust was also conceived towards Jhenida and Magura, the capture of which was considered of vital importance to split and paralyze the Pakistan forces operating in this Sector. The troops required for these two independent thrusts were assessed at two divisions, and it was decided to place them under a corps headquarters too for effective control and coordination.

- **Eastern Sector.** In this Sector, early control of the main crossing sites over River Meghna at Ashuganj, Daudkandi, and Chandpur was considered of vital strategic importance, since it would isolate Dacca from the entire area east of the Meghna. It was assessed that the tasks conceived for this Sector required three divisions: one for the thrust towards Sylhet; one for the Ashuganj-Bhairab Bazar Complex; and, one for Chandpur-Daudkandi thrust. The entire force would obviously have to be commanded by a corps headquarters.

- **Central Sector.** Dacca, the geopolitical heart of East Pakistan was naturally the prime objective of the entire operation. A thrust from the north along Jamalpur-Mymensingh-Tangail-Dacca axis was considered the best option to achieve this objective. As a measure of strategic deception, it was decided that initially only two brigades would be launched in the Sector, to be upgraded to a division later.

- Considering the strategic and psychological importance of Chittagong, it was initially considered to develop a thrust along Feni-Chittagong axis but resource and time constraints forced them to explore other options. However, at this stage the Indian Naval Chief Admiral S M Nanda came to their rescue and offered to blockade both Chittagong and Khulna. This offer was gratefully accepted and thus the strategic importance of these two ports was considerably reduced in their subsequent planning.

Articulation of Command

71

At this stage of planning, General Manekshaw took basic decisions on the command and control of this huge force, which was to launch complex offensive operations in every operational sector in East Pakistan. Accordingly, he articulated the command and control of this force as follows:

- The overall command and control of the entire operation against East Pakistan was delegated to HQ Eastern Command, located at Calcutta. It was then being commanded by Lt General Jagjit Singh Aurora with Major General (later Lt General) J FR Jacob as his Chief of Staff.

- The responsibility for the offensive in the Northwestern Sector was entrusted to HQ XXXIII Corps, located at Siliguri, commanded by Lt Gen M L Thapan. 20 Mountain Division, already a part of this Corps, was allocated for the main effort in the Sector. In addition, 340 Brigade ex Southern Command, Rajisthan and 71 Mountain Brigade from Nagaland were also made available for this Sector.

- In the absence of any existing controlling headquarters to command the operations in the Southwestern Sector, a new Corps HQ, designated II Corps, was raised in record time and entrusted with this responsibility; Lt General T S Raina was named as the Corps Commander. 9 Division, already located in Calcutta, and 4 Mountain Division, then deployed in West Bengal on internal security duties, were earmarked for offensive operations in this Sector as part of II Corps.

- To command the operations in the Eastern Sector, Headquarters IV Corps commanded by Lt General Sagat Singh, located at Tezpur, was split into two; the Main HQ was moved to Agartala for operations in this Sector under General Sagat Singh; the Rear HQ, under the Corps Chief of Staff, Major General O P Malhotra, continued to remain at Tezpur a holding role along the Chinese border. This Corps was allocated 57 Division, 23 Mountain Division and 8 Mountain Division for the task.

- Headquarters 101 Communication Zone Area was nominated to control operations in the Central Sector. It was allocated two brigades, including one East Bengal Brigade (Mukti Bahini). One infantry battalion was separately earmarked for demonstration against Sylhet in the adjoining Khasi and Jaintia Hills.

Throughout this process, General K K Singh, the DMO, remained skeptical of the feasibility of capturing Dacca within the time frame of a short war, envisaged at that stage to last no more than 21 days.

"He felt rather strongly that the Indian Army, with its inherent inhibitions against anything unorthodox and a speedier type of manoeuvre, and very short of the bridging equipment required to span the mighty rivers, lacked the capability to reach Dacca before the cease fire likely to be brought about by international pressures. At his insistence, the task was limited to occupying the major portion of Bangladesh instead of the entire country."[48]

The task, thus, originally allotted to Eastern Command by the Army Headquarters was to destroy the bulk of the Pakistan forces in the Eastern Theatre and to occupy major portion of East Pakistan, including the entry ports of Chittagong and Chalna/Khulna. There was no mention of capturing Dacca at this stage.

That Dacca was not the objective of the Indian offensive in the original planning is credibly borne out by Air Chief Marshal P C Lal, the then Indian Chief of Air Staff, as well:[49]

"Here I must clarify one doubt that has existed in my mind and also in the minds of others as to what the objectives of the 1971 war were. As defined by the Chiefs of Staff and by each respective service chief, it was to gain as much ground as possible in the East to neutralize the Pakistani forces there to the extent we could and to establish a base as it were for a possible state in Bangladesh. The possibility that Pakistani forces in East Pakistan would collapse altogether as they did and that Dacca would fall and that the whole would be available to the leaders of the freedom movement in East Pakistan was not considered something likely to happen."

The above embryonic plan had been formulated by about the middle of July 1971 and was then formally presented to the Indian Navy and the Indian Air Force so that they could formulate their own plans accordingly. It was at that stage that General Aurora, Commander Eastern Command, was officially brought into picture personally by General Manekshaw. The comprehensive briefing by the Army Chief covered in detail the political environment, Indian aims and objectives, the outline operational plan, and the emphasis on speed, vigour and determination required for its execution.

---

[48] Maj Gen Sukhwant Singh, Op Cit, page 72.
[49] ACM P C Lal, My Years with the IAF, as quoted by Lt Gen J FR Jacob, Op Cit, page 160.

This briefing *ipso facto* signified the formal assignment of the task to the Eastern Command by the Army Chief.

The ball had been set rolling!

Planning at HQ Eastern Command

Lt General Jagjit Singh Aurora, Commander Eastern Command, was thus destined to command the combined land forces of India and Bangladesh in the Eastern Theatre; he was also responsible to coordinate the functions of the Indian Air Force and the Indian Navy in this Theatre. Aurora was endowed with a smart and impressive bearing, a pleasing personality, a sound professional background and an incisive mind. Despite that, rather surprisingly, his contribution to the success of this campaign in the final count remained suspect in the professional eye within the Indian Army; perhaps because he did not display the flamboyance of a soldiers' general in the field. Many others, notably Lt General J FR Jacob, the then COS Eastern Command, have claimed the credit in giving the final shape to the operational plan and his claims have not met any serious challenge from any quarters.[50]

In this context, General Jacob himself has, rather brazenly, claimed:[51]

"In the planning period and during the operations, Manekshaw for the most part bypassed Aurora and dealt directly with the Chief of Staff, except for matters pertaining to Mukti Bahini."

General Jacob has also claimed that he had anticipated the eventual certainty of waging the war in East Pakistan soon after the Pakistan Army crackdown and the heavy influx of the large number of refugees. He claims the credit for the initiation of the planning process in HQ Eastern Command soon thereafter; he also claims the development and completion of a draft plan by as early as the end of May 1971. This draft plan was based on the following broad strategic guidelines, conceived and set for himself and his staff:

"1. Dacca, the geopolitical and geostrategic heart of East Pakistan, would be the final objective.

2. Such offensive thrust lines would be selected as will isolate and bypass Pakistani

---

[50] Maj Gen Sukhwant Singh, *Op Cit*, page 78.
[51] Lt Gen J FR Jacob, *Op Cit*, page 67.

forces to reach the final objective as early as possible.

3. Subsidiary objectives would be selected with the aim of securing communication centres and the destruction of enemy's command and control capabilities. Fortified centres of resistance would be bypassed and dealt with later.

4. Preliminary operations would be launched in all the sectors, which would be aimed at drawing out the Pakistani forces to the border area, leaving key areas in the interior lightly defended."[52]

As General Jacob and his staff set to formulating a strategic plan for this complex operation, he was *ab initio* beset with two major limitations. His first limiting factor was almost self-imposed. In his own mind, he had arbitrarily prescribed the maximum timeframe of 12-15 days, in which to reach the culminating point of his manoeuvre. The main rationale behind it was to avoid the contingency of intervention by the United Nations, forcing India to call a premature halt to its offensive.

General Jacob's second limitation was relatively more complex. By training and tradition, the Indian Army's operational technique, mainly based upon the doctrines evolved during the Second World War, was generally confined to the following cycle: set-piece battles; phased offensive plans; and, resumption of advance only after grouping, regrouping and reinforcement. The Indian planners were also quite confident that General Niazi, whose own professional training was limited to similar concepts, would almost certainly expect the Indians to adopt this very technique in their offensive operations. As such, Niazi too was expected to have mounted his defensive manoeuvre on this very assumption.

Thus, the basic conceptual challenge confronting General Jacob was to conceive such a scheme of manoeuvre as would enhance the speed of their operations by overcoming this systemic inertia in the Indian infantry and mountain formations. In his view, executing traditional offensive manoeuvres in the difficult terrain of East Pakistan would be tantamount to playing into Niazi's hands. As such, the cardinal requirement of the entire operation was to overcome the mental barriers of established operational and tactical doctrines; and, to develop the ability to generate flexible, mobile thrusts, bypassing enemy strong points and fortresses, to be dealt with at a later stage.

India enjoyed two very potent advantages in the Eastern Theatre, which

---

[52] *Ibid*, page 58.

would prove to be of decisive importance in ensuring the success of the above technique: first, the overwhelming air superiority in this theatre of operations; and second, a very favourable local population, which could provide the Indian forces accurate and timely information about the deployment of Pakistan Army as well as intimate guidance on local terrain. Both these factors were to come in very handy during the war.

The operational concept eventually evolved by General Jacob and approved by General Aurora was as bold in essence as it was simple. However, its essential requirement, its *sine qua non*, was that the offensive must be executed with drive and determination, accepting calculated risks along the way. Without that, there was an acute possibility of the entire offensive manoeuvre hopelessly grinding to a halt amidst pitched battles and slow, phased advances. It was certainly a tall order for a conventional army, thus far trained essentially on a very rigid pattern of operations! The scarlet thread of the plan was to contain enemy strong points at the border while powerful mobile thrusts undertook a series of bypassing moves to sever the lines of communication; and race towards their strategic objectives.

The scheme of manoeuvre, evolved by HQ Eastern Command, essentially conceived three main thrusts, launched in Northwestern, Southwestern and Eastern Sectors by one army corps each, and complemented by an auxiliary thrust in the Central Sector. Each thrust would launch broad front offensive operations, tasked to bypass major resistance en route and press on towards their strategic objectives; adequate detachments would, however, be left behind to contain and then eventually liquidate the bypassed strong points and towns. With maximum support from the IAF, they expected to isolate Dacca from the bulk of the defending Pakistan Army, so as to ensure that in the end it remained inadequately defended.

General Jacob's leading hypothesis of the strategic courses open to Pakistan Army was that they would try to defend every inch of East Pakistan particularly main towns and cities, based on their assumption that the primary Indian objective of the offensive would only be to capture a sizeable chunk of territory to set up a credible Bangladesh Government. Accordingly, Jacob elected to mount his manoeuvre on this hypothesis. His assessment stood fully vindicated as it became confirmed even before the commencement of the war, when the Pakistan forces started fortifying the road approaches to major towns and later the towns themselves. That was rather fortunate for India; had Pakistan instead chosen to defend approaches leading to crossing sites over major rivers and vital communication centres, the Indians would not have been able to threaten Dacca so early and so quickly.

The next step in Jacob's planning process was the identification of main objectives and thrust lines in each operational sector; these will be discussed in greater detail in the plans of the respective corps and need not be repeated here.

At this stage, Jacob discussed his draft plan, still hand written for reasons of security with Major General K K Singh, the Director Military Operations at the Army Headquarters on telephone. As per Jacob, his plan provided a major input into the planning process of the Army Headquarters. Meanwhile, he had also tasked his staff to plan the development of the logistic infrastructure in the entire area of the Eastern Command in anticipation of the huge demands which would soon be generated for the imminent conflict. This included road and rail infrastructure particularly in Assam and Tripura states and buildup of the requisite level of re-enforcement stocks.

At the beginning of August 1971, General Manekshaw, accompanied by Major General K K Singh, came to Headquarters Eastern Command at Fort Williams, Calcutta to discuss his proposed Operational Instruction, the draft of which had already been sent to General Aurora a few days earlier. The meeting was held in the main operations room of the Command Headquarters, attended by Manekshaw, Aurora, K K Singh, and Jacob.

The main briefing was conducted by the DGMO General K K Singh on behalf of Manekshaw. He went on to indicate Khulna and Chittagong as the initial strategic objectives of the offensive. His basic rationale was that these were the main ports for reinforcement and evacuation of the Pakistan garrison; the early capture of these ports would inculcate a sense of isolation and demoralization, thus bringing the war to a quick end. In his assessment, Khulna was the key which must be the main objective of their main effort in the Southwestern Sector. The Hardinge (Paksey) Bridge was also indicated as an early objective to prevent any inter-sector movement by Pakistan reserves and reinforcements.

At this point, General Jacob interrupted the proceedings and objected to the very concept of these two ports being the main objectives, on the following rationale:[53]

---

[53] *Ibid,* page 66.

- Since India had an overwhelming naval superiority, it must be employed to the fullest potential and both Khulna and Chittagong be effectively blockaded.

- Khulna was, in any case, only a subsidiary port; its main anchorage lay further downstream at Chalna.

- A direct offensive towards Khulna would be against the grain of the ground. The terrain here restricted manoeuvre, being interspersed by several subsidiary water channels. It was hardly possible to generate fast moving operations here.

- Chittagong was located well east of the main theatre of operations, almost peripheral. It would thus consume a fairly large number of troops.

Instead, he strongly advocated that Dacca, being the geopolitical heart of East Pakistan, must be captured if the Indian aim was to ensure control of East Pakistan. This led to a heated discussion among the participants. Eventually, General Manekshaw agreed to downgrade the capture of Khulna and Chittagong in his overall plan. At this point, the meeting came to an end.

Following this planning conference, the Army Headquarters finally issued its Operational Instructions on 16th August 1971, which included provisional objectives, main offensive thrust lines, initial concentrations, and deployments. Based on this Army Operational Instruction, Outline Plans were drawn up by HQ Eastern Command soon thereafter, and sent to the concerned corps headquarters in draft form to be studied in detail by them.

This was followed by formulation of detailed plans for each Sector by the Eastern Command. However, in formulating these plans, a rather presumptuous and domineering Jacob entirely ignored the normal methodology of allotting tasks and resources to subordinate commanders and delegating to them the liberty of drawing up their own plans, followed by final coordination by the higher commander. General Jacob even issued such mundane details as allotment of troops to each axis of advance within the Sectors as well laying down programmed progress along each axis on a D-day basis. This methodology hardly left any initiative with the corps commanders to plan operations in their own sectors based on the local knowledge of terrain, enemy dispositions and their own aptitudes.[54] As we shall see, it would lead to some problems later.

Planning at Corps/Sector Level

The stage was then set to fine tune the operational plans for each sector/corps and to work them out in complete detail, covering the identification of objectives, finalization of thrust lines, and sub-allocation of resources. This was carried out at each corps headquarters during the greater part of September 1971. These plans were then critically examined and analyzed during war games held in each corps down to the brigade level and this process continued right up to the end of October. After the evaluation of the conclusions reached in these war games and in the light of the latest information on dispositions of Pakistan forces, necessary modifications were incorporated through Confirmatory Orders issued by HQ Eastern Command, separately for each corps.[55]

The Final Plan

The final plan that emerged as a result of the preceding planning process is summarized hereunder.

1. **Scheme of Manoeuvre**

   a. **Main Effort._** IV Corps with under command three divisions and one Mukti Bahini Brigade to launch an offensive in the Eastern Sector and capture Chandpur, Daudkundi, and Bhairab Bazar in the shortest possible time with a view to threatening Dacca.

   b. **Secondary Effort-1.** XXXIII Corps with under command one division and an independent brigade group to launch an offensive thrust in the Northwestern Sector with a view to capturing Bogra at the earliest.

   c. **Secondary Effort-2.** II Corps with under command two divisions to launch an offensive in the Southwestern Sector with a view to capturing Jessore and then exploiting up to the line of River Ganges.

---

[54] Maj Gen Lachhman Singh, *Victory in Bangladesh*, Natraj Publishers, Dehradun, page 61.
[55] Maj Gen Sukhwant Singh, *Op Cit*, page 79.

d. **Auxiliary Effort.** 101 Communication Zone, using up to three brigades, to make a thrust in the Central Sector with a view to capturing Mymensingh and Tangail and thereafter posing a threat to Dacca.

2. Northwestern Sector- XXXIII Corps

The resources allocated to XXXIII Corps, commanded by Lt General M L Thapan, comprised 20 Mountain Division, 71 Mountain Brigade, and 340 Mountain Brigade Group, supported by 6 and 7 Sectors of Mukti Bahini.

The plan for 20 Mountain Division, with under command 340 Mountain Brigade Group, was to advance along Phulbari-Nawabganj-Pirganj Axis, thereafter swing south to capture Bogra, and with further exploitation, up to the line of River Brahmaputra. The fortifications at Hilli and Gaibanda were initially to be bypassed and the axis of maintenance to be opened later.

Later, however, on the insistence of Generals Manekshaw and Aurora, an attack on Hilli was also included in the plan as one of the preliminary operations.

71 Mountain Brigade was to capture Thakurgaon from the north and thereafter capture Dinajpur and Saidpur. Dinajpur was initially to be contained by para-military forces.

Elements of 6 Mountain Division, normally deployed for the defence of Bhutan border, were to simulate a threat towards Rangpur by capturing the area north of River Teesta. However, they were to remain in a state of readiness to move to Bhutan at short notice, as and when ordered by the Army Headquarters.[56]

The Inland Waterways Flotilla in Assam was moved to Dubri on the border to support 20 Mountain Division, as well as the troops moving in the Central Sector on Jamalpur-Tangail axis, on as required basis.

2. Southwestern Sector – II Corps

Newly raised II Corps, commanded by Lt Gen T N Raina, with under command 9 Division and 4 Mountain Division, and supported by 8 and 9 Sectors of Mukti Bahini, was to launch an offensive in the Southwestern

---

[56] Ibid, page 74.

Sector.

9 Division was to capture Jessore and later assist 4 Mountain Division in the capture of Magura. One of its brigades was to be prepared to capture Khulna on orders.

4 Mountain Division was to capture Jhenida, Magura, Faridpur and Goalundo Ghat. A task force was to capture Hardinge (Paksey) Bridge.

Contingency plans were also made for elements of II Corps to cross the Brahmaputra at Goalundo Ghat. For this purpose, the Inland Waterways Flotilla was moved from Calcutta to Farakka in order to facilitate its movement down the River Padma to Faridpur and later to Dacca, if required.

3. Eastern Sector – IV Corps

IV Corps, commanded by Lt General Sagat Singh, with under command 8 Mountain Division less one brigade, 23 Mountain Division, and 57 Mountain Division was to launch an offensive in the Eastern Sector.

8 Mountain Division, comprising two brigades, was to secure Shamshernagar and Maulvi Bazar. Thereafter, to contain Sylhet city with one brigade. The other brigade was to be detached to form Corps Reserve, to be used only with the permission of HQ Eastern Command. It was to be supported by 'Z' Force as well as Numbers 4 and 5 Sectors of Mukti Bahini.

23 Mountain Division would advance along Feni-Chauddagram-Laksham axis, avoiding Comilla complex, and capture Chandpur. It was supported by 'K' Force as well as 1 and 2 Sectors of Mukti Bahini.

57 Mountain Division was to contain Comilla with one brigade while the rest of the Division to swing towards Daudkundi. It was supported by 'S' Force as well as Number 3 Sector of Mukti Bahini.

An infantry battalion ex 101 Communication Zone, located at Shillong was to assist 8 Mountain Division operation against Sylhet by posing a threat from Dauki in the north.

IV Corps would also pose a heliborne threat to Dacca at an opportune moment. For this purpose, they were allotted fourteen Mi 4 helicopters much prior to the operations for training.

(At this stage, there was no mention of any IV Corps operations along Akhaura- Brahmanbaria Axis nor was any operational importance accorded to this sub-sector. But as we shall see, IV Corps plans underwent massive changes during the course of the operations, which in effect changed the dynamics of the entire campaign.)

4. Central Sector- 101 Communication Zone

General Manekshaw did not consider the capture of Dacca as a priority objective at this stage and held the view that after being isolated and surrounded from all sides, its fall would be automatic. As such, Army Headquarters had not allocated any troops for the Central Sector. Even after it had been decided to launch an auxiliary effort in this Sector, Manekshaw did not agree to release either 6 Mountain Division or 2 Mountain Division to spearhead this effort despite several requests from the Eastern Command.

Consequently, HQ Eastern Command had no option but to employ HQ 101 Communication Zone, commanded by Major General Gurbux Singh Gill, as a coordinating headquarters for this purpose. The following troops were assembled in an ad hoc manner and placed under its command:

- 95 Mountain Brigade, which was made into a brigade group of four infantry battalions with supporting artillery.
- Two brigades were planned to be pulled out from NEFA at the commencement of hostilities.
- A battalion ex 50 Para Brigade was placed on priority call for an air drop at Tangail, an area controlled by 'Tiger Siddiqui' group of militants.
- It was to be supported by Number 11 Sector of Mukti Bahini.

Comment: An analysis of the preceding plans makes it clear that the plans were aimed at clearing territory only up to the lines of the three major rivers; these did not give any clear indication that Dacca was the ultimate objective. In fact, the macro planning in Delhi as well as Calcutta did not indicate focusing sights on Dacca at this stage.[57]

Logistics

In an operation of this magnitude, with large forces operating along

---

[57] Maj Gen Lachhman Singh, *Op Cit*, page 63.

exterior lines over great distances, Logistics were bound to be a critical factor. The success of the impending Indian campaign too depended upon diverse logistic factors: the ability to equip the troops adequately; move them in time to their respective concentration areas; and, create administrative complexes with adequate resources to sustain the troops. Furthermore, all these tasks had to be accomplished in many areas which had inadequate road/rail communications and without much supporting infrastructure. Roads had to be constructed, ordnance and supply depots established and adequately stocked, and accommodation fabricated in time. All in all, it was a logistician's nightmare.

One of the major problems confronting HQ Eastern Command was bridging; it had worked out the requirement of bridging resources based upon its draft outline plan and submitted it to the Army Headquarters as early as in June 1971. However, no physical movement of bridging had taken place until mid-August.[58] The bridging they eventually did receive was nearly all of World War II vintage and, in many cases, in dire need of heavy repairs, which were completed barely days before the hostilities commenced. Ironically, all the modern and serviceable bridging equipment that the Indian Army possessed was allocated for the western front, where it was never utilized!

Another major problem faced by the Eastern Command was the movement of stores to the respective corps maintenance areas. The assembly areas earmarked for the troops were located in places which had never been used for troop concentrations in such numbers; of these Tripura State proved the most problematic. Some 30,000 tons of stores/supplies were moved to various locations in Tripura for IV Corps where corps dumps were established at Teliamura, Udaipur and Dharamnagar. Similarly, some 14000 tons were moved to Krishannnagar for II Corps; 7000 tons to Raigarh for XXXIII Corps; and, 4000 tons to Tura for the thrust in the Central Sector. In many cases, particularly in Tripura, new road networks had to be created to support impending operations, for which special task forces of the Corps of Engineers were raised.[59]

Signal Communications in Tripura and Meghalaya states were highly underdeveloped and the civil communications network was barely sufficient for the civilian requirements. An entirely new signals communication infrastructure had to be created for IV Corps and its divisions even before these formations had even moved to their assembly areas. Similarly, II

---

[58] Lt Gen J FR Jacob, *Op Cit* page 78.
[59] *Ibid*, page 79.

Corps which had yet to be created at Krishananagar in West Bengal had to be provided with an elaborate network. Telecommunications facilities had also to be created at Tura and Cooch Behar.

In addition to these, there were a host of logistic problems which had to be tackled before the commencement of the war. These may be enumerated as follows:

- Shortages of weapons and equipment like machine guns and recoilless rifles and the spares for all infantry weapons.
- Provisioning of tank tracks and links for PT-76 tanks.
- A large variety in the types of artillery held by mountain divisions and the consequent problems of the stocking and supply of their spares and ammunition.
- Belated issue of Government Orders for raising of HQ II Corps, which were issued on 31st October 1971.

As General Jacob comments, prosaically:

"Perhaps the greatest achievement of this War was the foresight shown in setting up a viable infrastructure, and providing communications and logistical cover for operations. Work had commenced before any operation order was issued."

4

THE TWILIGHT WAR

As the monsoon clouds receded from the skies of East Pakistan, the clouds of war began to appear on its horizon with ominous intensity. As mentioned, October onwards the Mukti Bahini activity had begun to increase in a progressive crescendo, both along the border as well as in the hinterland. Large scale sabotage, attacks on police stations and other government installations, as well as the numerous killings of Razakars (volunteers) and their families created a sense of insecurity in the populace at large.

This is how this entire activity has been described by an Indian planner:

"The pattern these forays followed was that Mukti Bahini operated inside Pakistan territory supported by Indian artillery deployed on our side of the border. If Mukti Bahini men got into difficulties, they were helped out by BSF and the Indian Army. To the extent possible, the use of regular Indian troops was avoided inside East Pakistan as this would have been an act of war, but there were occasions when the intensity of operations-- --like those at Boyra, Hilli, Kamalpur, Akhaura and Belonia------- made this unavoidable. These Mukti Bahini actions were so numerous in terms of numbers and spread of time and space that it is difficult to describe them individually. It may be said however that by the time Yahya Khan declared war, the net gains of these nibbling operations were considerable. "[60]

Alarmed by this heightened activity and apprehending even greater support to these activities by the Indian Army, President Yahya Khan warned India in October that if the Indian troops attempted to enter East Pakistan, it would be considered open war against Pakistan and dealt with accordingly. Predictably, this warning fell on deaf ears. By this time, the

---

[60] Maj Gen Sukhwant Singh, *Op Cit,* page 123.

Indian Government, emboldened by the Indo-Soviet Peace and Friendship Treaty, signed on 19th August 1971, had already decided upon the future course of events in the sub-continent and were determined to implement it without any interference or hindrance from any foreign quarters. The Indian High Command too, emboldened by this major geo-political achievement of their Government, decided to escalate the crisis one step higher.

All this while, despite several potent indications to the contrary, General Niazi remained fixated in his assessment that India would not launch a full-scale offensive against East Pakistan. He remained rigidly fixated with the delusion that the Indian effort would remain confined to merely providing active support to the Mukti Bahini operations and not get involved in a major war. He was also certain that the real Indian aim was limited to capturing a major chunk of adjacent territory in which to establish a credible Bangladesh Government on the soil of East Pakistan.

Consequently, General Niazi's operational thinking remained restricted only to this course of action being adopted by the Indians, and remained blissfully oblivious to the possibility of any other contingency. Accordingly, he remained stuck with the strategy of orienting his tactical and operational dispositions to an extreme forward defensive posture. This involved occupation of the BOPs strongly and backing them up with adequate local reserves. In the process, he sacrificed strategic depth as well as the creation of operational reserves at the altar of this extreme forward posture; this was to prove a fatal strategic blunder for which his entire Command had to pay very dearly in due course.

By this time, HQ Eastern Command (India) had identified several areas/localities in vicinity of the border, nevertheless situated well within Pakistan, which would prove of immense operational advantage to them as and when the war commenced. These areas were so chosen so as to provide firm bases and launching pads for their eventual offensive and they decided to capture them before the commencement of formal hostilities between the two countries. Thus, the seemingly isolated and random operations by the Mukti Bahini were in fact part of a well-orchestrated strategy, which would eventually facilitate the smooth jump-off of the impending Indian offensive and ensure a rapid advance thereafter.

In the third week of November, the Pakistan forces, unwittingly, provided the pretext the Indians were looking for. In accordance with General Niazi's policy, Pakistani troops had been reacting in force to every provocation by the Mukti Bahini. In the process, some artillery fire from

Pakistani guns inadvertently landed in the Indian territory despite GHQ's explicit instructions to the contrary. This unintended incident precisely became the pretext, based on which the Indian High Command permitted their forces to enter the Pakistan territory up to a distance of ten miles from the border, ostensibly to silence these guns.

The Indian Eastern Command, however, took advantage of these rather vague instructions and proceeded to carry out the preliminary operations already planned by them to secure the identified areas to improve their offensive posture. Initially, these remained confined to limited objectives only in each Sector; but soon the orders were issued to expand these bridgeheads as per the dictates of the tactical situation, entirely at the discretion of the local commanders. This is how an Indian planner describes this creeping strategy:

"Due to shelling of our border posts by Pakistan, it was decided in November to allow our troops to go into East Pakistan up to a depth of ten miles to silence these guns. We took advantage of these instructions to secure specific areas to improve our offensive posture. Initially we instructed formations to carry out the following tasks, expanding them as the situations developed. ......"[61]

According to General Jacob, the following tasks were allocated by the Eastern Command to their formations on this pretext:

- II Corps (Southwestern Sector): Invest Pakistan defences in area Afra and capture Mohammadpur. Secure the Khalispur Bridge and then capture Uthali.

- XXXIII Corps (Northwestern Sector): Clear Pachagarh and advance as far south as possible towards Thakurgaon. Capture Hilli.

- IV Corps (Eastern Sector): Capture Gangasagar and clear area up to Saidabad. Establish a battalion block in area Debigram. Isolate Akhaura and Brahmanbaria. Eliminate Pakistani posts in Narayanpur area. Capture Rajpur and threaten Akhaura. Secure Shamshernagar and Kalhura. Isolate Feni.

- 101 Communication Zone Area (Central Sector): Capture Jaintiapur. Capture Kamalpur and advance to Bakhshiganj.

---

[61] Lt Gen J FR Jacob, *Op Cit*, page 71.

Intensify Mukti Bahini activity in Tangail and threaten Mymensingh, Haluaghat, Phulpur, Shamganj and Durgapur.

(The detailed accounts of these operations will be covered in subsequent chapters relevant to each Sector.)

An accurate and perceptive analysis and interpretation of these seemingly isolated and dispersed tactical actions by the Indian Army by General Niazi could have enabled him to accurately predict the direction and likely objectives of the Indian offensive. Yet he and indeed the GHQ in Pakistan completely failed to do this. On the other hand, these isolated and diverse gains did indeed manage to accrue several important operational advantages to the Indians even before the formal war commenced as follows:

- Several useful jump-off points well inside the East Pakistan territory were captured by the Indian Army in the areas where their main offensive was to be launched in each Sector, particularly where obstacles had to be crossed in the initial phases. For instance, the action at Boyra in the Southwestern Sector ensured that the Indian troops reached almost half-way to Jessore and came into direct contact with the main Pakistani defences west of the city.

- Pakistani troops were progressively being sucked into rigid fixed positions in an extreme forward posture along the border in a long thin line; in the process, they continued to lose their ability to manoeuvre and, thus, lost their freedom of action. The original concept of fighting from fortresses and strong points became hopelessly compromised even before the formal declaration of war.

- The Indian Army, in the process, had imbibed several useful lessons from these preliminary actions and suitably modified their original tactical plans. They came to realize that wherever their troops attacked fortified defensive positions, the Pakistani troops fought tenaciously and courageously, as at Hilli and Kamalpur. In such positions, the attacking troops had suffered heavy casualties and taken a long time to clear the positions. Thus, it became clear to the Indians that fortified positions must be avoided and bypassed to attain a speedy victory within the stipulated timeframe. This early lesson was put to good use in the impending war. Besides, these operations also gave realistic battle inoculation to their troops before the formal war commenced.

Thus, from 21st November to 3rd December 1971, a full scale but undeclared war raged on in East Pakistan between the two sides, which may well be called the Twilight War. During this period, India and Pakistan had not officially declared war on each other; yet the Indian forces brazenly entered the sovereign territory of Pakistan and launched a relentless operation designed to improve their offensive posture. The Government of Pakistan did call it a war imposed by India on East Pakistan but never reacted at that point of time on the western front. Just a day after the first blatant Indian incursion in Jessore Sector, President Yahya Khan had declared a national emergency but curiously enough the Government of Pakistan did not make any formal complaint before the UN Security Council at that time.

On receipt of reliable intelligence assessment from the GHQ that the Indian invasion of East Pakistan was imminent on 21st November 1971 (the Eid-ul-Fitre day), Pakistan Eastern Command had ordered all its formations and units on 19th November to immediately occupy their battle positions. The assessment proved to be accurate and the invasion did indeed commence on that day.

The information of the commencement of the invasion was duly conveyed on telephone by Brigadier Baqir Siddiqui, COS Eastern Command, to the VCGS at the GHQ, Major General Anwar Ahmed Qureshi. The VCGS in turn personally informed General Hamid, the COS Army, at his residence. After a discussion lasting about two hours, General Hamid sent him back without any orders or instructions. General Gul Hasan Khan, the CGS, was away to Lahore where he had gone for Eid despite knowing the imminence of Indian offensive precisely on this very day. He learnt about the attack only on his return.[62]

On his return, the CGS arranged a briefing conference in the GHQ for the next morning but both the President and the COS declined to attend as they were visiting Sialkot, ostensibly to visit the troops but in fact for a partridge shoot. On return from Sialkot, they were accosted on the airport by Air Marshal Rahim Khan, the C-in-C Air, and General Gul Hasan who both prevailed on the President to come to the MI Operations Room; even at this critical time, General Hamid was suggesting to the President to take an afternoon siesta. The briefing was finally held late in the evening but the President appeared completely 'non-chalant, casual and almost

---

[62] Maj Gen Fazal Muqeem Khan, *Op Cit*, page 159.

89

unconcerned'. At one stage, he remarked, *"What can I do for East Pakistan? I can only pray."*[63]

General Gul Hasan has described the proceedings of this critical conference in some detail. According to him, right at the beginning, the President queried him as to the course of action to be adopted to deal with the current situation. Gul Hasan replied that *'this as well as our previous governments had directed GHQ that, in case of an attack on East Pakistan, it should plan to rescue that part by an offensive from the west.'* He went on to say that the plans for this contingency had been drawn up and already approved by him (the President). *The time was of an essence. So, the sooner he gave us the green light for putting our plans into operation the better, because the chances of imposing caution on the Indians were now propitious'.*

The CGS indicated to the President that since India had shifted some formations normally deployed in the Western Theatre to the Eastern Theatre, it had thus created an imbalance in the west; once the offensive was launched in the west, there was every likelihood of their shifting these formations back to the west, thereby providing some relief to our forces in the east. The President listened to the exposition of his CGS very patiently and then remarked, *"You must be informed that serious negotiations are in progress at this time and if we opened a front in the west, these would be jeopardized."*[64]

The only tangible action emanating out of this non-chalant conference was that a meaningless dispatch was sent to the United Nations on the emerging situation. However, over the next few days, the pressure on President Yahya Khan kept mounting and, much against the advice given him by the USA and China, he was eventually forced to declare an all-out war with India. The fateful war thus officially commenced at 5.30 PM on 3rd December 1971.

Let us now take a detailed look at the operations as they occurred in various Operational Sectors of East Pakistan.

---

[63] *Ibid*, page 160.
[64] Lt Gen Gul Hasan Khan, *Op Cit*, page 322.

SOUTHWESTERN SECTOR

(JESSORE-KHULNA)

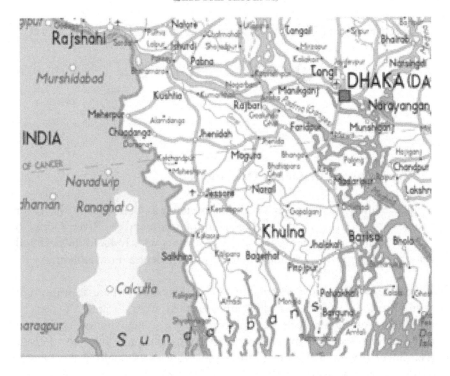

5

OPERATIONS IN SOUTHWESTERN SECTOR

(JESSORE-KHULNA)

Topographical Impact on Operations

The Southwestern Sector of East Pakistan was bounded by the River Ganges in the north, the Bay of Bengal in the south and the River Padma to the east. It had a border of about 320 kilometers with India to its west and generally lay opposite the Indian metropolis of Calcutta (now Kolkutta).

Jessore was the most prestigious city in this Sector where an important cantonment as well as an all-weather airfield were located. It was an important communications centre from where a network of roads and railway lines spread in various directions, providing links to: Paksey (Hardinge) Bridge in the north; Dacca in the east, (though all the Dacca-bound traffic had to cross River Padma by ferry at Goalundo Ghat); and Khulna in the south.

The next city in importance was Khulna in the south, which possessed a very large industrial complex; it was also linked to Chalna, a major seaport, next only to Chittagong in importance.

Jhenida, another town in the northern half of this Sector, was an important communications centre too, located at the intersection of two main roads; one linking Jessore with Paksey Bridge, and the other linking Mehrpur- Chuadanga-Jhenida with Magura and Goalundo Ghat. Paksey Bridge was operationally very important as it provided the only lateral link between the Northwestern and Southwestern Sectors over the mighty Ganges.

The grain of the ground in this Sector lay from north to south, the area south of Jessore becoming progressively more deltaic. The Sunder Ban forest area in the south comprises numerous water channels interspersed with thick forest. There are a number of marshy lakes, locally called Bheels, along the border which limit maneuverability, particularly in the south. The terrain north of Jessore is relatively more suited to mobile operations, but only in winter.

The most important road in this Sector, which ran almost parallel to the border, linked Paksey Bridge in the north with Jhenida, Jessore and Khulna in the south; its distance from the border varied from 45 to 70 kilometers, except at one point opposite Jessore where it was only about 18 kilometers.

The River Padma is a formidable obstacle in any weather against an advance towards Dacca from this Sector. In the absence of any bridge, the main ferry on this mighty river was at Goalundu Ghat, which was linked both to Jessore and Jhenida through the town of Magura. Another important river to the west of River Padma was the Madhumati (Gorai), flowing parallel to and about 30 kilometers east of the Jessore-Jhenida road. Another smaller river, the Kobadak, about seventy-five yards wide and 3 to 4 feet deep in winter, ran north to south just east of the border. It was a major obstacle to infantry but could be easily crossed by the amphibian PT-76 tanks.

Jessore was the linchpin of defence in this Sector; next to Dacca, it was also the most prized objective in East Pakistan. Moreover, the Jessore area could potentially provide a convenient base for generating a substantial threat to Calcutta, situated only 45 kilometers to the west from the border. This further enhanced its importance in the Indian perceptions. (After the war, Major General Dalbir Singh, GOC 9 Indian Division, confided to Brigadier Muhammad Hayat, Commander 107 Pak Brigade, that had Pakistani troops advanced even three miles towards Calcutta, a major exodus from the metropolis may have taken place.)[65] Jessore thus emerged as an obvious and critical Indian objective; its capture would not only provide a perimeter of security to Calcutta but would also be a shattering blow to the morale of the Pakistan forces. Khulna, Jhenida and Paksey Bridge also emerged as important objectives.

---

[65] Lt Gen Kamal Matinuddin, *Op Cit*, page 378.

For launching an offensive from the west in this Sector, the Indian forces could use any of the following major axes of advance:

1. **Bangaon- Jessore Axis.** Emanating from the metropolis of Calcutta, this highway was indeed the traditional, pre-Independence road from Calcutta to Dacca. It provided the shortest and most direct approach to Jessore and then on to Jhenida and beyond.

2. **Krishananagar-Kaliganj-Jhenida-Magura Axis. This** road-based approach took off from Krishananagar on the Indian side of the border and connected with the Jessore-Kushtia Highway at Kaliganj. Thereafter, it provided a convenient approach to Jhenida and then on to Magura and Goalundo Ghat.

3. **Meherpur- Jhenida-Magura Axis.** This road ran west to east linking Meherpur-Chuadanga- Jhenida-Magura. A road running parallel to and near to the border also linked Meherpur to Paksey Bridge.

In addition, the following two relatively minor track-based approaches were also available:

- **Beharampur-Kushtia** in the north of the Sector.

- **Satkhira-Khulna-Jessore** in the south of the Sector.

Pakistan Forces

Pak Eastern Command had entrusted the defence of Southwestern Sector to 9 Pak Division, commanded by Major General Muhammad Hussain Ansari, an artillery officer from the former State of Bahawalpur. In March 1971, he was commanding the East Pakistan Logistics Area, located at Chittagong and had displayed commendable personal courage during the critical stages of the counter-insurgency operations there; he captured the important Tiger Pass in the city while commanding essentially a company level force. Niazi has proudly asserted that he promoted Ansari to the rank of Major General *"because of his brave action against the rebels"*[66].

---

[66] Lt Gen A A Khan Niazi, *Op Cit*, page 146.

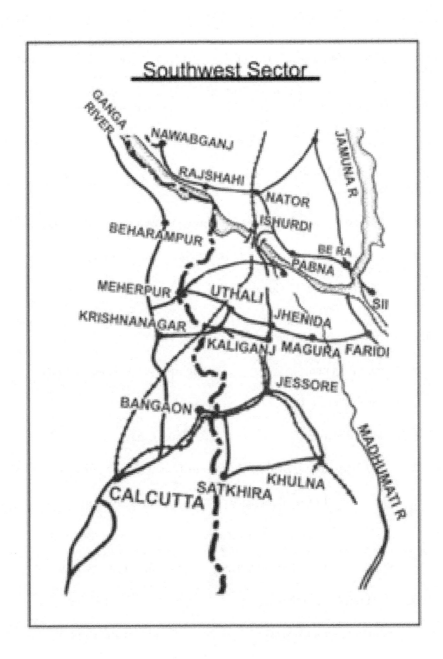

Southwest Sector

9 Pak Division had only two brigades under its command at that time instead of the normal three. It could boast of an Ad-hoc brigade too but without any combat potential. According to the Theatre plan, Jessore and Jhenida had been designated as Fortress Towns while the Road Jessore-Jhenida was laid down as the Line of No Penetration in this Sector.

The composition and locations of 9 Pak Division on the eve of the war was as follows:

1. 57 Brigade   Brigadier Manzoor Ahmed   Jhenida

a. 18 Punjab   Lt Col Matloob Husain   Mehrpur-Chuadanga-Darsana

b. 29 Baluch   Lt Col Atta Ullah   Bheramara- Kushtia

c. 50 Punjab   Lt Col Aijaz Ahmed   Jhenida-Kotchandpur (Reached only on 29th November)

d. 49 Field Regiment   Mehrpur-Chuadanga-Kushtia

d. Squadron 29 Cavalry   Kushtia-Bheramara

f. 211 Mortar Battery   Chuagacha

2.   107 Brigade   Brig Muhammad Hayat   Jessore

a. 15 FF   Lt Col Yusafzai   Satkhira-Kalaura

b. 22 FF   Lt Col Shams uz Zaman   Jhingergacha-Benapole

c. 38 FF   Lt Col Saeed Ullah   Afra-Sajiali-Asangar

d.   12 Punjab less company   Jessore

e. 55 Field Regiment Artillery   Satkhira-Jhingergacha

e.   Industrial Security Force   Lt Col Khattak

f.   Mujahid Battalion   Lt Col Ihsan ul Haq

3.   314 (A) Brigade   Col Fazal Hameed   Khulna

    a.   Sector HQ EPCAF   Lt Col M H Bhatti Khulna

    b.   Mujahid Battalion   Lt Col Sher Zaman Khulna

4.   Divisional Reserve

    a.   6 Punjab   Lt Col Sharif Malik Jessore

    b.   21 Punjab R & S   Lt Col Imtiaz Waraich Jessore

    c.   3 Indep Armoured Squadron   Maj Maqsood Ahmed Jessore

    d.   Section SSG   Capt Asif

5. Naval Base Khulna   Commander Gul Zarin

4 x Gun Boats

In his appreciation of the situation, General Ansari appears to have expected two major Indian thrusts in his area: one towards Jessore in the south and the second towards Paksey Bridge in the north. Accordingly, he divided his area of responsibility into two sub-sectors: Jessore and Jhenida. He entrusted Jessore Sub-sector to 107 Pak Brigade and Jhenida Sub-sector to 57 Pak Brigade; the obvious bias of his main deployment lay towards Jessore in the south and Paksey Bridge in the north. In the process, he exposed some operational weakness in the middle of the Sector opposite Faridpur and the Goalundo Ghat. Initially, he placed his Divisional Headquarters at Jessore but, at the outbreak of hostilities, shifted it rearwards to Magura; his tactical headquarters, however, remained at Jessore.

As in all other sectors too, the core weakness of 9 Pak Divisional defences was their deployment in an exaggerated forward posture, almost along the line of the BOPs. Based on Niazi's concept of defence, the operational strategy in this Sector theoretically visualized that these two brigades would carry out a fighting withdrawal towards the two fortress towns of Jessore and Jhenida, and then take a stand there to the last man, last round. Ironically, however, both the designated fortress towns were neither adequately manned nor properly prepared.

Another glaring omission was that the Pak Eastern Command had not issued any clear instructions regarding the eventual routes of withdrawal to be adopted by the brigades in case the capture of either Jessore or Jhenida by the Indians became inevitable. Apparently, General Niazi had decided to omit this critical detail from his orders and instructions under the apprehension that such coordinating instructions might adversely affect the troops' resolve to put up a last- ditch battle in the designated fortresses. This omission eventually caused a lot of confusion in subsequent phases of the operation, as we shall later see. Inherently implicit in this omission was the fact that no rear positions behind the fortresses had been designated or prepared in advance; thus, when and if the fortresses were lost, the withdrawal could potentially turn into a haphazard retreat.

Indian Forces

The Indian High Command had entrusted the operations in this Sector to the newly raised II Corps, commanded by Lt General T N Raina. He had been recently promoted in October 1971 to raise this corps headquarters; by that time most of the operational planning had already been carried out at the Indian Eastern Command, yet General Raina still had enough time to understand the plan as well as to affect changes in it where considered necessary by him.

The composition of II Corps was as under:

1. **4 MOUNTAIN DIVISION.**   **Maj Gen Mohinder Singh Brar**

    a. **7 Mountain Brigade**   **Brig Zail Singh**

       22 Rajput
       5 Jat
       1 Naga

    b. **41 Mountain Brigade**   **Brig Tony Michigan**

5 Guards
9 Dogra
5/1 Gurkha

c. 62 Mountain Brigade   Brig Rajendra Nath

5 Maratha Light Infantry (LI)
4 Sikh Light Infantry (LI)
2/9 Gurkha Rifles

d. 4 Mountain Artillery Brigade

22 Mountain Regiment (76 mm guns)
194 Mountain Regiment (76 mm guns)
7 Field Regiment (25 pounder guns)
181 Light Regiment (120 Tempella mortars)
Battery 78 Medium Regiment (130 mm guns)

e. A Squadron 45 Cavalry (PT 76 amphibian tanks)

2. 9 INDIAN DIVISION   Maj Gen Dalbir Singh

a. 32 Indian Brigade   Brig M Tewari

7 (Mech) Punjab
8 Madras
13 Dogra

b. 42 Indian Brigade   Brig J S Goraya

14 Punjab
19 Maratha LI
2 Sikh LI

c. 350 Indian Brigade   Brig H S Sandhu

26 Madras
4 Sikh
1 J & K Rifles

d. 9 Artillery Brigade

6 Field Regiment (25 pounder guns)
14 Field Regiment (25 pounder guns)
67 Field Regiment (25 pounder guns)
78 Medium Regiment less battery (130 mm guns)
88 Light Regiment (120 mm Brandt mortars)

e. 45 Cavalry less Squadron (PT-76 amphibian tanks)

f. Squadron 63 Cavalry (T 55 tanks)

A numerical comparison of the forces available to the two sides has been shown in the Table below. It shows that 9 Pak Division had some nine infantry battalions (including later reinforcements), one independent tank squadron, two field artillery regiments and a mortar battery compared to the Indian forces opposite them which comprised 19 infantry battalions (including a motor battalion), four armoured squadrons, eight field regiments artillery and one medium artillery regiment.

COMPARISON OF FORCES

Type	Pakistan	India
Infantry Battalions	9	19
Armour Squadrons	2	4
Artillery	2 Field Regiments 1 Mortar Battery	8 Field Regiments 1 Medium Battery

Thus, in terms of relative strength, the odds were heavily in favour of the Indian II Corps in this Sector, much more so compared with other sectors in the Eastern Theatre. Moreover, the airfield at Calcutta could provide efficient and timely close support to the ground troops. The fairly well developed road and railway networks around Calcutta were also very conducive for a quick buildup and maintenance of the advancing force. Ordnance and supply depots too were suitably located to provide maximum support to the operations.

In his initial conception of the operations in this Sector, General Manekshaw at the Army Headquarters had accorded great importance to the early capture of Khulna and had emphasized this point again and again. He was also anxious for the early capture of the Paksey (Hardinge) Bridge in order to isolate the Pakistan forces fighting in Northwestern and Southwestern Sectors. In his perception, this would, eventually, help in piecemeal destruction of the two forces by avoiding inter-sector movement of troops. Ironically, these early considerations eventually proved a setback to the strategic performance of this Corps when a possibility to advance towards Dacca on 7th and 8th December was lost due to confusion caused by these very perceptions. But we shall come to that later.

General Raina planned his main effort predictably against Jessore and entrusted it to 9 Indian Division commanded by Major General Dalbir Singh. The secondary effort of II Corps was aimed at Jhenida in the northern half of the Sector, to be launched by 4 Mountain Division, commanded by Major General M S Brar. In addition, in order to tie down maximum Pakistan forces in the Sector, General Raina had tasked Major General P Chowdhry, Commander Bengal Area to execute diversionary fixation along the Satkhira- Khulna approach.

The original Indian plan for offensive operations in this Sector was based upon the operational concept advocated by General Jacob, COS Indian Eastern Command. It emphasized making use of secondary roads and generally unknown tracks for launching its thrusts. Thus, the main thrust of II corps was to be launched in the south by 9 Indian Division along the Boyra-Jessore axis, while the secondary thrust was to be launched in the north by 4 Mountain Division along the axis Behrampur-Kushtia-Jhenida.

However, as Major General Dalbir Singh, GOC 9 Indian Division, studied the area of operations in greater detail, he apprehended that road network beyond the Boyra salient may not be sufficient to support his operations. Consequently, he decided to launch his offensive along the Bangaon-Jessore axis. This change, however, further increased the gap between the thrusts being made by 4 Mountain and 9 Indian Divisions. The consequent physical dispersion between his two divisional thrusts was, however, unacceptable to General Raina, Commander II Corps. He, thus, came to oppose the very concept and direction of the northern thrust because of apprehensions about the protection of its southern flank. So, he decided that 4 Mountain Division must launch its thrust along an axis in closer proximity to 9 Division, so that the two thrusts were mutually supporting.[67] An unintended consequence of this change was that the offensive of 4 Mountain Division fell almost exactly on the inter-brigade boundary between 57 and 107 Pak Brigades; we shall talk about it in greater detail later.

Operations in Jessore Sub-sector

---

[67] *Ibid,* page 68.

The defence of Jessore Sub-sector had been entrusted to 107 Pak Brigade, commanded by Brig Muhammad Hayat, a Yusufzai Pashtun officer from the Frontier Force (FF) Regiment, posted to this command only in May 1971. His area of responsibility extended in the north to the line joining the towns of Jibannagar, Kotchandpur and Kaliganj; and, in the south, to the edge of the Sunder Ban Forest on the shores of the Bay of Bengal. The tasks entrusted to his Brigade were somewhat contradictory. Whereas his primary task was to defend Jessore as a fortress at all costs, he had also been directed to *"keep the enemy as far away as possible by occupying all BOPs and not to permit any infiltration"*.[68]

---

[68] Ibid, page 379.

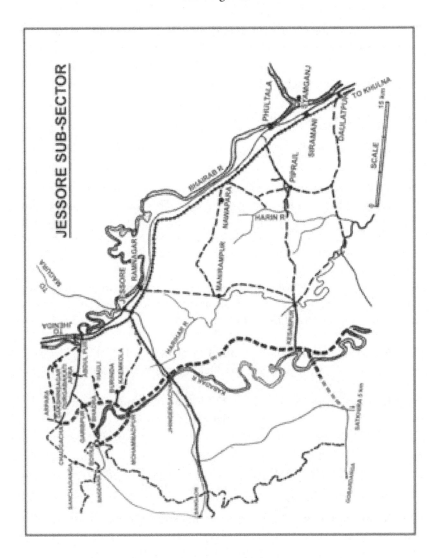

JESSORE SUB-SECTOR

Brig Hayat had appreciated that there were three main approaches open to the Indian forces in his area of responsibility. Starting from the north:

- Mehrpur-Chuagacha-Jessore axis.

- Bangaon-Benapol-Jhingargacha-Jessore axis.

- Satkhira-Karole-Jessore axis.

- In addition, there also existed a secondary approach leading from Kaliganj towards Khulna over a track. (There are two towns by the name of Kaliganj in this area; one is located just south of Jhenida on the road to Jessore; however, Kaliganj mentioned here is located south of Satkhira, very close to the border.)

Keeping in view his tasks and the nature of terrain in his area, Brig Hayat decided to deploy his forces so as to provide a balanced defence along all the above approaches as under:

1. **Mehrpur Approach.**   38 FF (Lt Col Saeed Ullah)
   55 Field Regt less two batteries

2. **Benapol Approach.**   22 FF (Lt Col Shamsuz Zaman)
   Battery 55 Field Regt

3. **Satkhira Approach.**   15 FF (Lt Col Yusaf Zai)
   Battery 55 Field

4. **Kaliganj Town**   Industrial Security Force (Lt Col
   Khattak)

   Mujahid Battalion (Lt Col Ihsan ul Haq)

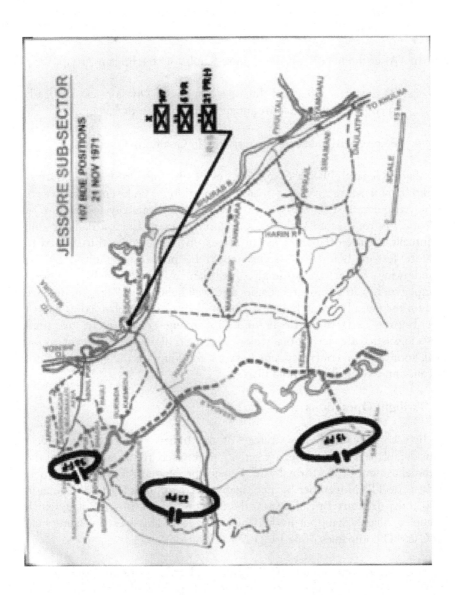

Indian Plan for Offensive

On the Indian side, General Raina, Commander II Corps, had entrusted the offensive operations in the Jessore sub-sector to 9 Indian Division and assigned him the following tasks:

a. Capture Jessore by D+7 along the main highway Bangaon-Benapol axis.

b. After the fall of Jessore, capture Khulna with a brigade group.

c. Be prepared to capture Jhenida/Magura by Division less a brigade in conjunction with 4 Mountain Division, on orders.

d. Be prepared to secure the ferry site in Goalundo Ghat area.

Major General Dalbir Singh was evidently fully informed, courtesy Mukti Bahini sources, that a major proportion of Pakistan forces were deployed quite close to the border. Thus, his basic strategy for capture of Jessore was to execute a double envelopment aimed at outflanking and eventually cutting off the Pakistani forces on this axis; he thus hoped to capture Jessore before its defence could be properly organized by the withdrawing forces. Accordingly, his plan was to launch a pincers manoeuvre towards Jhingargacha, located well behind the Pakistani defence line on the main highway Bangaon- Benapol- Jessore; he planned to launch one brigade each from Boyra and Gobardanga respectively; his third brigade was to advance frontally along the main highway.[69] However, as we shall soon see, the course of actual events unfolding on the ground did not permit him to execute this bold plan.

Twilight Operations

In accordance with the strategy of the Indian Eastern Command, a considerable level of preliminary activity took place in this area prior to the commencement of the formal war. A major probing attack was launched as early as on 11th November by a company of 1 Jammu & Kashmir Battalion (350 Indep Infantry Brigade) from the direction of the Boyra Bulge, which occupied village Chandpur in the Chuagacha area. This area was being held by C and D companies of 38 FF (107 Pak Brigade).

Brig Hayat, commander 107 Pak Brigade, learnt of this encroachment at about 1100 hours on 12th November and moved the rest of 38 FF Battalion, supported by a battery of 55 Field Regiment, to deal with the encroachment. By then, another Indian battalion had also captured the nearby Masalia BOP and some area around it. To deal with this evolving threat, Brig Hayat formed a composite task force, composed as follows:

---

[69] Maj Gen Lachhman Singh, *Op Cit*, page 135.

- Company 38 FF, commanded by Major Anis.
- Company 22 FF, commanded by Maj Bokhari.
- Platoon 21 Punjab (R & S).
- Battery 55 Field Regt.
- Troop 120 Mortars.

This task force launched a spirited counter-attack on Masalia BOP at dawn on 13th November, led by both the company commanders in person. The attack, however, was repulsed; in the process, Major Anis was killed while leading his company and Major Bokhari severely wounded. Major Anis was later buried with full military honours by General Dalbir Singh, who personally recited Fateha (funeral prayers) over his grave - a befitting tribute from one soldier to another.[70]

While this attack was still in progress, an Indian tank squadron too had appeared on the scene of battle and engaged the defensive positions of 38 FF with heavy fire, knocking down most of its bunkers in the process. 38 FF, however, quickly readjusted its positions and managed to contain further Indian encroachment. Meanwhile, 4 Mountain Division, operating in the Jhenida sub-sector in the north, also commenced its preliminary twilight operations in this very area. 4 Sikh LI (62 Mountain Brigade) established a road block behind the positions of A and B Companies of 38 FF. By then, the Indians had also come in a position to threaten Gharibpur and Chuagacha in the rear.

By this time, the gravity of the developing situation had eventually begun to dawn upon General Ansari, commander 9 Pak Division, and he came to the conclusion that 107 Pak Brigade would require additional resources to deal with these Indian encroachments. Consequently, on 16th November, he decided to employ the following troops from his Divisional Reserve to deal with the situation:

- 6 Punjab.
- 21 Punjab (R&S)
- 3 Indep Armoured Squadron.

Initially, General Ansari had intended to form two task forces out of these units, each mainly based upon 6 Punjab and 21 Punjab respectively, to deal with the dual encroachment. While the counter- attack was still being planned, the entire situation was overtaken by other considerations. On 19th

---

[70] Maj Gen Shaukat Riza, *Op Cit*, page 126.

November, General Niazi ordered all formations and units of Pak Eastern Command to occupy their battle locations in view of the imminent Indian invasion of East Pakistan. Consequently, 38 FF and 6 Punjab took up defensive positions in Chuagacha and Kaliganj respectively and the task forces never came to be launched.

The Twilight War was imposed by India on East Pakistan in real earnest on 21st November 1971. On the morning of 20th November, General Dalbir Singh ordered Brig J S Goraya, 42 Indian Brigade, to secure Gharibpur during the ensuing night so as to dominate Road Chuagacha-Afra. Brig Goraya in turn allotted the task to 14 Punjab. At about 7:30 AM, the unit began to cross the River Kobadak in assault boats near Boyra (a small village 32 kilometers to the northwest of Jessore in a salient jutting into East Pakistan). At this point, the river almost flowed along the border and was not secured by Pakistan troops. The entire Battalion managed to cross the river by afternoon; by last light 20th November, the engineers had laid a 200 foot, class 40 bridge on the river. The Battalion along with PT-76 tanks then reached Gharibpur by the last light. Since daylight reconnaissance had not been carried out, the companies of 14 Punjab took up a linear defensive position in the dark along Track Gharibpur-Jagannathpur. At this time, Gharibpur was held by a company of 38 FF spread out thinly over a 10-kilometer front; it was also augmented with some elements of EPCAF spread over three BOPs in the area.

Since the orders of the Pak Eastern Command were not to allow even an inch of penetration, Brig Hayat was ordered by General Ansari to launch a counter-attack on the intruding force and regain the territory captured by them. Hayat immediately arrived at Afra, and planned a quick counter-attack as follows:

- Two companies of 6 Punjab to attack from the direction of Chuagacha.

- 3 Indep Armoured Squadron and two companies of 21 Punjab (R&S), moved from Jessore, to attack from the direction of Afra.

- 201 Field battery and troop of 120 mm Mortars to provide fire support.

- The attack to be launched at first light.

According to the original orders, Lt Colonel (later Lt General) Imtiaz Waraich, CO 21 Punjab, was to command this force but since he could not be contacted in time, the command was entrusted to Major Yahya Hamid, second-in-command of 6 Punjab. [71]

Brig Hayat had issued his orders for the counter-attack at 2 AM on 21st November, while the attack had to be launched at 6 AM; this gave hardly any time to Major Yahya Hamid to plan the attack properly. At the prescribed time, the PT 76 tanks of 3 Indep Armoured Squadron assaulted 14 Punjab (42 Indian Brigade) from the north and east and closed up to within 100 meters of their positions. Despite poor visibility, tanks and artillery on both sides were very active. At this point it appears that the companies of 21 Punjab failed to follow the assaulting tanks closely and thus, without the infantry cover, the tanks became exposed to the dug in Indian tanks and anti-tank weapons; eight out of 12 Pakistani tanks were soon knocked out in the fray while three tanks were abandoned and captured intact by 4 Sikh Battalion; only two tanks were lost by the Indians on the other side. It was a very heavy blow, not only to the Squadron but to the entire 107 Pak Brigade, which was deprived of its entire armour support at this, the earliest, stage of the operation.

The other prong of the attack relatively met with more success. Major Yahya Hamid at the head of two companies of 6 Punjab led the attack from the direction of Chuagacha and attacked 14 Punjab (42 Indian Brigade) on its western flank. The attack was successful and the assaulting troops managed to enter the built-up area of Gharibpur. The Indian troops withdrew from the village with heavy casualties: 19 killed, and 44 wounded.

Brig Hayat's handling of this important counter-attack has since come under heavy criticism. After the surrender, even Major General Dalbir Singh mocked Brig Hayat for his poor handling of this inaptly launched counter-attack. Subsequently too, after the repatriation of prisoners of war from India, his personal and professional conduct was to come under much criticism. Even the Hamood ur Rahman Commission found him prima facie guilty, inter alia, of the following lapses:

- Neglect to obtain full information about the enemy strength before launching the Gharibpur counter-attack.

- Failure to personally command this important Brigade counter-attack.

All this while, the remainder of 42 Indian Brigade had continued to cross River Kobadak unchecked and managed to concentrate in the Boyra

---

[71] Maj Gen Shaukat Riza, *Op Cit*, page 136.

salient. At this point, General Ansari realized that the strength of the enemy was much more than he originally assessed, particularly in armour, and began to clearly perceive the mounting danger to Jessore city. He therefore decided on 22nd November to withdraw 6 and 21 Punjab from Gharibpur and ordered them to take up defensive positions along the line of Afra Nullah, a few kilometers to the rear; incidentally, these positions were in close proximity of Jessore Cantonment.

Under increasing pressure, Gharibpur, thus, had to be vacated by Pakistani troops and 14 Punjab (42 Indian Brigade) re-occupied it. The same day, 22nd November, the Pakistan Air Force also went into action over this Sector. Four F-86 Sabre aircraft attacked the Gharibpur position after it had been re-occupied by 14 Punjab. They were, however, intercepted by a flight of Indian Air Force Gnat aircraft and in the ensuing dogfight, two sabre jets were lost. One of the pilots bailed out and landed near the positions of 4 Sikh Battalion near Gharibpur and was captured by Captain H S Panang (later, Lt General) of that unit. The name of this pilot was Flight Lieutenant Pervez Mehdi Qureshi, who after repatriation from India continued an illustrious career in the PAF and rose to be the Chief of Air Staff in due course.

On 23rd November, the company of 38 FF in Chuagacha came under attack by a squadron of 63 Cavalry and was soon overrun. Remnants of the company were withdrawn to the Afra position; Chuagacha was occupied by the Indians on the next day.

Under the progressive, cumulative pressure of these events, 107 Pak Brigade became completely unbalanced at this point. The Brigade had already lost all its armour component and the path to Jessore almost lay open.

Clearly, there was an urgent need to re-align and strengthen the defensive positions of 107 Pak Brigade at this time. Curiously enough, although Jessore had been designated a Theatre Fortress since July 1971, no efforts had been made to develop and organize its defences. The only ostensible preparation comprised the dumping of ammunition and rations but nothing else had been done to make it a "fortress", except in name. An Indian breakthrough from any point on the thinly-held defensive position could have potentially created an extremely serious hazard for Jessore. This stark danger to the second most prized objective in East Pakistan now suddenly loomed very large on the horizon.

Consequently, a planning conference was held by General Ansari in

Jessore at the Tactical Headquarters of 9 Pak Division on 24th November to consider the serious developing situation. Both Brig Hayat and Colonel K K Afridi, Colonel Staff 9 Pak Division, recommended a readjustment of the entire defensive position as the Indians had by then established themselves in strength across River Kobadak and were now re-organizing for a strong push towards Jessore. Brig Hayat also requested the GOC to release the full complement of 6 Punjab from Divisional reserve to his command so that he could organize a proper defensive position along Afra embankment.

He claims that he also asked General Ansari to permit him to withdraw one battalion to Jessore to develop its defences as it would not be possible to defend the city after a withdrawal in contact against the heavy offensive that the Indians were eventually expected to launch. According to Brig Hayat, the GOC did not accede to his request because he (GOC) felt that this would leave a dangerous gap and the possibility of the establishment of Bangladesh on East Pakistan soil would increase. The GOC also felt that such a move would have an adverse effect on the soldiers' morale.[72]

Brig Hayat has also claimed that as there were no fighting troops in the city at that time, he also requested his GOC to allow him to withdraw 15 FF from the less threatened Satkhira axis in the south to Jessore; this permission was, however, not accorded by General Ansari, who reportedly said, *"you have effectively contained the enemy. Let us wait and see."*[73]

In Dacca, the Pak Eastern Command was also monitoring this serious situation developing against Jessore. It ordered the immediate move of a fresh battalion, 12 Punjab, from 16 Pak Division to 9 Pak Division. The Battalion moved from Pabna and reached Jessore on 25th November. It was placed under command 107 Pak Brigade, which employed it to further strengthen the Afra position.

In a strange quirk of coincidence, which could only occur in these two opposing armies of that period, Major General Dalbir Singh, GOC 9 Indian Division, was originally commissioned in 12 Punjab Battalion, which would now face him as part of 107 Pak Brigade. Moreover, Brig H S Sandhu, Commander 350 Indian Brigade was a class-mate of Brig Hayat, Commander 107 Pak Brigade; both were then studying in Military College Jhelum when it was part of British India; now of course Jhelum was part of West Pakistan. Sandhu was said to speak fluent Pashto too.

---

[72] Lt Gen Kamal Matinuddin, *Op Cit*, page 382.
[73] *Ibid,* page 384.

111

By 26th November, 107 Pak Brigade had fallen back and taken up defensive positions along the general line Afra-Jhingargacha. Brig Hayat had deployed 38 FF in Kotchandpur-Khalispur area, 12 Punjab in Arpara area, 6 Punjab in Durgabarkati-Afra area, and 22 FF in Jhingargacha area; 15 FF continued to remain deployed in Satkhira area. The company of 22 FF in Benapol, being in danger of being surrounded, was also withdrawn to the Battalion main position at Jhingargacha. 21 Punjab (R&S) was held in Brigade Reserve at Jessore. All the units in line were engaged in developing their defensive positions with a feverish activity, with even the local villagers were employed, albeit forcibly, in large numbers to dig anti-tank ditches ahead of the positions. The entire undertaking was further facilitated by the presence of bheels and marshy areas which were integrated with their defensive positions by the Pakistani troops. Consequently, making full use of this reprieve in time, fairly strong defences based upon village complexes around Arpara, Durgabarkati, Afra, Burinda and Jhingergacha had been developed.

By this time, 50 Punjab had also been inducted from 16 Pak Division to reinforce 9 Pak Division.

No major activity, however, took place over the next two days, 26th and 27th November; 9 Indian Division merely remained content with creeping forward towards Jessore, improving their tactical posture for the impending assault on the city. During the period 28th November to 3rd December, an un-announced operational pause seemingly ensued in the battle as the Indians carried out their regrouping and replenishment while the Pakistanis remained feverishly engaged in improving their defensive positions. General Dalbir Singh had, however, utilized this period to concentrate one brigade at Bangaon- Benapol, while the rest of his Division remained concentrated in the Boyra salient.

General Niazi paid a visit to HQ 107 Pak Brigade on 29th November. While briefing him on the operational situation, Brig Hayat made the recommendation to pull some troops back to Jessore in view of the developing threat to the city. Niazi reportedly replied, *"No! No Shera! You do not understand. If you vacate any more territory, the Muktis will declare Bangladesh."* [74]

Another opportunity to defend Jessore properly was thus lost.

This was the opportune time when 107 Pak Brigade could have fully readjusted its defensive posture by occupying Jessore in strength while

---

[74] *Ibid,* page 387.

112

maintaining strong screens and delaying positions to the west of the city. Furthermore, 15 FF deployed along Satkhira approach was hardly facing any threat and could perform a more useful operational role had it also been pulled back to Jessore. But the short-sighted and rigid policy of 'no withdrawal' kept Jessore devoid of combat troops at a time when they were critically needed.

The War Commences

This period of minimal activity was to last till the evening of 3rd December when Pakistan made a formal declaration of war by launching an air strike against the Indian airfields in the Western Theatre. The Indians were already prepared to launch a full-scale offensive in East Pakistan in such a contingency and their armed forces swung into full action immediately.

By about 8:30 PM on 3rd December, orders and coordination for commencement of the full-scale offensive had been completed at HQ Indian Eastern Command. All the Corps Commanders were briefed telephonically by General Jacob, the Chief of Staff. The allocation of the air effort and the allotment of sorties to the respective corps had also been completed by then. On the fateful day of 3rd December, 107 Pak Brigade also received a signal message from HQ Pak Eastern Command which stipulated:

"no withdrawal from present location(.) brigade commander can only withdraw screens).) GOC can withdraw only one company(.)fight on present positions till 75 % casualties have been suffered".[75]

At the outbreak of the war, Major General Ansari, GOC 9 Pak Division, moved his Tactical Headquarters from Jessore back to his Main Headquarters at Magura. In hindsight, one can say, this move actually precipitated the doomsday for Jessore. Poor Brig Hayat was left stranded to fend for himself and atone for all the strategic blunders of his superiors!

Reverting to operations by 9 Indian Division, General Dalbir Singh at that point had three approaches open to him for an advance towards Jessore:

- Northern Approach along Road Chuagacha-Jessore in conjunction

---

[75] *Ibid,* page 384.

113

with Track Chuagacha-Arpara-Durgabarkati, which bypassed the Afra position of 107 Pak Brigade altogether.

- Central Approach along Track Burinda- Kaemkhola-Jessore.

- Southern Approach along the main highway Benapol-Jessore.

His initial decision was to carry out fixation of Pakistan troops along the Northern approach and advance in strength along the Central approach directly on to Jessore. Accordingly, on 4th December, 42 Indian Brigade began its advance but was held up against strong resistance by 6 Punjab at Arpara and Durgabarkati. 350 Indian Brigade under Brig Sandhu simultaneously began to move along the Central approach but was held up by 22 FF and the day of 5th December witnessed a number of determined Indian attacks, matched by equally fierce resistance by 107 Pak Brigade troops along this approach.

This defiant and strong resistance put up by 107 Pak Brigade troops revived the Indian fears and apprehensions of suffering very high casualties when attacking well-prepared Pakistani defensive positions. Clearly, a change in operational approach for the capture of Jessore was strongly indicated. The Indian Eastern Command at this time was already thinking of planning an air drop on Jessore in conjunction with ground assault at an opportune time; they urgently obtained the permission of Army Headquarters for employment of 50 Para Brigade, so far held back as the Army Reserve. Accordingly, 50 Para Brigade less a battalion was directed to be prepared for an air drop on Jessore in the rear of the main Pakistani defensive positions on orders. However, a quick breakthrough on the ground by 9 Indian Division obviated the requirement for this air drop.

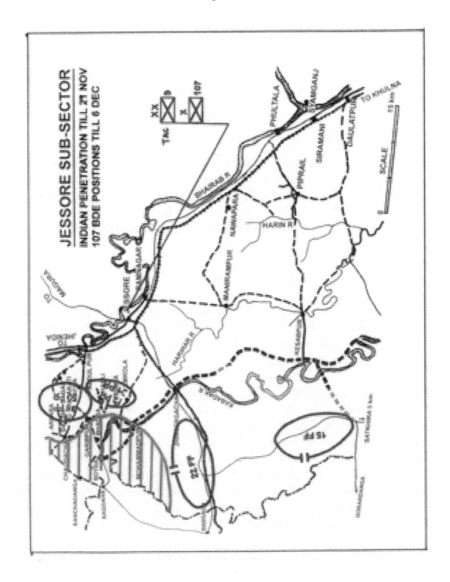

JESSORE SUB-SECTOR
INDIAN PENETRATION TILL 21 NOV
107 BDE POSITIONS TILL 6 DEC

By this time, General Dalbir Singh had also come to realize that a breakthrough along the Central approach would be time-consuming and very costly in lives and decided to swing the full weight of his Divisional offensive along the northern approach. So, he ordered the move of 32 Indian Brigade from Bangaon-Benapol area to Boyra salient, leaving only one battalion behind at Bangaon. The plan he now conceived was to force a breakthrough around Durgabarkati using 42 Indian Brigade and then launch 32 Indian Brigade through the gap so created to capture Jessore. Accordingly, 42 Indian Brigade was ordered to clear a passage around Durgabarkati by launching a day attack so that maximum use of air support could be made to soften up the defensive positions. 32 Indian Brigade was to be poised behind the assaulting brigade to exploit its success and capture Jessore as soon as possible.[76]

Brig Goraya, Commander 42 Indian Brigade, in turn nominated 2 Sikh LI for the capture of Durgabarkati and then to clear a passage for the follow up brigade. The H hour was fixed at 8 AM on 6th December; however, it had to be postponed because of heavy fog due to which air support could not be made available. In desperation, eventually, it was decided to launch the attack at 9:30 AM, still without the air support. By this time, an artillery duel from both the sides had been in full swing. On the Pakistan side, the main thrust of the attack was mostly borne by 6 Punjab and partially by 12 Punjab. 2 Sikh LI cleared its objective by 10 AM with 27 casualties. By about mid-day, three safe lanes had been breached opened by the Indian Engineers after clearing the mines. The route for the eventual dash to Jessore, only 10 kilometers away, had finally been opened.[77]

At this stage, 32 Indian Brigade were given the green light to resume their advance through these three safe lanes. 7 (Mech) Punjab and B Squadron 63 Cavalry led the advance. The ground in this area was very marshy and so the progress of the advance was rather slow; despite that the armour managed to cut Road Chuagacha-Jessore by last light near

---

[76] Maj Gen Lachhman Singh, *Op Cit*, pages 138-139.
[77] *Ibid.*

Abdulpur, some six kilometers east of Afra. However, on their northern flank, 6 Punjab was still holding on stoutly to their defensive positions around Afra, thus making further advance by the Indians hazardous. Another worrying factor for General Dalbir Singh at this stage was his artillery getting out of range and so unable to support further advance towards Jessore. In view of these complications, General Dalbir Singh decided to clear Afra position first so as to open the main axis for the move forward of artillery guns before launching an attack on Jessore itself.

Accordingly, he directed Brig Tewari, Commander 32 Indian Brigade, to clear Afra area by advancing from the Abdulpur direction to attack the defensive positions of 6 Punjab from the rear. At the same time, he also directed 350 Indian Brigade to exert pressure on Afra position frontally along the main axis. Under heavy pressure from both the sides, 6 Punjab had to vacate their positions before midnight, but not before they had blown up the bridge on Afra Nullah (stream). Since the vacated area had been heavily mined, the Indian engineers got engaged in de-mining the area with the help of some willing locals, who appeared to know the position of the minefields quite well; they had probably earlier been forced by the Pakistan troops to help laying them.

On the Pakistan side in Jessore, the situation was totally confused, ruled by the usual fog of war and full of panic. The information about the initial breakthrough of 7 (Mech) Punjab and B Squadron 63 Cavalry (32 Indian Brigade) was received at the brigade Headquarters in a highly-exaggerated form; it is said that an officer of 12 Punjab had panicked and sent in very inflated information about the actual number of the breaking out tanks. HQ 107 Pak Brigade being out of communication with 6 Punjab at that time was hardly in a position to counter-check and verify these reports.

At this point of time, the bulk of 107 Pak Brigade was deployed south of Jessore, strung over an area of almost 100 kilometers. There was simply no possibility of its being concentrated in the Jessore fortress in time to check the anticipated attack; even if some elements did manage to move back, there would still be no time for them to prepare proper defensive positions. One cannot really blame Brig Hayat for being in a state of panic in this situation. He carried out a quick assessment of the situation and came to the conclusion that he would have to abandon Jessore and live to fight another day.

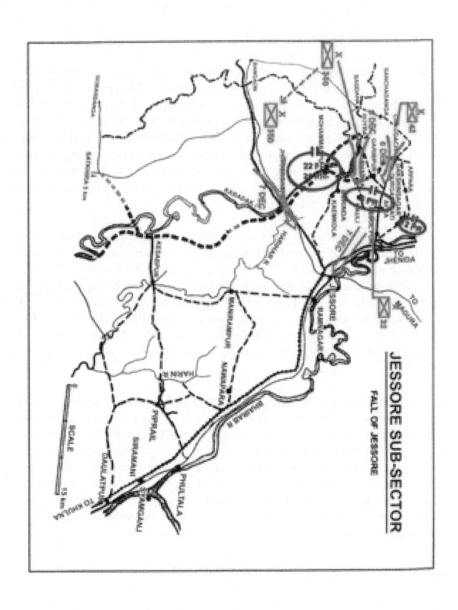

JESSORE SUB-SECTOR

FALL OF JESSORE

At this time, Brig Hayat had the choice of two axes along which to withdraw from Jessore; either towards Magura/Faridpur; or, towards Khulna. It is generally accepted that he had never received any clear orders, instructions, or guidance from either General Niazi or General Ansari on the axis of withdrawal to be adopted in case he had to abandon Jessore under heavy enemy pressure. However, as a senior brigade commander, he should have been well aware of the Theatre Commander's strategic plan and the vital importance of defending Dacca at all costs. Any professional soldier with even a working knowledge of operational strategy would easily have come to the conclusion that a withdrawal towards Magura and Faridpur would certainly confer a measure of superior strategic orientation not only on his own Brigade and Division, but to the entire Eastern Command. His Brigade, in that scenario, would have been able to take up a strong defensive position at Faridpur-Goalundo Ghat Ferries and to hold the Indians at bay for a fairly long time. Thus, it would have certainly served the strategic interests of his Theatre Commander in a more positive way. In his state of panic, perhaps, Brig Hayat could not give proper consideration to these critical factors.

He was essentially a simple infantry officer who had spent most of his professional life in regimental soldiering. His professional expertise had remained confined primarily to the tactical domain only; as such, he adopted the easy course and took the decision to withdraw towards Khulna. This decision was taken despite the fact that the route from Jessore to Magura had remained open to 107 Pak Brigade throughout 6th and 7th December; as we shall see, 4 Mountain Division captured Magura only on 8th December. Thus, till then, there was hardly any hindrance to his withdrawal towards Magura or Faridpur. (There are some views suggesting that Brig Hayat was conveyed the false news that the Indian tanks had already cut the Road Jessore-Magura as well. However, Brig Hayat himself never made that claim, not even before the Hamoodur Rahman Commission.)

At about this time, in the Jhenida sub-sector, 57 Pak Brigade was also facing intense pressure from 4 Mountain Division and it too could have easily withdrawn to Magura, fairly intact. It was thus a great opportunity for both these Brigades to take up a strong Divisional defensive position at

Magura and subsequently at Faridpur-Goalundo Ghat; in due course, a substantial part of this combined force could have also have detached for defence of Dacca too. As we mentioned before, strategy is essentially an interplay of Time, Space and Relative Strength. There is hardly a doubt that General Ansari as well as both his brigade commanders failed to analyze the emerging scenario in a proper strategic context. In the end, Brig Hayat simply fell a prey to his instinct for survival at all costs!

Apart from the question of whether his decision was right or wrong, it is very instructive to evaluate the actual conduct of the withdrawal itself. The stark fact is that Brig Hayat just did not issue any proper orders to his unit commanders for the contemplated withdrawal; nor were all of them even aware of his intention to withdraw. Thus, the operational and tactical procedures for an organized withdrawal to Khulna were simply not adopted. By all available accounts, he just left his Jessore Headquarters in his jeep and took off for Khulna. Two of his units, 15 FF and 22 FF were already on the move to Khulna but out of communication with the Brigade; when and how they were conveyed the orders for withdrawal has never been fully clarified. The other three infantry battalions were still in their positions, hardly knowing what to do next. The vast dumps of ammunition and other stores in Jessore were also left intact because of this panic withdrawal.

After the surrender, Brig Hayat narrated his own version of the battle in Jessore to some Indian officers who were rather curious on the erratic way the battle had been conducted. This is how one such account describes Brig Hayat's version of his actions:

"On 6 December, when Hayat Khan got the news of the breakthrough at Durgabarkati, he ordered the withdrawal of his Brigade to Khulna. 22 FF, which was in Jhingergacha area, was ordered to fall back to the Ramnagar area on the Jessore-Khulna Road on the afternoon of 6 December. The rest of the brigade withdrew before midnight of 6/7 December. The Pakistanis made no effort to destroy the vast dumps of ammunition and other stores in Jessore."[78]

But that was hardly the whole story. Here is an eye-witness account of what was actually happening on the ground, narrated by a responsible and highly credible officer Major (later Brig) Syed Masudul Hasan, then the second-in-command of 21 Punjab (R&S) in Jessore (Major Masud had already been promoted Lt Colonel and posted to Dacca but he opted to stay on with his unit during these critical times.):

---

[78] *Ibid,* page 141.

120

"Brig Hayat and his BM were absolutely clueless. At one stage, I offered to my CO to act as BM because BM was totally out of picture about the fast moving situation. The only sane and brave person in the Brigade HQ was GSO-3 Capt Hafeez Malik, who retired as a Brigadier.

"Brig Hayat and his BM were the first to run to Khulna without informing any unit. When CO and myself went to Brigade HQ, there was no officer available to tell us what to do. Some clerk told us that the Commander and BM had gone towards Khulna. We contacted CO 6 Punjab who was on our right. He also expressed his ignorance about move to Khulna. CO 12 Punjab said the same thing. COs of 15 FF and 22 FF could not be contacted. These two COs were always seen with the Commander and were his main advisors. So, they probably knew of his plans.

"We kept deliberating the future course of action. Then we learnt that 15 FF and 22 FF had already moved to Khulna. CO 12 Punjab then decided to move to Khulna. Then moved 21 Punjab. 6 Punjab was the last to move. ...." [79]

Major General Shaukat Riza has also hinted, albeit obliquely, to this state of affairs:

"Brig Hayat ordered the troops to withdraw towards Khulna. In fact, the troops were already doing so." [80]

As described above, the withdrawal to Khulna was initially a haphazard and uncoordinated affair. The battalions rushed back whenever they could and simply had no idea whether any delaying position en route to Khulna had been planned to be occupied and by whom. The whole intricate mechanics of conducting a withdrawal while in contact with the enemy, taught so painstakingly by the Command & Staff College Quetta had been totally neglected by the Brigade Commander and his Brigade Major, Major Fakhar Alam. By this time, 22 FF had reached the Y-junction just outside Jessore, where the road from Satkhira joined the Jessore-Khulna Road. They took up the semblance of a defensive position there; apparently to await the arrival of 15 FF from Satkhira, where it was still deployed. Meanwhile General Dalbir Singh, still unaware of the hasty withdrawal of the Pakistan forces from Jessore city, was busy planning a major assault on the city.

By first light 7th December, the minefield at Afra position had been

---

[79] *Email to the author* by Brig Syed Masudul Hasan.
[80] Maj Gen Shaukat Riza, *Op Cit*, page 139.

cleared and a bridge constructed on the Afra Nullah (stream). This development had also enabled the out of range artillery guns to move forward and support the final attack on Jessore. Soon thereafter 7 (Mech) Punjab and B Squadron 63 Cavalry pressed forward towards the Jessore airfield from the west and by 8 AM the tanks had driven across the main runway without meeting any opposition. At the same time, 14 Punjab pushed forward on the main road to Jessore while 350 Indian Brigade was directed to move along the Jhingargacha axis to press on the city from the southern flank. 32 Indian Brigade secured the Cantonment area by midday and the advancing Indian forces were pleasantly surprised to find the city totally evacuated by Pakistan troops. Jessore was the largest and the most important city of East Pakistan to have been captured before the surrender. It was doubtlessly a great prize and its reverberations were felt even in the faraway, august halls of the United Nations, as we shall later see.

After the fall of Jessore and the withdrawal of 107 Pak Brigade to Khulna, the route to Magura and then on to Goalundo Ghat lay open to II Corps; only a weak, ad hoc task force comprising remnants of 50 Punjab and 38 FF, supported by an artillery battery, stood in between; these troops had become separated from their parent units during the operations. Subsequently, General Ansari grouped them under his Colonel Staff, Colonel K K Afridi, to protect his Headquarters at Magura and to guard the approaches to Faridpur and Goalundo Ghat. A rather belated after-thought, though!

At this time, General Dalbir Singh had the option to merely mask the move of 107 Pak Brigade towards Khulna and move the bulk of 9 Indian Division towards Magura and Faridpur in accordance with the strategic plan conceived by HQ Indian Eastern Command. Coincidentally, at about the same time, a similar situation had also materialized on the Jhenida Front where 4 Mountain Division too could have moved unchecked towards Magura and on to Faridpur. This was a great opportunity offered to II Corps, along the fronts of both its divisions, for a concerted advance towards Goalundo Ghat, en route to Dacca. This would have changed the entire dynamics of war at that early stage. But here also, narrow tactical considerations ruled the day and the strategic vision neglected with a gay abandon. Through a stroke of luck for the Pak Eastern Command, both the Indian divisions instead chose to wheel outwards: 9 Indian Division towards Khulna and 4 Mountain Division towards the Paksey Bridge; a great opportunity was thus squandered by the Indians.

There is some explanation available, however nebulous, why General Dalbir Singh chose to go towards Khulna and not Faridpur. From the information received at HQ 9 Indian Division from intelligence agencies as well as some local Mukti Bahini sources, General Dalbir Singh had been led to believe that at best only up to one battalion had withdrawn towards Khulna and the rest of 107 Pak Brigade had withdrawn towards Magura. Inexplicably, Dalbir Singh also lost sight of strategic imperative and decided to push towards Khulna; perhaps he was lured by the prospects of an easy victory at Khulna. This is what General Jacob, COS Indian Eastern Command, had to comment on this situation:

"Despite our plan of operations, and contrary to our instructions, the whole of 9 Infantry Division unnecessarily became committed to this area instead of concentrating on its specified thrust line to Magura-Faridpur."[81]

According to the original plan of the Indian Eastern Command, one of the tasks allocated to 9 Indian Division after the capture of Jessore was for the Division less a Brigade to assist 4 Mountain Division in its operations towards Magura and Faridpur. In view of wheeling south of the entire 9 Indian Division, it was hardly in a position to do so. But as we shall later see, 50 Para Brigade was instead ordered to move on Magura axis.

Back to operations of 9 Indian Division. General Dalbir Singh tasked Brig Tiwari's 32 Indian Brigade to advance towards Khulna, and concentrated the rest of his Division in Jessore.

32 Indian Brigade, with a squadron of 45 Cavalry under command, commenced its advance at about 2:30 PM on 7th December, with 7 (Mech) Punjab leading. On the Pakistan side, as discussed earlier, 22 FF had by then taken up a defensive position along the Jessore-Khulna Road at Ramnagar near the Y junction, about four kilometers southeast of Jessore city. Meanwhile, 15 FF, from its earlier position at Satkhira, had already passed through the Y junction during the preceding night and taken up a defensive position at milestone 7 on Jessore-Khulna road.

By 4 PM, the leading Indian elements had contacted the 22 FF position at Ramnagar. Sensing strong opposition at this position, Brig Tiwari decided to make an outflanking move in order to cut off 22 FF from the rear. Accordingly, one battalion moved out to the east at about 8 AM on 8th December while 7 (Mech) Punjab kept up the pressure frontally; by 1 PM it had succeeded in cutting off the road a few kilometers east of Ramnagar. 22 FF was thus isolated from the rest of 107 Pak Brigade and encircled by the Indian troops.

---

[81] Lt Gen J FR Jacob, *Op Cit*, pages 198-109.

Major Azmat Hayat, an artillery officer commanding 201 Battery of 55 Field Regiment rose to the occasion in this desperate situation, and rescued 22 FF by a heroic action. He personally directed intense fire on the advancing Indian troops and forced them to withdraw. Using open sights and direct fire, he destroyed a number of tanks as well. 22 FF thus managed to come out of the encirclement because of the bravery, courage and determination of this brave officer, who in the process laid down his life. He was later found by the Indians still clinging to his gun even in death. Azmat was deservedly recommended for Nishan-e-Haider but his citation was perhaps misplaced somewhere along the line.[82]

By mid-day 8th December, Brig Hayat and his Headquarters had reached Khulna. By then, the infantry battalions of 107 Pak Brigade were strung along the Jessore-Khulna Road as follows:

- 15 FF   Milestone 7.
- 6 Punjab   Milestone 9.
- 21 Punjab   Milestone 14.
- 22 FF   Milestone 17.
- 12 Punjab   Milestone 21.

From Ramnagar to Khulna, the Jessore-Khulna Road runs along the west bank of River Bhairab. With the River on one side and the railway line embankment on the other, the road becomes almost a defile at most places. As the locale of the operation gradually moved southwards towards Khulna, the area also became progressively marshier, covered with dense foliage. Movement off the road for wheeled as well as tracked vehicles became more difficult accordingly. These terrain conditions naturally helped the defenders and made offensive actions correspondingly more difficult by imposing severe limitations on the maneuverability and speed of the advancing troops

While gradually withdrawing towards Khulna, the units of 107 Pak Brigade took up a number of delaying positions along this Road, albeit in a rather haphazard and hasty manner since these had never been reconnoitered or prepared earlier. They did however make a good use of the surrounding terrain, which provided natural help to the defender. Thus, throughout 8th and 9th December, even these hastily-prepared delaying positions successively became formidable impediments against the advance

---

[82] Maj Gen Shaukat Riza, *Op Cit*, page 139; Lt Gen Kamal Matinuddin, *Op Cit*, page 389.

of the units of 9 Indian Division.

By 10th December, Brig Hayat had finally managed to establish full control over his units. He had, by now, also prepared a plan for a strong defensive position at Daulatpur, some eight kilometers north of Khulna; he had also decided to place a strong screen at Phultala, about 17 kilometers from Khulna. (A screen position is basically established to impose delay on the advancing enemy for a specific period of time, after which it is expected to fall back to the main position.)

Thus, on the evening of 10th December, 107 Pak Brigade had for the first time got an opportunity to be in a position to fight as a compact formation in a textbook deployment. The Brigade deployment at this point of time was as under:

1. Screen Position: Company 21 Punjab (R&S) and Two companies 15 FF, at Phultala near Milestone 14, with Major Nazar of 21 Punjab as overall commander.

2. 12 Punjab at Miksimil, facing west.

3. 15 FF at left of road at Daulatpur.

4. 6 Punjab at Right of road at Daulatpur.

5. 22 FF in depth, covering Daulatpur from the south.

6. 55 Field Regiment deployed in the middle of the defensive position for effective fire support to all the infantry units.

Major Nazar, commander of the screen position, was an experienced and competent infantry officer. He deployed his force very soundly and quickly mined all the likely approaches along which the Indians could mount an attack on his position. He also identified the likely assembly areas around his position where the attacking force could assemble prior to launching an attack, and laid mines and booby-traps there.

32 Indian Brigade had meanwhile continued with its advance along the Khulna Road and contacted the Phultala screen position at about last light on 10th December. An impulsive Brig Tiwari, over-confident with easy successes so far, sought to rush the position during the same night; Major

Nazar's troops put up a fierce resistance and the attack was repulsed. Captain Ahmed Bilal of 15 FF became a casualty during this action; he was gallantly trying to adjust the forward most positions of his Company while the attack was still in process.

107 PAK BRIGADE
LAST STAND AT KHULNA

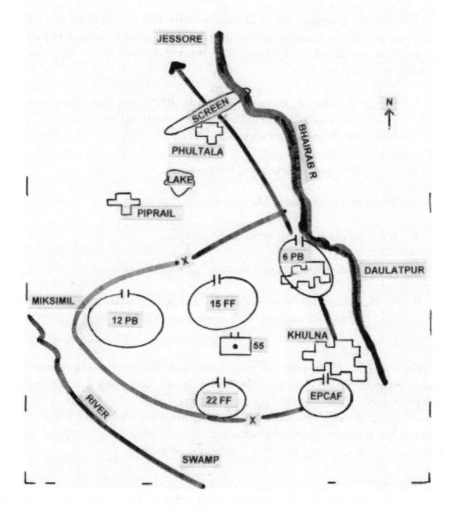

The fierce and determined resistance put up by this screen position managed to convince Brig Tiwari that he was dealing with indeed a much bigger force than it actually was. Consequently, he decided to launch a major attack at dawn the next day with 7 (Mech) Punjab and a squadron of 63 Cavalry, preceded by heavy artillery and air bombardment. Even this attack was beaten back with heavy casualties.

Major Nazar and his troops held this screen position against heavy odds for full two days and gained that valuable time for the rest of 107 Pak Brigade to prepare their defensive positions properly at Daulatpur. After this job well done, he was ordered to withdraw to the main positions during the night 11th /12th December. During the course of these two days of constant engagement, his force had suffered almost 100 casualties; most of his officers had also been killed or severely wounded.

The withdrawal of the Phultala screen position enabled 32 Indian Brigade to resume their advance at first light 12th December along the main road. In addition, Brig Tiwari had also sent a mobile column comprising 7 (Mech) Punjab and a squadron of 45 Cavalry on an outflanking move towards Piprail with the mission to threaten Daulatpur position from the west. At Piprail, this column was sighted by a patrol of 15 FF and engaged at long range with two recoilless rifles; the Indian mobile column lost two tanks and a couple of APCs in this quick melee and their further advance was stalled.

The rest of 32 Indian Brigade had by then come into contact with the main positions of 107 Pak Brigade. During the night 12th/13th December, Tiwari launched an attack on a flank of Srimani Village, held by 6 Punjab but it was beaten back. Two separate mobile columns were also sent out to outflank this strong position but could hardly make much progress due to marshy terrain. By this time, General Dalbir Singh too had come to realize, through air reconnaissance and input from the friendly locals, that he was facing the bulk of 107 Pak Brigade at Daulatpur and not merely an isolated unit as earlier appreciated by him. But this was hardly the only problem confronting him at that time.

Daulatpur, a suburb of Khulna, had sprung up astride the main road as a long, continuous, and narrow built- up strip of about two miles. The area around was covered with thick groves and creepers which restricted visibility to hardly more than 30 meters. River Bhairab on the east of the main road was a major obstacle and on the western side, movement was severely restricted due to extensive impassable marshes. Thus, he realized, much to his chagrin, that this was a position very well selected by Brig

Hayat, which could not be easily outflanked.

Faced with these problems, General Dalbir took a typically reactive decision; he concentrated the entire strength of his Division for the impending battle. His eventual scheme of manoeuvre for his Divisional attack was as follows:[83]

- 32 Indian Brigade to hold a firm base astride the main road.

- 42 Indian Brigade to secure the ferry at Syamganj and then cross River Bhairab with Brigade less a battalion and with half a squadron of PT-76 amphibious tanks. After crossing the River, the Brigade to advance southwards along the eastern bank of the river, re-cross it in the rear of Daulatpur and then capture Daulatpur/ Khulna in conjunction with 350 Indian Brigade.

- 350 Indian Brigade to attack from the north and overrun the main enemy position at Daulatpur in conjunction with 42 Indian Brigade.

According to this ambitious plan, 42 Indian Brigade moved at 3 PM on 12th December to secure Syamganj Ferry but could make very slow progress due to thick vegetation and marshy ground. The leading battalion eventually captured the Ferry site by the afternoon of 13th December after suffering some 30 casualties. However, soon after this, they came under heavy observed fire from the depth company of 6 Punjab, which was dominating the crossing site. Meanwhile, another battalion of this Brigade attacked the Srimani positions held by 6 Punjab but suffered heavy casualties and so made little progress. Thus, even after suffering over 70 casualties, the Indian Brigade did not succeed in making an outflanking move southwards.

This setback forced General Dalbir Singh to modify his plan. He ordered that 42 Indian Brigade should now cross River Bhairab further up north during the night 13th /14th December and then to move south towards Daulatpur/Khulna in accordance with the original plan. This change proved more successful and by the morning of 14th December, the Brigade had managed to cross the River without much difficulty. However, the area being very marshy, their southwards progress along the River remained extremely slow. Thus, it could not reach the point from where it had to re-cross the River in time to support the Divisional attack. The

---

[83] Maj Gen Lachhman Singh, *Op Cit*, pages 143-144.

consequent delay forced the Divisional H-hour to be postponed several times since 350 Indian Brigade had to launch its attack in conjunction with 42 Indian Brigade. A desperate and frustrated General Dalbir Singh finally decided to launch the attack only by 350 Indian Brigade on 14th December, without waiting any further for 42 Indian Brigade.

On 15th December, in the first phase of the Divisional attack, 1 J&K commanded by Lt Colonel Surinder Kapoor, fully supported by tank and divisional artillery fire, was launched to clear the positions around Syamganj held by 6 Punjab. By 4 PM, the position had been cleared after fierce fighting during which the attacking unit had suffered very high casualties.

Soon thereafter, leaflets were thrown by helicopters over the 22 FF positions advising the defending troops to cease fire in view of the imminent surrender by Pak Eastern Command. Brig Hayat, however, decided to ignore these messages and to continue with the battle.

The second phase of the attack was launched after a heavy preparatory bombardment of about 45 minutes on the positions of 6 Punjab and 15 FF by tank, artillery, mortars, as well as continuous air support. For this phase, 4 Sikh Battalion was tasked to establish a roadblock south of Srimani village. It launched the attack at about 4 PM on 15th December and succeeded in dislodging the left-forward company of 6 Punjab, commanded by Major Nadir Pervez, after suffering some 70 casualties. It, thereafter, continued to exploit forward and, by first light on 16th December, it had managed to reach the road behind the 6 Punjab positions. At this stage, 13 Dogra was launched, through the 4 Sikh positions, on the 15 FF positions holding the western side of Srimani village. The right-forward company of 15 FF was badly mauled and had to fall back. In the confusion that followed, four officers, one JCO and 26 soldiers of 15 FF were taken prisoner. One young officer of 15 FF, Captain Arjumand Yar Khund, was killed while still firing from his machine gun. Major Thakkar of 13 Dogra paid tribute to his gallantry in these words:

"One young looking soldier who was bleeding from all over body was leaning on his machine gun, his right thumb pressing the firing mechanism. Ammunition had been exhausted. This young officer said in a whisper 'fetch me some water'. Before I returned he was dead. One of his arms had been shot off. Later, while searching the body, we identified him as Capt Arjamand Yar Khund." [84]

Reacting to this penetration by the Indians, Brig Hayat planned a heavy

---

[84] Maj Gen Shaukat Riza, *Op Cit*, page 140.

129

counter-attack on the captured positions during the succeeding night, 16th /17th December. He ordered a company of 22 FF to move behind 15 FF and provide a firm base for this counter-attack.

By this time, the news of the surrender at Dacca were being received from different sources. A message from the Indian Brigade Commander had also been handed over to an officer of 15 FF, which asked the Pakistan Brigade Commander to meet him at 9:30 AM on 17th December to discuss the modalities of cease fire and surrender. Brig Hayat called a conference of his commanding officers to decide the future course of action. At about this time, he also received a message from Commander Pak Eastern Command directing the Brigade Commander to surrender.

Brig Hayat surrendered with about 3700 all ranks to Major General Dalbir Singh on 17th December 1971 at the Circuit House of Khulna. The battle for Jessore and Khulna was finally over.

Despite his initial fumbling during the defence of Jessore, Brig Hayat and his Brigade acquitted themselves well in the battle for Khulna, which has been acknowledged by even the Indian chroniclers. Lt General Jacob has this to say about it:

"The Pakistanis had apparently intended to fight to the last in this last- ditch fortress and the operation for the capture of Daulatpur and Khulna, therefore, turned into a hard- slogging match."[85]

Major General Sukhwant Singh comments as follows:

"He (Brig Hayat) had kept the (9 Ind) Division at bay on his own for a good ten days, and yet the real fight for Khulna had not begun. He was justifiably confident of holding out for another week or so till the much- promised American help materialized. He felt badly let down by the Pakistani Higher Command, he said later in interrogation."[86]

In his apologia 'The Betrayal of East Pakistan', General Niazi has claimed that Brig Hayat, being out of communication with his Divisional Commander, General Ansari, had instead sought his permission to withdraw his Brigade from Jessore. Niazi asserts that not only he accorded this permission but also directed him to withdraw towards Khulna instead of Magura and Faridpur. He has thus tried to claim the credit not only for

---

[85] Lt Gen J FR Jacob, *Op Cit,* page 108.
[86] Maj Gen Sukhwant Singh, *Op Cit,* page 143.

the epic defence of Khulna by 107 Pak Brigade but also the strategic deflection of 9 Indian Division, which followed the Pak Brigade to Khulna instead of moving towards Magura-Faridpur-Goalundo Ghat.[87]

After analyzing the entire situation in detail, we are of the considered opinion that General Niazi's assertion is just an after-thought and factually incorrect. We are further strengthened in making this assessment because Brig Muhammad Hayat himself never mentioned this very significant fact while giving his testimony during the proceedings of Hamood ur Rahman Commission. He did not proffer this rationale even when the Commission charge-sheeted him, inter alia, for withdrawing towards Khulna and not towards Magura.

Operations in Jhenida Sub-Sector

The defence of Jhenida sub-sector had been entrusted to 57 Pak Brigade, commanded by Brig Manzoor Ahmed. His area of operations was defined on the north by the River Ganges, which line also demarcated the boundary of Southwestern Sector with the Northwestern Sector. His southern boundary was defined by the line connecting Darsana- Jibannagar-Kaliganj-Jhenida-Faridpur. Originally, the inter-brigade boundary between the two Brigades of 9 Pak Division lay along line Darsana – Jibannagar, but as soon as the hostilities commenced, the entire area north of Chuagacha perforce had to be made the responsibility of 57 Pak Brigade because of the thrust made by 4 Mountain Division.

There were two main rivers in this area. The Padma (Ganges) on the east was a major obstacle sprawling over miles. The Madhumati, west of the Padma, was another substantial obstacle and was not bridged anywhere in the Sector. A number of subsidiary rivers also flowed north to south. The two important ferry sites over the River Padma (Ganges) en route to Dacca were located at Faridpur and Goalundo Ghat, both falling in this sub-sector.

---

[87] Lt Gen A A Khan Niazi, *Op Cit*, page 146.

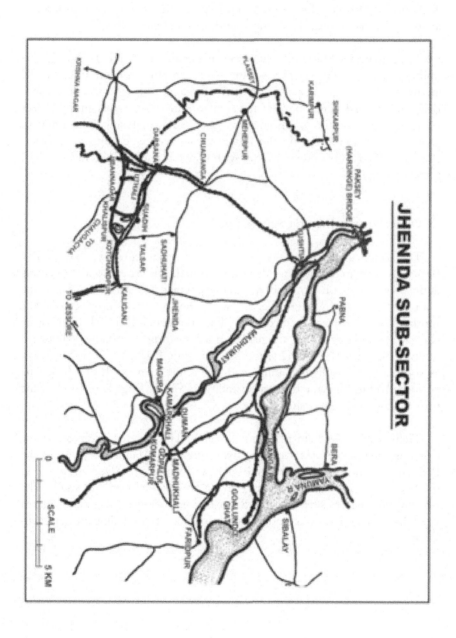

JHENIDA SUB-SECTOR

Operationally, the most important road in this area ran south to north, linking Jessore- Jhenida- Kushtia- Paksey (Hardinge) Bridge. Its alignment was generally parallel to the border with India and lay approximately 40 to 50 kilometers east of it. The area along the border from Meherpur to Chuagacha, up to a depth of about 20 kilometers along the general line Chuadanga-Kotchandpur-Chuagacha, was dotted with numerous bheels (small, marshy lakes). Despite that, this area on the whole was better suited for mechanized and mobile operations as compared to Jessore Sub-sector.

Jhenida was the most important communications centre in the area, lying at the intersection of two important roads: Jessore-Kushtia Highway; and, Road Meherpur-Faridpur/Goalundo Ghat. Considering its importance, Jhenida had been declared a fortress town by Pak Eastern Command. Kushtia was another important communications centre. Pak Eastern Command had designated the Jessore-Kushtia Highway in this sub-sector as the Line of No Withdrawal.

There were two main axes of advance open to the Indian forces in this Sub-sector, both converging at Jhenida and then leading towards the main ferry sites of Faridpur and Goalundo Ghat on the Padma (Ganges). North to south, these were:

1. **Meherpur-Chuadanga-Jhenida-Faridpur.**

   Relatively a longer approach to River Padma. Chuadanga, a town en route, was the home town of the Governor of East Pakistan Dr. Abdul Malik, and as such possessed some political sensitivity; besides it was also an important rail communications centre.

2. **Jibannagar-Kotchandpur-Kaliganj-Jhenida-Faridpur.**

   Relatively the shorter route to Jhenida and onwards to Faridpur. A number of lateral link roads linked this approach with Chuagacha-Jessore Road as well as Chuadanga-Jhenida Road.

In order to cover the large frontage of his area of responsibility, Brig Manzoor Ahmed had been constrained to deploy his battalions over wide frontages, primarily in company groups, mixed with EPCAF personnel and the Razakars. His basic deployment was as under:

- **29 Baluch.** Paksey (Hardinge) Bridge area.

- **18 Punjab.** Meherpur-Chuadanga-Darsana area.

- **50 Punjab.** Suadih-Kotchandpur axis. (Some elements placed in reserve at Chuadanga).

- **38 FF (minus).** Jibannagar-Kaliganj axis. (This unit was originally part of 107 Pak Brigade but after the Battle of Gharibpur during the Twilight phase of operations, two of its companies were isolated and so were placed under 57 Pak Brigade. The rest of the Battalion continued to form part of 107 Pak Brigade.)

- **Squadron 29 Cavalry.** Paksey Bridge. (It was detached from 16 Pak Division and placed under command 57 Pak Brigade. Equipped with Chaffee tanks.)

- **Brigade HQ.** Jhenida.

From the pattern of his deployment, it would appear that Brig Manzoor was relatively more concerned about the security of Paksey Bridge as well as Meherpur-Chuadanga area; thus, the emphasis of his deployment leaned more towards the north.

As already mentioned, General Raina, Commander II Corps, had tasked 4 Mountain Division, commanded by Major General Brar, to launch an offensive in this area for the early capture of Jhenida and Magura. General Brar was, however, to accomplish his task with two brigades only. His third brigade had been detached to form Corps Reserve; it was initially to be deployed in a defensive role opposite Meherpur area; later, on orders, it was to simulate a show of threat against Paksey Bridge.[88] The Division was allotted one squadron of tanks, one medium battery artillery and one company APCs for this operation.

---

[88] Maj Gen Lachhman Singh, *Op Cit*, page 118.

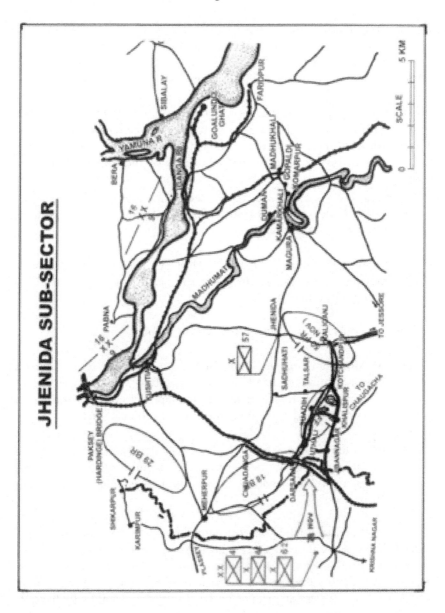

JHENIDA SUB-SECTOR

In retrospect, it is fairly obvious that General Raina as well as both his divisional commanders were extremely conscious of maintaining mutual support between the two divisional axes of advance. In the case of 9 Indian Division, as we have seen, the main thrust was eventually launched along the Boyra axis and not along the main road Benapol-Jessore despite his earlier inclination to do so. Similarly, the main weight of the 4 Mountain Division was oriented towards the southern side of its allocated sector.

135

Despite this, it is surprising that General Raina failed to concentrate the strength and combat potential of his divisions at any point during the campaign; thus, both these divisions essentially fought their independent battles and hardly ever functioned as a corps.

The task entrusted to General Brar was to capture Kaliganj by D plus 6 and Jhenida by D plus 8. This was to be followed by capture of Magura and Maduakhali ferry site over River Madhumati by D plus 11. Subsequent to this, he was to be prepared to perform either of the following tasks on orders:

- Secure Faridpur and Goalundo Ghat ferries with a view to posing a threat towards Dacca.

- Capture Kushtia and Paksey (Hardinge) Bridge with a view to moving to Bogra (Northwestern Sector) for mopping up operations in that Sector.

The plan conceived by General Brar was as follows:

- 41 Mountain Brigade, under Brig Tony Michigan, to advance on Uthali-Suadih-Kotchandpur axis. After the capture of Kotchandpur, this Brigade was to approach Jhenida through a cross-country advance along the Talsar-Sadhuhati track.

- 62 Mountain Brigade under Brig Rajinder Nath to advance on Jibannagar-Kaliganj axis. After the capture of Kaliganj, this Brigade was also to advance towards Jhenida along the Kaliganj-Jhenida axis.

General Brar had reached his concentration area by 15th November. He utilized the available time to thoroughly study and reconnoiter his area of operations with the help of Mukti Bahini sources. His main interest at this stage, was to identify the areas in the vicinity of the border whose capture would facilitate his eventual main offensive. Initially, he identified Khalispur and Darsana as two likely objectives. However, intense reconnaissance indicated that Khalispur area across River Bhairab was being held in sizeable strength and 57 Pak Brigade troops had also blown up the bridge leading to it. On the other hand, it transpired that Darsana was being held by only a company of 18 Punjab. This led General Brar to select Darsana as his initial objective.

Accordingly, he ordered Brig Rajendar Nath, commander 62 Mountain

136

Brigade, to secure Darsana. The attack was launched on 28th November and succeeded in breaking through the defences of the company of 18 Punjab deployed there. The next night, the village of Uthali, a few kilometers to the east of Darsana, was also attacked. This village was held by another company of 18 Punjab and was also protected by a minefield. The squadron of armour supporting the Indian attack was held up by the minefield and a few tanks sustained damage; the attack on Uthali thus failed. The Brigade however launched yet another attack on 30th November and this time succeeded in securing Uthali as well as nearby Jibannagar. However, on 2nd November, 18 Punjab counter-attacked and re-occupied Darsana position.

This development was viewed seriously by General Brar, who apprehended that these Pakistan troops in Darsana would effectively disrupt his axis of maintenance. Moreover, they could potentially impede his contemplated advance towards Jhenida by causing harassment in the rear areas of his brigades. He, therefore, ordered Brig Tony Michigan, commander 41 Mountain Brigade, to clear this position on 4th December.

As mentioned earlier too, the attack on Jibannagar and probing actions towards Khalispur coincidentally fell exactly on the inter-brigade boundary between 57 and 107 Pak Brigades and thus engaged some positions of 38 FF (107 Pak Brigade) as well. The Battalion thus got split; some of its troops fell back to the area of their parent Brigade, while the bulk of the unit had no option but to withdraw north towards Jhenida, thenceforth forming part of 57 Pak Brigade.

As the official war started in the evening of 3rd December, Brig Michigan was already engaged in planning for the re-capture of Darsana as ordered by his GOC. His plan was to launch his attack in two phases: in Phase I, 5/1 Gurkha Battalion, supported by a squadron of PT-76 tanks, was to capture Darsana Railway Station; and, in Phase II, the second battalion of his Brigade was to clear the rest of the town. To completely ensure the success of this attack, General Brar also decided to establish a roadblock on Road Darsana-Chuadanga, so as to mask Darsana area from Pakistani troops in Chuadanga; this roadblock was to be established under the Divisional arrangements.

As a preliminary operation, 22 Rajput Battalion (7 Mountain Brigade), with a squadron of tanks, began to advance from the direction of Uthali on 3rd December but were held up by 18 Punjab troops while still about 1000 meters southeast of Darsana. The Indian tanks then moved up at just about the last light on 3rd December and destroyed some of the forward bunkers held by 18 Punjab. This encouraged a company of 22 Rajput to advance surreptitiously to occupy these bunkers, but they came under accurate machine gun fire from the defenders in the depth. The preliminary attack on Darsana thus stalled with heavy casualties inflicted on the Rajputs, but in the process the Indians did come to know about the exact layout of the defensive position.

By about 4 AM on 4th December, the promised roadblock was reported to be in position as planned at a crossroad area some three kilometres northwest of Darsana and so Brig Michigan decided to launch his Brigade attack. The excellent layout of 18 Punjab defences, with both its flanks resting on natural obstacles, forced Michigan to attack the position frontally. The Phase I attack by 5/1 Gurkhas went in at first light on 4th December; the squadron of tanks again played havoc with the first line of 18 Punjab bunkers, clearing the path of the advancing Gurkhas and Darsana railway station was secured by 8 AM. However, by then the 18 Punjab troops had regrouped along a rear row of bunkers, which were shielded from the tanks being in a defilade position; from there they were in a position to bring down heavy fire on the attackers. Eventually, a lane in the mined area east of Darsana was soon cleared by the Gurkhas to enable the tanks to pass through and effectively engage these depth bunkers as well.

Instead of waiting for the second unit to pass through, as per the original plan, Colonel Venugopal, CO 5/1 Gurkha, volunteered to clear out the rest of Darsana town and thus save time. This was permitted by Brig Michigan and the Gurkhas succeeded in clearing the entire position by 11 AM; in the process, the Gurkhas suffered heavy casualties: 93 dead and wounded.[89] The company of 18 Punjab withdrew towards Chuadanga, but not before facing yet another misfortune as they ran head along into the ambush laid by the Indian troops at the roadblock established earlier on this road.

By 3rd December, Brig Manzoor Ahmed, Commander 57 Pak Brigade, had come to realize that 4 Mountain Division was engaged in establishing a bridgehead in Uthali and Darsana area. He appreciated that having captured Darsana, the Indians would be in a position to directly threaten Chuadanga, the hometown of Governor Abdul Malik. He was fully aware that besides the political and psychological sensitivity of this town, the capture of Chuadanga would potentially open the route to Kushtia as well as Jhenida to the Indian troops. He therefore moved his Tactical Headquarters to Chuadanga to control the operations there personally. When Darsana fell

---

[89] Maj Gen Lachhman Singh, *Ibid,* page 119.

around midday 4th December, he ordered the remnants of 18 Punjab to fall back on Chuadanga. 18 Punjab thus consolidated their position at Chuadanga, where a troop of 29 Cavalry under Lt Aslam Panhwar also joined them on 7th December.[90]

Meanwhile, leaving behind 22 Rajput in Darsana, the rest of 41 Mountain Brigade had concentrated in area Uthali by last light 4th December, poised for operations towards Kotchandpur and onwards to Jhenida.

While 41 Mountain Brigade was still around Darsana, 62 Mountain Brigade had commenced probing its way forward towards Khalispur; however, it faced stiff and determined resistance there. General Brar, apprehending heavy casualties to his troops, decided to make some changes in his original plan. He decided that 62 Mountain Brigade would now advance along Khalispur- Suadih axis; this was a subsidiary axis, based only on a dirt track. In Brar's view, it was not likely to be held in strength by the Pakistan troops since they would hardly expect a major force to move on it. He was, however, soon to be surprised.

Brig Rajendar Nath left one battalion in Khalispur to provide a firm base to his Brigade and advanced towards Kotchandpur along the Khalispur-Suadih axis with 9 Dogra Battalion leading. 9 Dogra had advanced only a little distance from Khalispur when it came under heavy fire from a high ground and the railway embankment near Suadih village. It soon became clear that, contrary to the expectations of General Brar, some elements of 18 Punjab had taken up a strong delaying position in this area, where the lay of the ground provided them a naturally defensible position. Probing actions by 9 Dogra attracted heavy machine gun and artillery fire from the defenders. Seeing this, Brig Rajendar Singh decided to mount a Brigade attack on the Suadih position.

He planned to launch his attack in two phases; in Phase I, 5 Maratha LI was to attack from the north and capture Suadih village; in Phase II, 9 Dogra was to attack from the west; its task was to clear the railway embankment, capture the railway bridge there, and then to link up with 5 Maratha.

The initial attacks by both these battalions were beaten back by the tenacious defenders. However, during the succeeding night, both the units renewed their attacks and succeeded linking up with each other around the

---

mid-night. 9 Dogra resumed its advance at first light and captured Kotchandpur by about 2 PM on 4th December, after clearing minor opposition en route.

Thus far, 41 Mountain Brigade was lying in concentration in Uthali; On 4th December, it also moved to an area just west of Suadih. Meanwhile, 62 Mountain Brigade had also concentrated in area Kotchandpur by last light 5th December. They were both now poised for further advance and the stage was thus set for the crucial battle for the capture of Jhenida.

General Brar, at this point, appreciated that as soon as Brig Manzoor came to realize that a major threat was developing towards Jhenida by these two Indian brigades, he would most likely vacate Chuadanga and try to concentrate all his forces at Jhenida. Brar, evidently, considered it vital to deny this option to the Pak Brigade Commander at all costs. So, instead of adopting the original, and time-consuming, plan of advancing along the main road towards Kaliganj and then on to Jhenida, he executed a brilliant manoeuvre at this time. He decided to use a little- known dirt track towards the north connecting Suadih, with Talsar and on to Sadhuhati, located on the Chuadanga-Jhenida Road. He planned to move a part of his force along this axis and effectively block Chuadanga-Jhenida Road before Brig Manzoor could concentrate his Brigade at Jhenida. Accordingly, the plan conceived by him was as follows:[91]

- One battalion ex 41 Mountain Brigade with a squadron less a troop to move along the Suadih-Talsar-Sadhuhati axis and establish a road block on Road Chuadanga-Jhenida with a view to blocking any move of Pakistan troops from Chuadanga to Jhenida.

- The rest of 41 Mountain Brigade to move along Track Kotchandpur-Talsar-Sadhuhati and capture Jhenida from the west.

- 62 Mountain Brigade with a troop of tanks to advance to Kaliganj and capture it as soon as possible.

In accordance with this plan, 5 Guards and a tank squadron moved cross-country from Suadih at 8 AM on 5th December. By last light the same day, they had succeeded in establishing a road block at Sadhuhati on Road Chuadanga-Jhenida, thus effectively blocking all moves between the two towns.

---

[91] Maj Gen Lachhman Singh, *Op Cit*, page 121.

To give credit to Brig Manzoor, he had perceived the developing threat to Jhenida fairly early and had already requested permission from General Ansari to move 18 Punjab to Jhenida during night 4th /5th December. The request was, as usual, initially refused but eventually approved for the next night. By then, of course, it was too late as the Indians had already blocked the Road Chuadanga-Jhenida.

In his mounting desperation and anxiety for Jhenida, Brig Manzoor then tried to reach it via Kushtia, as it was linked by rail with Jhenida via Chuadanga. However, the Mukti Bahini had already blown up most of the railway bridges in this section and the train move was no longer possible. Mukti Bahini had also blown up most of the bridges along the Road Meherpur-Kushtia, thus effectively cutting off 29 Baluch, deployed in the Paksey Bridge area, from the rest of the Brigade. However, the hectic efforts of Brig Manzoor and his staff eventually enabled him to concentrate 18 Punjab and 29 Baluch at Kushtia, but only on 8th December. By that time, it was simply too late for them to influence the battle at Jhenida in any way. Being a Theatre Fortress, Jhenida should have been held strongly from the beginning; instead, it was now being held only by some remnants of 38 FF, which had withdrawn there since after the attack on Jibannagar on 30th November.[92] Despite being devoid of troops, Jhenida, however, was well stocked with ammunition and other stores, in anticipation of a last- ditch battle.

Meanwhile, 41 Mountain Brigade, leaving behind a battalion at Sadhuhati for rear protection, had resumed its advance at last light on 5th December, along a very difficult dirt track, in accordance with the Divisional plan. The advance was led by 5/1 Gurkha Battalion, which succeeded in establishing a bridgehead across River Chitra by first light the next day.

At first light 6th December, 9 Dogra Battalion also moved from Kotchandpur area on foot along the Talsar track. By about 9 AM on 7th December, having marched continuously for 28 hours, they finally made contact with the outskirts of Jhenida. 9 Dogra launched a quick attack on the 38 FF positions at about 1 PM and soon captured the position easily. 38 FF troops had meanwhile withdrawn hurriedly without even demolishing the huge dump of ammunition; it had, however, succeeded in setting the POL dump on fire. Even the bridges on River Banaganga, flowing through the town, were abandoned intact. The last Pakistani vehicle had left the town by midday 7th December.[93]

---

[92] Lt Gen Kamal Matinuddin, *Op Cit*, page 396.

In retrospect, 6th and 7th December marked the nadir of the 9 Pak Division in the Southwestern Sector. Brig Manzoor, commander 57 Pak Brigade, had been totally out-manoeuvred by General Brar and found himself sequestered from the Theatre Fortress of Jhenida, which had thus fallen with merely a whimper, while Brig Hayat, commander 107 Pak Brigade, had also decided at about this time, to abandon the Theatre Fortress of Jessore without a fight.

Back at his Divisional HQ in Magura, General Ansari had been viewing these ominous developments with growing apprehension. On 4th December, in desperation, he had directed his Colonel Staff, Colonel K K Afridi, to collect elements of 50 Punjab and 38 FF, both of which had become detached from their parent brigades, and to form a task force to check the Indian advance towards Kaliganj. One artillery battery, already deployed in Kaliganj, was also grouped with this force.

By the evening of 6th December, however, Ansari had fully come to realize the criticality of his position; his Division was no longer in a position to defend either Jhenida or Jessore. By now, his command had been split in three and became totally paralyzed: 107 Pak Brigade had withdrawn south to Khulna, 57 Pak Brigade was forced to move north to Kushtia, while the remnants of his Division had withdrawn across the Madhumati. He had perhaps expected his brigades to join him at Magura at this stage but had never ever indicated any such contingency to them. He had thus been totally out-manoeuvred; 9 Pak Division had ceased to be a cohesive fighting force and Ansari had totally lost control of it. So, in desperation, he decided to move his HQ to Faridpur on 7th December and ordered Colonel K K Afridi to delay the advance of the Indian forces as much as possible, eventually denying the ferry site on River Madhumati, but without risking his force.

While to a certain extent, Brig Manzoor's predicament was understandable, the decision by Brig Hayat to move south to Khulna was totally inexplicable. For the whole duration of 6th and 7th December, the road from Jessore to Magura lay open to Pakistan forces as the Indians had fortuitously made no attempt to cut it till then. Brig Hayat could certainly have withdrawn to Magura on either of these two days. Had he done so, the course of subsequent operations in this Sector would have been entirely different. As it happened, by 8th December, II Corps had become masters

---

93 Maj Gen Shaukat Riza, *Op Cit*, page 142; Maj Gen Lachhman Singh, *Op Cit*, page 123.

of the operational situation. This was primarily due to the follies of Brig Hayat; undue delay had also been caused by the GOC's referring matters of essentially tactical nature to General Niazi in securing permissions, which authority, in the first instance, should never have been arrogated by the Theatre Commander.

Meanwhile, 62 Mountain Brigade resumed its advance as per the Divisional plan. At last light 5th December, 5 Maratha Battalion led the advance from Kotchandpur and captured Kaliganj by the morning of 7th December. The rest of the Brigade also concentrated there by last light. It was then ordered to link up with 41 Mountain Brigade at Jhenida and advance to Magura with a view to capturing it as soon as possible. It resumed its advance from Jhenida at first light 8th December; it had been allotted a squadron less a troop of tanks and a motorized company to speed up its advance. It captured Magura by 4 PM the same day after brushing aside minor opposition en route. After the capture of Magura, 62 Mountain Brigade commenced the advance towards Faridpur. The remnants of 9 Pak Division, led by Colonel K K Afridi, had demolished the bridge over River Kumar and withdrawn east of the River Madhumati. 62 Mountain Brigade concentrated on the west bank of Madhumati by last light 9th December and commenced preparations for the river crossing.

The capture of Magura marked the high tide of success for II Corps. This was also a great strategic opportunity for the Indian Eastern Command to undertake a rapid advance to Faridpur and then onwards to Dacca. 9 Pak Division at this time had no prepared defences and no organized force to check such an advance; both its brigades having already moved waywardly on divergent axes. This great opportunity was however permitted to slip away when the two divisions of II Corps also decided to wheel on divergent axes; 9 Indian Division towards Khulna and the bulk of 4 Mountain Division towards Kushtia. In the process, they even ignored the capabilities of 50 Para Brigade, which could be dropped in support of a determined manoeuvre towards Dacca. Thus, II Corps at this stage failed to exploit this strategic opportunity and simply failed to make any serious effort to reach the ferry sites on the Padma en route to Dacca.

That any such strategic manoeuvre towards Dacca was still very far from their minds is further indicated when General Brar, GOC 4 Mountain Division, requested his Corps Commander General Raina to release to his Division its third brigade, 7 Mountan Brigade, so far lying idle as II Corps Reserve. Brar wanted to use this fresh force to quickly clear Kushtia and Hardinge Bridge. The ostensible rationale that he advanced for this request was that he apprehended a flank threat from the north to his over-stretched line of advance to Faridpur.

General Raina readily agreed to the request; accordingly, 7 Mountain Brigade, less 1 Naga Battalion, was concentrated at Jhenida by mid-night 8th December. Brig Zail Singh, commander 7 Mountain Brigade, was entrusted with the task to advance on Jhenida-Kushtia axis to capture Kushtia the earliest. To make up for 1 Naga, he was allotted 5 Guards as his third battalion. He was to be supported by two troops of tanks and one medium battery artillery and had been allocated sufficient transport to make one battalion mobile.

Brig Zail Singh, however, had been given only scanty information about the strength and dispositions of Pakistan troops. He had been simply conveyed the general notion that they were utterly disorganized and on the run; and, that the bulk of the Pakistan forces had withdrawn towards Faridpur. The presence of a largely intact 57 Pak Brigade in Kushtia was simply never indicated to Brig Zail Singh nor did he ever realize it on his own.

On the other side, Brig Manzoor had, by then, managed to move the bulk of his Brigade to Kushtia. After the fall of Jhenida, his initial intention was to join up with HQ 9 Pak Division at Faridpur by using the Kushtia-Faridpur rail link. But with the destruction of the rail bridges on this line too, he was effectively stranded in Kushtia. Oddly enough, like 57 Pak Brigade in Dalatpur-Khulna, Brig Manzoor too had finally got an opportunity to deploy his Brigade as a compact fighting formation and decided to take up a defensive position there as follows:

- 29 Baluch deployed astride road coming from Jhenida.

- 18 Punjab deployed to prevent enemy access to Paksey (Hardinge) Bridge.

- Company 21 Punjab (R&S) pushed ahead to establish a screen position on Road Jhenida-Kushtia.

- 50 Punjab minus in reserve.

22 Rajput Battalion (7 Mountain Brigade), with two troops of tanks, commenced their advance from Jhenida to Kushtia at about 6 AM on 9th December. The unit had been provided adequate transport to make it mobile. After some skirmishes en route, they reached the outskirts of

Kushtia by 2 AM, where they debussed. At this stage, Generals Raina and Brar landed by helicopter in the middle of the Battalion position. Raina was in high spirits; he exhorted the unit officers and troops to speed up the capture of Kushtia as the enemy was on the run everywhere. The words (in Punjabi) that he used were "Charh Jao" (press on regardless). Thus motivated, the troops rushed forward in a spirit of reckless aggression in the expectation of hardly meeting any worthwhile opposition. But there the disaster awaited them!

At about 2:45 PM, six Indian tanks, moving in almost a single file formation, with gaps of only 20 to 30 meters, led the advance with the vanguard company also moving forward, grouped with the tanks. They found no signs of any Pakistan troops even when they reached the town centre, a relatively open area with many shady trees. They were completely oblivious of the fact that a company of 21 Punjab (R&S) had laid a very well sited ambush around this location. Brig Manzoor also had made available to them the combined firepower of all the tanks, artillery, and medium machine guns that he could scrounge under the circumstances. They let the tanks come well ahead without any resistance and then sprung the ambush. The fifth tank in the line was the first to be hit by a recoilless rifle and then all hell broke loose with every type of available weapon opening up at the same time. Only the sixth tank managed to extricate itself; all other tanks were either hit or captured by the defenders. 22 Rajput suffered heavy casualties; in all, 111 Rajput soldiers including six officers lost their lives in this brief encounter.

According to General Jacob, this setback would not have occurred:

"had II Corps agreed to our suggested thrust line of Shikarpur-Kushtia. The Hardinge Bridge could have been taken intact and the withdrawal of Pakistani troops across the river would not have taken place."[94]

This unexpected Pakistani action and the high number of Indian casualties unnerved the entire 4 Mountain Division and resulted in over-reaction on part of both Generals Raina and Brar; they became overly apprehensive that 57 Pak Brigade might try to exploit the situation by now launching a counter-attack on their extended axis of maintenance. Raina instructed Brar to move the bulk of 62 Mountain Brigade to Kushtia, leaving just one battalion along the Madhumati River to contain the remnants of 9 Pak Division. 4 Mountain Division was also allotted two troops of tanks to this Brigade to make up for the loss of tanks at Kushtia;

---

[94] Lt Gen J FR Jacob, *Op Cit*, page 110.

these were grouped with 45 Cavalry. The orders to 4 Mountain Division at this stage were to capture Kushtia and clear the area up to Hardinge Bridge. [95]

In retrospect, 9th December was overall quite a critical day for the Indian forces then operating in East Pakistan. As 4 Mountain Division wheeled north towards Kushtia, 9 Indian Division was also wheeling south towards Khulna the same day. This was happening at precisely the time, when 57 Indian Division (IV Corps) was poised in the Eastern Sector to take the decisive step of crossing River Meghna, for making a thrust towards Dacca. With this massive shift in their centre of gravity, the strategic initiative was thus lost by II Corps and instead passed on to IV Corps. Commenting on this situation, General Jacob says:[96]

"More serious was the delay caused in getting the Division back to its original thrust line. Consequently, the advance to Faridpur was delayed by at least three days and the contingency plan of crossing the Padma at Goalundo Ghat to Dacca could not be put into effect."

After making careful preparations, General Brar mounted his Divisional offensive against Kushtia at midday 11th December. He launched two of his brigades in roughly a pincers move as follows:

- 7 Mountain Brigade to attack from the south.

- 41 Mountain Brigade to be launched to roll the defences from west to east in an effort to prevent the escape of 57 Pak Brigade across the Hardinge Bridge.

- 62 Mountain Brigade held in reserve.

The birds, however, had flown the coop by then. Completely isolated and with no hopes of any relief or replacement, Brig Manzoor had decided to make a clean break and moved across the Ganges over the Paksey (Hardinge) Bridge. He had also blown up the Bridge behind them as they withdrew. The Indian attack was thus launched in a void and Kushtia was captured the same afternoon without any resistance.

Surprisingly however, even after crossing into the Northwestern Sector, 57 Pak Brigade was never allotted any task by 16 Pak Division operating there or even by Commander Eastern Command; it entirely remained out

[95] Maj Gen Lachhman Singh, *Op Cit*, pages 128-129.
[96] Lt Gen J FR Jacob, *Op Cit*, page 110.

146

of the war thereafter as if it had simply ceased to exist. This happened at a time when General Niazi was desperately looking for troops everywhere which could be moved to Dacca for its defence. The move of this Brigade to Dacca would certainly have improved its defensive capability considerably. This laxity remains one of the unsolved mysteries of this war.

On 12th December, in a bid to regain the lost strategic initiative, General Brar ordered his Division, less 41 Mountain Brigade, to move back to Magura; their concentration there was completed by midday 14th December. The only remnants of 9 Pak Division holding the east bank of River Madhumati at this stage were elements of 38 FF and 50 Punjab, supported by a battery of artillery. They had been loosely organized as an ad hoc brigade under Colonel K K Afridi. Afridi had made a very good use of the respite of last six days that fortuitously came his way due to the diversion of Indian attention towards Kushtia; he had organized his meagre force fairly well. They were at that time holding an extended line of villages along the eastern side of the river.

General Brar decided to attack by crossing River Madhumati with two brigades. 62 Mountain Brigade was ordered to cross the River in the north opposite Village Duman on night 14th /15th December and to clear the area up to Road Magura-Faridpur as well as the ferry at Kumarkhali. 7 Mountain Brigade, was ordered to make the crossing the same night from a crossing site about 25 kilometers down south.

The crossing by 62 Mountain Brigade met heavy resistance initially but the Brigade kept up the pressure and secured Kumarkhali ferry site by first light 16th December. 7 Mountain Brigade, however, managed to complete its crossing by about midday 15th December without much resistance.

General Brar ordered both the Brigades to establish blocking positions well towards the east, in order to seal off the escape of the Pakistan troops deployed along the River. Both the brigades were subjected to heavy artillery shelling as well as three spirited counter-attacks by the besieged troops. Ultimately, as the defenders ran out of ammunition and without any hopes of relief, they gave up. Five officer, five JCOs and 187 soldiers surrendered while 83 of their comrades lay dead on the ground.

About 2 AM on 16th December, General Niazi, Commander Pak Eastern Command, dictated a message for General Manekshaw, the Indian Army Chief, and GOC 9 Pak Division was ordered to have it delivered. About midday on 16th December, a Pakistani officer strode towards the Indian positions east of Kumarkhali waving a white flag. He was followed by Lt Col Mansoor ul Haq Malik, GSO-1 of 9 Pak Division.[97]

General Ansari, GOC 9 Pak Division, surrendered the same day to General Brar, GOC, 4 Mountain Division, with some 3000 troops. The bulk of them comprised administrative and support troops and there were hardly any fighting troops among them. [98]

As a passing consideration, what part did II Corps operations play in influencing General Niazi's decision to surrender? According to Niazi himself, it was negligible, as these operations neither threatened Dacca nor impaired his fighting capability. In fact, he heard of General Ansari's surrender only after he himself had asked for a ceasefire.[99]

---

[97] Maj Gen Shaukat Riza, *Op Cit*, page 143; Maj Gen Lachhman Singh, *Op Cit*, page 132.
[98] Maj Gen Lachhman Singh, *Ibid.*

[99] Maj Gen Sukhwant Singh, *Op Cit*, page 146.

6

OPERATIONS IN NORTHWESTERN SECTOR (BOGRA-RAJSHAHI-RANGPUR)

Topographical Impact on Operations

The Northwestern Sector of East Pakistan, commonly known as North Bengal, comprised civil districts of Bogra, Rajshahi, Rangpur, Dinajpur and Pabna. The Sector was bounded by the narrow Indian corridor of Siliguri in the north, River Brahmaputra (Yamuna) in the east, and River Ganges (Padma) in the south. To the west lay the Indian province of West Bengal, comprising the civil districts of Malda and West Dinajpur.

Two major rivers, Ganges and Brahmaputra, effectively isolated this Sector from the rest of East Pakistan; the only ground link then available was the Paksey (Hardinge) Bridge over the Ganges, near Pabna. These rivers, however, did have a number of ferry sites which were the main means of transportation across them. The ferry sites across the Brahmaputra located at Phulchari, Sirajganj and Bera were the main crossing points leading to the cities of Jamalpur, Tangail and the capital city of Dacca respectively.

Strategically, the Siliguri Corridor was a critically sensitive area from the Indian point of view; it was a narrow belt in the plains over-looked by the mountains of Sikkim and Nepal in the north. Through this belt passed all the road, rail and air routes from mainland India to the eastern Indian states of Assam, Nagaland, Meghalaya and Arunachal Pradesh; these included the main railway line to Gauhati, the Assam oil pipeline, as well as the Asian Highway to Burma and beyond. The northwestern tip of this Sector, near the Titulaya BOP, lay fairly close to Siliguri. Thus, any pre-emptive strike by

149

Pakistan in this corridor could potentially disrupt all movements to/from the eastern states of India. Pachagarh was a notable town in this sensitive area on the Pakistan side.

Another important strategic consideration for the Indian planners was the close proximity of this Corridor to Chumbi Valley, a major Chinese base to the north. In the event of any collusive operations by Pakistan and China against India, this area would assume critical importance as it could then serve as an anvil for the Chinese hammer blow. Thus, India had a strategic compulsion to ensure the security of this critical and sensitive area at the earliest.

Operationally sensitive area in this Sector, from Pakistan's point of view, was the narrow waistline linking Hilli with Gaibanda and Phulchari Ferry on River Yamuna; this was formed by the Balurghat bulge, which protruded eastward as a prominent salient into East Pakistan, with the border town of Hilli situated at the tip of the bulge and provided the shortest approach to bisect this Sector horizontally. Any offensive effort by India against Hilli and leading to Gaibanda would in effect isolate the Pakistan troops in the Rangpur-Dinajpur area in the north from all the troops in the south and thus effectively unhinge the Pakistan defences. As such, Hilli-Gaibanda axis provided an ideal but obvious thrust line to the Indians.

Hilli was a small town as well as a railway station right on the border with India; the main railway line from Calcutta to North Bengal during the British period passed through Hilli. Besides, it was an important communications centre as well; several tracks emanated from here leading towards Bogra in the south and to Dinajpur in the north. Thus, holding Hilli in strength was an obvious operational compulsion for Pakistan.

The grain of the ground in this Sector lay north to south; most of the rivers too flowed south from the Himalayas in the north. The prominent rivers flowing through the Sector are:

- Teesta, west of Lal Munirhat and Kurigram.
- Dhepa, west of Dinajpur.
- Karatoya, west of Pirganj and running west to east near Gobindganj.
- Atrai, running north to south, through the Indian salient of Balurghat.
- Mahananda, runs north to south on by the side of Nawabganj.
- Ichhamati, runs west and north of Bogra. (This river was not marked on Indian maps.)

NORTH EASTERN SECTOR

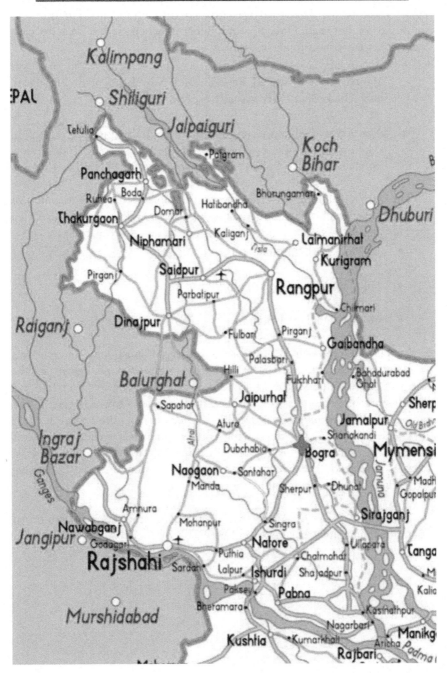

This Sector could boast of only one all-weather highway, which ran from Titulaya in the extreme north, all the way to Nagarbari in the south; en route, it connected with the towns of Thakurgaon, Rangpur, Bogra and Pabna respectively. This road was bridged throughout and ran north to south except between Dinajpur and Rangpur where it ran west to east. Some other important roads in the area were:

- A tarmac lateral road ran along the eastern bank of River Mahananda and linked Rajshahi and Nawabganj with Nagarbari, near which Bera Ferry was also located.

- A concrete road connecting Dinajpur to Phulbari, which ran within a kilometer of the border opposite Samjia on the Indian side; Samjia in turn was linked by a tarmac road with Balurghat.

The Samjia-Phulbari-Charkai axis offered an alternative thrust line to reach the main highway at Pirganj and then on to Gaibanda, thus avoiding the Hilli approach. Some important tracks in the area were as follows:

- Domer-Nilphamari-Saidpur.

- Hilli-Jaipurhat-Naogaon-Bogra.

- Goraghat- Khetlal-Bogra.

Two key objectives in the Sector were Rangpur and Bogra. Rangpur was a major cantonment and an important communications centre in the northern part of this Sector while Bogra was a very important operational objective in the south as it controlled communications towards Dacca. The capture of Bogra would jeopardize the defence of the entire Sector; it could also serve as a base for developing further offensive operation towards Dacca, albeit it would be the longest approach to the capital of East Pakistan; it would also involve crossing several water obstacles of varying size including the mighty Brahmaputra (Yamuna).

This Sector was relatively more suited to mobile and armoured operations than any other sector in East Pakistan.

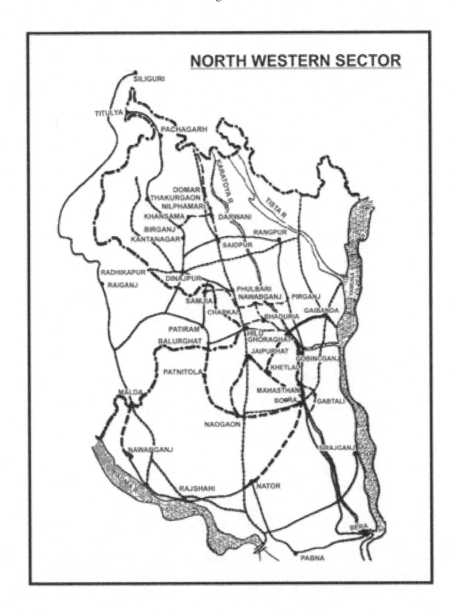

NORTH WESTERN SECTOR

Pakistan Forces

The defence of this Sector was entrusted to 16 Pak Division, commanded by Major General Nazar Husain Shah. The Divisional HQ was initially located at Bogra but subsequently shifted to Natore, near Rajshahi. The composition of this Division in November 1971 was as follows:

1. **23 Brigade**   **Brig Akhtar Ansari**   **Saidpur**
   a.   8 Punjab
   b.   25 Punjab
   c.   48 Punjab
   d.   26 FF
   e.   Squadron 29 Cavalry
   f.   34 Punjab (R & S) less company
   f.   48 Field Regiment

2. **34 Brigade**   **Brig Mir Abdul Naeem**   **Rangpur**
   a.   32 Punjab
   b.   32 Baluch
   c.   13 FF
   c.   Squadron 29 Cavalry
   d.   117 Mortar Battery

3. **205 Brigade**   **Brig Tajammul Husain Malik**   **Bogra**
   a.   8 Baluch
   b.   4 FF
   c.   13 FF
   d.   Squadron 29 Cavalry
   e.   80 Field Regiment

In his Appreciation of the Situation, General Nazar Husain Shah had concluded that the Indians would launch their main effort against the waistline of his Sector along the Hilli-Gaibanda axis as well as towards Rangpur. After the surrender, as described to his Indian interrogators, his expectation of the likely Indian manoeuvre was that they would employ up to two divisions in this Sector as follows:[100]

- Launch the main effort by a division along the Hilli-Goraghat-Gaibanda axis to split the 16 Pak Division's defences in two.

- Advance with two brigades along Domer - Saidpur axis towards

---

[100] Maj Gen Lachhman Singh, *Op Cit*, page 84.

Rangpur.

- Advance with at least one brigade along Pachagarh-Thakurgaon axis towards Dinajpur and, in the process, provide security to their Siliguri corridor.

- In his own mind, he had ruled out any direct major threat to Bogra from the direction of Patnitola or Naogaon because of poor means of access from Balurghat and Malda districts of India.

Keeping this threat assessment in view, General Nazar had divided his area of responsibility amongst his brigades as follows:

- 23 Pak Brigade, commanded by Brig Akhtar Ansari, was made responsible for the defence of the area north of the Hilli-Gaibanda waistline; it included cities/towns like Rangpur, Saidpur, Thakurgaon, Dinajpur and Domer.

- 205 Pak Brigade, commanded by Brig Tajjamal Husain Malik, was made responsible for the defence of the waistline including the towns of Hilli, Goraghat, Patnitola and eventually, at a later stage, Bogra.

- 34 Pak Brigade, commanded by Brig Mir Naeem, was allocated the responsibility of southern cities like Rajshahi, Nawabganj and Nator.

- 29 Cavalry, commanded by Lt Col Bukhari, was split up to support the operations of 23 and 205 Pak Brigades. Its regimental HQ was located at Rangpur.

Indian Forces

The Indian High Command had entrusted the operations in this Sector to XXXIII Corps, commanded by Lt General M L Thapan. Besides being responsible for this Sector, he also continued to remain responsible for Sikkim and Bhutan borders in the north against the Chinese. His HQ, therefore, remained at Siliguri, from where he could adequately control both sides.

General Thapan was a veteran of World War II and the only general officer in this theatre to have commanded a division in the 1965 Indo-Pak

War; however, according to the Indian sources, his performance then as Commander 25 Indian Division was rather lackluster. He had the reputation of being a pedantic and copybook general and operationally prone to be rather over-cautious. In view of this reputation, General Aurora had initially tried to split HQ XXXIII Corps and to entrust the East Pakistan operation to his Chief of Staff, Major General J S Nakai. However, General Thapan stoutly resisted this suggestion and in the end succeeded in retaining these dual responsibilities.[101]

The composition of XXXIII Corps at the time of as allocated for this offensive was as follows:[102]

1. **20 Mountain Division**   **Maj Gen Lachhman Singh**

    a. **66 Mountain Brigade**   **Brig G S Sharma**
        1 Guards
        6 Guards
        17 Kumaon

    b. **165 Mountain Brigade**   **Brig R S Pannu**
        20 Maratha LI
        16 Rajput
        6 Assam

    c. **202 Mountain Brigade**   **Brig Farhat Bhatty**
        8 Guards
        22 Maratha LI
        5 Garhwal

    d. **6 Mountain Artillery Brigade**
        94 Mountain Regiment
        98 Mountain Regiment
        184 Light Regiment less battery

2. **340 Mountain Brigade Group**   **Brig Joginder Singh**
    4 Madras

---

[101] Maj Gen Sukhwant Singh, *Op Cit*, page 162.
[102] Lt Gen J FR Jacob, *Op Cit,* page 190.

2/5 Gurkha
5/11 Gurkha
97 Mountain Regiment Artillery

3. 71 Mountain Brigade Group   **Brig P N Kathpalia**   **(**
Under Corps HQ)

7 Maratha LI
12 Raj Rif
21 Rajput
5 Grenadier   (Allotted on 14 December)

4. 471 Engineer Brigade Group

3 x Engineer Regiments
Army Engineering Regiment

5. 63 Cavalry less squadron

6. 69 Armoured Regiment

In addition, XXXIII Corps was also permitted to use one brigade ex 6 Mountain Division, then concentrated in Siliguri Corridor, for limited tasks, with the caveat that it must be extricated in 24 to 48 hours, if required for the Chinese border.

A comparative analysis of the forces available to the two sides would show that 16 Pak Division had a total of ten infantry battalions, three squadrons of tanks (PT-76), two artillery regiments and one mortar battery. Opposed to this, the Indian XXXIII Corps had available for this offensive fifteen infantry battalions, five squadrons of tanks (T-55 and PT- 76) and four artillery regiments. In addition, it could use one brigade ex 6 Mountain Division, which comprised three infantry battalions, albeit for limited tasks only. Glaring weakness of the Pakistan forces, thus, lay in armour and artillery units.

The major strategic compulsion of the Indians in this Sector was to ensure effective defence and security of Balurghat, Malda and Siliguri areas. The ground configuration and the layout of the road network in this area further accentuated this vulnerability. Moreover, Balurghat area had been selected to serve as the firm base of their main operations and thus had to be secured.

The offensive plan for this Sector as originally drawn up by the Indian Army Headquarters underwent several major changes while being subjected to detailed analyses at HQ Indian Eastern Command and then in a war game held at HQ XXXIII Corps. Based upon the conclusions of this war game, the original concept of launching the main thrust along the Hilli-Gaibanda axis was abandoned. The capture of Rangpur and Dinajpur was also relegated to a later stage of the offensive. The strategy now adopted was to bypass the Pakistan strong points in the initial stages and to concentrate, instead, on the earliest capture of the main objective, Bogra.

This modification in strategy was essentially facilitated by a stroke of good luck. General Jacob had somehow managed to secure Survey of Pakistan maps of this area, which clearly showed an un-metalled road along the Phulbari-Nawabganj-Pirganj alignment, leading south on to Bogra, which was hitherto unknown to the Indians. They gleefully decided to exploit this lucky discovery since a thrust along this axis would entirely bypass the heavily fortified positions of Hilli and Gaibanda, thus facilitating a speedy advance to Bogra.

The question of attack on Hilli, a heavily fortified defensive complex, continued to be hotly debated throughout the planning process. General Thapan, Commander XXXIII Corps, was of the view that since the new strategy visualized avoiding the Hilli-Gaibanda axis altogether, there was hardly any compulsion to attack Hilli in the initial stages of the operation; his objections, however, were brushed aside by General Aurora as Manekshaw was personally very keen on the early capture of Hilli.

The main offensive in this Sector was to be launched by 20 Mountain Division, commanded by Major General Lachhman Singh, an artillery officer from East Punjab. The strategy evolved for this Sector was based upon classic Liddel Hart theory of *Expanding Torrent*: to break through the Pakistani defences on a narrow front so as to turn their defences and then to get to their rear as soon as possible. The scarlet thread of the Indian planning was to prevent the withdrawal of Pakistan forces operating in the north to the Theatre Fortress of Bogra in any significant numbers.

The detailed Indian plan in this Sector was as follows:[103]

- Operating directly under HQ XXXIII Corps, 71 Mountain Brigade, commanded by Brig Kathpalia, to advance south along Mirgarh-

---

[103] Maj Gen Lachhman Singh, *Op Cit*, page 87.

Pachagarh-Thakurgaon axis to secure Pachagarh and Thakurgaon; then exploit up to Kantanagar Bridge and capture Dinajpur, if possible.

- 20 Mountain Division to launch the main effort as follows:

  a. 165 Mountain Brigade, under Brig Pannu, to establish a firm base in the Balurghat bulge to defend the Indian districts of Balurghat and Malda.

  b. 202 Mountain Brigade under Brig Farhat Bhatty to capture Hilli, and then advance to capture Palasbari along the Goraghat axis in conjunction with 66 Mountain Brigade.

  c. 66 Mountain Brigade under Brig Sharma to advance from Samjia to Charkai via Phulbari, and capture Pirganj and Gaibanda.

  d. After the capture of Palasbari and Gaibanda, thrusts to be launched to capture Rangpur or Bogra, situation permiting.

- 340 Mountain Brigade Group, under Brig Joginder Singh, to contain Dinajpur and be available as Corps Reserve.

- 63 Cavalry less a squadron (T-55 tanks) was grouped with 202 Mountain Brigade while 69 Armoured Regiment (PT-76 tanks) was grouped with 66 Mountain Brigade, in such a way as the two regiments could provide mutual support to each other, and produce overwhelming superiority at any chosen point.

Operations in 23 Pak Brigade Area

On the commencement of hostilities, 23 Pak Brigade was being commanded by Brig Akhtar Ansari. This Brigade was responsible for the defence of the area bounded by Phulbari in the north, the Brahmaputra in the east, the border with India in the west, and Dinajpur in the south. It thus was responsible for a frontage of 230 kilometers and a depth of 165 kilometers. The Brigade HQ was located at Saidpur with the following composition and initial deployment:

- 8 Punjab — Lt Col Saleem Zia — Hathibanda-Kurigram

- 25 Punjab — Lt Col Muhammad Hussain Malik — Rangpur

- 26 FF — Lt Col Hakeem Arshad Qureshi — Dinajpur

- 48 Punjab — Pachagarh

- 34 Punjab (R&S) Lt Col Amir Muhammad Thakurgaon (less company)

- 86 Mujahid — Lt Col Mumtaz Elahi Jauhri — Rangpur

Twilight Operations

The first, and obvious, Indian operation in this Sector was aimed at protecting, at the earliest, their strategic vulnerability at the Siliguri Corridor. This task was entrusted to 71 Mountain Brigade, released to XXXIII Corps for this very purpose and was to operate directly under the Corps HQ.

As a preliminary operation, Brig Kathpalia, Commander 71 Mountain Brigade, had planned the capture of Pachagarh, an important town in the salient just about 3 kilometers from the border. At the end of November 1971, Pachagarh was held by a company of 48 Punjab, commanded by Major Khurshid; two artillery guns had also been located there. Brig Kathpalia planned to use two of his battalions to isolate the Pakistani troops from the south, and one battalion to attack them frontally from the north. His apparent intention was to surround them there from all the sides and thus induce them to surrender or to force them to launch a costly counter-attack to extricate themselves.

Accordingly, during night $20^{th}/21^{st}$ November, 21 Rajput and 7 Maratha LI (Light Infantry) crossed the international border with the orders to cut the main highway south of Pachagarh. The Rajputs commenced their move along the west bank of River Kartoya, flowing a few kilometers east of Pachagarh, and established a roadblock off the main road. Meanwhile, 7 Maratha LI continued to advance further south along the riverbank and succeeded in securing an important road junction southwest of Pachagarh. During the next day, both the units made attempts to close the ring tighter around Pachagarh but met with stout resistance from Major Khurshid and

160

his men.

During night $22^{nd}/23^{rd}$ November, Brig Kathpalia ordered 21 Rajput to cut the main highway at Boda, a small town south of Pachagarh, but they did not quite succeed in that due to a valiant action by the elements of a company of 34 Punjab (R&S).

Kathpalia, now at the end of his patience, ordered his third unit, 12 Raj Rif (Rajputana Rifles), to advance directly to Pachagarh on 24th November. The three units now began to put a concerted squeeze around the town; eventually 7 Maratha LI succeeded in entering Pachagarh on 25th Novemeber. To their utter disappointment, however, the Pakistan troops had already flown the coop; they had pulled out their guns and vehicles during the night $21^{st}/22^{nd}$ November, and the company of 48 Punjab slipped out on night $23^{rd}/24^{th}$ November on foot along the river bed.

After securing Pachagarh, 71 Mountain Brigade was ordered to resume its advance along Pachagarh-Thakurgaon-Dinajpur axis. On the other side, 23 Pak Brigade had tasked 34 Punjab (R&S) to impose maximum delay on the Indian advance towards Thakurgaon, a designated strong point. 34 Punjab (R&S) at this stage comprised only three companies; its fourth company having been detached to 205 Pak Brigade already. It was however being supported by a battery of 48 Field Regiment, commanded by Major Mazari.[104]

On 27th November, 12 Raj Rif commenced its advance towards Thakurgaon, supported by a squadron of 69 Cavalry, a distance of some 20 miles; ordinarily, it should have been covered by the Indian brigade in about 48-72 hours. That it took 71 Mountain Brigade almost six days to cover this distance by itself speaks volumes about the stiff and skillful resistance put by the officers and men of 34 Punjab. The credit for this performance mainly goes to Major Nisar Bukhari, commanding D Company, and Major Saeed Azam Khan commanding A Company. Both these companies, between themselves, imposed a delay of over four days on the Indians before they could advance further even from Boda area; Thakurgaon was still twelve miles away from there. It took the Indian Brigade yet another two days before they came into contact with Thakurgaon defences; sometimes late on 2nd December.

Considering the anticipated strength of Thakurgaon defensive position, Brig Kathpalia had planned a Brigade attack on the town with 21 Rajput

---

[104] Colonel Nazir Ahmed, *East Pakistan 1971: Distortions and Lies*, page 95.

and 7 Maratha LI. However, before it could actually materialize, GOC 16 Pak Division presented 71 Mountain Brigade with a very pleasant surprise.

The War Commences

As noted, the war between India and Pakistan was formally declared on 3rd December. Soon after that, Lt Col Amir Muhammad, CO 34 Punjab, holding the town of Thakurgaon, received the orders to vacate the town and, instead, to take up positions along River Dhepa, near Birganj, a town some 20 miles away. This message was passed to him on telephone by Major Abdul Haq Mirza, Brigade Major 23 Pak Brigade, late in the evening of 3rd March. Despite protests by the CO, the order prevailed because it had been given to the Brigade Major personally by the GOC, Major General Nazar Husain Shah.[105]

Despite these unexpected orders, 34 Punjab managed to withdraw intact from Thakurgaon during the night 3rd /4th December and took up defensive positions around Kantanagar Bridge over River Dhepa, just south of Birganj. Finding Thakurgaon vacated, 71 Mountain Brigade resumed its advance towards Birganj on the next day.

Making a skillful use of the mobility and firepower of his R & S (reconnaissance and support) unit, Lt Colonel Amir Nawaz, the competent and determined CO of 34 Punjab, placed several delaying positions en route; thus, he succeeded in holding the advancing Indian Brigade at bay for full two days. consequently, they could not come into contact with the defensive positions around Kantapur Bridge before 6th December. The next three days were to witness the mettle of the officers and men of 34 Punjab to the full. They gallantly withstood three concerted attacks by the units of 71 Mountain Brigade, launched successively at 9 PM 6th December, 8 AM 9th December, and then, last light 9th December. In the last attack, 7 Maratha LI suffered heavy casualties including its CO, adjutant, artillery observer as well as some 70 other ranks. After these three days of intense fighting, Brig Kathpalia was forced to carry out a detailed reorganization of his force and to ask for reinforcements before coming in a position to advance further towards his main objective, Dinajpur. 34 Punjab meanwhile continued to remain in control of Birganj.

At about this time, commander XXXIII Corps ordered 9 Mountain Brigade ex 6 Mountain Division to undertake advance in an enclave formed by River Brahmaputra and River Teesta in the extreme northeastern corner

---

[105] *Ibid*, page 96.

162

of this Sector with the mission to simulate a threat towards Rangpur. GOC 16 Pak Division was certainly sensitive to this important enclave as Lalmunirhat, the only airstrip serving this Sector, was also located there. However, by this time, General Nazar Hussain Shah was facing several other problems too and could hardly react there in a meaningful manner.

A company of 8 Punjab was defending Hathi Banda in this enclave. It came under a heavy attack by a unit of 9 Mountain Brigade on 4th December. After holding out for a night and a day, this company was withdrawn to its parent unit. Consequently, 9 Mountain Brigade continued to develop its operations further to the south unchecked and captured Lalmunirhat and Kurigram by 7th December. [106] After accomplishing this task, 9 Mountain Brigade was pulled out of this enclave and was moved to the area south of Dinajpur in order to relieve 340 Mountain Brigade for further offensive operations. [107]

Commander Pak Eastern Command was somewhat unhappy with the performance shown by Brig Akhtar Ansari, commander 23 Pak Brigade, and so replaced him with Brig Muhammad Shafi at about this time.[108] It is generally believed that this change was made as a sequel to the hasty vacation of Thakurgaon. However, credible evidence indicates that the new brigade commander had already arrived to take up his new assignment before the fall of Thakurgaon; indeed, both the commanders were present in HQ 23 Pak Brigade when the brigade major, Major Abdul Haq, actually passed the vacation orders to CO 34 Punjab.[109] Moreover, according to Major Abdul Haq, he had been given the orders to vacate Thakurgaon personally by the GOC, Maj Gen Nazar Hussain Shah and as such Brig Ansari could hardly be held responsible for the fall of Thakurgaon.

Emboldened by the quick and easy success achieved at Thakurgaon, the Indian High Command decided to shift 6 Mountain Division to the Western Theatre. Had this move actually materialized, it would have significantly altered the numerical balance in favour of the Indian forces opposite West Pakistan. It appears that the Pakistan High Command too became aware of this contemplated move; the GHQ consequently directed General Niazi, by a signal on 5th December, to somehow engage 6 Mountain Division and try to hold it in the Eastern Theatre. However, following the resolute defence of Birganj by 34 Punjab, the Indians,

---

[106] Lt Gen Kamal Matinuddin, Op Cit, page 375.
[107] Lt Gen J FR Jacob, *Op Cit,* page 113.
[108] Lt Gen A A Khan Niazi, Op Cit, page 137.
[109] Col Nazir Ahmed, *Op Cit,* page 98.

meanwhile, had already decided to review this move, and to retain 6 Mountain Division in the Eastern Theatre.

Ironically, General Niazi has tried to claim credit for this success in his book.[110] We are really at a loss to understand what role, if any, he could have played in the heroic defence of Birganj by 34 Punjab. As a sequel to this entire episode, 71 Mountain Brigade, so far operating directly under the command of HQ XXXIII Corps, was reverted to the command of 6 Mountain Division on 3rd December. [111]

On 9th December, Brig Kathpalia was informed by some friendly locals that Dinajpur too had been vacated by Pakistani troops. In the wake of the surprise vacation of Thakurgaon still fresh in his memory, he tended to place reliance on this piece of information and immediately dispatched two companies of 12 Raj Rif under Major Naresh Chandra to occupy the vacant city. The companies reached the outskirts of the city the same night and tried to enter it at first light on 10th December. They were soon subjected to heavy tank and artillery fire by the troops of 26 FF, who were obviously still there. So, Major Naresh Chandra prudently decided to fall back and managed to reach his unit position in small parties. The Indian plan to capture Dinajpur, which all this time had been stoutly defended by 26 FF under Lt Colonel Hakeem Arshad Qureshi, was eventually abandoned on 10th December and it was decided henceforth to merely contain it.

After the war, Brig Kathpalia was prone to claim credit that it was his relentless pressure that kept the Pakistani garrisons tied down in the strong points of Dinajpur, Saidpur, Parbatipur, and Rangpur, and thus prevented a pullout of these troops to reinforce threatened areas farther south. Major General Sukhwant Singh, however, has more rational comments to make regarding this claim, as follows:

"If these fortresses were not denuded to reinforce these areas, this was due more to the inept conduct of battle by the General Officer Commanding 16 Division than to Kathpalia's pressure. For at no time was 71 Mountain Brigade Group able to sever the routes of withdrawal of the Pakistani troops deployed in Dinajpur, Parbatipur, Saidpur, and Rangpur fortresses. In the later stages, 9 Mountain Brigade and two battalions were also moved South of Dinajpur, but despite encirclement by both these brigades, the garrison held out till the end of the war."[112]

---

[110] Lt Gen A A Khan Niazi, *Op Cit,* pages 138-139.

[111] Maj Gen Lachhman Singh, Op Cit, page 89.

[112] Maj Gen Sukhwant Singh, *Op Cit,* page 165.

Brig Kathpalia now planned to cross River Dhepa, but not from the vicinity of Birganj. He crossed this river after moving further south and then attempted to advance direct towards Saidpur.[113] Consequently, 71 Mountain Brigade resumed its advance led by 21 Rajput towards Khansama on 13th December. The leading troops were soon held up by the advance position of 48 Punjab there. Rather than risking an immediate night attack, Brig Kathpalia ordered 21 Rajput to mount a daylight attack from a flank, fully supported by tanks and artillery. The Pakistani troops were forced to withdraw when their rear was threatened by a simultaneous outflanking move by Indian tanks and infantry. A bridge was immediately launched over River Dhepa; 12 Raj Rif moved across and took up positions there. Early the next morning, the Indian air aviation reported the move of a tank and infantry column from the south towards the 12 Raj Rif positions. This was a composite force of 26 FF and 48 Punjab from Dinajpur, which had been ordered by Brig Shafi, commander 23 Pak Brigade, to eliminate the Indian bridgehead across the Dhepa. However, Indian air force and medium artillery managed to foil the effort before it became effective.

On 15th December, 5 Grenadier Battalion was also allotted to 71 Mountain Brigade and took over the advance from 12 Raj Rif. By last light, they had managed to reach Darwani railway station near Saidpur. Brig Kathpalia concentrated the rest of his Brigade there too during the night.

However, at 10 AM on 16th December, as 21 Rajput was preparing to resume its advance from Darwani, they spotted a man coming towards them, waving a white flag. He was a washer man from 48 Punjab carrying the message of surrender. The war for 23 Pak Brigade was over.

Operations in 34 and 205 Pak Brigade Area

205 Pak Brigade was commanded by Brig (later Major General) Tajjamal Husain Malik. Earlier on, he had proved his mettle in the 1965 Indo-Pak War when as CO 3 Baluch, he had gallantly stopped the advance of the invading Indian forces towards Lahore on 6th September 1965. Now his main task was to prevent them from reaching Bogra. According to Lt General Kamal Matinuddin, one of his contemporary colleagues:

"He was known in the army for his doggedness and his determination to pursue a course of action, which he perceived to be correct, to the limit irrespective of its consequences. A streak of religious fanaticism made him unmindful of his personal safety. It also gave him perseverance in adversity. It was this trait in his character which made

---

[113] Maj Gen Lachhman Singh, *Op Cit*, pages 89-90.

him insist that every inch of the area assigned to him would be defended and that there would be no withdrawal to the designated fortress of Bogra. (A correct attitude at the company and battalion level but not necessarily so when fighting a corps or theatre battle.)"[114]

205 Pak Brigade had the following units under its command on the eve of the war:

- 4 FF   Lt Col Akhlaq Abbasi   Area Hilli

- 8 Baluch   Lt Col Beg   Area Jaipurhat

- 13 FF   Lt Col Amir Nawaz   Area Naogaon

- 80 Field Regiment

- Troop 29 Cavalry

This Brigade was initially deployed in the central zone of the Northwestern Sector and was guarding ostensibly the most obvious and the most dangerous approach (Hilli-Gaibanda axis). The task entrusted to Brig Tajjamul was to defend his area of responsibility by taking a defensive position as close to the border as tactically sound. The line of denial designated for his Brigade was Nawabganj-Maheshpur-Khetlal; this obviously implied that his main battle had to be fought on or ahead of this line, a fair distance from Bogra.

The total frontage of Brig Tajjamul's area of responsibility was about 100 kilometers, well above the normal 5- kilometer yardstick for a brigade in defence. He was, consequently, forced to deploy all three of his battalions forward in a classic shop window deployment: everything placed forward with no depth or any reserves.

In November, 34 Pak Brigade commanded by Brig Mir Naeem was also moved from Nator to Rangpur but did not take any part in the operations till the first week of December.

The Battle of Hilli

---

[114] Lt Gen Kamal Matinuddin, *Op Cit,* page 364.

This Sector witnessed the epic Battle of Hilli, the only occasion when the Indian forces directly attacked a well-prepared Theatre Fortress head on. It is therefore considered appropriate that this battle be studied in some detail.

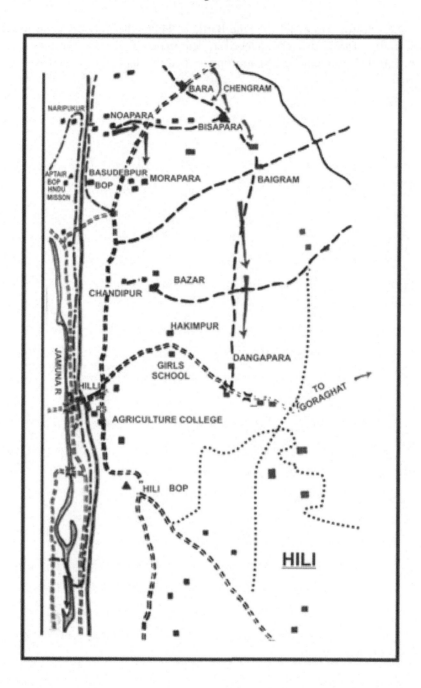

Hilli is a small town situated on the apex of the Indian salient of Balurghat; the town was spread in a north to south configuration along the railway line. The railway line itself lay immediately to the east of the international border.

Lt Col Akhlaq Abbasi had deployed his unit 4 FF as under:[115]

- C Company at Charkai.

- D Company at Hilli.

- Battalion HQ and A and B Companies at Maheshpur.

The tasks assigned to 4 FF were as under:

- Defend area of responsibility by taking up defensive position as close to the border as tactically possible.

- Deny line Nawabganj-Maheshpur-Khetlal within the area of responsibility.

- Be prepared to detach a company on orders.

The pattern of defence adopted by 4 FF at Hilli was based upon a line of platoon-sized screens placed along the railway line at Noapara, Basudeopur BOP, railway station complex, and Hilli BOP. Behind them were sited compact defended localities at Morapara, Bara Chingram, Baigram, Chandipur, and Dingapara, which covered all the approaches emanating from the tip of the Balurghat Bulge. The frontage of the entire complex was 3-4000 meters while the total depth of the unit did not extend more than 200 meters from the border. It was thus a very tight, compact and strongly held position.

The directive for Indian offensive operations along Hilli-Gaibanda axis was issued by General Aurora during his visit to Balurghat in mid-November; he, in particular, insisted upon the capture of Noapara, Morapara, and Basudeopura localities in the Hilli complex. Both General Thapan, Commander XXXIII Corps, as well as General Lachhman Singh, GOC 20 Mountain Division, were all along opposed to an attack on Hilli. They were fully aware that Hilli was a very strongly fortified and well

---

[115] Article by Maj (later Brig) Asif Haroon of 4 FF, written for Command & Staff College Magazine 1979. He was a veteran of this battle. The Author was then the editor of this magazine.

prepared defensive position; they also felt that this being an obvious and anticipated thrust line, an offensive here would fully preclude any possibility of tactical surprise.[116] General Aurora, however, was adamant and persistent in his views, perhaps because General Manekshaw, the Indian Army Chief, too had indicated his strong desire for the early capture of Hilli. Since formal war had yet to begin, General Aurora had originally permitted the use of only one battalion for this operation and also prohibited the use of tanks, unless first used by the Pakistan troops. However, as a concession to the vehement protests of his commanders, he permitted the use of only one squadron of armour.

General Lachhman Singh planned the attack on Hilli to be launched in three phases by 8 Guards Battalion, commanded by Lt Col Shamsher Singh, supported by a squadron of 63 Cavalry; 5 Garhwal Battalion was also released to 202 Mountain Brigade at this time to act as reserve. The attack was finally launched during night $23^{rd}/24^{th}$ November on D Company of 4 FF, commanded by Major (later Major General) Julian Peter. Fierce and furious battle continued throughout the night. The Guards had to mount two successive battalion attacks before they eventually succeeded in over-running just one platoon position located at Noapara; the troops located at Morapara, however, continued to defy them. During the course of this horrific night, 8 Guards suffered very heavy casualties; 4 officers killed, 3 wounded, 2 JCOs, 61 other ranks killed, 85 wounded.[117] Despite that heavy cost, all that it had achieved in the end was merely to secure a mere foothold, and 4 FF continued to tenaciously hold on to Morapara.

Just before dawn, however, Brig Farhat Bhatty, commander 202 Mountain Brigade, in an effort to secure the western flank of Morapara position, decided to capture Basudeopura with 5 Garhwal Battalion. The Garhwalis managed to surprise the EPCAF troops in Basudeopura BOP and captured it easily. However, the 4 FF troops at Morapara still remained defiant despite hectic attempts by 8 Guards to dislodge them. As the day finally dawned, the tank squadron of 63 Cavalry was sent forward to support the attack, but it got bogged down in the muddy paddy fields around the position. Amidst heavy casualties mounting by the hour, the Brigade attack on the Hilli complex thus stood stalled in its very first phase and the exhausted troops fell back helter-skelter.

At this time, strong religious convictions, rather than professional acumen, of Brig Tajjamul came to the fore. Under his orders, a rather ill-

---

[116] Maj Gen Lachhman Singh, *Op Cit*, page 90.
[117] Maj Gen Sukhwant Singh, Op Cit, page 168.

advised counter-attack was launched by two companies of 4 FF on Noapara at first light 26th November. However, it petered out under heavy Indian resistance, duly supported by tanks and heavy artillery fire.[118] Thereafter, a sort of stalemate set in around Hilli, during which both the sides took stock of their respective positions, and revised their plans. Thus, till 3rd December, no major operation was undertaken by either side and they merely resorted to daily fire duels.

The bitter struggle and the heavy casualties suffered by the Indians at Hilli at this initial stage forced the Indian Eastern Command to carry out a major re-appraisal of their operational strategy for this Sector. It was consequently decided that heavily fortified positions like Hilli should not be directly attacked and their capture be instead relegated to the subsequent phases. Accordingly, the offensive plan of 20 Mountain Division was also reviewed and it was decided to launch its main effort northwards towards Charkai.

Brig Farhat Bhatty, commander 202 Mountain Brigade, was accordingly ordered to link up with Brig Sharma's 66 Mountain Brigade at Dangapara-Charkai area instead of Palasbari, as originally planned. Thereafter, these two brigades would advance along Charkai-Nawabganj-Pirganj and Charkai-Bhaduria-Goraghat axes respectively to cut the waistline at Gaibanda and Gobindganj. These two axes were selected primarily because they were close enough for mutual support; this would also facilitate concentration of armour and artillery in time and space, as and when required. [119]

In order to ensure that the Pakistan commanders were unable to perceive this change of plans in time to mount any effective reaction, it was also decided to maintain the pressure on Hilli complex as a deception measure. Consequently, 202 Mountain Brigade was directed to hand over Hilli front to 165 Mountain Brigade at an opportune moment and extricate itself for further operations. Thereafter, 165 Mountain Brigade would continue with the fixation of the Pakistani troops at Hilli.

The deception plan worked fairly well under the circumstances. Both General Nazar and Brig Tajjamul, for the next few days anyway, did continue to operate under the impression that they were still facing the main effort of 20 Mountain Division against Hilli. Thus, they continued to reinforce 4 FF with elements of 13 FF till 11th December when, in view of

---

[118] Maj Gen Shaukat Riza, *Op Cit,* page 149.
[119] Maj Gen Lachhman Singh, *Op Cit,* page 92: Maj Gen Sukhwant Singh, *Op Cit,* page 169.

the deteriorating situation elsewhere in the Sector, 4 FF group was ordered by Brig Tajjamul to totally withdraw from Hilli.

In accordance with the modified plan, 66 Mountain Brigade, under the command of Brig Sharma, made a rapid advance along Samjia-Bajai-Phulbari axis on 3rd December, led by 20 Maratha LI. By the afternoon of 4th December, the Maratha Battalion had captured Phulbari, some 20 kilometers away. Tanks of 69 Armoured Regiment continued with further advance and, later the same night, succeeded in securing Charkai as well, some 10 kilometers away.

Meanwhile, 202 Mountain Brigade under Brig Farhat Bhatty, still at Hilli, had continued making determined efforts on 3rd and 4th December to affect a breakthrough at Hilli; their objective at this stage was then to link up with Brig Sharma's 66 Mountain Brigade at Charkai, in accordance with the modified plan. He had planned to achieve this breakthrough by containing 4 FF with just one battalion 5 Garhwal Battalion, and extricate the rest of his Brigade for further operations in conjunction with 66 Mountain Brigade.

5 Garhwals, under Lt Col Subhash Chander, struggled hard to make a breakthrough but were held up by stiff resistance offered by C Company 4 FF, commanded by Major Muhammad Akram at Debkhanda, midway between Hilli and Charkai. Bitter fighting followed over the next two days; the only award of Nishan-i-Haider in East Pakistan was made posthumously to Major Akram in this very battle. To the everlasting credit of 4 FF Battalion, Bhatty's Brigade remained entirely committed at Hilli and just could not extricate from there despite several attempts. This was a classic example of an attacking force being pinned down by a smaller besieged force; a true reversal of roles.

General Lachhman Singh had no option at this stage but to modify his plan once again. He now decided to employ 340 Mountain Brigade, commanded by Brig Joginder Singh in the same role as earlier assigned to 202 Mountain Brigade. The two main tasks entrusted to Brig Joginder at this stage were:

- To advance towards Pirganj and capture the town.
- Thereafter, establish roadblocks to isolate Rangpur from Bogra and Nator in the south.

At this time, however, 340 Mountain Brigade was scattered all over the Divisional Sector in accordance with the earlier plan and it took Brig Joginder Singh all of the next 36 hours to concentrate and regroup his Brigade; an inexcusable delay in fast moving operations.[120]

(A word of clarification here. There are two towns by the name of Pirganj in this Sector, which may create some confusion. There is one Pirganj in the northwestern part of the Sector, almost midway between the towns of Thakugaon and Dinajpur; for ease of reference, we have spelt it as Birganj. The second Pirganj, to which we are referring now, lies almost along the axis Hilli- Gaibanda, situated just north of Palasbari. Author.)

Reverting now to the operations of 66 Mountain Brigade. After the capture of Charkai, while 20 Maratha LI, was still engaged in trying to establish a bridgehead across River Karatoya, 6 Guards Battalion, the follow up battalion of 66 Mountain Brigade, had on its own initiative, exploited the area further north. It came to discover that the town of Nawabganj had already been vacated by the Pakistan troops and so occupied it on 5th December; it is also possible that they were acting on information given by some friendly locals. Pushing ahead the same night, they also secured the ferry site at Kanchdaha; by midday 6th December, it had finally succeeded in establishing a bridgehead across the Karatoya.

By this time, Brig Joginder Singh had also managed to concentrate his 340 Mountain Brigade and so could build up into this bridgehead over the Kartatoya. At midday on 7th December, a combat group of this Brigade comprising 2/5 Gurkha Rifles and 69 Armoured Regiment, less a squadron, commenced their advance along Nawabganj-Chandipur-Laldighi Bazaar-Pirganj axis; while one squadron of tanks led the advance, the second squadron was used as mobile carriers for the Gurkha Battalion, thus speeding up the advance. The follow up battalion of the Brigade was however to follow this combat group on foot.

The combat group made rapid progress and secured Chandipur in a couple of hours while Pirganj was secured by the same evening; the light opposition encountered en route was brushed aside. Roadblocks were soon established along Rangpur-Bogra Highway at Laldighi Bazaar in the north and near Barabia Lake in the south, in addition to the roadblocks at Chandipur in the west and Bahadurpur in the southwest.

At about 5 PM on 7th December, while the roadblock at Laldighi Bazaar was still being established, a Pakistani vehicular column tried to pass that point at high speed. This was the column comprising General Nazar Husain Shah and Brig Tajjamul; they were both returning to the Divisional HQ at Bogra after attending a planning conference and an Orders Group at

---

120 Maj Gen Sukhwant Singh, *Op Cit*, page 171.

Rangpur. As they approached the roadblock at high speed, they were fired upon by the Indian tanks. The two senior officers jumped into ditches and eventually managed to escape with the help of some Bengali guides. General Nazar returned to Rangpur while Brig Tajjamul boldly managed to reach Hilli after passing through the area held by the Indians. General Nazar's driver and batman along with his jeep were captured by the Indians and they gained access to his marked maps and some other useful documents.

34 Pak Brigade at Rangpur had not come under Indian attack till then and was still intact. During the planning conference at Rangpur, General Nazar had taken the decision to split it into two, with Brig Mir Naeem and Brig Nawab Ahmed Ashraf commanding a battalion group each. These two ad hoc groups were tasked to take up defensive positions along River Kartatoya astride Gobindganj. [121]

These positions at Gobindganj were occupied on 8th December, well in time to block the Indian advance to Bogra. Brig Mir Naeem learnt about the ambush on his GOC some two hours after its occurrence. He immediately organized a rescue force comprising two troops of 29 Cavalry, two companies of 25 Punjab and two companies of 8 Punjab. They located and rescued the GOC but Brig Tajjamul had already managed to escape. The GOC preferred to return to Rangpur instead and reached his Divisional HQ the next day by a helicopter.

At this stage, Brig Tajjamul's assessment of the situation was that Pirganj had perhaps been captured by a mere raiding Indian column. Based on this hasty assessment, he ordered Lt Colonel Raja Sultan Mahmud, CO 32 Baluch Battalion, to launch a quick counter-attack on Pirganj from two directions, north and south. Colonel Sultan Mahmud launched a company each in this attack from the two sides and himself led the southern prong. The attacks faced fierce resistance from 2/5 Gurkha Battalion, already in position there. Both the attacks were eventually repulsed; Colonel Sultan Mahmud and seven of his men lost their lives in the process.[122]

General Lachhman Singh at this stage decided to exploit these successes relentlessly and to deal a crippling blow to the Pakistan forces in one master stroke. His revised plan at this stage was to launch a three-pronged attack from the north against the rear and flank of all Pakistan positions from along the waistline Hilli-Gobinda down to Bogra as follows:[123]

---

[121] Lt Gen Kamal Matinuddin, *Op Cit,* page 370.
[122] Maj Gen Lachhman Singh, Op Cit, page 98.

- 202 Mountain Brigade to capture Hilli and then advance eastward to link up with 66 Mountain Brigade in Goraghat area; thereafter advance to and capture Bogra via Khetlal.

- 66 Mountain Brigade to advance from Nawabganj to capture Bahaduria and then advance to Goraghat and Gobindganj to link up with 340 Mountain Brigade.

- 340 Mountain Brigade to advance from Pirganj to capture Gobindganj and then advance along the main road to Bogra and capture it.

This plan possessed the inbuilt advantage of reducing the lengthy axis of maintenance of 20 Mountain Division, which it otherwise would have encountered during the eventual operation for the capture of Bogra. This would enable the Division to be in a position to use the Hilli-Goraghat-Gobindganj axis, some 55 kilometers shorter than the existing Charkai-Pirganj-Gobindganj axis of maintenance.

In accordance with this plan, 340 Mountain Brigade made a rapid advance and captured Palasbari on the 9th and Gaibanda and Phulchari Ferry on 10th December. This quick success completely secured the waistline in the Indian hands and isolated all the 16 Pak Division forces in the Dinajpur-Rangpur area from the rest of Division in the south.[124] General Lachhman Singh at this stage decided to hold Pirganj as a strong pivot with a battalion plus and a squadron of armour so that it could face any likely reaction from the Pakistan forces operating from Rangpur.

Meanwhile, on the Pakistan side, Brig Tajjamul had carried out some regrouping too. He pulled out a company each from the less threatened sectors of 8 Baluch and 13 FF and grouped them with the depth company of 4 FF. This composite force was then tasked to prepare a strong blocking position at Bahaduria.

In the afternoon of 8th December, the Bahaduria blocking position was attacked by 17 Kumaon (66 Mountain Brigade) and a squadron of 69 Armoured Regiment. This engagement witnessed, perhaps, the bitterest fighting of this war, after which the attack was eventually beaten back. A fresh but still unsuccessful attack was then launched by 8 Guards on

---

[123] *Ibid,* pages 98-99.
[124] Lt Gen J FR Jacob, *Op Cit,* page 114.

9th December as well.

The next day, both 8 Guards and 17 Kumaon made a concerted effort to push through but met with minor success only. Major Sabir Kamal Meyer was killed in this battle after personally knocking out three Indian tanks and was awarded Sitara-i-Juraat for his gallantry. It gives me great pride to say that Major Sabir Kamal was from my PMA course! General Aurora has himself acknowledged that one of the bloodiest battles in East Pakistan was fought at Bahaduria where according to him 17 Kumaon had suffered 55 dead and 27 wounded.[125] Pakistan lost 82 dead including two officers.[126] On 11th April, the remnants of these gallant Pakistan troops fell back to HQ 205 Pak Brigade, a few miles away.

With the Indian capture of Palasbari, the route of withdrawal of 205 Pak Brigade had been cut. So, while the Battle of Bahaduria was being so gallantly fought, the Indian forces were already ensconced behind Brig Tajjamul's Brigade and well established on Road Rangpur-Bogra.

Totally out-manoeuvred, Brig Tajjamul had no option but to withdraw his 205 Pak Brigade from the Hilli area and ordered the remnants of 8 Baluch, 4 FF and 13 FF to withdraw to Bogra. The long hard battle of Hilli was finally over after 19 days of hard slog and 202 Mountain Brigade was eventually free to develop its operations further. At about the same time, General Nazar Husain Shah also moved his HQ from Bogra to Nator. Some writers in Pakistan, notably Major General Fazal Muqeem Khan, appear to be under the impression that Hilli was captured by the Indians on 9th December; they are obviously mistaken as even the Indian authors have not claimed this.[127]

Full Indian attention in this Sector was now focused on their main objective, Bogra. All the three mountain brigades, 66, 202 and 340, were directed to exploit every available axis to get to Bogra. However, only 340 Mountain Brigade managed to unshackle itself from the tenacious defenders and was thus in a position to make a rapid advance.

By this time, 16 Pak Division had been split into three independent sub-sectors: 23 Pak Brigade holding out at Rangpur; elements of 34 Pak Brigade under Brig Ashraf in Rajshahi; and, 205 Pak Brigade in Bogra. Thus, the command of General Nazar Husain Shah more or less stood disintegrated

---

[125] Lt Gen Kamal Matinuddin, *Op Cit*, page 369.
[126] Maj Gen Sukhwant Singh, *Op Cit*, page 171.
[127] Maj Gen Fazal Muqim Khan, *Op Cit*, page 179.

at this stage. The defence of Bogra eventually devolved upon Brig Tajjamul, who had with him 32 Baluch as well as remnants of his other units. By 14th December, his weak brigade was ready to fight a last- ditch battle in the built-up area of Bogra.[128]

At last free from Hilli, 202 Mountain Brigade under Brig Farhat Bhatty advanced on Goraghat-Saidpur-Khetlal axis and captured Khetlal on 12th December. Its further operations were, however, held up as the route beyond had been extensively demolished by the withdrawing Pakistan engineers. This Brigade was to face a lot of problems as well in grouping/regrouping. By the time it started moving again, the ceasefire had already been announced. According to Sukhwant Singh:

"It appeared as though the spirit of Bhatty's troops had been sapped in the defensive operations at Hilli."[129]

A great tribute to the valiant officers and men of 4 FF indeed!

340 Mountain Brigade under Brig Joginder Singh made a rapid advance towards Gobindganj and captured it on 12th December after a two-pronged attack on the position; only some troops of 32 Baluch were there to put up a spirited defence but were heavily outnumbered. His advance continued on the next day as well; he contacted the Bogra defences during the night 13th /14th December and encircled the city from all directions.

The attack on Bogra commenced on 15th December with three Indian battalions clearing the built-up area, block by block. Heavy resistance was put up by the besieged troops and some bitter hand to hand fighting was witnessed. The Indians, however, prematurely announced the capture of Bogra while the fight had continued to rage till the time of surrender.[130]

On 14th December, while the battle for Bogra was still in progress, General Thapan, commander XXXIII Corps decided upon the capture of Rangpur. Plans were made for a two-pronged attack on this town by 66 and 202 Mountain Brigades simultaneously along Mitapukar-Rangpur and Mitapukar-Nasirabad-Fatehpur- Rangpur axes respectively. Brig Sharma's 66 Mountain Brigade captured Mitapukar by midday on 15th December and had reached the outskirts of Rangpur by the time of ceasefire.

---

[128] Lt Gen Kamal Matinuddin, *Op Cit*, page 371.
[129] *Ibid*, page 177.
[130] Maj Gen Sukhwant Singh, **Op Cit,** pages 176-177.

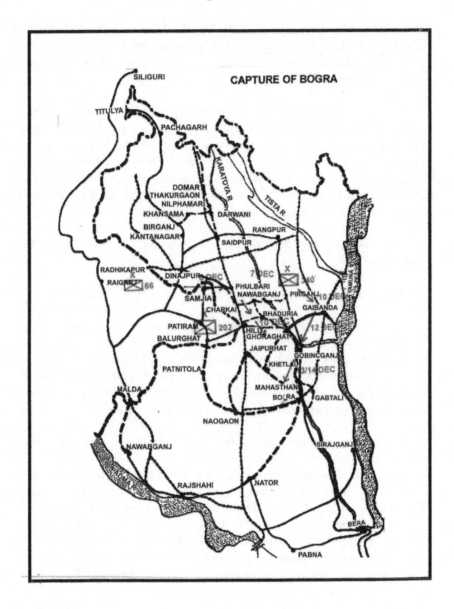

CAPTURE OF BOGRA

INDIAN CAMPAIGN AT A GLANCE

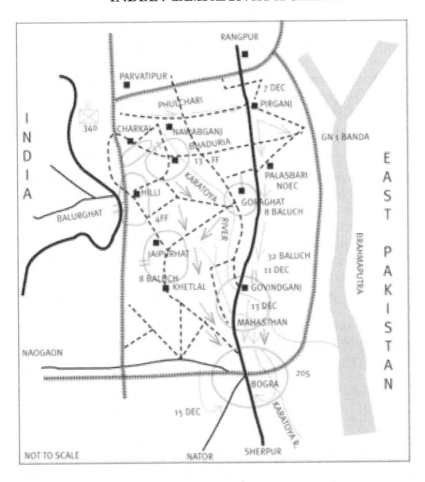

An Assessment of the Campaign

The Indian operational planning, despite some successes, was fairly ambiguous and it is difficult to discern the Corps Commander's actual strategic design during this entire operation. The scarlet thread underlying the operational plan of XXXIII Corps, in a nutshell, was first to secure general area of Thakurgaon, Dinajpur, and Hilli and cut the Hilli-Gaibanda waistline by D plus 8; THEN and ONLY THEN to advance towards Bogra.

Thus, the Indians spent almost the first ten crucial days of the offensive entirely in the northern half of the Sector before moving on their main strategic objective, Bogra. Even in the realm of operational strategy, General Thapan could not exploit his numerical superiority and failed to develop the full combat power of his formations. Of some six brigades available to him in this Sector after 7th December, only one brigade group at a time was performing actual offensive tasks while the remaining five were either on the defensive or engaged in investing various fortresses and strong points. It was only after 12th December, after 340 Mountain Brigade Group's rapid operations in the rear areas, that two more brigades were to become available. But at that late stage, they failed to play any significant part in the campaign. The primary credit on the Indian side should go to Brig Joginder Singh of 340 Mountain Brigade Group who introduced the power of manoeuvre on the battlefield, thus breaking away from the typical World War II concepts, deeply ingrained in the Indian military psyche.

The conduct of the defensive battle by General Nazar Husain Shah also suffered from glaring weaknesses. Conceptually speaking, he had planned to block the main routes of Indian ingress with a brigade group each in three distinct complexes: Dinajpur-Saidpur-Rangpur complex in the north; Hilli-Ghoraghat complex in the centre; and, Bogra-Nator complex in the south. All these fortresses and strong points were well-sited, and located on nodal points of communication. This posture certainly bestowed upon him the capability to check the Indian thrusts before reaching the sensitive interior area from any direction. However, he failed to identify the direction of the main Indian offensive in time and thus was unable to create adequate reserves from relatively less threatened areas. Had he done so, he could check the main Indian thrust and frustrate its further progress. But he entirely failed to comprehend the Indian design of battle holistically and permitted his brigades to fight their own battles independently. In the process, the role and effectiveness of 34 Pak Brigade became totally ambiguous and it failed to make any meaningful operational contribution.

His biggest mistake, however, was not to react strongly after the capture of Pirganj on 7th December. He should certainly have launched a strong counter-attack on Pirganj the same night or latest by first light 8th December; even if it meant pulling out troops from Rangpur. At that point of time, the Indian strength at Pirganj was fairly thin and a strong, well-organized counter-attack could have unhinged the Indian offensive before it gathered momentum. After that, it did not remain possible to execute any effective check on operations of 340 Mountain Brigade Group.

Between 8th and 12th December, the Indians just had 340 Mountain Brigade Group operating along Rangpur-Bogra Highway and nothing more. General Nazar had the option of strengthening Bogra complex by moving his troops from Rajshahi-Nator complex as by then Paksey Bridge had been demolished and there was no possibility of any threat developing from the Southwestern Sector. He also totally neglected to utilize 57 Pak Brigade, which by then had crossed over the Paksey Bridge and was lying without any employment.

As a result of these lapses on part of the Divisional Commander, only 8 Baluch was left to oppose the 340 Mountain Brigade Group during this critical period. However heroic may be the actions of 8 Baluch and its officers, they just could not contain a strong force like this brigade group, supported by a regiment of armour.

It is at times like this when the operational acumen and the tenacity of field commanders are put through the supreme test; it is at such times when Rommels, Pattons, and Guderians distinguish themselves from run of the mill, text book commanders. The impetuosity with which the Indians advanced towards Bogra, leaving their own lines of communications vulnerable and the base of their operations denuded, presented General Nazar Husain Shah with two great opportunities in the closing stages of the operation. General Nazar had these options available to him, any of which would have totally unhinged the Indian operations in this Sector; a Mark Clark would call it a 'Calculated Risk':

- He had the opportunity of mustering up to a brigade strength by denuding the garrisons at Dinajpur, Saidpur and Rangpur to mount a strong counter-attack aimed at severing the lines of communication of 340 Mountain Brigade at the precise time it was making a rapid advance towards Bogra; it was by then already some 65 kilometers away from its pivot at Pirganj. It would have certainly impeded Brig Joginder Singh's speed of advance and given some precious time to Brig Tajjamul's 205 Pak Brigade to improve their defensive posture at Bogra. With almost a certain defeat staring him in the face, General Nazar could certainly have endeavoured to buy more time for General Niazi as well as the Pakistan High Command in Rawalpindi. He might have still lost but could at least have lost with his head high.

- His second and even bolder opportunity was to launch a strategic riposte towards the base of the XXXIII Corps, which lay totally exposed and denuded at this time. He still had almost two brigade strength, including 57 Pak Brigade, which could be mustered and launched towards Malda and Bansibari, located at the base of the Balurghat Bulge. This was precisely the time when General Thapan had committed all his brigades deep inside the Northwestern Sector and had no reserves available to him in the vicinity. This would have been a classic manoeuvre, which almost certainly would have forced 20 Mountain Division to recoil from its relentless offensive in order to guard sensitive Indian territory.

His inexplicable failure to make any operational use of 57 Pak Brigade ex 9 Pak Division also came at a heavy cost to his formation. At the very least, he could have dispatched it for the defence of Dacca.

EASTERN SECTOR

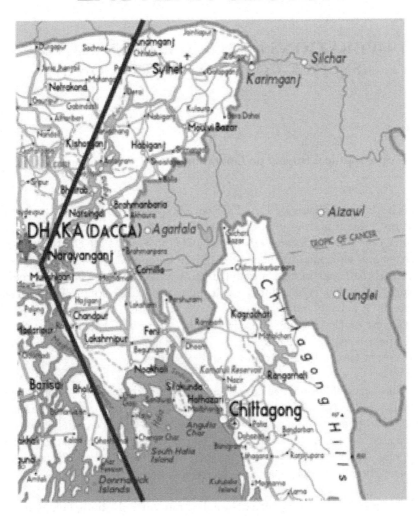

7

OPERATIONS IN THE EASTERN SECTOR (SYLHET-COMILLA-CHITTAGONG)

Topographical Impact on Operations

The Eastern Sector of East Pakistan comprised the area east of River Meghna encompassing the districts of Sylhet, Brahmanbaria, Comilla, Chittagong and Chittagong Hill Tracts (CHTs). Comparatively, the area is narrow and elongated in shape; it could be compared to a stretched bow, with its broad apex in the centre bulging towards Dacca and its two corners resting on Sylhet in the north and Chittagong in the south. The area is generally low lying and waterlogged by paddy fields except for the Lalmai Hills west of Comilla and the CHTs. Like the rest of East Pakistan, it is interspersed with numerous rivers and streams, making cross-country movement fairly difficult except in winter months.

The central zone of this Sector, lying between Comilla and Brahmanbaria, provided the shortest approach to Dacca from the Indian state of Agartala. The aerial distance from Agartala to Dacca is about 75 kilometers; however, en route it has to cross the major obstacle of the Meghna, a river of great width, ranging from 4000-4500 meters even in winter. The only bridge over it was the railway bridge at Ashuganj.

A single- track meter-gauge railway line ran north to south, linking most all important cities/towns situated between Sylhet and Chittagong. It crossed the Meghna over the Ashuganj Bridge, connecting it with Dacca as well as Mymensingh; besides, it also served the river port and ferry site of Chandpur. The marshy terrain around the Ashuganj bridge as well as Brahmanbaria area in its proximity formed a bottleneck in this Sector. However, the capture of Brahmanbaria- Ashuganj complex could effectively cut off all Pakistan forces operating north in the Sylhet- Maulvi

Bazar area from the rest of East Pakistan. Laksham, situated south of Comilla, was the hub of road and rail communications to Chittagong; its capture would isolate Chittagong from the rest of East Pakistan. The capture of the rail and road bridges at Feni would also have the same effect on communications from/to Chittagong.

On the Indian side too, only a single track, meter gauge railway line branched off from the Trans-Assam railway at Lumding, near Gauhati, and terminated at Dharampur; it ran for a considerable distance quite close to the border. The two rail systems of Pakistan and India could be linked with each other only by connecting Latu railway station near Sylhet with Karimganj railway station in Assam.

The main arterial road on the Pakistan side ran parallel to the railway all the way from Sylhet to Chittagong, well connected with a number of feeder roads linking most towns and important river ferries. Both the road and rail tracks ran over embankments four to eight feet high.

By the time hostilities with India commenced, most of the bridges on this road had been blown up by Mukti Bahini guerillas, making road movement tedious and time consuming.

On the Indian side too, a single north-south arterial road connected Silchar in Assam with Belonia in Tripura via Teliamura, a major communication centre from which feeder roads branched off to Kamalpur, Khowai, Agartala, Sonamura and other border towns. In addition, a recently constructed road ran parallel to the border from Agartala to Chauddagram, which fairly eased logistic buildup and movement of troops. In contrast to the railway lines, the road networks of the two countries could be connected at any point across the border.

The grain of the ground generally lay from north to south, except in Sylhet area where it lay east to west, sloping down from the Lushai Hills in Indian Assam towards the River Meghna. Consequently, road and rail networks generally tended to conform to the grain of the ground to avoid too many bridges and culverts. This was one reason why the alignments of major roads and railway ran so close to the international border and susceptible to interdiction from either side.

The operational, jet-capable airfields available to Pakistan were at Sylhet, Shamshernagar, Comilla, Chittagong and Cox's Bazar, which could handle F-86 Sabre jets. On the Indian side, Silchar was the only jet-capable airfield while Agartala, Kamalpur, Khowai, and Kailashahar were fit for transport planes only. Most of the Indian airfields were located quite close to the border; the Agartala airfield was actually within small arms range of the Pakistani BOPs at Akhaura.

Dacca could be accessed from the Eastern Sector only by crossing River Meghna, mainly through the following three points:

- The railway bridge at Ashuganj.
- The ferry site at Daudkundi.
- The river port of Chandpur.

The Meghna was almost three kilometers in width, the Ashuganj Bridge itself being about 3000 feet long; it was thus a formidable obstacle in any weather from every point of view. On the western bank of the Ashuganj Bridge lay the town of Bhairab Bazar, connected with Dacca only by rail. Any force trying to reach Dacca from the direction of Bhairab Bazar would have to move cross-country till the town of Narsingdi from where the road system serving Dacca took off. Further to the west of Narsingdi lay a minor branch of the Brahmaputra, which, however, was bridged for road traffic. The last obstacle to Dacca along this route was the River Lakhya, which had no road bridges but could be crossed at a number of ferry sites around Demra.

Comilla, located on the main Chittagong - Sylhet highway, was an important hub of road communications; three east-west roads emanated from here which led towards Daudkundi Ferry Site, Chandpur riverport, and Ashuganj respectively. It also had a rail link with Akhaura, Bhairab Bazar and Ashuganj Bridge, the only rail link connecting Dacca with the Eastern Sector. A large number of subsidiary roads and tracks crisscrossed around Comilla, one of which linked it with Agartala in India as well. Comilla was also linked with Chandpur by rail. Despite all these obvious strategic advantages, Comilla, lay too close to the border for being defensible.

This Sector offered the shortest approach to Dacca. Its ground configuration was in effect a great strategic disadvantage for the Pakistan forces; they perforce had to operate with a major obstacle, the Meghna, at their back. This configuration ipso facto created an opportunity for the invading force to defeat the defenders in detail by fixing them against this obstacle. The linear dispersion forced on the defenders by the great length of the Sector was yet another great disadvantage since it forced them to operate along exterior lines, thus precluding intra-sector mutual support and switching of forces between the zones; on the other hand, it enabled the invaders to operate along interior lines. The bulging configuration in the middle from Comilla to Ashuganj provided a great natural geographical opportunity to the invader for developing an enveloping pincers manoeuvre towards the Meghna.

Despite these obvious operational advantages, this Sector did nevertheless pose great logistic challenges for the invading force as well. The area of the contiguous Indian states was underdeveloped and very far from any major army depot in India. A large number of roads had to be constructed in the border zone as an operational requirement but the region was devoid of commensurate local resources. Everything, thus, had to be transported from great distances, over difficult terrain, and at the peak of the monsoon season. Indian logistic staff can rightfully take pride in achieving this goal with a fair degree of success.

Considering the large frontages as well as the independent nature of operations taking place there, it appears advisable to divide the area into three zones or sub-sectors as follows:

- Northern Zone, comprising areas Sylhet- Brahmanbaria-Kasba but excluding Comilla.

- Southern Zone, comprising Comilla- Laksham- Feni.

- Chittagong Zone comprising the districts of Chittagong and Chittagong Hill Tracts.

Pakistan Forces

General Niazi, commander Pak Eastern Command, had rightly appreciated that the main offensive effort of the Indian Eastern Command would be launched in the Eastern Sector. He was also fully conscious of the relatively early strategic threat which could develop from this direction towards Dacca. Keeping this in view, he made several changes in the articulation of command of his forces in this Sector. He entrusted 14 Pak Division with the defence of the Northern Zone (Sylhet-Bhairab Bazar). He employed the ruse of creating HQ 39 (Ad Hoc) Division in late October and entrusted it with the defence of the Southern Zone (Comilla-Laksham-Feni). In view of the possibility of Chittagong being isolated by an Indian thrust at Feni, he placed an ad hoc brigade at Karerhat, only nominally under the command of 39 (A) Division. The composition of the Pakistan forces in this Sector was as follows.

187

Northern Zone (Sylhet-Brahmanbaria)

This Zone was held by 14 Pak Division, commanded by Major General Qazi Abdul Majeed, with its Headquarters at Bhairab Bazar. It had the following troops under its command:

1. **27 Brigade**   **Brigadier Saad Ullah Khan**
   Brahmanbaria

   a. 12 FF   Lt Col F R Khilji
   b. 33 Baluch   Lt Col Aftab Qureshi
   c. Platoon R & S ex 34 Punjab.
   d. 4 x Chaffee and PT 76 Tanks.
   e. Mix of guns from 4 (Lahore) Battery, and 47 Field Battery; and 210 Mortar Battery.

2. **202 (A) Brigade**   **Brigadier Saleemullah**
   Sylhet

   a. 31 Punjab   Lt Col Sarfraz Malik
   b. 91 Mujahid Battalion
   c. 2 x companies EPCAF
   d. ½ Wing Frontier Corps
   e. 500 Razakars
   f. Battery 31 Field Regiment

3. **313 Brigade**   **Brigadier Iftikhar Rana**   **Maulvi**
   Bazar

   a. 22 Baluch   Lt Col Muhammad Yasin
   b. 30 FF   Lt Col Amir Mukhtar
   c. Wing Frontier Corps
   d. 210 Mortar Battery
   e. 3 x 105 mm howitzers ex 4 (Lahore) Battery

Southern Zone (Comilla)

This Zone was held by 39 (A) Division, a formation hastily raised on the eve of the war. It was commanded by Major General M Rahim Khan with its headquarters located at Chandpur, and had the following troops under its command:

1. 117 Brigade   **Brig M H Atif**   **Comilla**

    a. 30 Punjab
    b. 25 FF   Lt Col Akbar Baig
    c. 23 Punjab
    d. 13 x guns ex 53 Field Regiment

2. 53 Brigade   **Brig Aslam Niazi**   **Feni**

    a. 15 Baluch
    b. 39 Baluch   Lt Col Naeem
    c. Battery 53 Field Regiment
    d. Company 21 AK (This unit landed at Dacca in the middle of November. Its battalion headquarters was detached and tasked to act as a headquarters for 91 (A) Brigade at Karerhat. Two companies were attached with 117 Brigade and one company placed at Chandpur to act as Divisional Reserve. Only one company thus became available for 53 Brigade.)

Chittagong Zone

This Zone was only nominally placed under command 39 (A) Division and had the following troops to defend it:

1. 91 (A) Brigade   **Brig Taskeen-ud-Din**
    Karerhat

    a. 1 x company 24 FF
    b. Wing EPCAF
    c. Rangers Battalion
    d. Mujahid Battalion
    e. 171 Mortar Battery less troop.

2. 97 (A) brigade   **Brig Atta Malik**
    Chittagong

    a. 48 Baluch   Commanded by a Maj
    b. 24 FF less company   Lt Col Ashiq
    c. 2 Commando Battalion   Lt Col Muhammad Hanif

d. Wing EPCAF
e. Marine Battalion
f. Troop ex 171 Mortar Battery

It must be noted however that none of the brigades in the entire Eastern Sector possessed full combat power since they comprised only one to two regular infantry battalions, complemented with up to a battalion strength of Para-military forces. The artillery support was provided by a motley mix of guns and mortars from different units and these too had to be deployed in penny packets due to the large frontages, even singly at places. To confuse the Indians, General Niazi had allocated the names of regular infantry battalions to these EPCAF and Rangers units; more often than not, these names belonged to units which were at that time also on the ORBAT of formations in West Pakistan.

"This was a clever ruse indeed as it confused Indian intelligence for quite a while with the same units appearing in their ORBAT in the eastern and western wings at the same time. This puzzle could not be solved till the end of the conflict." [131]

Indian Forces

The responsibility for conducting offensive operations in this Sector had been entrusted to IV Corps commanded by Lt General Sagat Singh, a well reputed general officer of the Indian Army. Since this Corps was also responsible for the defence of the Indo-Chinese border in the NEFA area, its HQ was split into two: Main HQ commanded by General Sagat Singh moved to Teliamura, east of Agartala; Rear HQ commanded by his COS remained at its peace location, Tezpur, for its original task.

For performance of this operation, General Sagat Singh had been allocated the following resources:

- 8 Mountain Division (two brigades only).
- 57 Mountain Division.
- 23 Mountain Division.
- KILO Force.
- Para-military Forces in area.

The detailed composition of the IV Corps forces in this Sector was as

---

[131] Maj Gen Sukhwant Singh, *Op Cit,* page 150

follows:

1. **IV Corps Troops**

    a. Armour
       1 Indep Squadron 7 Cavalry
       5 Indep Squadron 63 Cavalry
       5   Ad Hoc Squadron Ferret Scout Cars

    b. Artillery

       HQ IV Corps Artillery Brigade
       24 Medium Regiment
       Battery 48 AD Regiment
       Troop 46 AD Regiment
       124 Locating Battery
       6 Air OP Flight
       11 ir OP Flight

2. **8 Mountain Division.**   **Maj Gen K V Krishana Rao**

    a. **59 Mountain Brigade.**   **Brig C A Quinn**

       9 Guards
       6 Rajput
       4/5 Gurkha Rifles

    b. **81 Mountain Brigade.**   **Brig R C V Apte**

       3 Punjab
       4 Kumaon
       10 Mahar

    c. **E Sector.**   **Brig Wadke**

This was an ad hoc force created with the following elements
under command:

       5/5 Gurkha Rifles
       86 BSF Battalion
       1 E Bengal Battalion (Mukti Bahini)
       Battery Mountain Artillery

191

d. HQ 2 Mountain Artillery Brigade

99 Mountain Regiment
93 Mountain Regiment
Battery 85 Lt Regiment
Battery 40 Medium Regiment

3. 23 Mountain Division.   **Maj Gen R D Hira**

a. 83 Mountain Brigade.   **Brig B S Sandhu**

2 Rajput
3 Dogra
8 Bihar

b. 181 Mountain Brigade.   **Brig Y C Bakhshi**

6 Jat
9 Kumaon
18 Kumaon

c. 301 Mountain Brigade.   **Brig H S Sodhi**

14 Jat
3 Kumaon
1/11 Gurkha Rifles

e. HQ 23 Mountain Artillery Brigade

57 Mountain Regiment
197 Mountain Regiment
198 Mountain Regiment
183 Lt Regiment

f. 1 Indep Armour Squadron

g. **'KILO' Force**

This was a force commanded by Brig Anand Swarup, the former commander of Counter-Insurgency and Jungle Warfare School, located at Mizo Hills. It comprised the following Units:

31 Jat
32 Mahar
2 E Bengal (Mukti Bahini)
4 E Bengal (Mukti Bahini)
BSF Battalions
CRFF Battalion

4. 57 Mountain Division.   **Maj Gen B F Gonsalves**

   a. 61 Mountain Brigade.   **Brig Tom Pande**

7 Rajputana Rifles
2 Jat
12 Kumaon

   b. 73 Mountain Brigade.   **Brig Tuli**

14 Guards
19 Punjab
19 Rajputana Rifles

   c. 311 Mountain Brigade.   **Brig Misra**

4 Guards
18 Rajput
10 Bihar

   d. 57 Mountain Artillery Brigade

23 Mountain Regiment
59 Mountain Regiment
65 Mountain Regiment
82 Lt Regiment

124 Locating Battery

e. **'S' Force Mukti Bahini**

The tasks originally allocated to IV Corps by the Indian Eastern Command were as follows:

- Capture Comilla by D+7.

- Secure the Line of River Meghna at Chandpur and Daudkundi by D+18.

- Secure the approaches leading to Sylhet.

- Sylhet to be captured, if possible. (No timeline prescribed).

- Capture Akhaura to provide security to Agartala.

- Isolate Chittagong initially, to be captured later.

Based upon the allocated tasks, the initial plan conceived by General Sagat Singh assigned the following broad objectives to his formations:

- 8 Mountain Division to initially capture Shamshernagar and Maulvi Bazar, and then invest Sylhet.

- 57 Mountain Division, after initially capturing Akhaura area, to swing south towards Daudkundi and to assist 23 Mountain Division in its operations.

- 23 Mountain Division to capture Comilla-Maynamati Complex and then to develop operations towards Chandpur, Daudkundi and Feni, in conjunction with 57 Mountain Division.

194

- Depending upon the situation then, operation to capture Chittagong was to be mounted.

In the war game held by HQ IV Corps for the finalization of their plan of operations in the Eastern Sector, there was considerable discussion regarding the advisability of capturing Comilla - Maynamati Complex in the initial stages of the offensive where the latest air photos indicated considerable fortification in progress. This discussion led to a quantum change in the IV Corps Concept of Operation, as reflected in the detailed Operational Instruction issued by General Sagat Singh on 12th November 1971 as follows:

- **8 Mountain Division**. While operating in the Sylhet area, to perform the following tasks:

  o Contain Charkai in the north.

  o In Phase I, advance with a brigade each on two convergent axes from the direction of Dharamanagar and capture Shamshernagar.

  o Isolate Sylhet from the south in six days by securing ferries at Sadipur and Sherpur.

  o In Phase II, Capture Sylhet, if possible.

  o Be Prepared Mission: Capture Brahmanbaria, on orders.

- **57 Mountain Division**. While operating in Akhaura-Brahmanbaria area with only two brigades under command, to perform the following tasks:

  o In Phase I, capture Akhaura and contain 27 Pak Brigade in Brahmanbaria area.

  o In Phase II, build up in area Maynamati with a view to capturing Daudkundi by D+8.

  o Be prepared to capture Chittagong, on orders.

- **23 Mountain Division**. While operating in Feni-Laksham area,

195

perform the following tasks:

- o In Phase I, capture the southern portion of Lalmai Hills and isolate the Maynamati Complex from south and west.

- o In Phase II, clear Comilla and capture Chandpur by D+8.

- o In Phase III, eliminate all Pakistan forces still operating in Lalmai Hills.

- **61 Mountain Brigade:**

  - o Operate directly under HQ IV Corps.

  - o Cut Maynamati-Daudkundi Road and isolate Maynamati Complex from the north.

  - o Establish a firm base for the 57 Division operations for the capture of Daudkundi.

- **'KILO' Force:**
  - o Operate in the Belonia Bulge.
  - o Isolate Chittagong.
  - o Capture Feni, if possible.

Curiously enough, at this stage the importance of Akhaura-Ashuganj-Bhairab Bazar axis for a rapid advance towards Dacca was appreciated neither by the Indian Eastern Command nor by Commander IV Corps. Perhaps, it was because intelligence information had then indicated that terrain around Brahmanbaria and Ashuganj was unfavourable for heavy traffic; furthermore, the approaches to the Ashuganj (Coronation) Bridge over the Meghna were known to be defended by a full infantry brigade.

It is also noteworthy that at this stage, there was no mention of crossing the Meghna or mounting any operation towards Dacca. Thus, the initial culminating point of the IV Corps manoeuvre was the line of River Meghna and NOT Dacca. After he had received the Eastern Command Operational Instruction in August 1971, General Sagat Singh is on record that he had personally queried General Aurora regarding tasking for capture of Dacca. Aurora's reply was that this will be decided later. At that time, Aurora's broad visualization of the future course of operations was that his three main offensive thrusts would reach the banks of the major rivers in their respective Sectors in about the same timeframe as follows:

- XXXIII Corps would reach the confluence of Rivers Brahmaputra and Yamuna near the Bera ferry site.

- II Corps would reach the line of River Padma at Goalundo Ghat.

- IV Corps would reach the line of River Meghna at Chandpur and Daudkundi.

At that time, Aurora's thinking appears to be that his formations would take an operational pause after reaching the line of major rivers and carry out extensive regrouping and replenishment. This would also have provided him an opportunity to carry out a fresh appreciation of the situation, and, then make a fresh plan for further operations.[132]

The possibility for an advance towards Dacca was certainly a later development and the credit for germinating that impetus in the fertile mind of General Sagat Singh is claimed by Major General Sukhwant Singh, then the Deputy Director Military Operations in the Army Headquarters in New Delhi. In his own words:

"I did not agree with the limited aims of the offensive but had failed to convince my superiors of the need to aim at the vital objective of Dacca. I suggested this to Sagat Singh indirectly. I said, 'General, why are you wasting your energies in knocking your head against Lalmai Hills defences? Why don't you secure the Brahmanbaria-Ashuganj area and then the road to Dacca will open itself for you to stage a triumphant march in the heart of Bangladesh polities?' 'But that is not my task,' he snapped back. 'I am only suggesting,' I said with a smile. A glint came into his eyes, and he took me away from his operations room in the darkness of the evening, beyond the hearing of eavesdroppers. 'Tell me, does India mean business this time or are they wasting our time?' he asked. 'It almost appears a certainty,' I replied. He said: 'Then leave it to me. I will get there.' We left it at that. I knew he would, orders or no orders."[133]

And with that conversation, the whole dynamics of the impending war changed. General Sagat Singh, a former paratrooper and commander of 50 Para Brigade, was a daring and energetic commander and reputed to be the most dynamic of all the Indian general officers participating in this war. And, at a critical and decisive time in this war, he certainly did rise to the occasion. After the capture of Akhaura, he was to make two critical changes to his plan with his renowned flexibility of approach. Such flexibility in

---

[132] Randhir Singh, *A Talent for War: The Military Biography of Lt Gen Sagat Singh*, page 232.
[133] Maj Gen Sukhwant Singh, *Op Cito*, page 151.

planning is reminiscent of General (later Field Marshal) Bill Slim advancing towards the River Irrawaddy on the way to Mandalay during the Burma campaign of World War II.

The first of these changes was the masterful strategy he adopted to ensure the early capture of Laksham by forcing General Niazi to unmask that pivotal city at a critical time. By this time, Sagat Singh had already come to appreciate the importance of initially bypassing the strong defences of Comilla-Maynamati Complex. Instead, he had decided to secure the nodal points of Chandpur and Daudkundi at the earliest, which would have effectively isolated the Pakistan troops operating in the entire Comilla Zone and thus completely unhinged 39 (A) Division.

The second major change of his modified plan was to completely modify the thrust line of 57 Mountain Division after it had captured Akhaura. Instead of wheeling south towards Comilla-Daudkundi, it was now ordered to develop its further operations along Brahmanbaria-Ashuganj-Bhairab Bazar axis.

Operations in 14 Pak Division Area

The responsibility for the defence of the Northern Zone of the Eastern Sector had been entrusted to 14 Pak Division, commanded by Major General Qazi Abdul Majeed, a rather heavyset and burly Frontier Force officer, hailing from the princely state of Bhopal in India. His area of responsibility extended from Sunamganj (Sylhet) in the north to Salda Nadi (Short of Comilla City) in the south and included towns like Sylhet, Maulvi Bazar, and Brahmanbaria; a frontage of about 320 kilometers. Geographically, it was hemmed in by River Meghna in the west and hilly Indian terrain across the border to the east. The Divisional HQ was initially located at Dacca but shifted to Bhairab Bazar in November 1971.

To defend this vast area, this Division had been allotted two regular brigades (27 and 313) and one ad hoc brigade (202), in all comprising just five infantry battalions instead of the normal nine; this deficiency was ostensibly sought to be compensated with para-military forces and mujahid troops. The supporting arms allotted to it were equally inadequate: just one troop of armour with only four PT-76 tanks; two regiments of field artillery (instead of normal three), and a mortar battery.

The main task entrusted to the GOC, Major General Qazi Abdul Majeed, was to deny Sylhet city and Bhairab Bazar at all costs. Because of extended frontages entrusted to his Division, he had no option but to deploy all his brigades in a forward posture to accomplish this task. Thus, all five of his regular battalions were deployed in a linear defence along the border. With the quantum of forces available to him, he just could not afford the luxury of having any depth in his Divisional layout despite the obvious consideration that the shortest approach to Dacca lay through his Division (Brahmanbaria-Ashuganj-Bhairab Bazar-Narsingdi).

Because of the independent nature of operations carried out in Sylhet and Bhairab Bazar areas, it is imperative that these be discussed separately for ease of understanding.

Operations in Sylhet Zone

Sylhet district lay in the northeastern corner of East Pakistan, contiguous to the Indian states of Meghalaya in the north and Tripura and Cachar on the eastern side. It was bounded by hilly terrain on the Indian side in the north and east. Within the district itself, the terrain is mostly a low lying plain, dotted with small hills at places and interspersed with numerous bheels and hoars (small perennial lakes). The rainfall in the area is very heavy, particularly during the monsoon period.

The major rivers in this area are the Surma and the Kushiara, which eventually fall into the Meghna. Both the rivers are navigable throughout, enabling riverine movement from Sylhet to Dacca via Ashuganj.

The railway line from Chittagong ran quite close to the border with India till Kulaura where it branched off towards Sylhet city while the main line continued to run parallel to the border up to Latu. A road also ran parallel to the railway line up to Latu.

Sylhet city, located on the north bank of River Surma, was the district headquarters as well as an important communications centre in the area. It was connected to the provincial rail network via Kulaura and linked to most of the important towns in the district like Charkai, Fenchuganj, Maulvi Bazar, Kulaura, Sadiganj, Sherpur and Shamshernagar by feeder roads and tracks. It was thus a junction for roads converging from Charkai, Fenchuganj and Maulvi Bazar and was served by an all-weather airfield as well. The city itself was surrounded by numerous tea gardens, mostly grown on low hills.

Maulvi Bazar in the southern part of the district was an important communications centre too. It controlled all road movement from Sylhet to Dacca through Sadipur and Sherpur ferries; once Sherpur ferry was captured, Sylhet would be isolated from the rest of East Pakistan except by rivercraft along the Surma river.

Kulaura was another important rail and road communications centre near the border, a railway junction connecting railway lines to Sylhet, Chittagong and Latu. Roads to Karimganj, Shamshernagar and Maulvi Bazar also emanated from here. It was a thus a key operational objective.

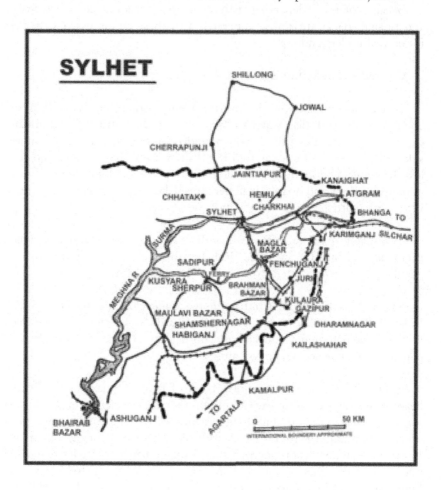

The important roads in the area were:

- Sylhet-Jaintiapur, which was the main route to Shillong in British India.

- Sylhet-Karimganj, a graveled road running east to west via Charkai.

- Sylhet-Fenchuganj-Kulaura-Dharamnagar.

- Sylhet-Maulvi Bazar-Shamshernagar- Kailashahar.

Pakistan Forces in Syhet Zone

On the Pakistan side, the area was defended by 202 (A) Brigade and 313 Pak Brigade under the overall command of 14 Pak Division. The composition of these two brigades on the eve of the war was as follows:

202 (A) Brigade   **Brigadier Saleemullah**   **Sylhet**

31 Punjab   Lt Col Sarfraz Malik   Sylhet
91 Mujahid Battalion   Sunamganj
2 x companies EPCAF
½ Wing Frontier Corps
500 Razakars
Battery 31 Field Regiment

313 Brigade   **Brigadier Iftikhar Rana**   **Maulvi Bazar**

22 Baluch   Lt Col Muhammad Yasin   Kulaura
30 FF   Lt Col Amir Mukhtar Shamshernagar
Wing Frontier Corps
210 Mortar Battery
3 x 105 mm howitzers ex 4 (Lahore) Battery

The defence of Sylhet city and the surrounding area was the responsibility of 202 (A) Brigade, commanded by Brig Salimullah. He was basically an artillery officer who had spent much of his early service in army aviation. He had been posted to East Pakistan on martial law duties but on 1st October found himself in command of a motley crowd of ragtag soldiers, designated as 202 (A) Brigade. Furthermore, he found himself pitted against an experienced and professional general like Major General Krishna Rao, a future Chief of the Indian Army.

As the defender of Sylhet Fortress, the defence of the approaches leading to Sylhet from the Indian border was thus the responsibility of Brig Salimullah. The two main approaches along which Sylhet could be threatened directly were:

- Jaintiapur-Hemu-Sylhet approach from the north.

- Atgram-Charkai-Sylhet approach from the east.

In addition, there were two relatively less important approaches from Sunamganj and Chatak to Sylhet. Despite his meagre forces, Brig Salimullah per force had to cover all these approaches.

Keeping in view the nature of his task and the diverse nature of the force under his command, he perhaps had no option but to create ad hoc groups by beefing up regular elements with second line forces. He employed these groups to cover all these approaches in a deployment pattern fully indicative of the inadequacy of his resources compared to the tasks allocated to him. His deployment was as shown below:

- **Akram Force**   **Sunamganj-Sylhet axis**

  Company Khyber Rifles
  Company Bajaur Scouts
  Company EPCAF

- **Riaz Force**   **Chatak-Sylhet axis**

  Company 14 AK

- **31 Punjab less 2 companies**   **Jaintiapur-Sylhet axis**

- **2 companies 31 Punjab**   **Karimganj-Sylhet axis**

- **Brigade Reserve**

  Company Khyber Rifles
  2 x companies EPCAF

- *Artillery Assets*

  23 Battery 31 Field Regiment

2x guns each on Jaintiapur and Charkai axes
2 x 6 Pounders on Sunamganj axis

313 Pak Brigade under Brig Iftikhar Rana, located at Maulvi Bazar, was responsible for defending the Kulaura and Maulvi Bazar area, a frontage of some 640 kilometers from Munshiganj to Shamshernagar. He had available with him just two regular infantry battalions and had no option but to make the following deployment:

- **30 FF**   Shamshernagar - Maulvi Bazar
  area

- **22 Baluch**   Ghazipur and Kulaura area

Indian Forces in Sylhet Zone

On the Indian side, 8 Mountain Division, commanded by Major General Krishana Rao, a future COAS of the Indian Army, was poised to operate in Sylhet area with the following forces under his command:

59 Mountain Brigade.   **Brig C A Quinn**

9 Guards
6 Rajput
4/5 Gurkha Rifles

81 Mountain Brigade.   **Brig R C V Apte**

3 Punjab
4 Kumaon
10 Mahar

E Sector.   **Brig Wadke**

5/5 Gurkha Rifles
86 BSF Battalion
1 E Bengal Battalion (Mukti Bahini)
Battery Mountain Artillery

HQ 2 Mountain Artillery Brigade

99 Mountain Regiment
93 Mountain Regiment
Battery 85 Lt Regiment
Battery 40 Medium Regiment

The main strategic interest of the Indian planners in this Zone was to prevent the two brigades in Sylhet area from withdrawing towards Bhairab Bazar and thus affecting a link up with 27 Pak Brigade operating there. Another important strategic interest of the Indians was to provide protection to the communication infra-structure in the contiguous Indian area. The Eastern Indian States were essentially reliant upon the rail and road communications from Silchar to Dharamnagar for the sustenance of their local population, which ran parallel to and very close to the border. Thus, these were quite exposed and vulnerable to disruption from Pakistan side, particularly in the Karimganj area. To ensure the security of these lines of communications was a critical compulsion for the Indian planners, more so because the logistic support of the entire IV Corps would be dependent upon them.

In a war game jointly carried out by HQ IV Corps and 8 Mountain Division, it had come to be appreciated that GOC 14 Pak Division would be very sensitive to the defence of Sylhet city because of its political importance. As such, he was likely to defend the approaches emanating from the north and east of the city in strength; thus, the Indian planners perceived great advantage in advancing from the southern direction. Moreover, an advance towards Maulvi Bazar and its capture would accrue the added advantage of splitting 14 Pak Division into two. Some rather transparent deception measures were also adopted in Karimganj area to convey the impression that the Divisional main effort was being launched along the Atgram-Charkai-Sylhet axis up north and not in the south towards Maulvi Bazar.

However, the pattern of deployment adopted by the Pakistan troops, as mentioned above, shows that the Indian appreciation in this instance was hardly accurate. In actual fact, 313 Pak Brigade placed two of its regular battalions precisely opposite the actual axis of the main offensive of 8 Mountain Division. Quite obviously, the Indian deception measures too had failed to achieve their objective.

At the end of the planning process, HQ IV Corps assigned the following tasks to 8 Mountain Division:[134]

- Main Effort to advance along two axes:

  o Dharamnagar-Kulaura-Fenchuganj axis.

  o Kailashahar-Maulvi Bazar axis.

- Capture Maulvi Bazar and secure the ferries at Sherpur and Sadipur.

- Develop an Auxiliary Effort along Jaintiapur-Sylhet axis.

- Contain Pakistan forces in Charkai and clear the area south of River Surma to ensure security of Karimganj in India.

- Be prepared to detach a brigade as Corps reserve after D + 5.

Major General Krishna Rao, GOC 8 Mountain Division, conceived the succeeding plan to achieve the assigned tasks:

- 59 Mountain Brigade, commanded by Brig Quinn, to advance along Fenchuganj axis; capture Kulaura and then advance to Sylhet via Fenchuganj.

- 81 Mountain Brigade, commanded by Brig Apte, to capture Shamshernagar and then advance to Sylhet via Maulvi Bazar.

- E Sector, under Brig Wadke, to advance along the Jaintiapur axis towards Sylhet with 4/5 Gurkha Battalion.

- Mukti Bahini Brigade (Z Force) to contain the Pakistan forces in Charkai.

- Deception Plan. To generate/simulate considerable activity in Karimganj area to give the impression that the Divisional main effort was being launched from the northeast against Charkai and Jaintiapur and not from down south opposite Kulhaura and Kailashahar.

---

[134] Maj Gen Lachhman Singh, *Op Cit*, page 179.

The Twilight war

During the last week of November, in their quest for executing a credible deception plan around Karimganj area in accordance with the Divisional Plan, the Indians initiated several border skirmishes mainly against Pakistan BOPs. Some of these skirmishes were fairly serious affairs involving regular troops from both sides as well as frequent resort to artillery fire; in the process, the Indian forces suffered fairly high casualties. In retaliation, General Sagat Singh took the decision to eliminate most of the Pakistani BOPs in the area, particularly along the railway line. This was accomplished by 1st December without any major reaction from Pakistan.

During the night of $28^{th}/29^{th}$ November, 8 Mountain Division launched its main offensive from its base in Kailashahar, aimed at capturing Shamshernagar. The offensive was led by Brig Apte's 81 Mountain Brigade, with 8 E Bengal Battalion and two troops of Ferret Cars under command, which began to advance towards Munshiganj. On the Pakistan side, this area was being defended by 30 FF.

3 Punjab Battalion, under Lt Colonel Rajasekharan, commenced its advance along the main axis towards Bagichara Tea Estate. Soon thereafter, 10 Mahar Battalion, under Lt Colonel Rajinder Singh, also began to advance from a flank towards the Chatlapur Tea Estate, the main hub of the 30 FF defensive position. Pakistani troops had prepared their defences very strongly, with double-storied bunkers and were well protected by wire obstacles as well as mines. By midday 30th November, 10 Mahar had captured Chatlapur after some determined fight put up by both sides. In the meantime, 3 Punjab had captured Bagichara without much opposition and then began to probe forward in order to link up with 10 Mahar. However, they were soon to come under heavy fire from a depth company of 30 FF.

Col Rajasekharan, CO 3 Punjab, mounted a quick attack on this company position, during which the defending company commander Captain Khusro laid down his life. In the melee that followed, Lt Zamir, the young artillery observer with this company, found himself surrounded by the Indian troops. He gallantly resorted to the measure of last resort by calling for defensive fire on his own location. The fire came in about 20 seconds; the Indian troops were caught in the open and suffered heavy casualties during their assault. The attack was beaten back but in the process Lt Zamir made the supreme sacrifice for his mother country. Eventually, however, 3 Punjab succeeded in capturing the position at first light 1st December and soon linked up with 10 Mahar.

While the attack on 30 FF positions was still in progress, Brig Apte, commander 81 Mountain Brigade, took the initiative to dispatch a company of 4 Kumaon Battalion to establish a roadblock on the Shamshernagar-Maulvi Bazar Road, in the rear of the 30 FF positions. His main aim was to cut off their route of withdrawal. By first light 30th November, this roadblock had been established about two kilometers northwest of Shamshernagar. By sheer coincidence, Brig Iftikhar Rana, commander 313 Pak Brigade, was then coming from Maulvi Bazar to visit 30 FF. His leading escort jeep came under heavy fire from this roadblock and he himself barely managed to extricate himself in the nick of time. Reacting promptly, he moved a platoon of 22 Baluch, supported by two mortars of 210 Mortar Battery, to contain the roadblock. Sustained fire from the mortars as well as continuous fire from infantry weapons eventually forced 4 Kumaon troops to abandon the roadblock.

By then, however, Brig Apte had come in a position to mount an attack directly on Shamshernagar. For this purpose, he decided to use 4 Kumaon; however, since one of its companies was still not combat-worthy after the experience of its roadblock, he decided to place two companies of 3 Punjab under its command. 4 Kumaon launched the attack on Shamshernagar during night 1st/2nd December, then defended by a company of 30 FF, commanded by Major Ehsan. The fighting continued for the entire night and the position was finally captured by midday 2nd December. In the process, 26 Pakistani soldiers were taken prisoner, while all the rest had laid down their lives including Major Ehsan and his mortar troop observer, Captain Altaf. The Indian casualties were also quite high: 31 killed and 87 wounded.

The War Commences

Meanwhile, 59 Mountain Brigade, command by Brig Quinn, had also become active opposite the Kulaura area; this area was being defended by 22 Baluch of 313 Pak Brigade. On 3rd December, 6 Rajput Battalion under Lt Colonel Hardev Singh came into contact with the positions of a company of 22 Baluch in Ghazipur Tea Estate area and launched a night attack on them. Baluchi troops fought back gallantly and the attack was repulsed.

At this stage, Brig Quinn ordered 4/5 Gurkha Battalion to capture Ghazipur town, which at that time was being defended by another company of 22 Baluch, beefed up with personnel from Tochi Scouts and EPCAF. Lt Colonel Harliker, CO 4/5 Gurkhas, planned to mount a silent attack (without preparatory artillery fire) soon after last light on 4th December to surprise the defenders. The surprise instead boomeranged on the Gurkhas as they were detected while still forming up for the attack and were subjected to heavy machine gun and mortar fire. Despite this setback, true to their reputation, the Gurkhas remained steadfast and still managed to launch a determined attack. After some very bitter fighting, they succeeded in capturing the position by midday 5th December; the bitterness of the fighting can be judged by the fact the Indians had to resort to heavy air and napalm bombardment on the Baluchi position before it could be secured.

While this operation in Ghazipur area was still in progress, Brig Apte (81 Mountain Brigade) ordered 9 Guards Battalion under Lt Colonel Raghbir Singh to clear and secure the right flank of the Brigade's line of advance towards Kulaura. However, as soon as the Guards began moving forward, they came under heavy fire from a tea garden east of Ghazipur, which was held by some 22 Baluch troops, part of the company at Ghazipur. Colonel Raghbir Singh ordered two of his companies to bypass the tea garden and to establish a roadblock behind it. The roadblock was placed in position by first light 4th December; however, the blocking troops had misjudged the depth of the defenders' position. Consequently, the roadblock too attracted heavy artillery and automatic fire from the Baluchis.

By this time, Major Aziz, the Baluch company commander, had come to appreciate the danger of being cut off from the rear, and so launched a spirited counter-attack on the roadblock, leading it personally. His attacking troops managed to reach within 200 meters of the objective but were beaten back despite repeated efforts. Soon after that, Colonel Raghbir launched a daylight attack on Ghazipur from the east and captured it after three hours of hand to hand fighting.

After the capture of Ghazipur, 4/5 Gurkhas began to advance towards Kulaura, meeting hardly any opposition *en route* and succeeded in occupying it by midday 6th December. The town of Kulaura was the key to the defences in this entire area as it controlled road communications from Dharamnagar to Fenchuganj and from Shamshernagar to Latu.

The main brunt of fighting in the Ghazipur area had been borne by 22 Baluch, which suffered heavy casualties and became disorganized in the process. Its Battalion HQ went out of wireless contact with the Brigade HQ as well as with its own companies. Brig Iftikhar Rana, commander 313 Pak Brigade made hectic efforts to re-establish contact with the unit but did not succeed. With most of their officers having been killed or injured during these operations, the hapless troops of 22 Baluch were left rudderless under the circumstances. They were forced to fall back helter-skelter in small parties, abandoning their heavy weapons; while most of them fell back on Maulvi Bazar, some of them even reached as far as Sylhet in the north and Bhairab Bazar in the south.

The virtual disintegration of 22 Baluch had effectively unbalanced the entire defensive posture of 313 Pak Brigade; consequently, even the critical Fenchuganj axis was left exposed and virtually unguarded. This was duly exploited by 6 Rajput Battalion (59 Mountain Brigade); it commenced its advance to Fenchuganj on 7th December, and captured it the same day after brushing aside minor opposition en route.

Let us revert now to 81 Mountain Brigade, which was by then poised to resume its advance on the Shamshernagar- Maulvi Bazar axis. Brig Apte had already learnt from intelligence reports as well as prisoner interrogation that a company of 30 FF, along with some EPCAF elements, was deployed as a strong screen position in front of Munshi Bazar, while Maulvi Bazar, a major town and communication centre, was being held as the main position.

Brig Apte ordered 3 Punjab to clear Munshiganj screen position as soon as possible. The unit launched its attack at first light 5th December after a cross-country night march. The 30 FF troops fought back tenaciously for the entire day; the position, however, was captured late in the evening, when the bulk of defenders had successfully withdrawn to Maulvi Bazar.

The further advance of 3 Punjab towards Maulvi Bazar was again checked by 30 FF troops at a ferry site on River Dhalai, just north of Maulvi Bazar. At this stage, 10 Mahar Battalion took over the advance and by last light 6th December managed to establish the firm base a few kilometers east of Maulvi Bazar. Intensive patrolling by Indian troops as well as Mukti Bahini sources had revealed that the Maulvi Bazar position was held by a battalion plus, comprising remnants of 30 FF, 22 Baluch, and some second line troops.

By then, Major General Qazi Majeed, GOC 14 Pak Division, had come to realize the futility of holding on to the entire Sylhet area; he had also become conscious of the serious strategic threat developing at this very time along Brahmanbaria-Ashuganj-Bhairab Bazar axis. Consequently, on 6th December, he directed Brig Iftikhar Rana to fall back towards Ashuganj and link up with 27 Pak Brigade there. Brig Iftikhar Rana, however, expressed his inability to comply as in his view the route to Ashuganj was insecure and unsuitable for moving his Brigade; he instead proposed to move his Brigade towards Sylhet. This move, of course, could hardly be acceptable to the GOC as it was not in conformity with his current strategic compulsion of blocking the Indian threat in strength at Brahmanbaria-Bhairab Bazar.

This difference in perceptions led to a number of radio messages being exchanged between the two on that day. They were, however, completely oblivious to the fact that these were being intercepted by the Indians too, who thus received a clear indication that the Pakistanis were actively contemplating a pullout from the Maulvi Bazar area and to concentrate either in Sylhet city or in Ashuganj/Bhairab Bazar area. Their first reaction was to hold back the impending attack on Maulvi Bazar, anticipating its imminent evacuation in either scenario. In the event, Brig Iftikhar Rana finally decided to fall back with his Brigade on Sylhet. The road to Maulvi Bazar and the two ferries at Sherpur and Sadipur thus lay open and exposed.

The refusal by Brig Iftkhar Rana to move his Brigade to Brahmanbaria was incomprehensibly surprising as, in that timeframe, there was no reported major Indian activity along Maulvi Bazar- Habiganj-Brahmanbaria axis. His indefensible decision not only compromised the defensive potential of the entire 14 Pak Division but, eventually, also enabled the Indian troops to make a convenient and almost unopposed crossing over the mighty River Meghna.

Even the Indians were pleasantly surprised by this development; according to General Jacob:

"The move of the Pakistani 313 Infantry Brigade from Maulvi Bazar to Sylhet had not been anticipated by us at Command Headquarters and came as a surprise. We had expected this Brigade would fall back to the Coronation Bridge on the Meghna for the defence of Meghna crossing and Dacca. Had they done so, IV Corps' progress across the Meghna would have been very difficult. When we got radio intercepts confirming their move to Sylhet we were very relieved. It meant for all practical purposes, that two infantry brigades were out on a limb at Sylhet where they could be contained and their effectiveness neutralized."[135]

These developments in the Sylhet area were also being keenly monitored by General Sagat Singh sitting in his HQ IV Corps at Agartala. On 7th December, he decided to further reinforce his effort opposite Brahmanbaria and to undertake the following measures to dissuade the

---

[135] Lt Gen J FR Jacob, *Op Cit,* page 118.

Pakistanis from thinning out the Sylhet Sector:

- He directed General Krishna Rao, GOC 8 Mountain Division, that a battalion should be heli-lifted as near to Sylhet city as possible and to capture it before 313 Pak Brigade could become effective there.

- He ordered 81 Mountain Brigade to continue with its operations to capture Maulvi Bazar and the ferries at Sherpur and Sadipur as this would isolate the Pakistan troops in Sylhet from rest of their forces down south.

- He ordered 59 Mountain Brigade, commanded by Brig Apte, then operating in Kulaura, to concentrate at Kailashahar for employment in the Brahmanbaria Sector; the Brigade was to be relieved from its present positions by the BSF in the area.

Now for the first time, the focus of the battle in this Zone was to shift towards 202 (A) Brigade, commanded by Brig Salimullah in Sylhet city. So far, this area had not witnessed any major activity as the Indians were content to merely contain the Pakistan forces there. Brig Wadke's E Sector had made a few tactical gains close to the border at Jaintiapur. But as he came into contact with Charkai defences, the situation had stalemated; neither side had the strength or the will to change this situation.

This hitherto relatively quiet sector was now to witness the first heliborne operation by the Indian Army in this war, for which nine MI-4 helicopters were made available to 8 Mountain Division. Major General Krishna Rao had already designated 4/5 Gurkha Battalion (81 Mountain Brigade) as the unit to be heli-lifted; it was essentially tasked to capture the railway bridge, radio station and the airfield in Sylhet. Krishna Rao's appreciation of the timeframe for a link up was based on the sole assumption that this heli-drop would force Pakistan troops operating north of Sylhet to recoil back to the city, enabling Brig Wadke's force, operating along the Jaintiapur axis, to affect an early link up, possibly within 48 hours.

Brig Quinn, along with the CO of 4/5 Gurkhas, flew over Sylhet city in a helicopter at about midday on 7th December and selected a landing site on the northern bank of River Surma, some two kilometers from the railway bridge. The heli-lift commenced at 2:30 PM the same day and by 4 PM, almost a company of Gurkhas, including the CO, had concentrated in the area.

Being daylight, Brig Salimullah, commander 202 (A) Brigade, immediately became aware of the heli-drop. There was some initial consternation as he hardly had any worthwhile force to launch a quick counter-attack. Eventually, he managed to collect an ad hoc force comprising some regular, Frontier Corps, and EPCAF troops and ordered them to bring fire on the helicopters from close range to interrupt their smooth landing process; one lonely artillery gun was also located and used to some effect. Despite that, the landings continued unabated; by the next day, they even managed to drop two mountain guns into the bridgehead.

By then, however, Brig Salimullah had managed to gather some more troops and positioned several small parties around the perimeter of the landing zone so as to bring sustained fire on the Gurkhas from all directions; this ensured that no further landings could take place. Though Brig Salimullah had, thus, managed to contain the bridgehead, he did not possess adequate strength to eliminate it altogether. Despite this, he successfully managed to reinforce his troops operating along the Jaintiapur axis to some extent. This, in turn, hampered the link-up of Brig Wadke's E Force with the bridgehead and by 10th December, Wadke had managed to reach only up to Hemu, still some 24 kilometers from Sylhet.

On the other side, in compliance with the orders of Commander IV Corps, 59 Mountain Brigade (less 4/5 Gurkha Battalion) had concentrated back at their base in Kailashahar by 8th December for the anticipated move to Agartala. Meanwhile, 81 Mountain Brigade had been making steady progress on the ground. It successfully secured Maulvi Bazar on 9th December and captured Sherpur Ferry in the afternoon of 10th December. Sadipur Ferry was also captured just the next day. However, then onwards, this Brigade faced resilient opposition from elements of 313 Pak Brigade during its further advance to Sylhet.

Back in Sylhet, Brig Wadke's troops were still stuck around Hemu while the Gurkhas in the bridgehead were under a lot of pressure due to the delayed link up. Surprisingly, however, the Pakistanis showed no inclination to eliminate the isolated Gurkha bridgehead even when Brig Iftikhar Rana's 313 Pak Brigade had fallen back on Sylhet and then possessed sufficient forces to accomplish this. Faced with a sense of creeping stalemate, Krishna Rao requested General Sagat Singh to permit 59 Mountain Brigade, now concentrated at Kailashahar, to advance on Fenchuganj-Sylhet axis. In his assessment, this axis was only lightly held by the Pakistanis and, thus, this Brigade would be able to affect an early link up with the beleaguered Gurkhas.

General Sagat Singh readily agreed and Brig Quinn was accordingly ordered to speedily advance to Sylhet via Fenchuganj. Against very light opposition, the units of 59 Mountain Brigade made good progress and contacted the outer defences of Sylhet City on 14th December. By about the same time, units of 81 Mountain Brigade had also made contact with the city along the Maulvi Bazar axis. Under increasing pressure, Brig Salimullah was thus forced to withdraw most of his troops operating along the Jaintiapur axis. This also enabled Brig Wadke's E Sector as well to contact Sylhet on 15th December.

On 13th December, while these operations were still in progress, Commander IV Corps issued the orders for the immediate transfer of one mountain brigade group to Agartala as Corps Reserve for eventual operations around Dacca. Krishna Rao decided to move 81 Mountain Brigade less 3 Punjab to Agartala. 3 Punjab was consequently placed under command 59 Mountain Brigade and Brig Quinn was nominated as overall field commander for operations against Sylhet city.

By 15th December, Sylhet had been completely invested from all directions by the Indian troops. At that time, there were some five depleted battalions, one artillery regiment and a mortar battery within this fortress town and could have held on for quite some time. But, like the Battle of Khulna, the Battle of Sylhet was lost by Pakistan elsewhere. In the early hours of 16th December, Brig Asghar Hassan, the Garrison Commander of Sylhet, sent two officers carrying a white flag to the positions held by 4/5 Gurkha, and offered to surrender. 107 officers including three brigadiers, 191 JCOs and about 6500 soldiers surrendered to General Krishna Rao at 3 PM on 17th December.

The battle for Sylhet was over!

Major General Sukhwant Singh highlights the only redeeming feature of this operation as far as Pakistan troops were concerned:

"It was remarkable that, despite battle fatigue and the prospect of an unequal fight, a company each at Shamshernagar and Kulaura, with a few paramilitary troops and very little artillery and air support, held Krishna Rao's brigades for days. And in spite of great odds against them, they managed to slip away to Sylhet."[136]

Operations in Bhairab Bazar Zone

---

[136] Maj Gen Sukhwant Singh, *Op Cit,* page 158.

The area to be defended by 27 Pak Brigade extended in the north from Shahbazpur Bridge to Salda Nadi in the south, a distance of some fifty kilometers by road. This area was the scene of some crucial and spectacular battles, particularly around Akhaura, which eventually changed the entire dynamics of the war. It will be therefore pertinent to describe these operations in some detail.

Akhaura, a small town, was located very close to the border, just opposite the Indian town of Agartala. Situated at the junction of three railway lines, it was a major communications centre in this area. The first of these railway lines connected Akhaura to Dacca via Brahmanbaria. Between Akhaura and Brahmanbaria, this line crossed the River Titas over a bridge that was not decked for vehicular movement. The line then crossed the River Meghna over the Ashuganj (Coronation) Bridge and went on to Dacca. The second of these railway lines connected Akhaura with Sylhet in the north while the third connected it to Comilla and then onwards to Chittagong in the south.

The main road from Comilla to Brahmanbaria ran via Kasba, crossing River Titas about 46 kilometers west of Akhaura. Thus, Akhaura had no direct road link from any direction, except a narrow and tenuous approach along the railway line embankment going to Brahmanbaria. Ironically, however, a direct road did link Akhaura with the Indian town of Agartala. The fact that Akhaura was connected to Brahmanbaria by rail only and that there was no direct road link between these two towns was to become a significant limitation in the ensuing operations. Since HQ 27 Pak Brigade as well as the Tactical HQ of 14 Pak Division were both located at Brahmanbaria, this limitation was to pose several command and control problems for them in the course of the impending battle.

River Titas meanders through the entire area forming several loops. During the monsoon season, it effectively isolates Akhaura from the rest of East Pakistan. During the winters, the flow of this river becomes sluggish, resulting in a wide marsh, making the Titas a formidable lake-cum-marsh obstacle. The area around Akhaura was also crisscrossed by a number of streams and ponds, particularly in the south up to Gangasagar.

Akhaura town lies barely three kilometers west of the border with India, just opposite the Indian town of Agartala. At that time, General Sagat Singh's HQ IV Corps had also been established there. Agartala airfield lay hardly a few hundred meters from the border and so remained under close observation as well as small arms fire from Akhaura. Thus, Akhaura in

Pakistani hands posed a serious threat to Agartala town as well as the airfield. The security of this airfield was, obviously, of critical importance to the Indians in order to keep the air traffic running smoothly, since it frequently carried senior Indian officers.

Brahmanbaria was also an important communications centre in the area, located on the western bank of River Pagla, in a narrow loop of River Titas. The Akhaura-Dacca railway line as well as Comilla- Kasba - Ashuganj Road both passed through Brahmanbaria and it was thus a crucial operational objective for the Indians.

At that time, 27 Pak Brigade, commanded by Brig Saadullah Khan, comprised two and a half regular battalions: 12 FF, 33 Baluch, and 12 AK less two companies. In addition, it also had some EPCAF and other second line forces, as already mentioned. It had available the support of only ten field artillery guns and four tanks: one Chaffee and three PT-76 (out of them, one had a cracked cylinder block and one needed a push by a dozer to start it.) This Brigade had been allocated 30 days' reserve ammunition; however, half of it was dumped at Brahmanbaria while the rest was at Bhairab Bazar, across the Meghna. Since Brahmanbaria had been nominated as a Theatre Fortress, to be defended to the end, Brig Saadullah had at one stage made a request that the entire reserve ammunition be placed at Brahmanbaria; however, this request was denied by the GOC, Major General Qazi Abdul Majid. In view of subsequent developments, this proved to be a wise decision.

Based upon the preceding broad topographic factors, Brig Saadullah deployed his Brigade as follows: [137]

1. **12 FF**

   a. Battalion less two companies at Akhaura, with two tanks under command.

   b. One company at Gangasagar.

   c. One company at Latumura (Twelve kilometers south of Akhaura).

2. **33 Baluch**

---

[137] Brig Saadullah Khan, *East Pakistan to Bangladesh*, pages 90-91

a. Battalion less one company from Kasba to Salda Nadi.

b. One company in area Shahapur-Kuti Chowk-Saidabad.

3. **12 AK**

a. One company with elements EPCAF, Razakars, simulating as a battalion, in area Mirzapur in the north, covering Shahbazpur approach.

b. One company behind Akhaura on home side of River Titas, with elements guarding its bridge.

4. **Platoon 34 Punjab (R & S).** Distributed between 12 FF and 33 Baluch.

5. **Company 21 AK.** This additional company was deployed for close protection of the Ashuganj (Coronation) Bridge on the Meghna. Although It had not been placed under the command of 27 Pak Brigade, yet the Brigade was allocated the responsibility for siting and coordination of its defences.

On the Indian side, 57 Mountain Division, commanded by Major General B F Gonsalves was to operate in the Akhaura-Bhairab Bazar area, with the following forces under its command:

61 Mountain Brigade.   **Brig Tom Pande**

7 Rajputana Rifles
2 Jat
12 Kumaon

73 Mountain Brigade.   **Brig Tuli**

14 Guards
19 Punjab
19 Rajputana Rifles

311 Mountain Brigade.   **Brig Misra**

4 Guards
18 Rajput

10 Bihar

57 Mountain Artillery Brigade

23 Mountain Regiment
59 Mountain Regiment
65 Mountain Regiment
82 Lt Regiment
124 Locating Battery

'S' Force Mukti Bahini

The plan of operations conceived by HQ IV Corps initially visualized only a limited role for 57 Mountain Division in the Akhaura- Brahmanbaria Sector and was mainly to operate in Comilla Sector. Accordingly, the tasks allotted to 57 Mountain Division at this stage were as follows:

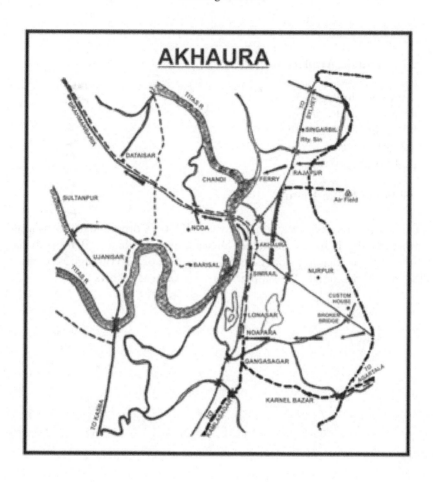

1. In Phase 1, 57 Mountain Division to capture Akhaura.

2. 311 Mountain Brigade to stay behind to contain the Pakistan garrison at Brahmanbaria.

3. Rest of Division to move south and build up in the Comilla-Maynamati area by $D + 5$.

4. 61 Mountain Brigade to isolate Comilla from the north.

5. In Phase 2, 57 Mountain Division to capture Daudkundi by $D + 8$.

6. In Phase 3, the Division, less 311 Mountain Brigade but with KILO Force (Mukti Bahini) under command, to capture Chittagong.

However, as we shall see later, this plan was to undergo radical transformation after the capture of Akhaura and fall of Brahmanbaria.

The Battle of Akhaura was the only battle fought as a divisional set piece battle by IV Corps. The outline plan drawn up by Major General Gonsalves for the capture of Akhaura was as follows:

- 73 Mountain Brigade to put in a holding attack on Akhaura along northeastern approach, from the direction of Agartala Airfield; this was the more obvious and expected direction.

- 311 Mountain Brigade to capture Akhaura using the southeastern approach, preferably in a single night.

This plan, however, underwent a dramatic change on 28th November in a manner which was to become characteristic of General Sagat Singh. At that time, Sagat Singh had come to learn, courtesy Mukti Bahini, that it was possible to wade through the River Titas at a specific point in the south of Akhaura. This meagre piece of information alerted Sagat Singh's agile mind to the possibility of isolating the Pakistan troops from Brahmanbaria in the west. At this point, he abandoned the original plan of a direct, costly assault against the main defences of Akhaura. The revised operation, named "NUTCRACKER" was planned as follows:

- In Phase 1 of the operation, 311 Mountain Brigade would now invest Akhaura not only from the south but from the west as well. (The task of crossing over River Titas from its vulnerable point and getting behind Akhaura was also entrusted to a battalion of this

219

Brigade.)

- In Phase 2 of the operation, 73 Mountain Brigade was to launch a two-pronged attack: one prong to attack from the direction of Agartala airfield; second prong to clear the southern and western flanks of 311 Mountain Brigade.

The scarlet thread of the modified plan was to extend the firm base in such a manner as to exert maximum pressure against the early warning posts and screen positions of the defending troops and thus forcing them back to their main defences. Thereafter, the investing troops would soften up the defences by accurate, directed artillery fire and destroy their bunkers with recoilless rifles, tanks and napalm bombing by the IAF. Finally, the main assault was to be mounted from the south after they had been sufficiently softened.

There is some confusion regarding the actual date on which 57 Mountain Division commenced its operations against Akhaura. The Pakistan side has consistently maintained that the operation commenced on the night 30th November/1st December while according to the Indian authors, the operation commenced one day later during the night 1st December/2nd December. We have carefully consulted several accounts from both sides, particularly Brig Saadullah Khan's *"East Pakistan to Bangladesh"* and Major General Ashok Kalyan Verma's *"Bridge on the River Meghna"*, both of them having participated in this battle from the opposite sides. Surprisingly, the descriptions of the ensuing battles by themselves do not differ much and the confusion is regarding the date of initial attack only. After a careful review and analysis, we tend to accept the Indian version of the date as correct. We have also discovered that before 28th November, the day on which the plan underwent the above-described modification, the D-Day was indeed night 30th November/1st December but on that day, it was delayed by one day. In any case, this difference is hardly a significant point in the current perspective.

Precisely at 6 PM on 1st December, 10 Bihar Battalion of 311 Mountain Brigade infiltrated cross-country, followed by a company of 4 Guards Battalion; the rest of 4 Guards having adopted a different route. Some half an hour later, a company of 18 Rajput Battalion followed 10 Bihar too, guided by the telephone line laid by the brigade signals.[138] On the Pakistan side, this area was held by elements of 12 FF Battalion. They eventually did detect some movement near Dhaturpalia, but by then the leading elements

---

[138] Maj Gen Ashok Kalyan Verma, *Bridge on the River Meghna*, page 49.

had already covered about 3 ½ kilometers towards their objective. Brig Saadullah quickly came to the conclusion that "the real show was on" and that the Indian attack on Akhaura had commenced.

As luck would have it, Lt Colonel Khilji, CO 12 FF, was running high temperature and lying in the makeshift field hospital in Brahmanbaria at that time. Major Yusaf, the second-in –command of the Battalion, was away too as he had already been placed in command of the company at Latumura. Sensing this weakness in the command arrangements, Brig Saadullah immediately decided to go to Akhaura himself.[139]

Meanwhile, 10 Bihar had captured Lonasar and Noapara without much resistance; it continued to probe forward till it came into contact with B Company of 12 FF in Simrail area, commanded by Major Aziz Bukhari. At this time, elements of 4 Guards also moved through the 10 Bihar lines to cross River Titas in order to establish a firm base in the rear.

At about this time, 73 Mountain Brigade also swung into action as 14 Guards Battalion moved cross-country and secured Maniad, 1 kilometer south of Gangasagar. In the north, 2 E Bengal Battalion (Mukti Bahini) secured Singarbil and captured Rajapur. By this time, 4 Guards too had succeeded in establishing the firm base across River Titas in Kodda area. So far, the operation had, by and large, gone according to the Indian plan.[140]

The major weakness of the Pakistani defence at Akhaura, indeed all over the Eastern Theatre, lay in their meagre artillery support. Due to extended frontages, 31 Field Regiment had split its batteries between 12 FF and 33 Baluch positions; thus, leave alone the divisional artillery, concentrated fire of even one regiment could not be brought down at any point in the ensuing battle.

In a highly unorthodox deployment, despite the protest of his artillery advisor, Brig Saadullah had placed a solitary field gun at a forward BOP in order to hit Agartala town in retaliation for the Indian bombardment on Comilla city; the exposed gun was being guarded just by a section of 12 FF. During the operations of the preceding night, this position had been directly hit by 10 Bihar and was quickly over-run. The gun crew, however, refused to surrender and continued firing their gun in a direct fire role at the attacking Biharis. When 10 Bihar soldiers eventually reached the gun, they found the bullet splintered bodies of Havildar Yasin, Lance Naik

---

[139] Brig Saadullah Khan, *Op Cit,* page 93.
[140] Maj Gen Lachhman Singh, *Op Cit,* page 198.

Ehsan and Gunner Aziz, still draping the breech and trails of their gun.[141]

At about 9 AM on 2nd December, 19 Punjab of 73 Mountain Brigade moved along Agartala-Gangasagar Track and captured Karnel Bazar after overcoming stiff resistance by a platoon of EPCAF and a section of 12 FF deployed there as a screen. The troop of tanks supporting 19 Punjab, however, had bogged down in a stream and so remained ineffective in this engagement.

At about this time, 12 Kumaon of 61 Mountain Brigade also advanced along the main Agartala-Akhaura Road and captured the area of Broken Bridge, about a kilometer across the border after its first attack had failed.

Alarmed by the infiltration of 4 Guards in Kodda area, which potentially could block the movement of Pakistan troops from Akhaura back to Brahmanbaria, Major General Qazi Abdul Majid, GOC 14 Pak Division, decided to react against this development before it was too late.

A small force comprising a company strength of infantry, engineers, military police and Divisional HQ troops, as well as two tanks were hurriedly scrapped up for this task. An armoured corps officer, Lt Colonel (later Brig) Abdul Basit, then the GSO-1 of the Division, was placed in command of them. Colonel Basit, making a good use of his tanks, launched a spirited counter-attack on 4 Guards at about midday on 2nd December. Till then, the Guards holding Kodda were not in possession of any anti-tank weapons and so were totally unnerved. Numerically handicapped as Basit's motely force was, he was hardly in a position to eliminate the Indians encroachment there, but he did manage to disperse them effectively. Thus, despite their physical presence in the area, the Guards could hardly interfere with the withdrawal of 27 Pak Brigade troops, even several days later, on 5th December.[142]

The following night of 2nd /3rd December was to provide the Indians with many anxious moments: 2 E Bengal abandoned its positions in Rajapur area in panic because of heavy shelling; 4 Guards in Kodda were still without anti-tank weapons and Basit's force was persistently exerting pressure; in addition, a company of 12 FF had managed to effectively contain 14 Guards in Gangasagar area in the south.[143]

---

[141] Maj Gen Shaukat Riza, *Op Cit*, page 152.
[142] Brig Saadullah Khan, *Op Cit*, page 101.
[143] Maj Gen Lachhman Singh, *Op Cit*, page 199.

During this night, there was hardly any significant Indian activity opposite the left forward company of 12 FF at Akhaura. However, they continued to exert heavy pressure opposite the right forward company, commanded by Major Aziz Bukhari, who managed to repulse several probing attacks. In the process, he inflicted heavy casualties on 10 Bihar, as verified by wireless intercepts. Later the same night, General Qazi Majeed visited Brig Saadullah in the Battalion HQ of 12 FF in utter disregard of his personal safety. It was only then that Brig Saadullah learnt about the infiltration of 4 Guards across the Titas; till then he had been under the impression that it was merely aggressive patrolling by the Indians. Despite this development, he showed no inclination to withdraw from Akhaura. [144]

Early in the morning of 3rd December, 14 Guards supported by a troop of tanks attacked Gangasagar railway station on a restricted frontage with two companies. The 12 FF company deployed there offered stiff and determined resistance but Gangasagar was finally cleared after some three hours of close fighting and conspicuous gallantry by both sides. It was in this action that the only award of Param Vir Chakra (the highest Indian gallantry award) in this war was given to Lance Naik Albert Ekka of 14 Guards. Two PAF aircraft also flew into the Gangasagar area but failed to engage the Indian tanks due to poor visibility; all the same, they did have some deterrent effect and the Indians failed to sever the link between Akhaura and Kasba, where 33 Baluch was deployed. At this point, Gonsalves moved forward 19 Punjab also to reinforce 14 Guards at Gangasagar.[145]

Meanwhile, Major Bukhari's B company at Akhaura also came under repeated heavy attacks by 10 Bihar; Bukhari not only held on stoutly but to a certain extent improved his posture in Simrail area. However, at this time, 12 Kumaon also moved forward from the Broken Bridge area and joined with 10 Bihar in Lonasar. Thus, a link up with 311 Mountain Brigade was finally established from the direction of Akhaura. By 2 PM the same day, 2 E Bengal also managed to recapture Rajapur area in the north of Akhaura. The position on the ground was rapidly deteriorating for the 12 FF troops despite their gallant defence so far but a stage does come when human endurance and physical capacity begin to drain fast. The stage was thus finally set for the final assault on Akhaura.

On 3rd December, Major General Gonsalves, GOC 57 Mountain Division, changed the plan yet again. He decided to capture Akhaura using

---

[144] Brig Saadullah Khan, *Op Cit*, page 103.
[145] Maj Gen Lachhman Singh, *Op Cit*, page 199.

311 Mountain Brigade only, with the Mukti Bahini 'S' Force under its command. 73 Mountain Brigade was now tasked to block the move back of 33 Baluch from Kasba towards Brahmanbaria by establishing a road block north of Kasba on Road Brahmanbaria- Kasba.

Brig Misra, commander 311 Mountain Brigade, planned a feint attack by 'S' Force and 19 Raj Rif in the north from Rajapur direction as a deception measure. Originally, the main attack against Akhaura was to be launched at 9 AM on 4th December but had to be postponed three times due to non-availability of air strikes. Eventually, General Gonsalves was forced instead to launch a night attack at 10 PM the same night.[146]

Since Lt Colonel Khilji, CO 12 FF, was still running high fever, the GOC sent forward Lt Colonel Muhammad Ashraf, CO 12 AK, to take over the command of 12 FF as an interim measure. However, fast moving events and intense, continuous Indian pressure ensured that he never became fully effective.[147]

As mentioned, 2 E Bengal Battalion ex 'S' Force along with 19 Raj Rif Battalion had been given the task to simulate the main attack from the north as a deception measure. They kept exerting pressure from Rajapur throughout the day of 4th December but were effectively held up at the anti-tank ditch by the left forward company of 12 FF at Akhaura. In the early hours of night 4th /5th December, all the artillery available with 57 Mountain Division also opened up in their support, which misled Brig Saadullah Khan to believe that this was the main attack by 57 Mountain Division. General Gonsalves, who was personally listening in to the radio transmissions being made by 12 FF and 27 Pak Brigade, soon came to the conclusion that his deception measure had been successful. This was the time for him to launch his real main attack.

The main attack was launched by 10 Bihar Battalion (311 Mountain Brigade) from the south at about 10:30 PM on 4th December and brought Maj Bukhari's company under intense pressure. Simrail fell by 3 AM on 5th December after some very fierce and bitter fighting. On the western flank of 10 Bihar, 18 Rajput Battalion too kept inching forward towards Akhaura railway station. Seeing the critical situation developing in 12 FF area and with no hopes of any reinforcement from anywhere, Brig Saadullah Khan came to realize that his position in Akhaura was now untenable. He sent a verbal message to his GOC, through Lt Col Muhammad Ashraf, seeking his

---

[146] *Ibid, page* 200.
[147] Brig Saadullah Khan, *Op Cit,* page 108.

permission to withdraw to Brahmanbaria.

The permission was duly accorded just before dawn on 5th December; it was quite late as it was but another hour's delay could really have been fatal for Saadullah's command. A fighting withdrawal while in contact with the enemy under an active battle situation is one of the most difficult and hazardous tactical manoeuvres. All credit to him, Brig Saadullah Khan conducted a masterly withdrawal and managed to extricate most of his surviving personnel back to Brahmanbaria by the morning of 5th December.

Thus, ended the Battle of Akhaura, which commenced with the start of the infiltration on 1st December and terminated at about 5:30 AM on 5th December; during this period, Brig Saadullah Khan held the complete 57 Mountain Division at bay with just two companies of 12 FF. For this outstanding performance, he was deservedly honoured with the second highest gallantry award of Hilal-i-Juraat.

The same night, 33 Baluch also succeeded in falling back on Brahmanbaria from Kasba since the road block by 73 Mountain Brigade had not been fully established by then. One of the lingering mysteries of this battle is that 33 Baluch had remained a passive spectator to the battle raging at Akhaura and was never employed to reinforce Akhaura or to counter-attack the Indian forces there. Surprisingly, neither the GOC nor the Brigade Commander ever thought of such an obvious possibility.

By early afternoon on 5th December, 12 FF and 12 AK troops at Akhaura had withdrawn to Brahmanbaria while 33 Baluch had taken up delaying positions between River Titas and Brahmanbaria to cover their withdrawal by impeding the imminent Indian advance to the maximum. Meanwhile, the evacuation of all wounded and non-essential personnel across the Meghna was also being carried out over the available river craft.

The capture of Akhaura brought with it an unexpected windfall for the Indians, which changed the entire complexion of the succeeding events. To their immense surprise and delight, they discovered that the Pakistan troops had lifted one of the two rail tracks between Akhaura and Brahmanbaria and were, thus, using the railway embankment as a road. This was an important discovery for the Indians as it provided them with a fairly good vehicular approach directly from Akhaura to Brahmanbaria and Ashuganj. This discovery, in effect, opened the shortest approach to crossing the Meghna from the east and onwards for an advance to Dacca.

At the time when this critical discovery was made, General Sagat Singh fortuitously happened to be present at HQ 57 Mountain Division for a meeting with General Gonsalves. The operational implications of this discovery were immediately obvious to both of them. They quickly came to the conclusion that this Division must now advance towards Brahmanbaria instead of swinging south for the capture of Daudkundi, as originally planned. They felt that their immediate objective should henceforth be the capture of Ashuganj and the eastern bank of the Meghna. Sagat Singh immediately spoke to General Aurora by telephone, who also accorded his approval to this change of plan.

Almost simultaneously, Brig Saadullah Khan, who had reached the Divisional Tactical HQ at Brahmanbaria, was having a meeting with General Qazi Majeed; the issue under discussion was whether Saadullah would now prefer to take up a defensive position at Brahmanbaria or instead base his defence on Ashuganj, on the eastern bank of the Meghna. When asked for his opinion, Saadullah's immediate response was to ask whether there was any possibility of 313 Pak Brigade moving from Maulvi Bazar to Brahmanbaria. General Qazi Majeed in reply briefed him about the current situation in Sylhet and Maulvi Bazar and also apprised him that there was just no possibility of any move south from Maulvi Bazar. On hearing this, Saadullah indicated that in this scenario, he would prefer to take up the defence at Ashuganj instead of Brahmanbaria, despite the latter being a designated theatre fortress.

Brig Saadullah had based his opinion mainly on the rationale that a defensive position at Brahmanbaria might lead to the possibility of an Indian heli-landing near Ashuganj in an attempt to capture the Meghna Bridge intact and/or to disrupt the supply route of his Brigade position. On the other hand, the main disadvantage was that the defensive position at Ashuganj would have to be completely prepared from the scratch whereas the Brahmanbaria position was partially prepared. Weighing these two factors judiciously, he had correctly taken his decision in favour of Ashuganj.

The GOC hardly had any objection to this plan in principle. His only caveat was that there was no existing road link between Brahmanbaria and Ashuganj at the moment and that it would take at least two days to cut a track with dozers. Consequently, Brig Saadullah undertook to hold up the Indian advance for this period to gain time for preparation of this track.[148]

By this time, courtesy Mukti Bahini, the Indian commanders had also

---

[148] Brig Saadullah Khan, *Op Cit*, pages 125-126.

been made aware that Brahmanbaria was only a delaying position and that 27 Pak Brigade intended to take up its final defensive position in Ashuganj or even in Bhairab Bazar, along the western bank of the Meghna. Sensing the prospects of an easy and early victory, General Gonsalves now issued the following orders to his Division:[149]

- 73 Mountain Brigade to press forward and establish contact with Brahmanbaria position by last light 6th December.

- 311 Mountain Brigade to be prepared to secure Brahmanbaria or the Meghna Bridge at Ashuganj.

- 'S' Force to advance along the northern approach and secure Ajabpur Ferry, located north of Ashuganj, so as to check any movement of Pakistan forces from Sylhet/Maulvi Bazar towards Ashuganj or Dacca. (Apparently, the Indians were still concerned about the possibility of 313 Pak Brigade reinforcing 27 Pak Brigade or moving to Dacca.)

Accordingly, early on 6th December, 73 Mountain Brigade commenced its advance to Brahmanbaria along the railway embankment with two battalions up on man-packed basis. The advance was slow because of determined resistance put up by 33 Baluch, which had organized several delaying positions along the way. However, by last light 6th December, the Brigade had reached about four kilometers short of Brahmanbaria.

At this time, General Gonsalves was mainly concerned with preventing 27 Pak Brigade from taking its troops and equipment across the Meghna through the Ashuganj Ferry. He also realized that the Pakistani forces would strive hard to gain as much time as possible by trying to impose maximum delay on his advancing troops in order to achieve this objective. To avoid that, Gonsalves sought to make an attempt to capture the Bridge intact. Accordingly, on 6th December, he decided to further strengthen the force carrying out the outflanking move from the north so as to credibly threaten the Ashuganj Bridge. Accordingly, he ordered 10 Bihar (311 Mountain Brigade) to join 'S' Force and to advance towards Ashuganj from the north. Meanwhile, the main advance towards Brahmanbaria was to be led by 73 Mountain Brigade, as already ordered, with 311 Mountain Brigade moving up gradually behind it.[150]

---

[149] Maj Gen Lachhman Singh, *Op Cit*, pages 202-203.
[150] *Ibid*, page 203.

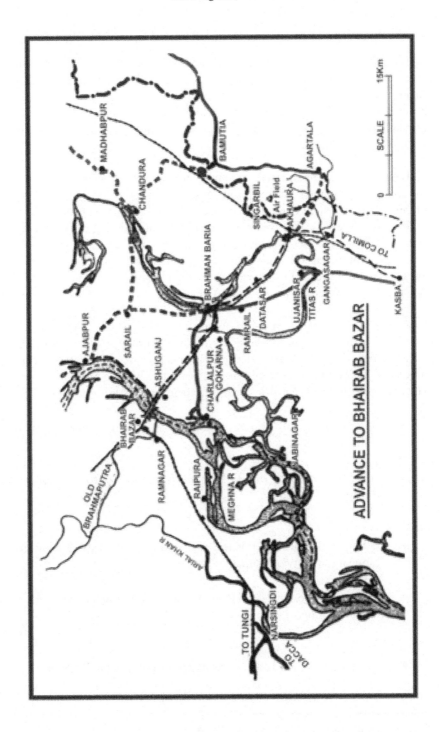

ADVANCE TO BHAIRAB BAZAR

On the other side, General Qazi Majeed and Brig Saadullah were also fully aware of the developing threat. Since they had already decided to fall back on Ashuganj, their main concern at this time was to gain maximum time for two purposes: improvise the track from Brahmanbaria to Ashuganj; and, preparation of defensive position at Ashuganj. Brahmanbaria was eventually abandoned during the night $6^{th}/7^{th}$ December, leaving behind 33 Baluch to continue resisting the Indian advance to gain maximum time.

Because of the determined resistance put up by 33 Baluch, the Indian commanders remained under the impression even on 7th December that Brahmanbaria was still being held in strength; most of their chroniclers too have been of the view that Brahmanbaria was vacated during the succeeding night, $7^{th}/8^{th}$ December and not a night earlier. The Indian commanders were thus quite careful and deliberate in their advance forward. This misunderstanding served to provide further time and opportunity to 27 Pak Brigade to organize their positions at Ashuganj.

Ashuganj was then a modern township with several blocks of high concrete buildings. It housed a big petroleum complex as well as an eight-storeyed rice silo, which provided excellent all-round observation over a large area. These buildings were put to a good use by Brig Saadullah Khan. The dispositions of 27 Pak Brigade at this stage were as follows:[151]

- One company of 12 AK established a screen position west of Brahmanbaria.

- An ad hoc company of 30 FF, comprising diverse troops, deployed in front of Talshehr.

- 33 Baluch deployed astride the railway track from Talshehr towards Ashuganj, with two companies on each side.

- Four companies of EPCAF in Ashuganj town, deployed north of the railway line.

- Two companies of 12 FF at Ashuganj as the Brigade Reserve.

---

[151] Brig Saadullah Khan, *Op Cit,* pages 140-141.

- Two Companies of 12 FF at Bhairab Bazar, across the Meghna, to protect the Refilling Point there.

- Brigade HQ established in Ashuganj near the Grain Silo.

- The solitary available tank placed near the Brigade HQ.

- Guns placed south of the railway line.

On 7th December, General Qazi Majeed came over to Ashuganj and conveyed the rather alarming news that General Niazi urgently wanted some troops from 27 Pak Brigade for the defence of Dacca. Consequently, two companies of 12 FF then in Brigade Reserve were dispatched to Dacca the succeeding night by river steamers. This deprived the Brigade of its only reserves and was left with only EPCAF troops within the town of Ashuganj to defend it. Brig Saadullah was rightly concerned about the security of Ashuganj, particularly from its left (northern) flank. In desperation and with hardly any resources in his hands, he created an ad hoc company under Captain Saeed, comprising one platoon of 33 Baluch and one company of EPCAF, and deployed them as a screen on this exposed flank; he called it as BB Company.

General Gonsalves arrived at 73 Mountain Brigade positions early on the morning of 8th December amid positive indications that Brahmanbaria had already been evacuated. He ordered Brig Tuli to cross the Pagla River immediately while 311 Mountain Brigade was ordered to resume advance beyond Brahmanbaria towards Ashuganj; they commenced their advance along the railway embankment with 4 Guards moving along the railway line and 18 Rajput along the road. Their intention was to reach the Meghna as soon as possible and capture the Ashuganj Bridge intact before the retreating Pakistan troops could have a chance to reorganize its defences there or to blow it up. At this stage, the Indians were facing a lot of difficulty in moving up their artillery and engineer assets due to demolished bridges en route. But the euphoria of their recent success at Akhaura had created an environment of over-confidence among the leading troops. Sensing quick victory, the Indian commanders had decided to press on regardless and began advancing without effective artillery cover.[152]

---

[152] Maj Gen Lachhman Singh, *Op cit*, page 204.

By midday of 9th December, 18 Rajput had swung north and were moving cross-country to Ashuganj from the northeast and, in the process, they too had moved beyond their artillery range. In their optimistic arrogance, they considered the Pakistani forces hardly capable of mounting any strong reaction to their swift advance. But, as soon as they reached the outskirts of Ashuganj, all hell was to break loose.

Brig Saadullah was a brave and competent commander who had sensed the desperation of the emerging situation. His major consideration at this stage was to ferry across his troops and equipment safely to the western bank of the Meghna. To gain the time to achieve this, the only option open to him at this stage was to stage a quick counter-attack to check the advancing Indians; he threw everything he had into this desperate counter-attack and led it personally. Lucky for him, he still had available to him two companies of 33 Baluch and their CO Lt Col Aftab, who were in a fairly good physical condition; in addition, he possessed a large number of EPCAF troops, such as they were. Saadullah's counter-attacking force brought down accurate and deadly machine gun, mortar and artillery fire on the exposed soldiers of 18 Rajput, some of whom panicked and ran helter-skelter. In a matter of minutes, the Indians had lost eight tanks while 120 of their men lay dead on the field in this sharp and sudden encounter. As luck would have it, this was the precise time when the northern task force, comprising 10 Bihar and 2 E Bengal, also reached Ashuganj from the north and rushed headlong into the melee in progress there. After suffering some casualties, they too fell back along with the troops of 18 Rajput in a state of total disarray.

Nonetheless, the sudden and rather unexpected appearance of 10 Bihar and 2 E Bengal from the northerly direction did serve to create some panic at HQ 14 Pak Division. By this time, the Indian heli-lift at Sylhet had already taken place and General Qazi Majeed had become very apprehensive of the possibility of a heliborne attack on the Meghna Bridge too. Perhaps somewhat unnerved by the emerging situation, he ordered the immediate demolition of the critical railway bridge over the Meghna, and thus abandoned the bulk of 27 Pak Brigade, still across at Ashuganj.

This time however the lady luck chose to smile on these hapless Pakistani troops. The deadly counter-attack and the huge number of casualties had resulted in considerable confusion and panic on the Indian side too, most visibly noticeable at HQ 57 Mountain Division. As such, they failed to react in time to exploit the desperate situation of the marooned Pakistani troops. The troops of 27 Pak Brigade eventually managed to safely ferry across the River to Bhairab Bazar during night

$9^{th}/10^{th}$ December. Ashuganj was thus occupied by the Indian troops early on 10th December without any opposition.

Brig Saadullah reached Bhairab Bazar in the morning of 10th December and was greatly encouraged to find that one company of 22 Baluch (313 Pak Brigade) had since managed to come through from Maulvi Bazar. In addition, a steamer carrying ammunition had also reached from Dacca during the same night. He immediately set about organizing the layout of his dilapidated Brigade for defence of Bhairab Bazar as follows:

- **Baluch Group.** Commander: Lt Col Aftab, CO 33 Baluch.

  33 Baluch
  Company 22 Baluch
  Companies of EPCAF and West Pakistan Police

  Task: To defend West, North and East of Bhairab Bazar.

- **FF Group.** Commander: Maj Yusaf, second-in-command 12 FF

  Two companies 12 FF
  Composite Company 30 FF and Mahsuds
  Company EPCAF

  Task: To defend Southwest and South of Bhairab Bazar

- **AK Group.** Commander: Lt Col Ashraf, CO 12 AK

  12 AK less two companies
  Company EPCAF

  Task: To defend Southeast and East of Bhairab Bazar including demolished Bridge

- **Brigade Reserve.** Commander: Maj Naeem

  Company 33 Baluch
  Company 22 Baluch

While Brig Saadullah was settling down in his new position, there was predictably a more hectic activity on the Indian side. On the same day as Ashuganj fell, the river port of Chandpur and the ferry site at Daudkundi had also fallen in the Comilla Zone; this, in effect, signified the complete

233

collapse of Pakistani forces in the entire Eastern Sector.

Sitting in his HQ at Agartala, Lt General Sagat Singh had two options in front of him for conducting further operations in this area: he could launch his troops in a costly opposed assault across the Meghna to capture Bhairab Bazar; or, he could bypass Bhairab Bazar altogether and somehow develop operations direct towards Dacca. Taking stock of the entire situation, he decided to act boldly and heli-lift his troops across the Meghna; he had available to him some 14 MI-4 helicopters and decided to use them to the fullest advantage. Here is how he arrived at this momentous decision:

"Around noon of 9 December, Sagat Singh discussed the tactical situation with Gonsalves at Brahmanbaria. He told Gonsalves that crossing the Meghna was inescapable to achieve a decisive victory. He had appreciated that Dacca was the political heart and tactical nerve centre of East Pakistan and its early capture would end the war in our favour. Both Sagat Singh and Gonsalves were convinced that no advantage would accrue from the capture of Bhairab Bazar, particularly as it was not even linked with Dacca by road. They agreed it would be better to contain the enemy at Bhairab Bazar and effect crossing farther south, where no opposition was expected."[153]

In a lucky coincidence, Major General Gonsalves was adequately qualified to command an heli-borne operation. He was a paratrooper as well as a qualified air observation pilot of considerable experience. In consultation with Brig Misra, commander 311 Mountain Brigade, he selected a landing zone a few kilometers southwest of Raipura, well outside the range of Pakistan artillery from Bhairab Bazar. The responsibility for the initial operation was allocated as follows:[154]

311 Mountain Brigade

- 18 Rajput to contain 27 Pak Brigade from the direction of Ashuganj.

- Rest of Brigade to perform the following tasks:

- Secure area Raipura by heli landing.

- Advance along the rail axis to capture Narsingdi, the nearest road head and riverport to Dacca.

---

[153] *Ibid*, page 207.
[154] *Ibid,* pages 208-209.

- Build up the remainder of the Brigade at Narsingdi by maximum use of available rivercraft and helicopters.

73 Mountain Brigade

- 19 Punjab to cross the Meghna southwest of Bhairab Bazar; contain 27 Pak Brigade from the south and ensure it could not interfere with the Heli landings.

- Rest of 73 Mountain Brigade to cross the Meghna by rivercraft and build up in Narsingdi area.

'S' Force

- Place 11 E Bengal under command 73 Mountain Brigade.

- Rest of the force to cross the Meghna and concentrate at Narsingdi.

Gonsalves was fully alive to the importance of logistics in such a complex operation. He organized a Riverine Logistic Support Organization under Lt Colonel Ganjoo, CO of 82 Light Regiment, to ensure an organized and methodical logistic buildup by rivercraft to provide adequate support for the heliborne and ground troops going across the Meghna.

The heli lift commenced at 3:30 PM on 9th December when 4 Guards and a troop of 82 Light Regiment were lifted from Brahmanbaria to Raipur area. By the evening, 4 Guards had secured the area west of Raipur without any opposition. The heli lift continued till moonset and then resumed at first light the next day; 110 sorties were thus flown in 36 hours. By 11th December, HQ 311 Mountain Brigade with four infantry battalions, one troop of PT-76 tanks, one mountain artillery regiment, one mortar battery and four medium guns had crossed the Meghna. It easily secured Narsigdi the same day and was then ordered to push forward to make contact with Pakistan troops as near to Dacca as possible.[155]

All this while, 27 Pak Brigade was kept engaged by a constant barrage of aerial bombardment and artillery shelling; napalm bombs were also used,

---

[155] Maj Gen Sukhwant Singh, Op Cit, page 203.

mostly against 31 Field Regiment. Thus, there was nothing General Qazi Majeed or Brig Saadullah could do to prevent the Indian buildup at Narsingdi or to impede their advance forward; all rivercraft in the vicinity had either been commandeered by the Indians or destroyed by them. Consequently, all the frantic calls made by General Niazi to Qazi Majeed to do something about the landings remained fruitless. For all practical purposes, war was over for this gallant Brigade.

Meanwhile, 311 Mountain Brigade advanced along Narsingdi-Demra axis and contacted Demra on 14th December. 2 E Bengal Battalion crossed the Lakhya River north of Demra and secured Rupganj the same day. At the same time, 73 Mountain Brigade advanced along the Narsingdi-Pubail-Tungi axis and secured Pubail on 14th December; it came into contact with the Pakistan troops at Tungi, the outer line of the so-called Dacca fortress defence, the same evening.

At this stage, further advance by 57 Mountain Division was halted on the express orders of General Aurora, who wanted to prevent the possibilities of its clash with the troops of 101 Communication Zone, advancing from the north and already in contact with the Dacca defences. Further progress of these operations will be covered in detail in the next Chapter.

Operations in Comilla Zone -39 (A) Division Area

The area of operations entrusted to 39 (A) Division could be roughly compared to gigantic triangle with its nodal points defined by Comilla in the north, Feni and Laksham in the south and the important riverport of Chandpur in the west. The Lalmai Hills, generally located within this triangle, dominated the surrounding area from Maynamati in the north to Lalmai village in the south; these low hills, thus, effectively lay across all major approaches from Tripura state towards Daudkundi and Chandpur.

Situated fairly close to the border, Comilla was an important communications centre from where a large number of roads and tracks emanated in all directions. The main Dacca-Chittagong highway passed through Comilla too and linked it with Daudkundi ferry site in the west. From Comilla to Feni, this Highway ran quite close and parallel to the border with India. Comilla was also linked with Chandpur by a road which passed through the Lalmai Hills.

Maynamati complex effectively dominated the main Comilla-Daudkundi Highway. It also visually dominated Comilla city and airfield.

Lalmai village was yet another important communication centre where roads and tracks from Comilla, Laksham, Chandpur and Barura converged. Laksham was an important nodal point too, connected by road and rail with Chittagong, Comilla, Noakhali, and Chandpur. There was, however, no direct east-west road linking Laksham and Chandpur; both, however, were connected by rail.

Comilla, despite its obvious importance, was situated too close to the border to be defensible. Thus, the most important strategic objectives for the Indians in the area were Daudkundi and Chandpur, both situated on the River Meghna. Other objectives of operational significance were Maynamati and Lalmai Village.

Pakistan Forces

Till the early autumn, the defence of the entire Eastern Sector was the responsibility of 14 Pak Division, commanded by Major General Rahim Khan. However, by mid-November, General Niazi had come to realize that, in case of an invasion, there was a strong possibility of the main Indian offensive being launched from south of Comilla, aimed at capturing Chandpur.

To meet this threat, he restructured the articulation of command in the entire Eastern Sector. 39 (A) Division was hastily raised under Major General Rahim Khan and given the responsibility to defend the area from Comilla in the north to Feni in the south. The area of responsibility of 14 Pak Division was thereafter limited to Sylhet-Brahmanbaria area, as already discussed. The inter-divisional boundary between the two divisions ran along the River Gumti inclusive to 39 (A) Division. The inter-brigade boundary between 117 and 53 Brigades was along the general line Chauddagram-Laksham-Chandpur, inclusive to 117 Pak Brigade.

At that time, the composition of 39 (A) Division was as under:

117 Brigade	**Brig M H Atif**	**Comilla**

30 Punjab
25 FF
23 Punjab
  12 x guns ex 53 Field Regiment

53 Brigade	**Brig Aslam Niazi**	**Feni**

15 Baluch

39 Baluch
Battery 53 Field Regiment
Company 21 AK

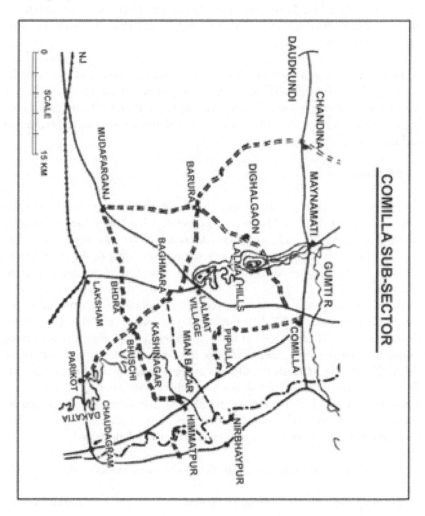

<u>Note</u>: 21 AK Battalion had landed at Dacca in the middle of November. Its battalion headquarters was detached and tasked to act as a headquarters for 91 (A) Brigade at Karerhat. Two companies were attached with 117 Brigade and one company placed at Chandpur to act as Divisional Reserve. Only one company thus became available for 53 Brigade.

Brig Atif, commander 117 Pak Brigade, had placed two battalions forward with 30 Punjab covering Comilla and 23 Punjab covering the approach to Laksham. However, due to wide distances, a yawning gap between the two units was left uncovered. He sought to rectify this by placing his third battalion, 25 FF, in depth in area Mian Bazar- Kashinagar, generally covering the road and railway track from Laksham to Daudkundi. Despite that, the gap between the two forward battalions proved to be a major operational weakness in his layout and as we shall see, it was exploited by the Indians to the full.

Brig Aslam Niazi, commander 53 Pak Brigade, had initially placed his HQ at Feni. He deployed his 15 Baluch Battalion in the Belonia salient while 39 Baluch was stretched out between Feni and Chauddagram.

Indian Forces

The composition of the Indian forces operating against 39 (A) Division was as follows:

23 Mountain Division.   **Maj Gen R D Hira**

a. **83 Mountain Brigade.**   **Brig B S Sandhu**
    2 Rajput
    3 Dogra
    8 Bihar

b. **181 Mountain Brigade.**   **Brig Y C Bakhshi**

    6 Jat
    9 Kumaon
    18 Kumaon

c. 301 Mountain Brigade. Brig H S Sodhi
14 Jat
3 Kumaon
1/11 Gurkha Rifles

d. HQ 23 Mountain Artillery Brigade

57 Mountain Regiment
197 Mountain Regiment
198 Mountain Regiment
183 Lt Regiment

e. 1 Indep Armour Squadron

f. 'K' Force.

This was an ad hoc force commanded by Brig Anand Swarup, the commander of Counter-Insurgency and Jungle Warfare School (Mizo Hills). It comprised the following Units:
31 Jat
32 Mahar
2 E Bengal (Mukti Bahini)
4 E Bengal (Mukti Bahini)
2 x BSF Battalions
CRPF Battalion

61 Mountain Brigade ex 57 Mountain Division had also been ordered to move south from Akhaura area and placed under command 23 Mountain Division to perform some specified tasks. Its composition then was as follows:

61 Mountain Brigade.   Brig Tom Pande

7 Rajputana Rifles
2 Jat
12 Kumaon

As already discussed, the original IV Corps plan was to secure Daudkundi by using concentric pincers by 57 Mountain Division from the north and 23 Mountain Division from the south. This plan was, however, changed by General Sagat Singh after the fall of Akhaura. Under the modified plan, the responsibility to launch the main offensive operation in this area was entrusted to 23 Mountain Division, commanded by Major General R D Hira. The task allotted to him was to initially capture southern part of Lalmai Hills and Laksham; his eventual strategic objective was Chandpur. Through air photos as well as input by the Mukti Bahini, General Hira had become fully aware of the natural strength of the Pakistan defences and wanted to avoid a frontal attack on a well- prepared position unless absolutely necessary. He was thus determined to find a way of bypassing prepared defensive positions by turning the flanks and infiltrating through gaps between them.

Considering all these factors, he decided to use the following two approaches for his offensive:[156]

1. **Northern Approach.** Along the Track Himmatpur (on the Indian border)- Kashinagar- Bhuschi-Bhora- Mudafarganj. (Bhuschi was an important nodal point east of Laksham-Comilla Road where several tracks converged.)

2. **Southern Approach.** Along the Track Radhanagar (on the Indian border)- Chauddagram- Laksham.

To perform the assigned tasks, General Hira conceived the plan to infiltrate a strong force through the Lalmai- Laksham gap, with another force advancing along Chauddagram- Laksham road. He planned to use Brig Pande's 61 Mountain Brigade in a flank protection role to preclude any threat from the north. The Scheme of Manoeuvre planned by him was as follows:

- 301 Mountain Brigade to infiltrate along the Northern Approach with 1 Armoured Squadron (PT-76 tanks) under its command.
- 181 Mountain Brigade to follow 301 Mountain Brigade and then advance to isolate Laksham from north and west.
- 83 Mountain Brigade to advance along the Southern Approach, Chauddagram-Laksham, and isolate Laksham from the south;
- After the isolation of Laksham, both 301 and 181 Mountain Brigades were then to capture Laksham.

---

[156] Maj Gen Lachhman Singh, *Op Cit,* page 216.

- After the capture of Laksham, 301 Mountain Brigade was to advance and capture Chandpur.
- 61 Mountain Brigade ex 57 Mountain Division to secure the northern flank of the Divisional operations.

Twilight Operations

The Indians commenced their probing attacks in this area on 21st November. Several BOPs were attacked and Mukti Bahini infiltrated to carry out subversive activities. By this time, Brig Pande's 61 Mountain Brigade too had concentrated in this area, while the other formations were already poised for action.

15 Baluch (53 Pak Brigade), with its Battalion HQ located at Feni, was initially deployed mainly within the Belonia salient but was very thin on the ground because of its extended frontage. The increasing Indian activity in the surrounding area, where 23 Mountain Division had by then concentrated, forced the unit to withdraw to Feni during night 24th /25th November. On 28th November, apprehending threat developing towards Laksham and Chandpur, Brig Aslam Niazi, commanding 53 Pak Brigade, also decided to withdraw his HQ from Feni and moved to Hajiganj, some 32 kilometers away.

During the night 1st /2nd December, Brig Pande launched 7 Raj Rif towards Pipulia, guided by Mukti Bahini scouts. A company of 30 Punjab (117 Pak Brigade) deployed there was surprised by the sudden attack and had to readjust its positions to the rear. Brig Pande then established his positions around Pipulia, thus not only providing flank protection to the operations of 23 Mountain Division but was also well-placed to pose a simultaneous threat towards Lalmai Hills and Comilla airfield.

The War Commences

As soon as the formal war commenced on 3rd December, Brig Sodhi's 301 Mountain Brigade launched the Divisional offensive by infiltrating through the gap between 30 Punjab and 23 Punjab. Apparently, Brig Sodhi had acquired very accurate intelligence about the exact positions occupied by these two battalions through Mukti Bahini sources and exploited it very skillfully. 14 Jat Battalion and 1/11 Gurkha Battalion moved cross-country astride the Northern Approach after last light 3rd December, with tanks following them. Soon these two battalions came into contact with B

Company of 25 FF near Mian Bazar. 14 Jats were ordered to tackle the positions of 25 FF Battalion from the south while 1/11 Gurkhas continued with their advance by infiltration to establish a block near Kashinagar on the west.

The company of 25 FF fell back hoping to occupy their prepared main defensive position at Kashinagar, only to find the Gurkhas already there. In the confused melee that ensued, a large number of unsuspecting Piffers fell into the hands of the Gurkhas; the entire Battalion HQ of 25 FF including its CO, Lt Colonel Akbar Beg and some 114 officers, JCOs and other ranks were taken prisoner.[157] This thrust had also served to create a wide gap between Laksham and the rest of 117 Pak Brigade in the Lalmai Hills. Through this gap, it became possible for a major part of 23 Mountain Division to easily move to the areas in depth.

After this successful action, Brig Sodhi concentrated his 301 Mountain Brigade at Bhuschi and cut the Lalmai-Laksham Road near Bhora by first light 5th December; and established roadblocks to the north and west of Laksham the same day. Meanwhile, 181 Mountain Brigade also came into a position to launch its operations.

Thus, within a span of just 24 hours, 23 Mountain Division had created a very dangerous gap in the defensive system of 39 (A) Division and succeeded in unbalancing it completely without any major effort on their part. The Indians at this point were well-poised to develop a major threat towards Laksham and Chandpur while the Pakistani forces had been deprived of any meaningful reaction capability, and that too so early in the war.

In view of the developing Indian threat towards Laksham and Chandpur, which potentially could pose a threat towards Dacca too, General Rahim Khan, in desperation, decided to concentrate his troops mainly for the defence of Laksham and Comilla fortresses only. Consequently, he ordered 53 Pak Brigade to fall back to Laksham with 15 Baluch, 39 Baluch and two companies of 21 AK, which was done during night 5th/6th December. Commenting on this situation, General Shaukat Riza, who had earlier commanded 9 Pak Division in this very area, says:

"53 Brigade was awkwardly deployed. 15 Baluch was scattered along the Belonia salient. It was an invitation for Indian troops to get to Feni without serious trouble. 39 Baluch was scattered between Feni and Chauddagram. It was in little position to seal off Indian infiltration. The unhinging of these two battalions virtually finished the war for 53 Brigade. Some of the remnants got through to Comilla while some remained in

---

[157] *Ibid*, page 219.

Laksham."[158]

At this point, possibly misreading the presence of Brig Pande's 61 Mountain Brigade at nearby town of Pipulia, Brig Atif, commander 53 Pak Brigade, appears to have formed the somewhat nervous misperception that the Indians had concentrated a large force north of Comilla with a view to attacking the Maynamati complex. Thereupon, he decided to consolidate his defences in Maynamati Complex by concentrating most of his troops there; in the process, he considered it prudent to evacuate Comilla city as well as the airfield. As soon as the Indians learnt of the vacation of Comilla through the Mukti Bahini sources, 14 Jat was ordered to secure Comilla from the south and clear the airfield; obviously, this was accomplished without any resistance.

While 301 Mountain Brigade continued with its advance along the northern approach, Brig Sandhu's 181 Mountain Brigade had also come in a position by 4th December to launch its offensive towards Laksham in accordance with the Divisional plan. However, since 23 Punjab (117 Pak Brigade) was still holding on to Chauddagram, Brig Sandhu considered it prudent to clear them out before advancing westwards so his artillery could also move forward along the Chauddagram-Laksham Road.

181 Mountain Brigade managed to clear Chauddagram by 10 AM on 5th December after stiff resistance by 23 Punjab. This brave unit made many attempts to break out but were effectively checked by roadblocks placed behind them on the Laksham Road and suffered many casualties in the process. Ultimately, they did manage to withdraw to Laksham along minor cross-country tracks, and joined 53 Pak Brigade there. While withdrawing, they did not neglect to blow up the bridge on River Dakatia near Parikot; this imposed some further delay on the advance of 181 Mountain Brigade towards Laksham.

After successfully dealing with 23 Punjab, 181 Mountain Brigade finally managed to commence its advance towards Laksham on 6th December. By first light on 7th December, they had succeeded in establishing roadblocks to the south and southeast of Laksham. These in effect complemented the roadblocks already established two days earlier to the west and north of this city by Brig Sodhi's 301 Mountain Brigade. Thus, by 7th December, Laksham had been surrounded by these two brigades of 23 Mountain Division from all the sides. Meanwhile, Sodhi's Brigade had captured Mudafarganj as well.

---

[158] Maj Gen Shaukat Riza, *Op Cit,* page 158.

At this stage, Pakistan's 39 (A) Division had chosen to box itself in a desperate situation. Under the orders of General Rahim Khan, most of its troops had been concentrated within the two fortresses: Maynamati in the north and Laksham in the south. The yawning gap in the middle of the two fortresses thus bestowed full liberty of action upon 23 Mountain Division to freely operate in the entire area.

As mentioned, Brig Sodhi had earlier managed to secure Mudafarganj but had been able to concentrate only two battalions (3 Kumaon and 1/11 Gurkha) with a squadron of tanks there; his artillery assets were still out of range. Sensing this situation, General Rahim Khan finally decided to react.

On 7th December, he ordered Brig Aslam Niazi, commander 53 Pak Brigade, to recapture Mudafarganj and to remove all the roadblocks set up by 301 Mountain Brigade. Brig Niazi decided to continue holding Laksham Fortress with 39 Baluch, and to attack Mudafarganj with two composite task forces. Each of these task forces comprised a mixed group of more than a battalion strength, commanded by the COs of 15 Baluch and 21 AK respectively.

15 Baluch Group attacked Mudafarganj after last light 7th December but were beaten back by 1/11 Gurkhas. 21 AK Group attempted to clear the roadblock set up by 3 Kumaon but were also beaten back. After these ill-planned and uncoordinated attempts at clearing Mudafarganj, Brig Niazi called 15 Baluch back to Laksham and ordered 21 AK Group to hold Hajiganj, little knowing that by then Brig Sodhi was already established there. In the event, even 15 Baluch could not make it back to Laksham under constant Indian pressure, and kept moving about in the countryside aimlessly.

21 AK Group, comprising elements of 21 AK and 23 Punjab, ran straight into an Indian gun position near Hajiganj at about midday 8th December. The Indian gunners resorted to direct fire over open sights and inflicted heavy casualties on them. Under the unexpected onslaught, the unit disintegrated and scattered into numerous small groups. These dispirited troops were by now short of rations and ammunition, and of course without any artillery cover; in utter desperation, they decided to abandon their heavy weapons so they could move about more easily. The Indian units, helped by Mukti Bahini, were having a field day picking up these hapless remnants as they moved helter skelter all over the area.[159]

---

[159] Lt Gen Kamal Matinuddin, *Op Cit,* page 413.

While operations around Laksham were still in progress, General Rahim Khan apparently came to the conclusion that it would be futile to continue making any efforts to defend the entire area; instead, he decided to concentrate all his available forces only within the Maynamati complex. Without giving any thought to all the serious strategic implications of his impulsive decision, he directed Brig Atif to vacate the southern portion of Lalmai Hills as well, including Lalmai village, and to move all his troops to within the Maynamati complex.

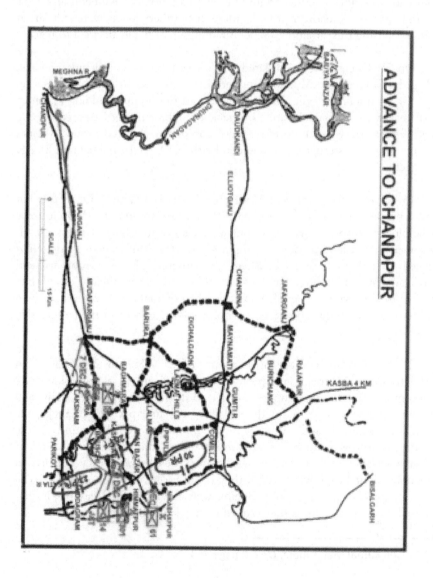

This decision was an unexpected bonanza for the Indians as it provided them with unhindered access to the vital road communications towards Chandpur. Capitalizing on this astonishing windfall, a jubilant General Hira ordered 181 Mountain Brigade to occupy the vacated Lalmai village and the surrounding hills immediately. The unhindered use of this road to Chandpur thus became available for all Indian vehicular traffic on 8th December. The availability of this critical axis immensely eased their logistic support problems. Eventually, it also facilitated the subsequent regrouping and move of their troops to Daudkundi, and then towards Dacca.

It is a noteworthy point that so far, the Indians had consciously avoided getting involved in any pitched battle with the troops of 53 and 117 Pak Brigades holed up in the fortresses of Laksham and Maynamati. Instead, Brig Sodhi's 301 Mountain Brigade was rapidly advancing towards the strategic objective of Chandpur, which at this time was virtually undefended. Soon enough, this Brigade had captured Hajiganj too, barely some 25 kilometers from Chandpur.

GOC 39 (A) Division, stranded at his HQ at Chandpur, had been left with no Divisional reserves to influence the battle in any way. His utility and role as the Divisional Commander was practically over by now. As a matter of fact, he did not even possess adequate troops to defend his HQ properly; only an infantry company and some maintenance personnel were all the troops left at his disposal. After the capture of Hajiganj, Chandpur was under direct threat by the advancing Indian forces. However, even before that, on 6th December Rahim Khan had already made up his mind to evacuate Chandpur as early as possible.

This, however, was a slow and tedious process as all moves had to be carried out by rivercraft and only at night. HQ 39 (A) Division with all its supporting elements finally evacuated Chandpur on night 8th /9th December. Its destination was Narayanganj, just a few kilometers southeast of Dacca on the west bank of River Meghna. To his credit, Rahim Khan's landing craft was the last one to leave Chandpur. This important river convoy was evidently a prime target and the slow process of move had been duly noticed by the IAF. By the time they reached Narayanganj, it was bright daylight and the boats became prey to direct hits from the attacking Indian aircraft. General Rahim Khan himself was wounded and evacuated to CMH Dacca. All other members of his Divisional HQ except for his ADC and one staff officer were killed or wounded. The casualties included the gallant Major Bilal Rana SJ, the captor of Sheikh Mujibur Rahman too.

Thus 39 (A) Division which had been raised on 20th November 1971 ceased to exist on 9th December the same year.[160] 301 Mountain Brigade reached an undefended, evacuated Chandpur on 9th December.

The brigades of 39 (A) Division were left rudderless with no one left in the field to guide them; the two brigade commanders had no option but to rely on their own judgements. Brig Aslam Niazi, commander 53 Pak Brigade was the first one to use his initiative. On night 8th/9th December, he took the precipitate decision to exfiltrate out of Laksham. He ordered his troops to slip out in small parties and head towards the fortress of Maynamati; he also took the highly questionable decision to abandon all his sick and wounded personnel behind with only one doctor and some nursing staff.

Predictably, the bulk of the exfiltrating personnel of Laksham garrison were taken prisoner by the Indians as they moved helter skelter in small parties. A few of these groups were lucky to reach Maynamati after some clashes with the Indians en route. Lt Colonel Naeem, CO 39 Baluch, however, had decided to defy his Commander's orders and instead chose to move out with his entire unit. Under his orders, they had left behind all their heavy weapons and moved out on man packed basis. Naeem took a circuitous route to avoid the Indians but finally had to surrender before Brig Pande on 12th December near Chandina.

However, Brig Niazi himself with about 200 men did manage to reach the Maynamati complex. The war for Brig Aslam Niazi and his 53 Pak Brigade was practically over. After the war, a rueful Brig Niazi was to tell Brig Pande: *"I was outmanoeuvred. The Indian Army was always 36 hours ahead of me."*[161]

A jubilant General Sagat Singh visited Chandpur on 12th December and discussed the developing situation. As there was still no possibility of arranging adequate rivercraft to cross the Meghna, Sagat Singh took the following decisions:

- 23 Mountain Division with 181 Mountain Brigade and 61 Mountain Brigade to reduce the Maynamati Complex where Brig Atif was still holding out.
- 301 Mountain Brigade to move to Daudkundi and cross the Meghna to secure Baidya Bazar on the western bank for developing

---

[160] Ibid.
[161] Brig Lachhman Singh, *Op Cit*, page 223.

operations against Dacca.

- The crossing to take place under the aegis of HQ 23 Mountain Division but the Brigade to come under command HQ IV Corps after crossing the Meghna.

Daudkundi was secured by 12 Kumaon and a troop of tanks on 9th December, brushing aside minor opposition en route. Thus, on this fateful date, the Indian troops had reached all the three key points on the Meghna: Ashuganj, Daudkundi and Chandpur. All approaches from the Meghna to Dacca were now open to them and the vital Meghna Bulge was fully secured within a period of about a week.

On this very date, Maynamati Complex had also been invested from all sides: 61 Mountain Brigade closed in from the north and west while 181 Mountain Brigade had closed in from the south.

This position remained essentially unchanged till 16th December when the Maynamati garrison surrendered with 86 officers, 175 JCOs and some 4000 other ranks.[162]

Operations in Chittagong Zone

It will be recalled that in the initial operational planning at the Indian Army Headquarters, General Manekshaw had accorded a very high priority to the early capture of Chittagong. This was ostensibly aimed at denying at an early stage the routes of supply, and even evacuation, to the Pakistan's Eastern Garrison. After the effective blockade of Chittagong carried out by the Indian Navy, this city lost much of its strategic importance in the eyes of the Indian Army planners. Furthermore, its distance from the scene of main operations in the Eastern Sector served to relegate it to a peripheral operational priority. This had been accurately appreciated by General Niazi and so reflected itself in the quantum and quality of troops allocated to this Zone.

This Zone was defined in the north by River Feni with two rail and road bridges over it and in the south by Chittagong city and port complex. Topographically, it was a rather narrow corridor formed on the western side by the Bay of Bengal and in the east by a range of hills. This corridor, between the hills and the sea, is quite narrow in the south; at Foujdarhat, it is only about 1000 meters but becomes progressively wider as we proceed north towards Chittagong. The main highway and the railway line run parallel to each other in this corridor all the way from Feni to Chittagong.

---

[162] Lt Gen J FR Jacob, *Op Cit*, page 121.

The ground here is generally broken with numerous water channels running east to west. Tracked and vehicular traffic would find it difficult to move cross-country and perforce have to remain confined to the road alignment, which is higher than the surrounding area. The growth is generally thick and visibility limited to about 200 meters at places.

The composition of the Pakistan forces placed in the Chittagong Zone was as follows:

91 (A) Brigade　　　　**Brig Taskeen-ud-Din**　　　　Karerhat (near Feni)

Company 24 FF
Wing EPCAF
Rangers Battalion
Mujahid Battalion
171 Mortar Battery less troop.

97 (A) brigade　　　　**Brig Atta Malik**　　　　Chittagong

48 Baluch
24 FF less company
2 Commando Battalion (-)
Wing EPCAF
Marine Battalion Pakistan Navy
Troop ex 171 Mortar Battery

The attack on Chittagong was predictably preceded by air action. Four aircraft of the IAF attacked Chittagong Port area at first light on 4th December; this pattern of air attacks was continually repeated for quite some time by waves of four aircraft each. The uncontested air attacks inflicted heavy damage, particularly in the port area. Two oil tanks of Dawood Petroleum and one civilian ship in harbour were set on fire and were observed burning over a large distance.

On this day, Lt Colonel Raja Asghar, in command of an ad hoc composite battalion, reached Karerhat to take up a defensive position along River Feni as part of 91 (A) Brigade. Three of his companies were deployed on the home bank of the river, while the fourth company was placed in depth. Colonel Asghar Raja placed his own HQ at Karerhat, quite close to where HQ 91 (A) Brigade was also located.

No further activity took place on this front till 6th December but the defenders could hear the artillery guns booming at a distance.

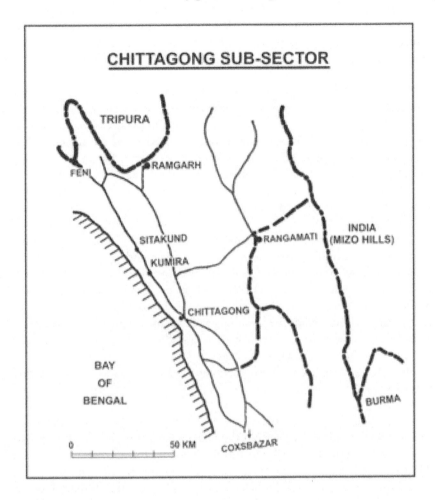

Following the capture of Laksham, the town of Feni too was vacated by the troops of 53 Pak Brigade at last light 6th December and the town was immediately occupied by the Indian 'KILO' Force. Brig Taskeen-ud-Din, commander 91 (A) Brigade, appreciated that the Indians would soon advance towards Chittagong on this axis. He considered discretion the better part of valour and ordered the withdrawal of his force during night 7th /8th December to take up a defensive position between Kumira and Foujdarhat, further south.

251

In order to give time to his troops to prepare the main position properly, he established two screens at Mirsarai and Sitakund with about a company each. The screen at Mirsarai was commanded by Major Hafeez of EPCAF and was tasked not to withdraw before last light 9th December. The screen at Sitakund was commanded by Major Shamshad, also of EPCAF, and was tasked not to withdraw before last light 10th December.

The main defensive position was taken up by Brig Taskeen between Foujdarhat and Kumira; the left forward company, commanded by Major Bangash, deployed from the sea up to the main road; the right forward company, commanded by Captain Tariq, deployed from the main road to the foot of the hills. Behind Tariq's company, Captain Sarfraz's company formed the second layer. An advance position was also established at Kumira and took up its positions at a high ground near a sanatorium there. And now they waited for the enemy.

Finding the Karerhat area vacated by the Pakistani troops, KILO Force advanced and captured the area up to Karerhat and Zurar Ganj on 8th December. Thereafter, they began to advance towards Chittagong and soon hit the main defensive position of 91 (A) Brigade. The untrained soldiers of different arms and services, hurriedly assembled into ad hoc units and sub-units, just could not stand before the sustained Indian attacks by troops of KILO Force trained in mountain warfare and the position was lost on 12th December. The withdrawing Pakistani troops then took up a defensive position at Kumarighat with two companies. This too was cleared during night 13th /14th December.

Meanwhile, it appears that Lt General Sagat Singh, commander IV Corps, became rather keen to add the feather of capturing this prize city to his cap at the earliest. In order to further speed up the advance, he directed 83 Mountain Brigade to concentrate in Sitakund area by 12th December. At about this time, General Manekshaw also directed the Indian Eastern Command to integrate Special Frontier Force, raised and trained by Major General Sujan Singh Oban, in operations against Chittagong. General Jacob, COS Eastern Command, directed this force to move from Mizoram into Chittagong Hill Tracts, capture Rangamati and then pose a direct threat to Chittagong from that direction.

With the induction of 83 Mountain Brigade in this sub-sector, the complexion of the entire operation completely changed. This force reached Foujdarhat the morning of 15th December. However, further operations were suspended thereafter in view of the anticipated surrender. On 16th December, the surrender became a reality when orders to this effect were received from Pak Eastern Command.

On that day, Brig Taskeen-ud-Din met Brig Sandhu of 83 Mountain Brigade to finalize the details of the surrender. It was a great irony of fate that Brig Taskeen had to surrender before Brig Sandhu, who as a cadet in the IMA was in the platoon of then Captain Taskeen. But such are the fortunes of war!

Amphibious Operation at Cox's Bazar

Cox's Bazar is a popular sea resort in the extreme south of Chittagong District, famous for its pristine beaches. From this town, a narrow road took off along the Teknaf peninsula, which was separated from Burma (now Myanmar) by the mighty River Naaf. This quaint, little town was chosen by the Indian High Command for an amphibian venture, the only one attempted by them during this war.

On 9th December, General Manekshaw directed HQ Indian Eastern Command to send a force by sea to Cox's Bazar area in order to prevent Pakistani troops escaping from that direction to neighbouring Burma. Apparently, this plan had been conceived by the three Indian Chiefs of Staff and as such the protestations made by the Eastern Command were simply ignored and the operation, code-named ROMEO was duly set to be launched, albeit with inadequate equipment and untrained troops. The following forces were hastily assembled for the purpose:

- HQ 8 Mountain Artillery Brigade, commanded by Brig S S Rai ex II Corps.
- 1/3 Gurkha Rifles.
- Two companies ex 11 Bihar Battalion.
- A detachment of artillery.
- A Naval contingent of 150, which however did not arrive in time.
- Air and fire support to be provided by aircraft carrier *Vikrant*.

A merchant ship *Vishwa Vijay* was requisitioned for the purposes of the operation and the whole force set sail from Calcutta on 12th December. Because of the troops' lack of training, the original plan was to transfer them from the ship using two Landing Craft, which were to be beached first and then refloated at high tide, so that the troops could land dry shod; this plan was however later changed by the Navy. The Indian Navy had instead decided on its own to disembark the troops on boats instead of the landing craft, as originally decided. The aircraft Carrier Vikrant also could not participate in the operation at all due to other commitments.

The operation was beset with several snags right from the beginning. The force while still at sea was transferred to INS *Gildar* and *Gharial* on 14th December. The landing itself proved to be a disaster and caused several casualties. Lucky for them, there were no Pakistan troops in Cox's Bazar area to offer any resistance and only a small Mukti Bahini camp was found active in the area. Eventually, the troops were disembarked from the ships on country boats provided by the local population. That was the ignominious end of this solitary amphibian operation by India in this war.

The Episode of PNS *Ghazi*

Just before the commencement of the war, HQ Indian Eastern Command had come to learn through signal intercepts that a Pakistani submarine PNS *Ghazi* had entered the Bay of Bengal. This to a certain extent had limited the freedom of action of the Indian Navy in that zone.

On 3rd December, General Jacob, COS Indian Eastern Command, was informed by Admiral Krishnan, Flag Officer Commanding-in-Chief of Eastern Naval Command, that the wreckage of a Pakistan submarine had been found by some fishermen on approaches to Vishakhapatnam Port. According to him, the blowing up of this submarine on 1st or 2nd December, while engaged in laying mines to block the Port, was an 'act of God'; he also opined that it would restore the freedom of action to the Indian Navy.

The next morning Admiral Krishnan rang up Jacob again in some panic and enquired if the above incident had been reported to New Delhi; General Jacob said that he had not done so as he was under the impression that the needful would be done through Naval channels. Krishnan thanked him and told him to forget about the whole thing.

The official Naval version given out later was that PNS Ghazi had been sunk by ships of the Eastern Indian Fleet on 4th December![163]

This is one way of seeking credit in a war.

---

[163] *Ibid,* page 104.

CENTRAL SECTOR

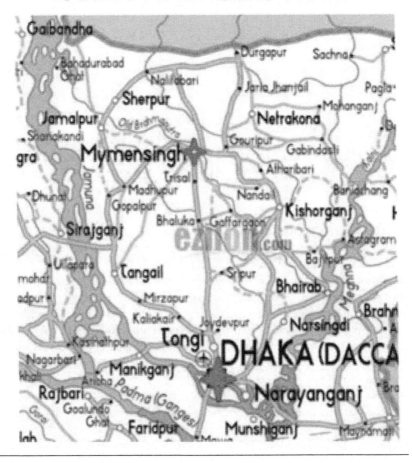

8

OPERATIONS IN THE CENTRAL SECTOR (MYMENSINGH-DACCA)

The Central Sector of the Eastern Theatre was generally shaped like a huge 'V' or an inverted triangle, with its apex resting around Dacca, and its two sides resting on Rivers Jamuna and Meghna. Important cities of operational significance in this Sector comprised Mymensingh, Jamalpur, Tangail and finally, Dacca itself. From the Indian point of view, in the absence of any major water obstacles en route, this Sector provided the easiest approach to Dacca with the least number of major natural obstacles en route. Moreover, the western flank of the advancing forces was secured by the Jamuna while the Meghna, and subsequently the Lakhya protected their eastern flank.

The eastern part of this Sector is generally low-lying and has several water obstacles, increasing in number and obstacle value as one nears the Meghna. The ground level in the western part is comparatively at a higher level from south of Mymensingh to east of Tangail, including the Madhupur Forest area, which comprises broken, hilly ground with heavy growth.

Most rivers in the Sector flow north to south along the grain of the country. The old course of River Brahmaputra runs diagonally from northwest to southeast bisecting the Sector horizontally, roughly about forty kilometers south of the border; locally, this river was called the Old Brahmaputra but compared to the great Brahmaputra (Jamuna) to the west, its obstacle value was rather insignificant. After skirting around Mymensingh, this river swings sharply south and then onwards, it is known as River Lakhya.

256

There were no bridges on the River Old Brahmaputra and only two main ferries over it were situated at Jamalpur and Mymensingh. These two ferry sites were linked by a lateral road and a railway line along the southern bank of the Old Brahmaputra, connecting Mymensingh and Jamalpur with Dacca. This railway line as well as most roads in the area generally conformed to the river lines to minimize bridges.

The area situated to the west and south of Old Brahmaputra was of great operational significance to Dacca. Since mid-1971, the countryside around Tangail and Madhupur had been under domination of the guerrilla force of Tiger Siddiqui, said to have as many as twenty thousand militants in his outfit.

On the Indian side of this Sector lay the Meghalaya state, which at that time possessed limited road network only. Tura was the main communication centre in the area, from where originated the two main roads leading into this Sector to Mymensingh and Jamalpur. Tura was also linked by a good road with the main railhead at Gauhati, a well-developed administrative base served by several airfields around it. Logistically, operations in this Sector could be better supported compared with areas further east.

A large number of routes led into this Sector from India but all of these eventually converged on to either of two focal communication centres: Jamalpur or Mymensingh. Jamalpur was a small town on the southern bank of the Brahmaputra while Mymensingh was the main city in the Sector. There were hardly any towns of importance north of this river.

The two main axes of advance available to the Indian forces into this Sector were:

- Kamalpur-Jamalpur- Tangail-Kaliakar-Tungi-Dacca axis, based on a metalled road from the border down to Dacca, skirting the western slopes of the high ground of the Madhupur Forest.

- Haluaghat-Phulpur-Mymensingh- Madhupur- Dacca axis, based on the main highway from the border running all the way to Dacca.

Note: Both these axes converged at Madhupur and from then on, only one main road led on to Tangail.

- Tangail, next to Mymensingh, was the most important city and communication centre in the Sector, situated at the junction of all the roads leading south towards Dacca. However, from Tangail onwards, only one road ran south to Kaliakar; notably, there were no water obstacles between Tangail and Kaliakar. Beyond Kaliakar, Dacca could be approached along the following two axes, while roads serving both these axes were properly bridged all the way:

:

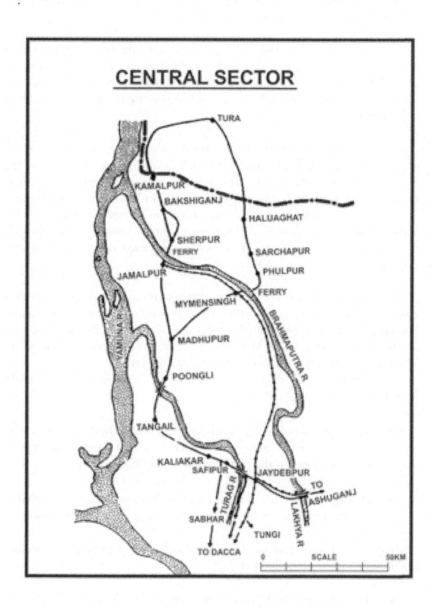

258

- Kaliakar-Chandina (across the River Turag)-Tungi-Dacca.

- Kaliakar-Dhamrai-Sabhar (across the River Dhaleshwari)-Mirpur (across the River Turag)-Dacca.

Despite these obvious operational advantages, the Indian planners persisted in according low operational priority to this Sector till very late in the war. One obvious reason, perhaps, was that in the initial stages, the Indians at the highest level were not considering Dacca as the culminating point of their manoeuvre. At that time, they were really more interested in other main cities like Jessore, Comilla and Rangpur rather than Dacca itself. Since there were no worthwhile prestigious cities north of the Old Brahmaputra, this Sector offered little attraction to the planners, who were then looking for the public relations value of early gains.[164]

Pakistan Forces

Initially, when 9 Pak Division was flown into East Pakistan in early April, the responsibility of this area had been entrusted to 27 Pak Brigade. Later, when General Niazi carried out his post-monsoon reorganization, this Brigade was moved out and the area was entrusted to 93 (A) Brigade, commanded by Brig Abdul Qadir Niazi. In late November, this Brigade was placed under command of the newly raised 36 (A) Division, commanded by Major General Muhammad Jamshed SJ, MC, already performing the duties of DG EPCAF and functioning as General Niazi's unofficial second-in-command as well.

It is, thus, obvious that the entire operational responsibility of this Sector was being handled in an entirely ad hoc and perfunctory manner by Pak Eastern Command. In hindsight, General Niazi appears entirely oblivious to the possibility of an unexpected breakthrough in this Sector, which could potentially generate a direct and dangerous threat to Dacca itself. In his arrogant overconfidence, he had totally neglected the conclusions and recommendations made by astute military minds like General Sahibzada Yaqub Khan and General Farman Ali Khan during the earlier planning process.

---

[164] Maj Gen Lachhman Singh, *Op cit*, page 148.

259

At the end of November 1971, the composition of the Pakistan forces operating in the Central Sector was as follows:

1. **HQ 36 (A) Division Dacca**   **Maj Gen Muhammad Jamshed**

2. **93 (A) Brigade Mymensingh**   **Brig Abdul Qadir**

    a. 31 Baluch Jamalpur   Lt Col Ahmed Sultan

    b. 33 Punjab Mymensingh   Lt Col Manzur Ahmed

    c. 2 Wing EPCAF Baluch   Under command 31

    d. 61 Wing WP Rangers Punjab   Under command 33

    e. 83 Mortar Battery   Maj Ghaffar Shah (12 x 120 mm Mors)

It would be readily obvious that the grandiose cover of an infantry division created in this Sector was just a hoax and the Indians had seen through the deception fairly early. With the rebel forces of Tiger Siddiqui active in this entire area, the Indians had gained accurate intelligence about the actual defensive layout of the Pakistan forces in this Sector. The Indian High Command had also correctly appreciated that the possibility of any major reinforcement to this Sector would be highly unlikely; General Niazi would be doing so only at the risk of denuding Dacca even further.[165] In fact, the actual plan conceived by General Niazi expected this Brigade to hold the Indian advance for as long as possible, and then fall back intact to strengthen the Dacca defences.

The deployment pattern of the Pakistani Brigade had, by itself, made it obvious to the Indians that Brig Qadir Niazi would fight his main defensive battle from behind the line of Old Brahamaputra, with his two regular battalions deployed at Jamalpur and Mymensingh in strong, fortified

---

[165] Maj Gen Sukhwant Singh, *Op Cit,* pages 185-185.

positions Moreover, several delaying positions had been prepared along both the axes between the border and the river.

Accordingly, Brig Qadir had, *ab initio,* deployed 31 Baluch at Jamalpur, and 33 Punjab at Mymensingh - Haluaghat. He had distributed his twelve mortars equally between these two units. In his own smug perception, Brig Qadir had taken up a very balanced defensive posture; his left flank was protected by the mighty River Jamuna while his right flank was secured from across the River Surma in Sylhet by 202 (A) Brigade, part of 14 Pak Division.

However, Brig Qadir, who used to teach us tactics at the PMA, could never have imagined, at that time, that it would be through his Brigade that the Indians would strike the final blow at Dacca; an ironic destiny had decreed that the weakest Indian force would push through this even more weakly held Sector and demand surrender from Commander Pak Eastern Command!

Indian Forces

The Pak Eastern Command was not the only one resorting to ad hoc measures in this Sector; the Indian Eastern Command too was taking recourse to similar expediency.

As discussed earlier, the Indian Army Chief, General Manekshaw, had refused to release 6 Mountain Division for taking command of Indian troops in this Sector. Consequently, General Aurora was left with no option but to employ HQ 101 Communication Zone Area for this purpose and to place it under his own direct command. This formation was essentially a static organization, which hitherto was responsible for providing logistic support to troops in the eastern regions of India. Now, almost overnight it was transformed into an operational HQ on an ad hoc basis, albeit with its existing staff. The only redeeming feature of this ad hoc formation was its commander, Major General Gurbax Singh Gill, known in the Indian Army as a competent and tough professional. He had earlier been, somehow, relegated to a logistic command and was now anxious to regain his position in the Army hierarchy by conducting a successful operation. [166]

101 Communication Zone Area was originally assigned the limited task to reach the line of the Old Brahmaputra, capture Jamalpur and Mymensingh, and, in the process, destroy the Pakistan forces deployed in

---

[166] Maj Gen Lachhman Singh, *Op cit*, page 149.

Tangail and Mymensingh districts within 14 days of the outbreak of hostilities. The words of an Indian planner succinctly describe the limited operational role visualized for General Gurbux Singh:

"It was visualized that the destruction and capture of 93 Infantry Brigade Group and other paramilitary troops under its command would deprive the Dacca fortress of its potential strength. If this was successfully achieved, it would contribute significantly to the campaign."[167]

For this purpose, General Gurbax Singh was allocated the following forces under his command:

1. **95 Mountain Brigade**   **Brig H S Kler**

       13 Guards
       1 Maratha LI
       13 Raj Rif
       5/5 Gurkha
       56 Mountain Regiment (76 mm guns)
       Battery 90 Mountain Regiment (75/24 mm guns)
       2 x batteries Light Regiment (120 mm mortars)

2. **Mukti Bahini Brigade (FJ Sector)**   **Brig Sant Singh MVC**

       6 Bihar
       Mukti Bahini Battalion
       83 SF Battalion
       11 Sector Mukti Bahini

3. This Sector was also allocated 5 and 167 Mountain Brigades from 6 Mountain Division but these, however, could not become available in time for the operations.

4. No armour was allocated for this Sector.

An ambitious and determined General Gurbux Singh could hardly be satisfied with such a limited role for his force. He made strong, repeated protestations to HQ Indian Eastern Command that his troops were capable of achieving much more than this limited task and in fact would be in a position to create a credible threat to Dacca from the north. Quite

---

[167] Maj Gen Sukhwant Singh, *Op cit*, page 185.

obviously, General Gurbux Singh looked upon this opportunity as a means to rehabilitating himself in the Army. His exuberance eventually succeeded in gaining a strong ally in the person of General Jacob, COS Eastern Command. Consequently, the task assigned to 101 Communication Zone Area was revised and made more ambitious:

- Capture Kamalpur by D plus 2.

- Capture Jamalpur by D plus 6/7.

- Air drop by a para battalion on Tangail on D plus 7.

- Capture Tangail by D plus 8.

- Contact Dacca defences by D plus 12/13.

General Gurbax Singh had quickly grasped the essentials of the task assigned him. It was obvious to him that while his own superiority in numbers was only marginal, the defender had been forced to accentuate his numerical weakness by the compulsion to defend two axes with almost equal strength. The best chance Gurbax Singh had was to exploit this weakness deftly.

Accordingly, he conceived the plan to launch his main thrust with 95 Mountain Brigade along Kamalpur-Bakhshiganj- Jamalpur axis, a relatively less expected approach. Simultaneously, he planned to keep the Pakistan forces fully engaged along the other available axes by simulating a brigade plus advance as follows:[168]

- Auxiliary effort with 6 Bihar, augmented by Mukti Bahini elements, under Brig Sant Singh's FJ Sector, along Haluaghat-Phulpur-Mymensingh axis.

- Auxiliary effort with 83 BSF Battalion along Baghmara-Mymensingh track.

The scarlet thread of his scheme of manoeuvre was to fix the Pakistan garrison operating along Haluaghat- Mymensingh axis by a show of force by FJ Sector and meanwhile to overwhelm the Jamalpur garrison by using the full strength of his 95 Mountain Brigade. After the capture of Jamalpur,

---

[168] *Ibid,* pages 185-186.

Gurbax Singh planned to press on to Tangail, while outflanking/ isolating the Mymensingh garrison. He had also been promised a para drop at Tangail to speed up his operations towards Dacca. General Jacob had visualized the air drop to take place on D+7 and the link up to be accomplished within twenty-four hours of that. Later events proved this assessment accurate. Once the bottleneck of Tangail was effectively secured, no force could pass through and fall back on Dacca, certainly not a cohesive force. The entire countryside around was, in any case, infested by the militant elements of Tiger Siddiqui Group, thus making it very unlikely even for small parties to pass through. Thereafter, his entire Brigade, along with the Tiger Siddiqui Force, was to advance towards Dacca with all speed.

Operations in Jamalpur Sub Sector

Kamalpur is a small town hardly more than 1000 meters from the border, which lay directly on the main thrust line of 95 Mountain Brigade. Brig Kler, therefore, decided to capture Kamalpur as a preliminary operation during the twilight phase; for this, he planned to use the Mukti Bahini Battalion, supported by regular troops, as and when necessary. Kamalpur post was then being held by a composite company of 31 Baluch Battalion, commanded by Captain Ahsan Malik.

The initial attack was launched on 18th November after heavy preparatory bombardment, followed by covering fire. The assaulting troops had almost reached the Pakistani bunkers under the artillery umbrella but as soon as the covering fire lifted, they came under heavy machine gun fire from the defenders. The attack had to called off after suffering heavy casualties.

In order to provide effective fire support to the defenders at Kamalpur during this attack, Captain Siddiqui of 83 Mortar Battery had taken four of his mortars forward. It appears that Brig Kler was somewhat familiar with the common Pakistani practice of keeping their mortars at one central position and moving them forward to the threatened sectors, as and when required. Making use of this knowledge, Brig Kler ordered elements of 1 Maratha LI Battalion to infiltrate and set up an ambush at a position behind Kamalpur, where the Pakistani mortars were likely to be deployed. As expected, as soon as the mortar troop came forward, it ran into the ambush headlong, thus losing all the mortars. This was a serious setback for 31 Baluch, which in any case had recourse to very limited artillery resources.

On 27th November, 31 Baluch launched a spirited counter-attack on these infiltrating Marathas, who had since taken a position behind

Kamalpur, and dislodged them. In this attack, Major Ayub lost his life while leading the attack. Somewhat piqued by this set-back, Brig Kler retaliated by putting the Kamalpur post under a close siege by a tight cordon formed by troops from two Indian battalions. The supplies and reinforcements of the isolated post were also intercepted by roadblocks established south of Kamalpur.[169] The Baluchis, however, continued to remain defiant and the Kamalpur post managed to hang on barely by its teeth.

Finally, on 3rd December, as the war formally commenced, Brig Kler decided to move forward in a more determined manner. 13 Guards Battalion, under Lt Col Sodhi, surrounded the Baluch company at Kamalpur from all sides; despite that, the company commander, Captain Ahsan Malik, refused to surrender. In desperation, Brig Kler asked for air support on 4th December.

Kamalpur Post was subjected to repeated heavy air attacks with rocket and cannon fire, interspersed with heavy artillery fire. Under the cover of this heavy air and artillery support, Sodhi's Battalion launched three successive attacks, each one beaten back with heavy casualties. Captain Ahsan Malik meanwhile had also refused repeated demands by Brig Kler to surrender the position. By then, an exasperated Major General Gurbux Singh had personally taken over the control of the battle which so far had only produced unsatisfactory results for his formation. In the afternoon of 4th December, General Gurbux Singh himself sent another message to the post commander, saying:

"Please let me know definitely by 1600 hours whether you wish to surrender. I cannot give you more time for certain reasons. It would be much better if you come along with the messenger. I give you my word of honour that you will come to no harm."[170]

In cold contempt, Captain Malik opened up with all the fire power at his disposal.

General Gurbux Singh was busy planning a night attack when at about 7 PM on 4th December, Captain Ahsan Malik came out with a white flag and offered to surrender. He said he was doing so only on the orders of his commanding officer. This gallant officer had kept an entire brigade at bay for more than two weeks with his force comprising regulars and second line troops totaling about 75 in all. His courage and gallantry were recognized even by his adversaries. His gallantry was brought to the notice of General

---

[169] *Ibid*, page 187.
[170] Lt Gen A A Khan Niazi, *Op cit,* page 161.

Manekshaw, the Indian COAS, who then sent a personal congratulatory message to Captain Ahsan Malik and instructed Gurbux Singh to treat him and his men with respect and kindness due to brave soldiers.[171]

While the Battle of Kamalpur was still raging, Gurbux Singh was already engaged in planning his future operations. His next objective was Bakhshiganj, a small town situated south of Kamalpur at the junction of two roads, both leading to Jamalpur: a direct Road Kamalpur-Jamalpur; and a looping Road Bakhshiganj-Sherpur-Jamalpur.

Meanwhile, 1 Maratha LI Battalion, commanded by Lt Colonel Brar, with a battery of field artillery, and 13 Raj Rif Battalion, under Lt Colonel Shanwal, with a light mortar battery, had commenced their advance by moving cross-country. At first light on 4th December, they came into contact with a composite company of 31 Baluch at Bakhshiganj. Brig Kler sent a company of Mukti Bahini to move south of Bakhshiganj and to establish a roadblock on the main road. The defending Baluchis engaged the advancing troops with intense fire using their long- range weapons but the attacking battalions continued to exert pressure from north and east throughout the day. During the ensuing night, the Baluch company managed to slip away without giving any inkling to the investing force. The Mukti Bahini troops manning the roadblock preferred to simply look the other way rather than expose themselves to the danger inherent in challenging these battle-hardened troops. After the withdrawal of the defending Baluchis, Bakhshiganj was secured by the Indian troops without any further loss.

Having received this news early on the morning of 5th December, an excited General Gurbux Singh went forward to personally view the situation at Bakhshiganj. He was accompanied by Brig Kler, driving him in a jeep, when it got blown up by an anti-tank mine. Kler escaped unhurt, though badly shaken while Gurbux Singh was seriously wounded. He was quickly evacuated and General Aurora decided to replace him with Major General Gandharv Nagra, commander 2 Mountain Division. He was hitherto stationed in a dormant sector on the Chinese border and was now moved post-haste to his new command.

General Nagra met Gurbux Singh at the military hospital in the morning of 6th December and received some briefing from him; he spent the rest of the day in visiting the forward troops and discussing the role and scope of his new assignment with Brig Kler and Brig Sant Singh. The same evening,

---

[171] *Ibid,* page 162; Maj Gen Sukhwant Singh, *Op Cit,* page 190.

266

he sent his recommendations to the Indian Eastern Command, indicating the strong possibility of his force making a very early contact with the Dacca defences provided he was allotted an additional infantry brigade, a squadron of tanks, a field regiment, a medium battery and some signals resources.

In his enthusiastic exuberance, he also spoke with General Jacob, the COS of the Indian Eastern Command, and tried to convince him of the bright chances of his force reaching Dacca before anyone else. Predictably, he received a rebuff from Jacob, who said that his plea was the normal reaction of all commanders trying to scrounge extra resources. Nonetheless, Nagra did manage to secure the permission to move some resources from his old formation (2 Mountain Division) to augment the resources of 101 Communications Zone; these included some staff officers, his engineer advisor along with a field company engineers, as well as some signals equipment.[172]

As noted, Bakhshiganj had fallen at first light 5th December. In the absence of any fresh orders, this entire day was spent by the battalions of 95 Mountain Brigade in regrouping and replenishment. The advance forward was only resumed from there at first light on 6th December.

Brig Kler was now keen to reach the north bank of Old Brahmaputra and get to grips with the Jamalpur Garrison as soon as possible. His plan at this stage was as follows:

- 13 Raj Rif to advance along the main Bakhshiganj-Jamalpur axis and secure the northern line of River Old Brahmaputra as soon as possible.

- 13 Guards to advance along the looping Bakhshiganj-Sherpur-Jamalpur axis.

- 1 Maratha LI to move cross-country to Shyampur area, some ten kilometers west of Jamalpur, ferry across the Old Brahmaputra and establish roadblocks on the likely escape routes of the Jamalpur garrison.[173]

13 Raj Rif resumed the advance at first light 6th December in accordance with the above plan. By last light 7th December, it had made contact with

---

[172] Maj Gen Lachhman Singh, Op cit, pags 152-153.
[173] Maj Gen Sukhwant Singh, *Op Cit,* page 193.

the river line. It was a painfully slow advance by any standard. This battalion consumed more than 48 hours to traverse a distance of some 20 kilometers only, despite having encountered just one platoon-sized delaying position en route.

Compared to this, 1 Maratha LI, commanded by Lt Col Brar, set off from Bakhshiganj at 1 PM on 6th December and by 5 PM the same day, it had reached Shyamnagar, a crossing site over the Old Brahamaputra; in the process, it covered some 22 kilometers in six hours! It managed to cross the river by 5 PM the next day and succeeded in establishing a roadblock some three kilometers south west of Jamalpur by 2 AM 8th December.

At this point, Brig Kler ordered 13 Guards as well to follow 1 Maratha LI to the south of the river and to establish another roadblock on the lateral road between Jamalpur and Mymensingh. By first light 10th December, both these battalions were in position and the encirclement of 31 Baluch position at Jamalpur had been accomplished as planned by Brig Kler. Surprisingly, all this while, these serious developments remained completely unnoticed by 31 Baluch.

But even this considerable achievement was hardly of much solace to Brig Kler as yet another major problem was now staring him in the face. In his relentless pursuit of cordoning off 31 Baluch, he had consumed all the three infantry battalions of his Brigade and was thus left with hardly any strength to storm the invested unit itself. His only option then was to continue with the investment in an essentially stalemated situation with the hope to squeeze out the Baluchis eventually.

In desperation, he tried to exert some psychological pressure on the besieged commander. At 3 PM on 9th December, Brig Kler sent a note to Lt Colonel Ahmed Sultan, CO 31 Baluch, through a Mukti Bahini courier asking him to surrender as all his escape routes had been blocked. Kler also threatened that in case of refusal, his unit would be subjected to an extremely heavy pounding as forty air sorties had been requisitioned for this position. In the evening, a defiant reply was received from Sultan (former BM 53 Brigade in Comilla), firmly and disdainfully rejecting the offer to surrender.

On 8th December, the Indian Eastern Command also placed 167 Mountain Brigade under the command of 101 Communication Zone. In order to end the stalemate at Jamalpur, General Nagra immediately contacted Brig Irani, commander 167 Mountain Brigade, and ordered him to report at his HQ at Sherpur along with one battalion as soon as possible.

Brig Irani duly reported to Nagra at about 10:30 PM on 9th December but by himself only; 6 Sikh LI Battalion, the unit designated by him for the purpose had been delayed; instead, it managed to arrive at first light the next day. It was directed by General Nagra to immediately join Brig Kler's Brigade on the south bank of the river.

Throughout the day of 10th December, 31 Baluch remained subjected to heavy artillery as well as air bombardment as Brig Kler prepared his plan and for the assault on Jamalpur. And then the situation changed dramatically at Dacca!

As noted in the previous chapter, the troops of 57 Mountain Division under General Gonsalves had commenced to cross the Meghna on 9th December and predictably General Niazi had begun to panic. In an unfortunate coincidence, General Ansari, commander 9 Pak Division, chose this very time to inform him that 50 Para Brigade, so far employed in his Sector, had been relieved from its ground role by the Indian High Command and moved out of his Sector. To Niazi, it indicated the imminent likelihood of a brigade level para drop somewhere around Dacca, most likely at Tangail. He also apprehended that if this para drop did materialize, it would certainly jeopardize the withdrawal of 93 (A) Brigade and thus deprive Dacca Fortress of this substantial force at a critical time. So, he permitted Major General Jamshed, GOC 36 (A) Division, to immediately pull back this Brigade from Mymensingh-Jamalpur area.

General Jamshed personally spoke to Brig Abdul Qadir, commander 93 (A) Brigade, and directed him to immediately withdraw his Brigade to Dacca. Brig Qadir, in turn, asked Lt Colonel Sultan, CO 31 Baluch, if he was in a position to withdraw his battalion back to Dacca. At that time, Sultan was still labouring under the impression that the Indians had a maximum of one battalion strength south of the river, and that too spread over a frontage of some 8000 meters. Thus, he did not expect to encounter more than two companies astride the road to Tangail. He, therefore, very confidently told his Brigade Commander that he visualized no problems in implementing these orders; that he would be able to conduct an orderly withdrawal from Jamalpur position and move his unit to Dacca.

Colonel Sultan revealed his thought-process to Brig Kler after the surrender; he said that being a staff college graduate he just could not comprehend how, in the absence of any bridging or proper rafting equipment, the Indians could put more than a weak battalion across the Brahmaputra. Brig Kler laughed and said that whereas Sultan had only attended staff college, he (Kler) had been an instructor at the Indian Staff

College, Wellington and was, as such, professionally more competent. According to the Indian sources, Sultan's decision to soften up the possible Indian roadblock positions with artillery fire prior to his withdrawal was a major blunder too since this had alerted the Indians about his intention.[174]

At about 11:50 PM on 10th December, the already alerted forward companies of 1 Maratha LI detected the movement of 31 Baluch troops on the road to Tangail. The Marathas held their fire till the Pakistani troops came to within about 20 meters of their depth company locality and then let loose a hail of machine gun fire. In order to clear their passage, the Baluchi troops mounted wave after wave of attacks, shouting their famous war cries of *Kai Kai,* throughout the night. In the process, they suffered very heavy casualties, but without success. With sunrise, as the fog lifted, the battleground was seen cluttered with dead bodies and abandoned weapons. The Indians counted 235 bodies, 23 wounded and also took 61 prisoners. [175]

Colonel Sultan, however, had managed to slip away with about 250 soldiers, though his vehicular column was not so lucky. Sometimes later, a wireless message from the second-in-command of 31 Baluch, offering to surrender, was received by the Indians. Eventually, a total of 376 all ranks surrendered on this occasion: out of them two officers, nine JCOs and 209 soldiers belonged to 31 Baluch; the rest belonged to artillery, para-military forces and a solitary doctor. The Indians had lost a total of ten killed and eight wounded from 1 Maratha LI and one JCO from 13 Guards during this terrible night of slaughter.[176]

Thus, ended the battle for Jamalpur.

Operations in Mymensingh Sub-Sector

It will be recalled that in addition to the main thrust towards Jamalpur, General Gurbux Singh had also planned two auxiliary thrusts along Haluaghat-Sarchapur-Mymensingh and Baghmara- Shyamganj-Mymensingh axes; both these auxiliary efforts were being commanded by Brig Sant Singh, commander FJ Sector.

On the Pakistan side, 33 Punjab under Lt Colonel Manzoor Ahmed, beefed up with 61 Wing Rangers and Razakars (volunteers), was defending both these axes. Colonel Manzur's plan was to give main battle to the

---

[174] Ibid, page 197.
[175] *Ibid*, page 197.
[176] *Ibid*.

270

Indians at Mymensingh. He had also organized strong delaying positions at Haluaghat, Sarchapur, and Phulpur along the main Haluaghat-Mymensingh axis, in order to impose maximum delay and attrition on the advancing Indians.

On the Indian side, Brig Sant Singh had planned to carry out his advance as follows:

- 6 Bihar less two companies to infiltrate and attack Haluaghat from the south.

- The remaining two companies of 6 Bihar to infiltrate further south and capture Sarchapur.

- Simultaneously, Mukti Bahini units to establish road blocks behind Haluaghat and Sarchapur in order to isolate Pakistani positions there.

- 83 BSF Battalion to advance along Baghmara- Mymensingh axis to simulate a show of force towards Mymensingh.

Haluaghat position was then being held by a company of 33 Punjab. During the night $4^{th}/5^{th}$ December, 6 Bihar less two companies managed to infiltrate successfully and by last light 5th December, they were in contact with the Haluaghat position from the south. During the succeeding night, the remaining two companies of 6 Bihar had also infiltrated towards the Sarchapur position. Heavy exchange of fire continued at Haluaghat throughout the day of 6th December in which the Indians relentlessly resorted to air strikes and napalm bombs to soften up the position. The next night, $6^{th}/7^{th}$ December, the Punjabis discreetly withdrew from Haluaghat under extreme pressure, leaving behind large quantities of ammunition and rations intact. The roadblock established by the Mukti Bahini south of Haluaghat, however, totally failed to interfere with the withdrawal; the Muktis conveniently looked the other way! 6 Bihar, having secured Haluaghat, had continued with its advance from Haluaghat along the main highway and contacted the Sarchapur position by evening of 7^{th}December.

At this stage, Brig Sant Singh carried out extensive reconnaissance to explore the possibility of bypassing the Sarchapur position. Consequently, he left behind the minimum strength to contain Sarchapur frontally and himself, along with two companies of 6 Bihar, crossed the Bughat River east of Sarchapur unopposed. Eventually, he managed to contact the

Sarchapur position from a flank. Meanwhile, he ordered the other two companies of 6 Bihar to infiltrate further south to pose a threat to Phulpur position. These developments unnerved the 33 Punjab company deployed at Sarchapur and Phulpur; they decided to withdraw discreetly during night $8^{th}/9^{th}$ December.

Sarchapur was occupied the next day and 6 Bihar resumed their advance towards Mymensingh. While withdrawing, the Punjabis had demolished three big bridges on the way to Phulpur and it took the Indians some 36 hours to restore the communications with the help of local population. The advance south of Phulpur could thus be resumed on 10th December.

It will be recalled that, by this time, Brig Qadir had already ordered the vacation of both Mymensingh and Jamalpur positions during the night $10^{th}/11^{th}$ December, which the Indians too had become aware of through wireless intercepts. At that time, Brig Sant Singh's force was still some 11 miles away from Mymensingh and he ordered them to push forward with all speed. Having marched all night, they managed to reach Mymensingh by first light on 11th December, only to find it already vacated.

33 Punjab appears to have evacuated Mymensingh in great haste and just in the nick of time. Brig Sant Singh's troops had found cooked food still in warm pots as well a large dump of ammunition and rations left intact. Meanwhile, the Indian force operating on the Baghmara-Shyamgarh axis also joined up by the same evening, without meeting any worthwhile resistance en route.

General Nagra was later to boast that he had duped the Pakistanis regarding the actual strength of his force. According to him, Brig Qadir felt that he was facing a division less a brigade. Nagra's overall performance thus far, however, belies his boasts. *The Pakistani troops had managed to impose a delay of more than 24 hours at every delaying position en route and each time, they managed to slip away intact.*[177] Factually, Brig Sant Singh had taken a great risk by splitting 6 Bihar again and again. He had thus managed to deny himself the capability of attacking any delaying position in strength. Indeed, he would have been in serious difficulties had the 33 Punjab troops decided to stay on and give fight on these successive delaying positions.

93 (A) Brigade Withdraws to Tangail

After withdrawing from Jamalpur, Colonel Sultan with the remnants of

---

[177] Maj Gen Sukhwant Singh, *Op Cit,* page 201.

31 Baluch had reached Madhupur Forest area by mid-day on 11th December, where HQ 93 (A) Brigade was already located. Shortly thereafter, they were joined there by 33 Punjab as well. Thus, by afternoon on 11th December, the whole Brigade, or what was left of it, had concentrated at Tangail.

Back in Calcutta, General Aurora was under intense pressure from General Manekshaw to secure Dacca as soon as possible, and preferably before its garrison was strengthened by withdrawing troops. In Aurora's assessment at this stage, Dacca could likely be reinforced by any or all of the following three Pak brigades fairly soon: 93 (A) Brigade, already near Tangail; 27 Pak Brigade at Ashuganj; and, at least one brigade from 16 Pak Division. Consequently, General Aurora decided to use his trump card, 50 Para Brigade, to interdict Brig Qadir's Brigade, which, in his view, could reach the outskirts of the capital the earliest.

Thus, it so happened that as Brig Qadir and Colonel Sultan were engaged in area reconnaissance to determine a suitable location for a delaying position at Tangail, the Indians began to air-drop 2 Para Battalion in their close proximity at 4 PM on 11th December.

The obvious reason for selecting Tangail for this airdrop was because of its proximity to Dacca. Besides, the countryside around was dominated by the 'Tiger Brigade' of Mukti Bahini under Qadir Siddiqui, whose presence around the drop zone was also expected to facilitate the contemplated para drop. The fact that 2 Para Battalion was dropped in broad daylight was because of this very advantage and the immediate task entrusted to the paras was to establish contact with 'Tiger' Siddiqui and, with his cooperation, to block all routes leading to Dacca.

This airdrop was seen from some distance by Brig Qadir, Colonel Sultan and many of their soldiers. Some of the troops mistook the dropping personnel as Chinese troops coming to help them and began to shout the slogans of 'long live Pak-China Friendship'. Brig Qadir and Sultan were, however, not deceived and managed to control their troops. 93 (A) Brigade subjected the dropping para battalion to repeated attacks by the troops immediately available to them at that time, but the paratroopers succeeded in hanging on regardless.

Meanwhile, 95 Mountain Brigade too was rapidly moving south from Jamalpur towards Tangail and soon affected a link up with 2 Para Battalion. Brig Qadir, his HQ and a small number of his troops were surrounded by the units of 95 Mountain Brigade on one side and the Para Battalion on the other and had to surrender. 31 Baluch, however, still managed to slip away towards Dacca with the bulk of their remnants.

To the surprise and utter delight of General Jacob at Indian Eastern Command, some foreign news agencies, while reporting the drop, erroneously mentioned that some 5000 paratroopers had been dropped in the vicinity of Dacca. Coming at the heels of the report, which he had recently received from Major General Ansari, GOC 9 Pak Division, this seemingly confirmatory news further unnerved General Niazi in Dacca; in panic, he sent a frantic message to the CGS at GHQ which stated:

"Enemy heli-dropped approx. one brigade south of Narsingdi and landed one para-brigade in Tangail area. Request friends arrive Dacca by air first flight 12 December."[178]

Apparently, in his confused and nervous state of mind, Niazi had linked the heli-crossing of IV Corps troops across the Meghna with the airdropping of 2 Para Battalion at Tangail as a concerted manoeuvre. After the surrender, he confided to General Jacob that he had been led to believe that a whole brigade had been dropped in the outskirts of Dacca and it was only because of that he had agreed to surrender. He had, evidently, realized that he just did not have adequate force to defend Dacca against such a force. He also confessed that once Chandpur fell in the Eastern Sector, he had come to realize that he had lost the war.[179]

The Race to Dacca

From then on, the race to reach Dacca at the earliest was on in real earnest. The advancing troops, now smelling an early victory, were in high spirits while the Pakistani resistance had become virtually non-existent. The only constraint on the advancing Indian troops, at this stage, was their logistic limitations, mainly transport. The ferry at Jamalpur could only permit a very limited number of vehicles to cross to the south; in addition, for moving their own troops forward, they only had access to eight civil trucks captured from the withdrawing Pakistanis. The POL for even their limited transport resources was in short supply too; the Indians had captured large quantities of rations and ammunition but hardly any fuel.

And then a lucky break came their way. With the help of the local population, they discovered a landing ground near Tangail, which was not marked on their maps. It was quickly repaired with the active help of the

---

[178] Lt Gen J FR Jacob, *Op Cit*, page 127.
[179] *Ibid.*

locals and made serviceable. From 13th December onwards, Indian aircraft began to drop massive volumes of supply and the logistic position of the advancing troops eased considerably.

By this time, the leading troops of General Sagat Singh's IV Corps had already reached the line of River Lakhya, the last obstacle before Dacca and only fifteen kilometers away from it. The PT-76 squadron of 57 Mountain Division had also crossed the Meghna and contacted River Lakhya on 14th December. General Niazi at this time was frantically busy collecting and organizing the remnants of his forces to stem the immediate threat from the east; the threat from the north was still a distant thunder for him, Tangail being 100 kilometers from Dacca.

At this critical time, General Nagra had come to correctly appreciate that notwithstanding serious logistic difficulties in moving forward his troops, the conditions on the Pakistani side were even worse. Prisoners of war reported shock, confusion and utter disorganization of their units and betrayed a state of paralysis in the minds of their commanders. They also indicated a severe loss of morale. Troops had been separated from their units, and the units from their officers; cohesiveness had thus been entirely lost among the withdrawing Pakistani troops.

Under this environment, Nagra decided to act boldly and to undertake a vigorous and relentless pursuit of the withdrawing units. He perceived a golden opportunity to rush into Dacca from the north while Niazi was busy mending fences against the mounting threat from the east. His immediate decision was to press on with Brig Kler to capture Kaliakar. His objective at this time was to contact the Pakistani positions along River Turag at the earliest and to execute an opportunity crossing over it, if at all possible.

There was only one road from Tangail to Kaliakar but thereafter two roads led from Kaliakar towards Dacca. The main approach was Kaliakar-Chandina crossroads- Tungi- Dacca and only involved a crossing over the Turag. The second approach was Kaliakar- Dhamrai- Mirpur- Dacca, which involved crossing of River Dhaleshwari east of Dhamrai and then the Burhi Ganga at Mirpur. Nagra decided to press on along the main Tungi approach in order to avoid crossing two rivers.

6 Sikh LI resumed advance from Tangail at 6 AM on 13th December with its two leading companies in transport while the rest followed on foot. Kaliakar was captured after a short skirmish by 10 PM. The advance continued during the night and the leading elements hit the Pakistani positions along River Turag at 8 AM on 14th December. The Pakistani

troops, mainly comprising remnants of 31 Baluch and 33 Punjab were holding defences on both banks of River Turag along with a troop of tanks. The advancing troops were held up and could not make any further progress. Two attempts to force an opposed crossing of the river were beaten back by the defenders, inflicting heavy casualties on the attacking troops.

And then another lucky break came the Indian way. Their patrols reported the existence of a hitherto unknown tarmac road taking off from nearby Safipur, which ran south and linked up with Dhamrai- Dacca road east of River Dhaleshwari. It led direct to Dacca without any water obstacle en route except at the Mirpur bridge on the outskirts of Dacca. Thus, this road permitted the advancing troops to reach Dacca without crossing either the Turag or the Dhaleshwari.

The position of the advancing Indian forces at midnight on 14th December was as follows:

- 95 Mountain Brigade had reached the line of River Turag with three of its battalions.

- FJ Sector with two battalions was concentrated in Safipur area.

- 2 Para Battalion was still at Tangail.

- 167 Mountain Brigade, which had recently been released to this Sector, was still at Tangail with two battalions. Their transport and other administrative echelons had yet to reach this Sector.

- None of the B echelons of any of the units had crossed over to the south bank of the Brahmaputra.

Meanwhile, in the east, the leading troops of 57 Mountain Division (IV Corps) had crossed River Lakhya on 14th December and the Indian artillery shelled Dacca for the first time. By then, General Nagra was also poised within striking distance of Dacca from the north. The final battle for Dacca was thus due to commence!

9

THE DAY OF RECKONING

The Endgame

The Battle for Dacca had, in effect, commenced from 9th December onwards with the heli-lifting of 57 Mountain Division troops across the Meghna to Narsingdi area. Till then, on the surface at least, life in Dacca gave the appearance of normalcy; despite the rapidly deteriorating situation of Pakistani forces in the entire Theatre, the threat was still considered a distant thunder.

To recapitulate, the actual situation of Pak Eastern Command formations in various Sectors on or around 9th December was as follows:

- 9 Pak Division in the Southwestern Sector had been inextricably split in three with 107 Pak Brigade fighting its own private war around Khulna; 57 Pak Brigade now lying idle after having crossed over into the Northwestern Sector; and, Major General Ansari at HQ 9 Pak Division precariously located at Faridpur.

- 16 Pak Division in the Northwestern Sector had been split in two with precious little hopes of any linkup between them. The gap in the middle of this Division was widening by the day from 7th December onwards.

- HQ 14 Pak Division as well as 27 Pak Brigade were holed up in Bhairab Bazar, with nowhere to go; the rest of this Division was bottled up around Sylhet. Thus, this Division was in no position to make any positive contribution to the impending operations around Dacca and was to remain a mere spectator.

- HQ 39 (A) Division had ceased to exist on 9th December, leaving its remaining troops holed up in Maynamati complex, soon to surrender.

On the other hand, the Indian forces had been making hectic efforts to reach Dacca. By 14th December, their situation in relation to Dacca was as follows:

- In the Eastern Sector, 57 Mountain Division commenced its trans-Meghna heli-lift operations on 9th December and had begun to land at Raipur area. By 11th December, it had secured Narsingdi, the road head to Dacca. On 14th December, the position of its Brigades was as follows:

  o 311 Mountain Brigade had contacted Demra on 14th December.

  o 73 Mountain Brigade had secured Pubail on 14th December and came in contact with Tungi the same evening, barely 15 kilometers away from Dacca city.

  o 2 E Bengal Battalion (Mukti Bahini) had crossed River Lakhya from a ferry site in the north and secured Rupganj the same day.

- 301 Mountain Brigade (23 Mountain Division) had by then moved to Daudkundi and was poised to cross the River Meghna with a view to securing Baidya Bazar.

- In the Central Sector, on 14th December, 95 Mountain Brigade had reached the line of River Turag and was in contact with Dacca defences. 167 Mountain Brigade was still at Tangail, awaiting its transport and B echelons to move forward. 2 Para Battalion too was at Tangail.

- Further operations of 57 Mountain Division were halted in the evening of 14th December on the orders of General Aurora to avoid clash and confusion with the troops of 101 Communication Zone Area.

The Indians had thus gained a decisive strategic advantage, particularly in Eastern and Central Sectors. In other Sectors too, wide gaps had been created in the Pakistani forces, with an all-pervading sense of paralysis. By then, a feeling of impending defeat and insecurity had encompassed Dacca as well. The United Nations further contributed to this environment by arranging an airlift on 8th December to evacuate foreign nationals and by requesting India to guarantee safe passage for it. The same day, General Manekshaw broadcast a special message to the Pakistani forces in the Eastern Theatre to surrender, pointing out the utter hopelessness of their situation. Thousands of leaflets with essentially the same message were also air- dropped on some other Pakistani garrisons as well.

By 10th December, it had finally become clear to General Niazi that the Indian forces were intent on moving on to Dacca itself. Though there were a fairly large number of Army personnel then present in Dacca but hardly any regular infantry troops were available for its proper defence; most of the available troops were from the services employed on various administrative and logistic duties. For details see Annexure D.

Earlier on, HQ Pak Eastern Command had vaguely conceived the design for the Battle for Dacca along two lines of defence around the Dacca metropolis. The outer ring was generally based along the general line of Sibalay in the northwest, Kaliakar in the north, Narsingdi in the northeast, Baidya Bazar in the east and Narayanganj in the southeast. General Niazi had vainly hoped that his formations would carry out a systematic and organized withdrawal from the theatre fortresses to position themselves along this fictional outer ring, and to defend the capital city to the last.

However, no serious thought had ever been given to planning, siting and preparation of these defences for fear of undermining the confidence and determination of his formations to fight to the last man and the last round in their theatre fortresses. Not a hint of this contingency and this plan had been indicated even to the divisional and brigade commanders.

The second or the inner ring of the perceived defences lay along the general line of Mirpur Bridge, Tungi, Demra ferry, and Narayanganj; but here too neither the defences had been prepared nor any troops allotted to man them.

Major General Jamshed, a brave and battle- tested soldier of the World War II as well as the 1965 Indo-Pak War, had been made responsible for the defence of Dacca in his capacity as GOC 36 (A) Division, a formation which in fact existed on paper only. He could perceive the impending disaster very clearly and was frantically making all possible efforts to organize the defence of Dacca. As the danger to Dacca loomed larger with every passing day, he undertook frenzied measures to collect all available forces to occupy the defensive perimeter of the city; in the process, he marshalled all and anyone in uniform for this task.

With hectic efforts, he managed to collect about 1000 regular soldiers, variously belonging to infantry, artillery, engineers, ordnance and the supply corps. In addition, he collected about 1500 soldiers of EPCAF as well as some 2000 West Pakistani policemen and razakars. The grand total of this motley force came to just about 5000; he diverted staff officers and any other available regimental officers from their routine duties and put them to command this poorly armed, disparate cluster of soldiers. He also managed to get hold of a couple of tanks, three inch mortars and light machine guns, mostly gathered from various workshops, depots and dumps in Dacca.

Without any doubt, at this time General Jamshed was facing an unenviable, almost impossible task. No divisional commander was prepared to send even a battalion from his Sector to Dacca; perhaps it was because of their apprehension that their troops could not reach Dacca safely even if ordered to move back, or maybe it was simply insensitivity on their parts. Major General Qazi Abdul Majid, GOC 14 Pak Division, had sufficient troops at Bhairab Bazar to effectively interfere with the Indian buildup in Narsingdi area; at one stage, he could even fall back via Tungi to Dacca. Instead, he wasted that window of opportunity and surprisingly elected to watch the situation passively, sitting comfortably in Bhairab Bazar and playing no part in the crucial events soon to take place in and around Dacca. Similarly, Major General Nazar Hussain Shah, GOC 16 Pak Division, could possibly arrange to send about a brigade strength from his Division, but even he did not agree to this. Surprisingly enough, he failed to send even 57 Pak Brigade, lying entirely idle, to Dacca. (It will be recalled that this Brigade was part of 9 Pak Division and was now simply camping near the Paksey Bridge in the area of 16 Pak Division.) All these divisional commanders had seemingly become oblivious to the paramount importance of defending Dacca at all costs, and remained busy with their own private wars. Curiously enough, even General Niazi failed to exert his full authority as the Theatre Commander and, in the end, was reduced to a mere spectator of unfolding events.

Under the heavy pressures playing on his mind, General Jamshed too committed a very costly blunder at this time. With the express permission of General Niazi, he precipitately ordered the immediate withdrawal of 93 (A) Brigade back to Dacca. Brig Qadir Niazi, the Brigade Commander, who had planned for this Brigade to take up a defensive position at Tangail, vehemently protested, pointing out his genuine problems. Yet, the General persisted and in the end the Brigade Commander was left with no alternative but to order the withdrawal at a time when most of his troops were still heavily engaged with the Indians. In fact, 31 Baluch at Jamalpur was, at that very time, entirely surrounded by the Indian troops. The result was that the Brigade disintegrated on the way and only its disorganized, disheveled remnants reached Dacca to tell their tale.

Back in Rawalpindi, the CMLA HQ as well the GHQ were both well aware of the serious military situation developing in East Pakistan. Unable to make any positive and tangible contribution to ameliorate their war effort in East Pakistan, all they could do was to resort to false promises of imminent foreign help. It was in this vein that General Gul Hasan Khan, CGS of Pakistan Army, rang up General Niazi and speaking in Pushto told him that "yellow from the north and white from the south" would soon intervene physically. This raised Niazi's hopes initially but when he did not see that hope being fulfilled, his morale sagged even further and the officers and men of his command too abandoned all hopes of any outside succour. Battles are often decided more by a commander's state of mind than the actual state of his troops. A spirit of despondency had by now gripped the minds of senior officers in Dacca rather than a heroic defiance born out of the despair engulfing them.

With the operations of IV Corps halted on the orders of General Manekshaw, the spotlight shifted to the Central Sector from 14th December onwards where General Nagra was making an all-out effort to reach Dacca at the earliest. It will be recalled that on this very day Nagra had decided to exploit a hitherto unknown road from Safipur area leading directly to Mirpur Bridge in Dacca, which could take him direct to the heart of Dacca without involving any river crossing operations. He, accordingly, directed Brig Sant Singh, commander FJ Sector, to make a push towards Mirpur Bridge along this newly discovered axis. Simultaneously, Brig Kler, commander 95 Mountain Brigade, was directed to continue with his operations along River Turag while Brig Irani, commander 167 Mountain Brigade, was directed to expedite his move from Tangail area as soon as possible and develop operations across River Turag in conjunction with Brig Kler.

At first light on 15th December, two companies of 6 Sikh LI (95 Mountain Brigade) crossed the Turag in country boats, well away from the 31 Baluch positions. Sensing a threat to their rear, the Baluchis withdrew from there, and after blowing up a bridge, took up prepared positions at Chandina cross-roads. 6 Sikh LI managed to secure a bridgehead across the Turag by about 3 PM but their further advance was effectively checked by the

Chandina position.

Meanwhile, the troops of 167 Mountain Brigade had started moving from Tangail the same day using any and every available transport and managed to concentrate at Kaliakar by the evening. At this point of time, General Nagra had available almost eight infantry battalions with which to threaten Dacca. But lack of adequate transport to bring his troops forward was proving to be a serious impediment even at that stage.

Brig Sant Singh was allocated 13 Guards with a battery of mountain artillery to advance to Mirpur via Sabhar; he was also promised the release of 6 Bihar as soon as he concentrated in Safipur area. 13 Guards commenced their advance at 10 PM on 14th December and secured the road junction east of Dhamrai ferry by 4 AM after a minor skirmish. Colonel Sodhi, CO 13 Guards, left one company to protect the ferry site and pressed on towards Sabhar at first light on 15thDecember. The Guards came under machine gun and mortar fire from around the military farms area located at Sabhar. It was ascertained from the locals that some 200 Razakars and some regular troops had reinforced Sabhar during the preceding night. Sabhar was cleared by the Guards during night 15th/16th December and large quantities of weapons and ammunition left behind by the withdrawing troops were captured.

By this time, it had become clear to General Aurora at the Indian Eastern Command that Dacca would likely be invested by Indian troops advancing from both the east as well as north. Visualizing coordination problems, he placed General Nagra and his troops under the overall command of Lt General Sagat Singh, commander IV Corps, effective noon 15th December. However, signal instructions like authentication and other details could not be issued in time with the result that wireless communications between HQ IV Corps and HQ 101 Communication Zone were never actually established till the time of surrender. Perhaps, Nagra deliberately magnified these problems as he was very keen to personally earn the glory of entering Dacca first of all.

Brig Kler had still not been able to make any headway towards Tungi because of stiff resistance being put up by 31 Baluch and remnants of other units at Chandina. So, General Nagra decided to induct 167 Mountain Brigade too in this area, so as to isolate the Pakistan troops at Chandina from Dacca. Brig Irani decided to cross the River at last light opposite Gacha with two battalions and established a strong blocking position by 3 AM 16th December; with one battalion facing north and the other facing south.

Despite the orders to cease operations given to IV Corps, some activity nevertheless did continue along River Lakhya as well. On 16th December, 1/11 Gurkha Rifles managed to cross the River north of Narayanganj as the area had been vacated by the defending Pakistan troops soon after first light 16th December. Major General Gonsalves, GOC 57 Mountain Division, had

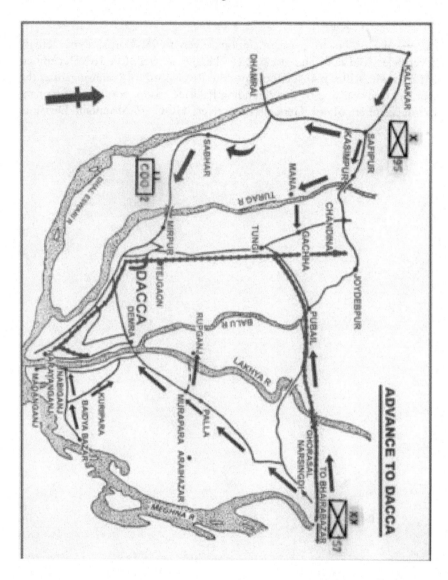

ADVANCE TO DACCA

meanwhile managed to move his medium artillery also to Demra in preparation for a final assault on Dacca.

Reverting now to the Central Sector. Brig Bashir Ahmed, an armoured corps officer then serving as DDG EPCAF, had been made responsible for the defence of Dacca along the Safipur- Mirpur axis. As soon as Brig Sant Singh's troops came in contact with Sabhar, Brig Bashir had come to realize, to his consternation, that his troops had evidently withdrawn in haste from the area and the route to Mirpur now lay exposed. After desperate efforts, he managed to collect some 200 odd troops, mainly from the EPCAF, and placed them on Mirpur Bridge by midnight 14th /15th December.

Meanwhile 2 Para Battalion had reached Safipur area from Tangail by the afternoon of 15th December and was placed under the command of Brig Sant Singh, who was now very keen to resume his advance towards the Mirpur Bridge. The advance from Sabhar was thus led by 2 Para Battalion at 10 PM 15th December. Major Sethi was appointed as the vanguard commander, with machine gun mounted jeeps leading the advance. They stopped after reaching a bridge east of Balipur, about three kilometers west of Mirpur Bridge, and sent forward a reconnaissance patrol towards the Bridge. The jeeps crept forward slowly; the leading jeep was creeping on the Mirpur Bridge itself when they surprised a sleeping sentry. Apparently, the Indian troops had not been expected to reach there so soon! Still, the surprised defenders, to their credit, opened up with everything they had and destroyed the two leading jeeps. 2 Paras did not attempt anything further during that night.

The BBC had announced in its evening news bulletin on 15th December that India had agreed to a temporary ceasefire in East Pakistan at General Niazi's request, effective from 5 PM 15th December to 9 PM 16th December. Early the next morning, 16th December, General Nagra was apprised by Brig Kler that his Signals Company had intercepted a wireless message from Niazi asking Pakistan troops to observe the cease fire. Rumours about the end of hostilities had already been rife in both the armies since the preceding midnight and General Nagra seized the initiative very boldly at this time. He immediately travelled to the position of 2 Para Battalion and sent Captain Mehta, his ADC, and the adjutant of 2 Para Battalion under a white flag to contact General Niazi in order to arrange a

285

cease fire. His famous message read:

"My dear Abdullah, I am here. The game is up. I suggest you give yourself up to me and I will look after you. Gandhrav."

The two officers drove forward in a jeep at about 08.30 AM; Major Sethi and two other officers also climbed into the jeep. The party was halted on the Bridge and taken to the Pakistan Sector HQ, some 400 meters away. General Nagra's message was delivered to the officer in command there, who sent it to HQ Pak Eastern Command. The Indians were meanwhile entertained to tea by the EPCAF officers there. After about one hour, they were informed that General Jamshed was coming himself to meet General Nagra.

When the car carrying General Jamshed arrived, Captain Mehta got into it while Major Sethi and the other Indian officers boarded their own jeep to lead the way. Captain Sharma, the adjutant of 2 Para, was driving the jeep while a Pakistani officer sat in the middle and Major Sethi sat on the left; Captain Gill and the RMO of 2 Para were in the rear seat. The white flag had since been removed, considering it unnecessary at this stage. The jeep was crossing the Bridge at about 10 AM when all of sudden it was fired upon from a flank.

Earlier on in the morning, soon after the party carrying the message to Niazi had left the position of 2 Para, the paratroopers had decided to improve their tactical posture by creeping forward. A platoon from one of the depth companies was moved forward to close in on the Bridge and had taken up positions a few hundred meters west of it; it had, however, not been briefed about the cease fire message or the imminent return of the party. So, when they saw a jeep and a staff car crossing the Bridge, they fired on the leading jeep with accurate LMG fire a burst of which hit Major Sethi in the legs while the Pakistani officer was also injured. Sethi was immediately moved to CMH Dacca in a Pakistani ambulance and thus gained the dubious distinction of being the first Indian officer to enter Dacca, though as a battle casualty; he Sethi lost his leg as it had to be amputated later.

General Niazi had meanwhile received the final instructions from Rawalpindi at midnight 15th /16th December to surrender to the Indian Forces. HQ Pak Eastern Command, in turn, ordered its formations at first light 16th December to contact the nearest advancing Indian Force to arrange for the surrender but, in the pervading confusion, this order could not be delivered to all the formations and isolated garrisons. In Dacca itself, the ceasefire had come into effect by 11 AM, but isolated, sporadic fighting continued in many sectors till 4 PM. Perhaps, the last act of defiance was exhibited by the intrepid Lt Col Ahmed Sultan, CO 31 Baluch, as he launched a spirited counter-attack from the direction of Chandina to clear the roadblocks setup by units of 167 Mountain Brigade.

General Nagra, eventually, met General Jamshed near the Mirpur Bridge. After a brief discussion on ceasefire modalities, Nagra sent a message to Calcutta apprising them of these developments. After that he joined General Jamshed in his staff car to proceed to HQ Pak Eastern Command, Dacca; Brig Kler, Brig Sant Singh and some other officers accompanied him. As they entered his office, General Niazi completely broke down and made some uncomplimentary remarks about the people who he thought had let him down.

After that, Niazi turned his attention to Brig Kler, who was wearing a maroon turban and wings, and asked him if he was the commander of the para brigade dropped at Tangail. When told that only one battalion had been dropped, Niazi found it hard to believe this. He then asked Kler to name his regiment. When told that he belonged to the Corps of Signals, Niazi quipped that in our Army, they did not give command of brigades to Signals officers. Kler retorted, *"No wonder you lost the war."*[180]

It was soon agreed to send officers to stop the ongoing fighting at Tungi and Chandina, so that troops of 95 and 167 Mountain Brigades could move into Dacca. However, the fighting could not be ceased till 4 PM when the orders about the surrender were finally conveyed to the Pakistan commanders at all levels. 2 Para Battalion entered Dacca at about 11:30 AM on 16th December, followed by 13 Guards and 6 Bihar at about 1 PM.

At about 12:15 pm, General Nagra received a message from Calcutta advising him that Major General J Fr Jacob, COS Indian Eastern Command, was flying in to settle the terms of surrender with General Niazi. Accordingly, General Jacob and his staff officer Colonel Khara, landed at Tejgaon airfield at about 1 PM on 16th December. By that time, 4 Guards and the Independent Armoured Squadron of 57 Mountain Division had also reached the airfield.

The Road to Surrender

Meanwhile, unknown to General Nagra, indeed to the entire IV Corps,

---

[180] Maj Gen Sukhwant Singh, *Op cit*, page 215.

rapid and critical developments had been taking place at Rawalpindi, Dacca, New Delhi and Calcutta during the preceding few days. All that while, General Manekshaw's calls for surrender were gradually beginning to have effect on the officers and troops of the Pak Eastern Command. Manekshaw had also addressed two such communications direct to General Farman, under the erroneous impression that he had since taken over the command of the forces in the Eastern Theatre.

The authorities in Pakistan eventually had been compelled to seriously consider and then accept these calls for surrender, but the circuitous path which led to this decision makes a kaleidoscopic study of political posturing and blame shifting among various power centres. For the sake of posterity, this entire process must be recorded in detail so that the reader may be able to draw their own conclusions and to place responsibility where it may actually be due.

In actual fact, ever since the war had formally commenced on 3rd December 1971, the acute possibility of a ceasefire or even a surrender in East Pakistan had been perceived as being inevitable by many sage minds in Rawalpindi and Dacca; yet there was hardly anything that could be done by anyone to prevent it. A lot many perceptive persons could clearly read the writing on the wall but simply chose to look the other way. The favourite pursuit then adopted by various numerous power centres in Pakistan then was to make a conscious effort to shift the blame of the inevitable catastrophe from one to the other.

At that time, there were three ostensible power centres operating in East Pakistan:

- Governor Dr. Abdul Malik, the head of the political government in the province and, theoretically at least, ultimately responsible for all its affairs.

- Lt General Amir Abdullah Khan Niazi, Commander Pak Eastern Command and MLA East Pakistan, responsible for all military matters and conduct of the war on the Eastern Theatre.

- Major General Farman Ali Khan, though on paper merely the advisor to the Governor on all civil and political affairs, but a power to be reckoned with in his own right, well respected for his long experience of East Pakistan affairs and his reputation for being a wise and capable military strategist.

Thus, the ultimate responsibility for all matters related to East Pakistan was bound to fall on the shoulders of one or the other of these persons. It is a matter of record, that they had all begun to develop widely differing views and perceptions when, soon after the commencement of the war, the forces in the field began to suffer one reverse after the other. All this while, HQ CMLA and the GHQ passively and nonchalantly continued to look at the unfolding tragic kaleidoscope. Yet, they were all keen to pass the eventual buck to one another with alacrity and this makes a fascinating, if tragic, study. Let us trace the contours of this intricate web for the benefit of the posterity.

Early on the morning of 4th December, Muzaffar Hussain, a senior and very astute civil servant who was then the Chief Secretary of East Pakistan, met Governor Malik in his office. The Governor had recently returned after a fruitless visit to Rawalpindi and was still very bitter at not being taken into confidence by the President about the imminence of the war. As soon as he saw the Chief Secretary, he angrily remarked, *"Yahya has bluffed us."* He then asked him to see General Niazi and to ascertain the operational situation.

Muzaffar Hussain met Niazi at his tactical HQ, located underground in a grove in a secluded part of Dacca Cantonment. At that time, Major General Farman, Major General Jamshed, Brig Baqir Siddiqui (COS Eastern Command), and Rear Admiral Shariff (commander East Pakistan Navy) were also present there.

Just about that time, a report emanating from the Dacca airbase was received announcing that Amritsar had just fallen. On hearing this news, and without in any way fretting to confirm its authenticity, a sense of euphoria immediately engulfed the room. Caps were thrown in the air and they all jubilantly became engaged in embracing and congratulating one another. After the situation had somewhat restored to normal, Muzaffar conveyed the Governor's message to Niazi. General Niazi readily agreed to brief the Chief Secretary every day, who in turn would keep the Governor informed. However, the perceptive Chief Secretary gathered the impression that even at that early stage, General Niazi appeared unsure of himself and grumbling on account of insufficient fire power, lack of armour, and having inadequate communications with his formation commanders. On his return, Muzaffar conveyed his shrewd assessment to the Governor concluding that, under the present circumstances, the Army may not be able to hold out for more than a week. The Governor thereon decided to bring the real situation to the notice of the President. A message to the President was duly drafted but General Farman was understandably reluctant to dispatch, as, in his opinion, Niazi would certainly not like it.

And there the matter rested for the time being.[181]

The GHQ, in any case, could hardly remain oblivious for long to the serious situation facing the Pakistan forces in East Pakistan. Soon enough, they too had come to notice, with mounting concern, the rapid advances being made by the Indians, and could sense the sagging morale in East Pakistan. At this time, the COS Army sought to elucidate the real role that the Eastern Garrison was expected to perform within the overall military strategy of Pakistan. In a message initiated at 11:15 AM on 5th December, the COS spelled it out very clear:

"COS Army signal No 9233 to Eastern Command(.) The enemy has stepped pressure against you and is likely to increase to max extent(.)He will attempt to capture East Pakistan as swiftly as possible and shift max forces to West Pakistan(.)This must not be allowed to happen(.)Losing of some territory is insignificant but you must continue to concentrate on operational deployment in vital areas aiming at keeping the max en force involved in East Pakistan(.)every hope of Chinese activities very soon(.) good luck and keep your magnificent work against such heavy odds

There was hardly anything new in this message per se! It had merely re-emphasized the basic doctrine of war cultivated and developed by the General Staff since the very inception of Pakistan; and this should have been already known to General Niazi in any case. However, whether he really comprehended the strategic import of this unambiguous message is a moot point. At this time, his primary objective should have been to adopt a strategy designed to gain maximum possible time. Only thus he could keep the invading Indian forces involved in East Pakistan till such time as the operational situation in West Pakistan was conducive for a strategic riposte to be launched there. Where he had failed *ab initio* was in his inability to evolve a strategy in harmony with this doctrine. Instead, to the very end, Niazi remained wedded to his doctrine of defending every inch of East Pakistan and thus failed to perform the primary role assigned him.

General Farman did in any case suggest to General Niazi the importance of carrying out a strategic adjustment in his posture in the spirit of this GHQ message. Soon after the daily briefing in Niazi's Tactical HQ on 6th December, Farman suggested to General Niazi to begin withdrawing his troops gradually towards the line of major rivers. Pointing on the map, he brought out the operational futility of keeping garrisons stuck up in exposed places like Dinajpur, Thakurgaon, and Comilla at that stage. His suggestion was that the troops at Dinajpur, Thakurgaon and Rangpur

---

[181] Hasan Zaheer, *Op Cit*, pages 363,364.

should be withdrawn to Bogra and from Comilla to the line of River Meghna. He suggested similar adjustments to be carried out in other sectors as well. Niazi immediately shot down the sound suggestion, commenting in chaste Punjabi, *"They have not even been attacked as yet."* Obviously, he had never heard of the term strategic withdrawal; he certainly had hardly a clue about the delicate relationship between 'time' and 'space' in operational strategy.[182]

The situation in East Pakistan continued to deteriorate at a fast pace. By 6th December, Pakistan forces in all the sectors had come under great pressure. A complete blockade by sea and air had already been enforced by the Indian forces. Dacca and Kurmitola runways had been bombed repeatedly and rendered out of service; the PAF's solitary squadron in East Pakistan had thus become completely grounded from the evening of 6th December onwards. General Niazi was constrained at this stage to send the following message G- 1233 to the GHQ at 10 AM the same day:

"Eastern Command to PAKARMY December 6(.)Enemy offensive intensified(.) IAF causing maximum damage(.)Rebels highly active(.)Local population also hostile(.)Main border towns and cities under pressure(.)Absence adequate firepower support aggravating situation which is becoming critical(.)Own forces now reaching pre-planned lines of defence(.)resorting to fortress/strong pt basis(.)will fight it out last man last round(.)Request expedite action on G-0235 of 5 dec"

Note: Message G-0235, referred above, had requested for early activities by the Chinese.

This was duly approved the very next day by a message from the CGS as follows:

"CGS Signal G-0907 dt 7 dec to Eastern Command(.)Position appreciated(.) Eastern Command's tactical concept approved(.)Hold position in strength without territorial considerations including Chittagong(.)Maintain entity of force intact and inflict maximum attrition on enemy(.)

(Evidently, what General Niazi had failed to realize even at this stage was that the GHQ was essentially advising him to carry out strategic withdrawal to defensible terrain, something akin to what General Farman had advised him two days ago.)

It was under these environment that the Governor held an important

---

[182] Maj Gen Farman Ali Khan, *Op cit*, page 120.

meeting in the Governor's House at 11 AM on 7th December, attended by General Niazi, General Farman and Muzaffar Hussain. Niazi was formally received by Farman and taken to the Governor's office where Muzaffar was also present. The normal custom in the Governor House was that as soon as a guest arrived in the office, tea or coffee was brought in automatically within a few minutes of his arrival. The Governor started the proceedings by making some placating remarks to the effect that in war, anything could happen; "When two sides fight, one wins and the other may lose. At times a commander may have to surrender and at other………." Before he could say anything more, General Niazi gave out a loud shriek and began to sob loudly with his hands covering the face. At that precise time, the butler entered with the tea and could see and hear what was taking place in the office. Muzaffar reacted quickly, took the tray from his hands and shooed him out rather awkwardly. When asked by the other staff about his abrupt exit, he remarked that the officers inside were weeping. This sensational news travelled all over Dacca quickly and conveyed the desperate situation of the Army to all and sundry.[183]

After some time, when some order had been restored in the room, the Governor said that he must convey the true situation in East Pakistan to the President and recommend to him the urgent need to negotiate a peaceful transfer of power so that unnecessary loss of life could be avoided. Accordingly, General Farman immediately set to drafting the following message to the President, sent at 12 AM 7th December:

"7 dec.
Governor A M Malik to President of Pakistan A- 6905
It is imperative that correct situation in East Pakistan is brought to your notice(.)I discussed with Gen Niazi who tells me that troops are fighting heroically but against hy odds w/o adequate armour and air sp(.)rebels cutting their rear and losses in equipment and men are heavy and cannot be replaced(.)The front in Eastern and Western Sectors has collapsed(.)loss of whole corridor east of Meghna river cannot be avoided(.)Jessore has already fallen which will be terrible blow to the morale of pro-Pakistan elements(.)civil admin ineffective(.)food and other sups running out(.)Dacca city will be without food in seven days(.)thousands of pro-Pakistani elms being butchered(.)millions of non-Bengalis await death(.)No amount of lip service except physical intervention by world powers will help(.)If any country is expected to help it should be within 48 hours(.)If no help is expected I beseech you to negotiate so that a civilized and peaceful transfer of power takes place and millions of lives are saved(.)Is it worth sacrificing so much when the end seems inevitable(.)If help is coming we will fight on whatever the consequences there may be(.)Request be kept informed

---

[183] *Ibid*, pages 123-124.

The President replied to this desperate message the same evening at 7:25 PM, as usual replete with vague platitudes and exhorted them to fight to the last while entrusting them to God with his prayers as follows:

"From President for Governor A-4555 DTG 071925
All possible steps are in hand(.)Full scale and bitter war is going on in the West Wing(.)World powers are very seriously attempting to bring about ceasefire(.)Subject is being referred to the General Assembly after persistent vetoes by the Russians(.)A very high powered delegation is being rushed to NEW YORK(.)Please rest assured that I am fully alive to the terrible situation that you are facing(.)Chief of Staff is being directed by me to instruct Gen Niazi regarding the military strategy to be adopted(.)You on your part and your Government should adopt strongest measures in the field of food rationing and curtailing supply of essential items as on war footing to be able to last for a maximum period of time and preventing a collapse(.)God be with you(.) We are all praying

This message was followed by another message from the GHQ to Eastern Command on 8th December, purporting to contain fresh operational guidance to General Niazi as promised to the Governor but hardly containing any new pearls of wisdom:

"COS to Comd Eastern Command
G-0910(.)Am very proud of your boys(.)hold defensive positions where possible regardless of loss of territory(.)all possible efforts being exerted on pol level"

In retrospect, the message from the Governor to the President on 7th December was indeed the first act in the game of shifting the blames among the various power centres, soon to become a rampant pastime in Rawalpindi and Dacca. In his book, General Niazi has alleged that this message was drafted by General Farman in consultation with the Governor, but without his (Niazi's) knowledge and sent to the President from the Governor House. He has in fact alluded to it as a grand conspiracy against him.[184] On the other hand, General Farman has categorically mentioned in his book that General Niazi was very much present in this meeting and the message was drafted in his presence. His contention is that it was dispatched from the Government House on Niazi's request who did not wish it to be sent from his HQ for morale purposes.[185] Hasan Zaheer, most likely relying on the memory of Muzaffar Hussain, has also verified the presence of General Niazi in that meeting.[186]

---

[184] Lt Gen A A Khan Niazi, *The Betrayal of East Pakistan*, OUP, page 176.
[185] Maj Gen Farman Ali Khan, *Op Cit*, page 124.

After analyzing the entire episode, we too are of the opinion that General Niazi was certainly present in that meeting and his attempt to deny it later was simply an attempt to shift the blame on to Farman. Our further comment is that General Niazi's whole book, on the whole, is simply an attempt at perceiving unfounded conspiracy theories and to blame others for his follies.

Meanwhile, some more ominous possibilities were being perceived in faraway Washington, which eventually would cast very long shadows on the outcome of this war. On 8th December, Henry Kissinger, the US National Security Advisor, briefed President Nixon and some other top US officials on the real Indian intentions about this war as follows:

"The Indian plan is now clear. The're going to move their forces from East Pakistan to the West. They will then smash the Pakistan land forces, and air forces, annex the part of Kashmir that is in Pakistan, and then call it off."

Kissinger's real concern and apprehension on the future of Pakistan actually went much deeper than this. His actual concern was that Pakistan's defeat in this manner would exacerbate the centrifugal forces in West Pakistan too and the already restless provinces of Baluchistan and NWFP might go their own way. He was already aware of the potential Iranian position that any massive instability and fragmentation of West Pakistan, particularly in Baluchistan, would be considered as 'posing a mortal threat to Iran'.[187]

The CIA too had concurred with Kissinger's view, based upon a report they had received just a day before from a 'reliable source'. According to this report, Indira Gandhi had spelt out the following three objectives for this war:

- Liberation of Bangladesh.

- The incorporation into India of the southern area of Azad (Pakistani held) Kashmir.

- The destruction of Pakistani armoured and air force strength so that Pakistan can never threaten India again.

By 9th December, the war had taken a tangibly disastrous turn in East

---

[186] Hasan Zaheer, *Op Cit*, pages 377-378.
[187] *US FR, 1969-1976, Volume E-7*, as quoted by Shuja Nawaz, *Op cit*, page 308.

Pakistan. The Indian IV Corps under General Sagat Singh had reached the banks of the River Meghna and captured all the three major ferry sites and river ports, and would soon begin to heli-lift their forces across the mighty river. II Corps under General Raina had reached the banks of the River Padma and looking for ways and means to cross the River. Similarly, XXXIII Corps under General Thapan had reached Bogra and poised to contact the river line at any moment. In the Central Sector, Pakistan's only Brigade was under extreme pressure by the troops of General Nagra, who were also straining to reach Dacca as soon as possible. And, on top of all this, General Niazi hardly had recourse to any regular fighting troops in Dacca; the famed fortress of Dacca was set to be held by phantom forces.

The message sent by General Niazi to the CGS at GHQ on 9th December, with a copy to the Governor, was reflective of the extremely grim situation on the ground as follows:

"Commander Eastern Command to CGS G-1255 dt 9 dec
ONE(.)Regrouping and readjustment not possible due to enemy mastery of skies(.)
(.)population getting extremely hostile and providing all out help to enemy(.)No move
possible during night due intensive rebel ambushes(.)rebels guiding enemy through gaps
and to rear(.)Air field damaged extensively, no air support missions possible in last three
days and in future(.)all jetties, ferries and river craft destroyed due enemy air
action(.)bridges demolished by rebels(.)even extrication most difficult(.)TWO(.)extensive
damage to heavy weapons and equipment due enemy air action(.)troops fighting extremely
well but stress and strain now telling hard(.)NOT slept for last 20 days(.)are under
constant fire artillery and tanks(.)THREE(.)situation extremely grim, we will go on
fighting and do our best(.)FOUR(.)request following(.)immediate air strike all enemy air
bases this theatre(.)if possible reinforcement airborne troops for protection Dacca(.)message
ends

As the operational situation continued to deteriorate almost by the hour, General Niazi sent another message to the President the same evening, which re-emphasized the extremely critical situation in even clearer terms. The copies of these two messages had been endorsed to the Governor too and assessing the gravity of the situation, Dr. Malik decided to take the matters in his hand. Accordingly, he too sent a message to the President in the late hours of 9th December. This was jointly drafted by General Farman and Muzaffar Hussain in the presence of General Niazi, though he did disagree with some of its contents. [188]

The message read as follows:

---

[188] Lt Gen A A Khan Niazi, *Op cit,* page 180.

"From Governor East Pakistan for the President A-4660 dt 091800dec
*Military situation desperate(.)enemy approaching Faridpur in the west and has closed up to the River Meghna in the east bypassing our troops in Comilla and Laksham(.)Chandpur has fallen to the enemy thereby closing all river routes(.)Enemy likely to be at the outskirts of Dacca any day if no outside help forthcoming(.)***Secretary General UN's representative in Dacca has proposed that DACCA CITY may be declared an open city to save lives of civilians especially non-Bengalis(.)Am favourably inclined to accept the offer(.)strongly recommend this be approved(.)Gen NIAZI does not agree as he considers his orders are to fight to the last and it would amount to giving up DACCA(.)***This action may result in massacre of the whole army, WP police and all non-locals and loyal locals(.)There are no regular troops in reserve and once the enemy has crossed the GANGES or the MEGHNA further resistance will be futile unless CHINA or USA intervenes today with massive air and ground support(.)once again urge you to consider immediate ceasefire and political settlement otherwise once Indian troops are free from East Wing in a few days even West Wing will be in jeopardy(.)Understand local population has welcomed Indian Army in captured areas and are providing maximum help to them(.)Our troops are finding it impossible to withdraw and manoeuvre due to rebel activity(.)with this clear alignment sacrifice of West Pakistan is meaningless(.)*   (Emphasis added.)

The President, despite his famed nocturnal activities, lost hardly any time in replying to this important message. His reply was received the same night at about 11 PM as follows:

*HQ CMLA to Governor East Pakistan and Eastern Command DTG 092300(.) G-0001(.)from PRESIDENT to GOVERNOR repeated to EASTERN COMMAND(.) your flash message A-4660 of 9 December received and thoroughly understood(.)***you have my permission to take decisions on your proposals to me(.)***I have and am continuing to take all measures internationally but in view of our complete isolation from each other decision about East Pakistan I leave entirely to your good sense and judgment (.)***I will approve of any decision you take and I am instructing Gen NIAZI simultaneously to accept your decision and arrange things accordingly(.)Whatever efforts you make in your decisions to save senseless destruction of the kind of civilians that you have mentioned in particular the safety of our armed forces, you may go ahead and ensure safety of our armed forces by all political means that you will have to adopt with our opponent(.)*   (Emphasis added.)

As indicated by the President, this message was followed by another

296

message this time from the COS Army to Commander Eastern Command just the next day on 10th December as follows:

"PAKARMY to EASTERN COMMAND DTG 100910
G-0237
*For Comd from COS Army(.)President's signal message to the Governor with a copy to you refers(.)President has left the decision to the Governor in close consultation with you(.)as no signal can correctly convey the degree of the seriousness of the situation I can only leave it to you to take the correct decision on the spot(.)**It is however apparent that it is now only a question of time before the enemy with its great superiority in numbers and material and the active cooperation of rebels will dominate East Pakistan completely(.)***meanwhile a lot of damage is being done to the civil population and the army is suffering heavy casualties(.)**you will have to assess the value of fighting on if you can, and weigh it, based on this you should give your frank advice to the Governor who will give his final decision as delegated to him by the President(.)<u>whenever you feel it is necessary to do so you should attempt to destroy maximum military equipment so that it does not fall into enemy hands</u>(.)**keep us informed(.) Allah bless you* (Emphasis added.)

Apparently, before the receipt of the preceding message (G-0237), General Niazi had already submitted another dismal report to the GHQ on 10th December, essentially similar as his earlier message.

Both these distress signals from General Niazi were a clear indication of the Pak Eastern Command's inability to continue the war beyond the next few days; they were also an accurate portrayal of Niazi's state of mind at this critical time. The very nature of modern warfare demands that if and when such a situation arises, it is then the job of the political governments to adopt ways and means to reduce its damaging effects as much as possible through concerted diplomatic/political manoeuvres. President Yahya Khan, instead of taking the requisite actions on his own had passed the buck to Governor East Pakistan and General Niazi, without considering that there was only one course of action which Governor Malik could possibly adopt under the circumstances. The following key words/phrases in the President's message (G-0001) and COS message (G-0237) deserve to be noted in particular:

• The President clearly and unambiguously delegated the authority to Governor Malik to "take decisions *about* East Pakistan. The use of word 'about' instead of 'in' East Pakistan certainly widened the scope of the delegated authority.

- In the message sent by COS to General Niazi, the key phrase was: *"Whenever you feel it necessary to do SO, you should attempt to destroy maximum military equipment......"* The use of word 'so' was a deliberate vagueness. Military equipment in war situations in only destroyed when the troops are about to surrender. So, in effect what the GHQ was conveying implicitly was that General Niazi could surrender when so decided by the Governor.

The above two signals were masterly worded with the sole intention to shift the responsibility of the inevitable surrender on to the Governor and the Theatre Commander. The apparent and rather transparent aim of this clever verbal charade was to absolve General Yahya and his coterie from the blame of actually ordering the surrender; and, thus enable them to continue ruling over West Pakistan even after the ignominy of surrender.

By this time, the senior civilian bureaucracy in East Pakistan, almost exclusively comprising West Pakistani civil servants, had shifted to the Governor House annex for their personal safety and protection. They were previously lodged in the Government Hostel, which had very poor security measures, comprising mostly Bengali policemen. Thus, they hardly had any choice but to avail the kind invitation of the Governor and shifted to the Governor House on 8th December.[189] Headed by the Chief Secretary Muzaffar Hussain, they were to become a formidable pressure group and a potent pro-ceasefire lobby within the Governor House itself.

The Governor, hard pressed from the civilian side, bureaucratic as well as political, now desperately wanted an early end to the war in East Pakistan with honour. He was very conscious of the fact that in the ever-increasing areas under Indian occupation, the life for patriotic Pakistanis of all ilk was pathetic. Prominent pro-Pakistan Bengalis were being butchered by the rebels and their properties confiscated. Biharis were facing unimaginable hardships, simply being hunted down like animals and viciously butchered. Seeing all this, the Governor was abysmally depressed but his mental faculties as a seasoned politician were still fully functional. His very rational view then was that compared to an outright surrender, a ceasefire was certainly a more honourable option. As soon as he received the above-mentioned President's message G-0001 and COS message G-0237, he apparently decided to act immediately. He called the Chief Secretary instantly and instructed him to draft a detailed message to the President,

---

[189] Hasan Zaheer, *Op cit*, page 379.

which was shown to General Farman the next morning. The Governor conveyed to him in clear terms that since the authority to reach a viable political arrangement had been delegated to him, he had decided to send this message to the UNO, but only *after approval by the President*. The fateful message read:

"FROM: GOVERNOR EAST PAKISTAN
TO: HQ CMLA   *A-*
7107
For President of Pakistan(.)your G-0001 of 092300 dec(.)as the responsibility for taking the final and fateful decision has been given to me I am handing over the following note to Assistant Secretary General Mr. Paul Mark Henry after your approval(.)NOTE BEGINS(.)It was never the intention of the Armed Forces of Pakistan to involve themselves in all-out war on the soil of East Pakistan(.)However a situation arose which compelled the Armed Forces to take defensive action(.)The intention of Government of Pakistan was always to decide the issues in East Pakistan by means of a political solution for which negotiations were afoot(.)The Armed Forces have fought heroically against heavy odds and can still do so but in order to avoid further bloodshed and loss of innocent lives I am making the following proposals(.)As the conflict arose as a result of political causes it must end with a political solution(.)I therefore having been authorized by the President of Pakistan do hereby call upon the elected representatives of East Pakistan to arrange for the peaceful formation of the Government in Dacca(.)In making this offer I feel duty bound to say the will of people of East Pakistan will demand the immediate vacation of their land by the Indian forces as well(.)I therefore call upon the United Nations to arrange for a peaceful transfer of power and request (.)ONE(.)an immediate ceasefire(.)TWO(.)repatriation with honour of the Armed Forces of Pakistan to West Pakistan(.)THREE(.)repatriation of all West Pakistan personnel desirous of returning to West Pakistan(.)FOUR(.)the safety of all persons settled in East Pakistan since 1947(.)FIVE(.)guarantee of no reprisals against any persons in East Pakistan(.)In making this offer I want to make it clear that this is a definite proposal for peaceful transfer of power(.)the question of surrender of Armed Forces would not be considered and does not arise and if this proposal is not accepted the Armed Forces will continue to fight to the last man(.)NOTE ENDS(.)Gen Niazi has been consulted and submits himself to your command(.)Request immediate approval (??)

The Governor directed both Farman and Muzaffar to take the above draft message to the Cantonment and secure General Niazi's approval to it. Accordingly, when Farman and Muzaffar reached General Niazi's Tactical HQ, they found General Jamshed, Admiral Sharif, and Brig Baqir Siddiqui present there too. The message was handed over to General Niazi by Muzaffar Hussain, who got it read out to all those present and then asked for their opinions. General Jamshed as well as Admiral Sharif both endorsed the proposal, saying that no other option was available under the circumstances. Finally, General Niazi queried Farman, *"In what capacity of mine you are asking for my approval?"* General Farman replied, *"In your capacity as Theatre Commander East Pakistan."* Niazi said, *"OK, you have my approval".* [190]

However, in his own memoirs General Niazi has given a somewhat different version of this meeting. His contention is that he did not accord his approval to the message but after a great deal of discussion, he only agreed to have the message sent if the sentence "Gen Niazi has been consulted and submits to your command" is included in the message. He also accuses General Farman of deliberately excluding the last sentence "Request immediate approval." from the text of this message as given in his (Farman's) memoirs, highlighted in the message above. He ascribes serious allegations of conspiracy and treason against General Farman for his conduct in this whole affair.[191] However, General Niazi is the only one making these assertions; all other reputed Pakistani sources too do not carry this disputed last sentence in their versions. Moreover, no other participant of this meeting has ever expressed any statement supporting Niazi's version, not even before the Hamoodur Rahman Commission.

As soon as General Farman reached the Governor House, a surprise development was awaiting him. He found Paul Mark Henry, the UN Assistant Secretary General, already present in the Governor's Office. Upon being informed by Farman that General Niazi had accorded his approval to the message, the Governor directed him to hand over a copy of the signal message to the UN representative, which he did after signing it. According to Farman, he signed it because a signal message has to signed by an Army officer before it can be transmitted over the Signals communications system and he was the only staff officer available at that time. In his own words:

" The communication was from the Governor to the President and not me. But I agreed with the proposals as their acceptance would have saved us from the humiliation of surrender". [192]

Thus, it was that this fateful message was unfortunately handed over to a UN representative even before its dispatch to the President, let alone his approval. The message had already been transmitted to New York before the President of Pakistan even became aware of its contents! As can be readily appreciated, this was soon to precipitate serious diplomatic repercussions.

---

[190] Maj Gen Farman Ali Khan, *Op cit*, page 131.
[191] Lt Gen A A Khan Niazi, *op cit*, pages 183-184.
[192] Maj Gen Farman Ali Khan, *Op cit*, page 131.

There was utter consternation in the GHQ and the CMLA Secretariat when the above message did eventually reach Rawalpindi on 10th December. The President was simply furious. He was apparently taken aback with open offers of transfer of power to the elected Awami League representatives as he had still not been able to overcome his dislike of the Awami League leadership and what they stood for. It is also possible that he was still hopeful of some form of intervention by either the Americans or the Chinese.

He, therefore, decided to disown and nullify the initiative taken by his Governor. He also directed the Foreign Secretary to deny the report immediately in the international fora. A radio broadcast was also made at this time which disclaimed all responsibility for the message and described it as an unauthorized message on part of General Farman.

The following message was immediately sent to the Governor in which he was conveyed a revised draft to be handed over to the UN:

President to Governor of East Pakistan   *G-002 dt 10 dec*
Your Message A-7107 of 10 dec
The proposed draft of your message has gone much beyond what you had suggested and I had approved(.)it gives the impression that you are taking decisions on behalf of Pakistan when you mentioned the subject of the transfer of power, political solution and repatriation of troops from East to West Pakistan etc(.)This virtually means the acceptance of an independent East Pakistan(.)the existing situation in your area requires a limited action by you to end hostilities in East Pakistan(.) Therefore suggest a draft which you are authorized to issue(.)QUOTE(.)In view of the complete blockade of East Pakistan by air and sea by overwhelming Indian forces and the resultant indiscriminate and senseless bloodshed of civilian population have introduced new dimensions to the situation in East Pakistan(.)The President of Pakistan has authorized me to take whatever measures I may decide(.)I have therefore decided that although Pakistan Armed Forces have fought heroically against heavy odds and can still continue to do so yet in order to avoid further bloodshed and loss of human lives I am making the following proposals(.)ONE(.)an immediate ceasefire in East Pakistan to end hostilities(.)TWO(.)guarantee of personnel settled here since 1947(.)THREE(.)guarantee of no reprisals against any person in East Pakistan(.)Safety of all armed forces personnel in East Pakistan(.)I want to make it clear that this is a definite proposal of ending all hostilities and the question of surrender of armed forces will not be considered and does not arise(.)UNQUOTE(.)within this framework you may make any additions and changes as you may desire(.)the question of transfer of power and political solution will be tackled at National level and is being done(.)

General Farman was also constrained to issue a complete denial on 12th December. An ISPR press release issued on 13th December ostensibly quoted him as follows:

"I have been quoted by various sources as having offered surrender terms. I wish to state, in the most categorical and emphatic terms, that surrender has never been offered to anybody. In fact, neither I, nor my colleagues here, at any time issued or conceived, the idea of surrender. Anybody or any agency, attributing to me surrender terms, is telling a blatant lie. I would like to challenge anybody to produce a document or statement, in which even the idea of surrender has been suggested,"[193]

While all this was going on, President Yahya appears to have become convinced of the imminent prospects of immediate military support by some foreign power; most likely, it was the news of the US Seventh Fleet setting sail from Singapore towards the Bay of Bengal. Entirely misreading its real purpose, the President felt emboldened to send the following message to Governor Malik:

President to Governor East Pakistan   *DTG 110430 dec*
Do not repeat not take any action on my last message to you(.)important diplomatic and military moves are taking place by our friends(.)It is essential that we hold on for another 36 hours at all costs(.)please also pass this message to Gen Niazi and Gen Farman

Unknown to Islamabad, the situation as being perceived by the United States at that point was in fact quite different. A CIA source report from within the Indian cabinet room had managed to acquire a copy of the actual minutes of a meeting of the Indian Cabinet on 12th December, and rushed it urgently on to Washington. These minutes not only confirmed the earlier CIA analysis of the Indian designs but had also quoted Mrs. Gandhi as follows: [194]

"Mrs. Gandhi asked her defence chiefs to be ready to drive into Sialkot and then proceed as deep as possible, even up to Rawalpindi, with the aim of destroying Pakistan".

Meanwhile, the charade of false self-confidence was continuing unabated in Pakistan. On 12th December, General Niazi received a call from General Gul Hasan Khan, the CGS, who conveyed to him in Pashto that *"Yellows are coming from the north and Whites from the south"*. Niazi took the message at its

---

[193] Brig A R Siddiqui, *Op cit*, page 207.
[194] Shuja Nawaz, *Ibid.*

face value and as such his confidence was bolstered no end. He decided it was high time to show some bravado to the outside world and this was the reason behind his famous statement to the effect that the Indian tanks would enter Dacca only over his chest. After the war was over, General Gul Hasan Khan found it convenient to blame General Hamid, COS Army, for directing him to pass along this false and misleading information to General Niazi; of course, by then General Hamid was hardly in a position to defend himself against an ascendant Gul Hasan.

General Niazi's response to the President's somewhat optimistic message of 11th Dcember was to send a series of bleak situation reports to the GHQ on 13th December as follows:

Commander Eastern Command to PAKARMY   G-1286   DTG 130130 dec
All fortresses under heavy pressure(.)No replenishment even of ammunition(.)Dacca under heavy pressure(.)Rebels have already surrounded the city(.)Indians also advancing(.)Situation serious(.)Promised assistance must take practical shape by 14 December(.)Will be effective at Silliguri on NEFA and by engaging enemy air bases

Just a couple of hours later, he sent another message as follows:

Commander Eastern Command to PAKARMY   G-1286 DTG 132300 dec
Moving to built up area for final battle"

Niazi's last message on 13th December was not only bleak and dismal but entirely false and misleading as well:

Commander Eastern Command to PAKARMY   G-1282 DTG 13 1500 dec
Dacca Fortress defence well organized and determined to fight it out"

In response to these distress messages, General Niazi was only to receive some platitudes from the COS during the night of 13th/14th December as follows:

COS to COMMANDER EASTERN COMMAND
Reference your G-1286 UN Security Council in session(.)Most likely will order ceasefire(.)Matter of hours(.)Hold out till UN resolution passed(.)Fully realize most critical situation Eastern Command "

In retrospect, it would appear that both the GHQ and the Eastern

Command were at that time engaged in a deadly game of bluff and deceit with each other; at stake was the entire East Pakistan garrison and in a broader sense, the entire Pakistani nation. This lethal charade was being played by both the sides with all apparent earnestness while the ominous boom of the Indian guns could clearly be heard in Dacca from 12th December onwards.

Through their vast intelligence network in Dacca, the Indians had remained well abreast with the fluctuating day to day perceptions not only in Dacca but within the Governor House as well. They were thus well aware of the wavering resolve of the Governor. In the process, they had also come to learn that Governor Malik had called a high- level meeting in his office at 11 AM on 13th December. Sitting in Calcutta, General Jacob, COS Indian Eastern Command, felt that a disruption of this meeting would make the Governor more amenable to the calls for surrender. Accordingly, he directed that the Governor House in Dacca be attacked by the IAF planes at the precise time of this meeting.

Thus, it was that exactly at the hour of 11 AM on 13th December, the Governor House in Dacca was heavily strafed and bombed by the IAF planes. Part of General Farman's office was gutted and the Governor House Library also caught fire. The irony inherent in this situation was that though this meeting had been postponed at the last minute, the bombing raid nonetheless achieve its purpose.[195]

The bombing raid in effect served as a stark reminder to Dr. Malik that fall of Dacca was only a matter of hours under the circumstances. It was also obvious to him that, in such a situation, his own life as well as those of his family members would be exposed to a grave risk, something he obviously wanted to avoid at all costs. Thus, he immediately resigned his high office and moved to the safety zone established by the International Red Cross in Hotel Intercontinental, Dacca. He was joined there by all the senior West Pakistani civil servants then in Dacca as well. Thus was brought the East Pakistan Government, established on 14th August 1947, to an ignominious end, simply a whimpering demise on 13th December 1971.

By 14th December, it had finally dawned even upon President Yahya Khan and his coterie that they would now have to reconcile with the writing on the wall and recognize that there was no alternative to the defeat of the Pakistan Armed Forces in East Pakistan. Consequently, he sent an unclassified message (in clear) to the Governor and Commander Eastern

---

[195] Lt Gen J FR Jacob, *op cit*, page 135.

Command, which was received in Dacca at 3:30 PM and read as follows:

PAKARMY to Governor CMM Eastern Command   *G-0013 DTG*
141332dec
For Governor and General Niazi from President(.)Governors flash message to me refers(.)you have fought a heroic battle against overwhelming odds(.)The nation is proud of you and the world full of admiration(.)I have done all that is humanly possible to find an acceptable solution to the problem(.)you have now reached a stage where further resistance is no longer humanly possible nor will it serve any useful purpose(.)it will only lead to further loss of life and destruction(.)you should now take all necessary measures to stop the fighting and preserve the lives of all armed forces personnel, all those from West Pakistan and loyal elements(.)Meanwhile I have moved UN to urge India to stop hostilities in East Pakistan forthwith and guarantee the safety of the armed forces and all other people who may be likely target of miscreants

General Niazi called a conference of his senior officers then in Dacca to discuss the implications of this message from the President; these included General Farman, General Jamshed, Admiral Sharif, AVM Inam and Brig Baqir Siddiqui. Admiral Sharif expressed his opinion by saying that the President had only given permission; it was not an order. He was supported by General Farman who also added, "*You should not surrender en masse, i.e, the whole theatre. You have the permission. Pass this permission on to the divisional commanders. Continue to fight and let local divisional commanders decide individually when to call a halt to the fighting.*"

General Niazi listened to all the views and said that he would contact the COS Army and get clarification. After that, he tried to talk to the President as well as the COS but neither was available. The only person he could talk to was Air Marshal Rahim Khan, C-in-C PAF, who told Niazi that the situation in West Pakistan was very serious as well and so he must surrender immediately.

The conference then decided that General Niazi and General Farman should meet with the US Counsel General and request him for help in arranging the surrender.[196]

The same evening, the two generals met Herbert D Spivak, the US Counsel General in Dacca, in his office. General Niazi initially pleaded with him for help as a friend, which the Counsel General flatly refused and coldly replied, "Why did you start the war? US cannot help you. The most I can do is to convey your message to the Indians and act as a message relayer.

---

[196] Maj Gen Farman Ali Khan, *Op cit,* page 149.

Not as negotiator. We have a worldwide communication system and could transmit your message to whomsoever and wherever you want. Give me a written message."[197]

The message was prepared then and there, written by General Farman ensuring that the word "surrender" was not mentioned at all; instead, the word "ceasefire" was used. It was signed by General Niazi; in order to meet the requirements of the American staff system, it was also authenticated by General Farman. The fateful message read as follows:

Lieutenant General A A K Niazi
Dacca, East Pakistan
December 14, 1971

Mr. Herbert D. Spivak
Counsel General of the USA
Dacca, East Pakistan.

Dear

In order to save further loss of innocent lives which would inevitably result from further hostilities in big cities like Dacca, I request you to arrange for an immediate ceasefire under the following conditions:
a). Regrouping of Pakistan Armed Forces in designated areas to be mutually agreed upon by commanders of the opposing force.

b). To guarantee the safety of all military and paramilitary forces.

c). Safety of all those who had settled in East Pakistan since 1947.

d). No reprisals against those who helped the administration since March 1971.

2. In those conditions, the Pakistan Armed Forces and paramilitary forces would immediately cease all military operations.
3. I would further abide by any resolution which the Security Council of the United Nations may pass for the permanent settlement of the present dispute.

4. I make this proposal with full authority vested in me by virtue of my position as Martial Law Administrator of Zone 'B' (East Pakistan) and Commander East Pakistan, exercising final authority over all Pakistani military and para-military forces in the area.

---

[197] *Ibid.*

Signed, Lt Gen A A K Niazi.

A copy of this letter was also sent to the GHQ vide message No. G-1305 at 12:30 AM on 15th December for information. The US Counsel General, instead of passing the message to the Indians at New Delhi, sent it to Washington. The US Government checked with President Yahya through Ambassador Farland and after his confirmation, instructed its Ambassador to the UN, George Bush, to pass it on to the Indian Delegation. The message eventually reached General Manekshaw on 15th December. Manekshaw decided to increase pressure on General Niazi so that there was no likelihood of a last- minute change of his mind; the air attacks on Niazi's headquarters were further intensified during the late afternoon.

The final communication received from the GHQ by Eastern Command in effect amounted to nothing more than shrugging off all further responsibility in the affair. The message (G- 0015) from COS Army to General Niazi sent at 11:50 am on 15th December read as follows:

"Reference G-1310(.) Saw your reply to President and heard Indian COAS reply on AIR(.)Suggest accept terms by COAS India as they appear to meet your requirements(.)Will however be local military decision with no bearing on political outcome(.)

Earlier in the day, GHQ had also directed Eastern Command for destruction of currency notes, travelers' cheques, National Bank treasury cheques, and Signals Crypto material. The State Bank was opened the night of 15th/16th December and the material was burnt. This was part of standard operating procedure of denial in the face of imminent occupation by the enemy.

General Manekshaw, the Indian Army Chief, received the above letter regarding the *ceasefire*, at about 14:30 hours on 15th December from the US Embassy in New Delhi. Manekshaw replied to the letter at 23:30 hours the same day, instead asking General Niazi to *surrender* to his advancing forces wherever they were located. The letter read as follows:

"For Lt Gen Niazi from S A M Manekshaw, Chief of Army Staff India   15 Dec 1971.
FIRSTLY- I have received your communication regarding a ceasefire in Bangladesh at 14.30 hours today through the American Embassy at New Delhi(.)SECONDLY. I had previously informed General Farman Ali in two messages that I would guarantee (A) The safety of all your military and para-military forces who surrender to me in Bangladesh. (B) Complete protection to foreign national, ethnic minorities, and personnel

of West Pakistan origin no matter who they may be(.)Since you have indicated your desire I expect you to issue orders to all forces under your command in Bangladesh to ceasefire immediately and surrender to my advancing forces wherever they are located(.)THIRDLY(.) I give you my solemn assurance that personnel who surrender shall be treated with the dignity and respect that soldiers are entitled to and I shall abide by the provisions of the Geneva Convention(.)Further as you may have many wounded I shall ensure that they are well cared for and the dead given proper burial(.)No one need have any fears for their safety no matter where they come from(.) Nor shall there be any reprisal by forces under my command(.)FOURTHLY(.)Immediately I receive a positive response from you I shall direct General Aurora the Commander of Indian & Bangladesh Forces in the Eastern Theatre to refrain from all air and ground action against your forces(.)As a token of my good faith I have ordered that no air action shall take place over Dacca from 1700 hours today(.)FIFTHLY(.) I assure you that I have no desire to inflict unnecessary casualties on your troops as I abhor the loss of human lives(.)Should however you do not comply with what I have stated you will leave me with no other alternatives but to resume my offensive with the utmost vigour at 1900 hours Indian Standard Time on 16 December(.)SIXTHLY(.) In order to discuss and finalize all matters quickly I have arranged for a radio link to be on listening watch from 1700 hours Indian Standard Time today 15 December(.)The frequency will be 6605 (6605) KHZ by day and 3216 (3216) KHZ by night(.)Call sign will be CAL(Calcutta) and DAC(Dacca)(.)I would suggest you instruct your signaler to restore microwave communication immediately"

The above message was received by General Niazi at 11:30 PM on 15th December and he immediately sent a copy of it to the GHQ. Radio links had been placed on listening watch in New Delhi in anticipation of Niazi's response to Manekshaw's above message soon after its dispatch. The whole night passed without any response and the seemingly endless wait was increasing Manekshaw's frustration by the hour. At 8 AM on 16th December, as Manekshaw was about to give orders for the daily operations, the radio suddenly came to life. It conveyed Niazi's request for an extension of the temporary ceasefire by six hours; he also asked for an Indian representative to visit Dacca to finalize the modalities of the **ceasefire.** The request for extension of the temporary ceasefire was immediately accepted and this time it was extended to ground operations as well. Soon after this, as General Niazi was perhaps contemplating his dwindling options under the prevailing circumstances, he also received the fateful message from General Nagra, as described earlier.

Generals Farman and Jamshed, Admiral Sharif and Brig Baqir Siddiqui were all present in the Tactical HQ of Pak Eastern Command when Nagra's message was received and read by all of them. There was a hush all around and finally General Farman asked Niazi if he (Nagra) was the negotiating team. He was still labouring under the impression that as a sequel to Manekshaw's message, General Nagra had arrived to discuss further modalities. No body at that time knew how he had managed to reach so close to Dacca but soon came to the conclusion that he could not be the negotiating team. The mystery was, however, soon cleared as a message was received from the Indian Army HQ advising that their negotiating team headed by General J FR Jacob would be arriving at about 12 noon the same day.

At this, General Farman asked Niazi as to what was his resistance potential in Dacca but received no reply. General Farman again asked, "How long can you resist?" Again silence. Admiral Sharif now spoke up in Punjabi, "Kuch Pallay Hai?" (Do you have anything in your pocket?). General Niazi looked towards General Jamshed who shook his head in negation. In exasperation, General Farman said, "*I can't give any advice. Go and do what you want to do.*" General Niazi told General Jamshed to go and meet Gen Nagra at the Mirpur Bridge. He put on his cap and went away.[198] The other participants of the meeting were also told to disperse and return at 12 noon.

At about this time, General Niazi also passed orders for a ceasefire to all his formation commanders and directed them to concentrate their commands in specified assembly areas. However, either his orders did not reach all concerned or some commanders deliberately ignored them. Consequently, at the time when formal surrender was taking place in Dacca, several local commanders at places like Khulna, Rajshahi, Nator, Dinajpur, Rangpur, Joydebpur, Sylhet, Maynamati, and Chittagong were still continuing to resist.

As General Farman returned to the command post at the appointed time, he found no one there. He enquired about their whereabouts from a staff officer, who very sarcastically and disapprovingly replied, "They are showing the Indians the Corps HQ's furniture and curtains." Farman proceeded to the peacetime office of General Niazi and, in his own words, was horrified to see the scene before his eyes there. General Niazi was seated in his chair and in front of him General Nagra was seated; on one side the famous rebel leader 'Tiger' Siddiqui was standing in a full general's uniform. General Farman saluted General Niazi and took a chair besides Admiral Sharif, who was also present there. General Niazi was in a jovial mood, reciting Urdu couplets. He then asked General Nagra if he could understand Urdu poetry. Nagra told him that he had a master's degree in Persian from Government College Lahore. Realizing that he was no match

---

[198] *Ibid*, page 151.

for General Nagra in this field, he immediately switched over to what he excelled at: dirty Punjabi jokes. In words of General Farman,

"In my opinion, he was behaving in a shameful manner; he was supposed to remain reserve and appear dignified at the time when surrender terms were to be discussed with the enemy. Instead he was behaving in a boisterous manner----telling filthy jokes to the Indians as if they were old chums." [199]

Meanwhile, at about 9:15 AM General Manekshaw had telephonically directed General Jacob to proceed to Dacca immediately to finalize all the details pertaining to the surrender and also to ensure that the formal surrender ceremony was held the same evening. At that stage, it was certainly a tall order but General Jacob had only one worry weighing on his mind. He had earlier received an invitation for lunch from General Niazi and queried whether he should accept it or not. Perhaps, Manekshaw did not want to commit himself without clearance from the prime Minister and so replied that he would think over it and convey his instructions to him in due course.

General Jacob immediately set about organizing this crucial visit. He asked Air Commodore Purushottam and his Colonel Intelligence Khara to accompany him. He took along with him a typed copy of the draft Instrument of Surrender which had been drawn up by his staff in anticipation of this eventuality and had already been sent to Delhi for approval. [200]

On their way to Dacca, the Indian team first landed at Jessore to change helicopters. While there, Jacob also received a message from the Army Headquarters directing him to accept General Niazi's invitation for lunch. At the Dacca airport, the Indian team was received by Brig Baqir Siddiqui, COS Pak Eastern Command, and driven to HQ Pak Eastern Command, reaching it at 1 PM. During informal discussion on the way, Brig Baqir came to realize that Jacob had brought a draft surrender instrument with him and NOT of a ceasefire. He escorted General Jacob to his own office and there the two held preliminary discussion on the subject. After ascertaining the contours of Indian proposal, Brig Baqir went into Niazi's office and apprised him of the essential details. At that time, Generals Jamshed and Farman as well as Admiral Sharif and AVM Inam were also present there. General Jacob was eventually received by General Niazi in his office in the presence of these senior officers. General Nagra was also

---

[199] *Ibid*, page 152.
[200] Lt Gen J FR Jacob, *Op cit*, page 138.

present in the office.

Colonel Khara read out the terms of surrender; there was dead silence in the room, as tears rolled down General Niazi's cheeks. The other Pakistani officers in the room, who expected the document to be on the lines of ceasefire as suggested by them, were visibly uneasy and fidgeting.

General Niazi eventually protested that what he was being asked to sign was an unconditional surrender. General Jacob in reply proffered the rather technical argument that since the Instrument included clauses about maintaining the dignity of the surrendering troops as soldiers and their treatment under Geneva Conventions, it could hardly be termed an unconditional surrender. According to him, inclusion of such terms was unique in an Instrument of Surrender and were very liberal indeed. General Niazi argued that General Jacob and his party had come to Dacca in response to the letter given to Paul Spivack and thus they were here only to discuss the terms of a ceasefire and withdrawal under the auspices of the UN. Jacob firmly replied that if they did not accept the terms as spelt out in their document, the Indians would have no alternative but to resume their full-scale offensive with full vigour. There was no response to this. General Jacob then said he would give them half an hour to make up their minds and walked out of the office.[201]

Unknown to Niazi at that time, General Jacob was in fact a very worried and apprehensive man. He was really extremely anxious about *"what would happen if he (Niazi) refused to agree to a surrender?"*. At that time, several critical considerations were weighing heavily on his mind at that point of time, such as:

- The UN Security council was currently in progress and the issue was still on the table.

- They Indians were well aware that General Niazi still had some 30000 troops in Dacca whereas they had just 3000 outside Dacca; though they had bluffed Niazi by saying that they had 15000 there. In their assessment, he could still hold them back for another two weeks.

- Had General Niazi refused to surrender at that time, and doggedly decided to continue the fight, the UN might have eventually enforced a ceasefire and withdrawal.

---

[201] *Ibid, page 142.*

311

- On top of all this, he was under great pressure from his own Chief to somehow arrange a surrender the same day. General Aurora and his wife were due to land at Dacca in just another two hours and he had to achieve results before then.

It was therefore imperative for General Jacob to somehow pressurize General Niazi to accept a surrender on their terms. In Jacob's own words,

"I felt lonely in an hostile environment wondering what the outcome would be if I failed to get a surrender."[202]

After some time, Jacob returned to General Niazi's office where he found the draft Instrument of Surrender lying at the table and the grim looking Pakistani generals sitting around. He quietly asked Niazi if he accepted the terms of the draft document; there was no answer. He repeated the question second and third time without any answer but he could see tears in Niazi's eyes. Jacob picked up the document and said that he took it as accepted. In words of General Jacob,

"I breathed a sigh of relief. We had been able to convert a ceasefire into a surrender." [203]

As borne out by General Niazi, General Jacob had used sheer blackmail in the process by telling him that if he did not comply, he (Jacob) would hand over the local loyal population and the West Pakistani civil officials, who had taken refuge in the Hotel Intercontinental, to the Mukti Bahini to bayonet and massacre them.[204]

General Jacob has justified it by saying that it was only due to his blackmail that General Niazi was compelled to accept the provisions of the Instrument of Surrender.[205] In the eyes of this Indian general, the end justified the means.

Once Niazi had given in, the modalities of the surrender ceremony were quickly finalized. Initially, General Niazi balked at the idea of a public surrender ceremony and insisted that it take place in his office but under relentless pressure from Jacob, he was constrained to agree. In the process, General Niazi did succeed in extracting two major concessions from a very reluctant Jacob:

---

[202] *Ibid, Page 143.*
[203] *Ibid,* page 143.
[204] Lt Gen A A Khan Niazi, *Op cit*, page 234.
[205] Lt Gen J FR Jacob, *Op cit*, page 143.

- The Pakistan troops would retain their personal weapons for self-protection as well as the protection of civilians till such time as adequate number of Indian troops were available for their protection in Dacca area.

- All Pakistani civil officials, civilians, and staff would be treated as civil internees and accompany the troops wherever they proceeded and would not left at the mercy of the Bengalis.

It was then decided by General Jacob that the ceremony would be held in Race Course ground, Dacca, where General Aurora would be presented a guard of honour by detachments of Indian and Pakistan armies. After that, both Aurora and Niazi would sign the surrender document and General Niazi would then surrender his sword. At this General Niazi pointed out that he did not have a sword; it was then decreed by Jacob that he should surrender his pistol instead. Niazi looked very unhappy at this but remained silent, which Jacob again took as assent.

This discussion was followed by lunch in the Pak Eastern Command officers mess. General Jacob had managed to surreptitiously take Gavin Young, a journalist of the daily Observer of London, with him to the mess. The lunch was typical mess fare with roast chicken as the main course. Gavin Young subsequently described this lunch in a scoop titled 'The Surrender Lunch'.

General Aurora and his party arrived at Dacca airfield at about 4:30 PM; he was accompanied by Mrs. Aurora, Air Marshal Dewan, Vice Admiral Krishnan, Lt General Sagat Singh, the Divisional Commanders of IV Corps and Wing Commander Khondkar of Bangladesh Airforce. Conspicuous by his absence was General Osmany, the C-in-C of the Bangladesh Forces, who could not be contacted in time. All of them then moved to the Race Course ground for the surrender ceremony.

After inspecting the guard of honour, Generals Aurora and Niazi proceeded to the table and the surrender document brought by Aurora from Calcutta was placed on the table. General Niazi looked at them casually and signed them, followed by Aurora. The time was exact 4:31 PM IST. General Niazi then undid his epaulette, removed his .38 pistol and handed it over to General Aurora with tears in his eyes. It was finally over.

Just before the ceremony had commenced, a French reporter managed to approach General Niazi and asked him, *"How are you feeling, Tiger?"* Niazi could barely utter, *"Depressed"*. Standing nearby, General Aurora remarked,

313

"He had an impossible task under extremely difficult conditions. Any other general in these circumstances could not have done better," A more befitting epitaph for Niazi could not be coined![206]

Sometimes later, when some senior Indian officers examined the pistol surrendered by General Niazi, they came to realize that it could not be Niazi's pistol. It was a normal Army issue revolver and its barrel was choked with mud; apparently, it had not been cleaned for quite some time. Its lanyard was also dirty and frayed. They felt that this just could not be the personal weapon of a commanding general and that most probably Niazi had just taken it from one of his soldiers and surrendered it to Aurora. Niazi's personal pistol was indeed a very fine, pearl-handled Italian weapon. Perhaps, in his own way, Niazi had got a little of his own back.[207]

In the gloom and confusion of surrender, someone had thought of 4 Army Aviation Squadron of Pak Eastern Command, then commanded by Lt Colonel Liaqat Israr Bokhari. It then comprised eight helicopters (four Mi-8s and four Alouettes). On 15th December, Bokhari told General Niazi that he was prepared to fly out his team in the hours of darkness to Burma, if permitted to do so. AVM Inamul Haq opposed the suggestion as he felt that in view of the total air supremacy enjoyed by the Indians, it would be hazardous. Admiral Sharif, on the hand, opined that Colonel Bokhari should be permitted to make this attempt as it would save eight helicopters from falling into Indian hands. General Niazi agreed and ordered Bokhari to take the wounded Major General Rahim with him, along with some important documents. He was also told that some nurses would also be sent with him.

Colonel Bokhari worked out his time and space calculations and decided that he must leave at 3 AM on 16th December, so that he could cross the border and enter the Burmese air space before the first light. Eventually, however, he was forced to take off without the nurses as they failed to reach the airfield at the appointed time; any further delay would have jeopardized the entire mission.

They reached Akyab in Burma at about 6:30 AM and then, with the cooperation of the Burmese authorities and the Pakistan Embassy in Rangoon, flew on to Thailand. From there the helicopters and all the people travelling on them were shipped to Karachi. Some 139 ladies and children along with the crew members as well as eight helicopters were thus

---

[206] Lt Gen A A K Niazi, *op cit,* page 235.
[207] Lt Gen J FR Jacob, *op cit,* page 148.

314

saved by the ingenuity and courage of one man, Lt Colonel (later Brig) Liaqat Israr Bokhari. [208]

Casualties

The total strength of the Pakistan Armed Forces, including para-military forces, in the Eastern Theatre immediately before the outbreak of war was 1833 officers, and 50,232 JCOs and other ranks. Out of them 354 officers, 192 JCOs, and 5320 other ranks lay dead on the battle fields.[209]

The Indian losses were 68 officers, 60 JCOs, and 1293 other ranks killed; and, 211 officers, 160 JCOs and 3690 other ranks wounded; and, 56 missing. [210] Slightly different figures, but of the same order of magnitude, have been mentioned by several other Indian authors.

Prisoners of War

A highly misleading figure of 93000 has somehow become the established number of Pakistani PWs in India. How this myth was created and stayed on in public minds is a different story. One thing is however very certain: the total number of Armed Forces all ranks in East Pakistan who became PWs was much less than this.

According to the figures quoted above on the authority of Lt Gen (retired) Kamal Matinuddin, the total number of all ranks in East Pakistan was 52,065. Out of them a total number of 5866 laid down their lives there. It simply means that the total number of armed forces PWs, including civil armed forces could not have been more than 46,199.

Several other Pakistani authors have worked figures variously from 43,000 to 46,000 in their own studies. Such variations are of course very normal, given the state of confusion in the Pak Eastern Command in the last few days, before and after the surrender. The figure of 93,000 as such is grossly incorrect. Probably it includes the number of families of the armed forces personnel, civilian internees and other people detained by the Indians.

This assessment is accorded further credence by the figures which came to light in 1974 as the process of repatriation of the prisoners of war was completed on 30th April 1974. The details of the total number of prisoners

---

[208] Lt Gen Kamal Matinuddin, *Op cit,* page 422.
[209] *Ibid*, page 430.
[210] Maj Gen Sukhwant Singh, *Op cit*, page 224.

repatriated from India were reported as follows:[211]

- Officers: 1818. (Army, Navy PAF and CAF).
- JCOs: 2138.
- Other Ranks (Army): 51,897.
- Naval Ratings: 1319.
- Airmen: 772.
- Rangers and Police: 20,766.
- Civilians Paid out of Defence: 882.
- Civilians: 10,389.
- Total: 89,981.

---

[211] Daily Dawn, Karachi, dated 1st May 1974

10

THE GAMES THAT NATIONS PLAY

Pakistan's ultimate hope of thwarting the Indian designs against East Pakistan lay in internationalization of the entire dispute, preferably through the auspices of the United Nations. However, the incompetence, displayed by the ruling military junta in the handling of the crisis within the country was even more vividly on display in the diplomatic realm too. The advice of seasoned diplomats of the Foreign Office was usually ignored by members of the junta like Major General Ghulam Umar, renowned for his ability to regale General Yahya with choice couplets from Urdu poetry to keep him in good humour. He had, thus, earned the reputation of being a 'literate general' amongst his peers, who were mostly famed for their Anglicized vocabulary only. As the virtual head of the National Security Council, he presumed himself to have become a past master of diplomatic manoeuvres as well. It was because of persons like him and his ilk that Pakistan's principled strong case was eventually lost in the corridors of the United Nations. Most of the Foreign Office mandarins usually found safety in obsequiously agreeing with the half-baked views of the junta; the only sane voice heard in this babel of cacophony was that of Agha Shahi, Pakistan's Permanent Representative at the UN, but even his advice was usually ignored by those who mattered.

Since 25th March, the international media regaled in circulating wild reports of atrocities, brutal killings and orgies of rape, mostly fed to them through the Indian sources or a few renegade Pakistani journalists like Anthony Mascranehas. Pakistan's case was going entirely by default following the initial public relations blunder of forcing the international media to leave East Pakistan immediately after the commencement of the Army action. This situation was tailor-made for exploitation by India in the absence of any credible rebuttal from Pakistan. What was essentially a civil war between the federal forces and the armed rebels, mostly comprising East Bengal battalions and the EPR, was being universally portrayed as the

317

ruthless genocide of a hapless populace.

Initially, the Yahya Regime was completely obsessed with the view that this 'domestic dispute' must be kept outside the UN purview at all costs. This illogical obsession with resisting the internationalization of this issue led to the adoption of some ridiculous and farcical postures at times. At one stage, the policy was to even deny that refugees had indeed crossed over from East Pakistan into India; accordingly, Agha Shahi was instructed to keep this issue out of the UN purview at all costs. Perhaps, even more absurd was the direction given him never to raise the issue of blatant Indian interference in the East Pakistan affairs in any UN forum. This was despite the fact that the entire diplomatic world was by then well aware of India being openly engaged in training, arming, and launching Mukti guerrillas inside East Pakistan from April onwards. Irrational obsessions are hard to overcome!

Despite these inhibitions, Agha Shahi, a very respected figure in the corridors of the UN, prevailed upon the Secretary General U Thant not to provide any humanitarian assistance to India till such time as their claims regarding the numerical level of the refugee problem were duly verified by a UN representative. On top of that, he even managed to persuade the Secretary General to send Ismat Khetani of Iraq as his Representative to verify the humanitarian relief requirements of East Pakistan. Ismat Khetani, in due course, strongly recommended immediate substantial relief to East Pakistan, including 28 Million dollars in cash.

Eventually, and rather reluctantly, the international community began to take the East Pakistan crisis seriously. The so-called "genocide" was the first issue to be taken cognizance of in a meeting of the United Nations Economic and Social Committee (ECOSOC), held in May 1971. Pakistan was ably represented in this meeting by Agha Shahi and Lady Viqar un Nisa Noon, wife of former Prime Minister Malik Feroze Khan Noon. To a certain extent, they did succeed in exposing the Indian designs of defaming Pakistan by baseless propaganda, but were greatly embarrassed when it came to defending a military crackdown in an essentially political dispute involving democratic rights of an ethnic community.

Yet another ECOSOC meeting was held on 3rd July 1971 in which the East Pakistan situation was again discussed. At this stage, it was hard and illogical for Agha Shahi not to concede that the refugees had indeed become a burden on India; however, he again finessed its decision successfully so that assistance was to be provided to India only after the actual scale of the problem had been assessed and verified by a UN representative. Eventually, a UK diplomat, John Kelly, reached Dacca on 19th July as the UN Representative to assess the situation on ground. However, his mission came to a dead end as the Indian Government impetuously refused him the permission to come to Calcutta to visit the refugee camps on the Indian side. At the Indian behest, Hussain Ali, the Head of the Consular Mission of the Provisional Bangladesh Government in Calcutta, refused to even guarantee John Kelly's safety during his proposed visits to the refugee camps. The mission thus had to be aborted.

Secretary General U Thant, highly concerned at the deteriorating situation on the sub-continent, was eventually constrained on 19th July 1971 to draw the attention of the Security Council members to it through a Memorandum to the President of the Council. Conscious of the limitations of the mandate of his office, he was, however, at pains to clarify that:

"The memorandum is not an official document of the Security Council and was intended to record my own deep concern with the wider potential dangers of the situation in the region....."212

In the event, the Council members felt disinclined at that stage to get involved in what they essentially perceived as 'yet another acrimonious dispute between India and Pakistan'.

As the months passed by without any success in finding a political solution to the crisis, Pakistan's reservations on internationalization of the East Pakistan issue gradually began to erode. Following this change in perception, Pakistan initially proposed that UN observers be posted on both sides of the border with India. After that, Pakistan also proposed that a 'Good Offices Committee' comprising members of the UN Security Council should visit both India and Pakistan to defuse the crisis. Both these proposals were rejected by India and the Soviet Union despite support from several other members of the Security Council.

In early October, Indira Gandhi, the Indian Prime Minister, visited Washington and held extensive talks with President Richard Nixon and Henry Kissinger, his National Security Adviser. Both Nixon and Kissinger used this opportunity not only to restrain the Indian Premier from the war path but also asked her to give a chance to these negotiations to succeed. But Indira Gandhi remained obdurate, and in Kissinger's astute assessment, war had become a certainty after her return from Washington. Kissinger at that time was already engaged in trying to arrange a meeting between the Awami League leadership and President Yahya Khan in order to arrive at a

---

212 Pakistan Horizon, XXIV, No. 3, pages 127-130.

mutually acceptable political solution. After Indira Gandhi's visit, he intensified his efforts to that end but without much success.

On 20th October, the Secretary General took the initiative to offer his personal good offices to find a solution. President Yahya accepted it with alacrity and invited U Thant to visit both the countries. He also made the proposal withdrawing both forces to a mutually agreed line in the rear. Both these proposals were firmly rejected by India. Several times during the month of November, Agha Shahi drew the attention of the President of the Security Council to the increasingly hostile activities by the Indian forces on the borders of East Pakistan. However, hardly any formal follow up action was ever initiated by the Council.

On the fateful day of 22nd November, regular Indian troops heralded the commencement of war in the Eastern Theatre when they formally entered the borders of East Pakistan. Yahya Khan brought this grave situation to U Thant's notice on 23rd and again on 29th November. Although on both these occasions Yahya did request for immediate UN intervention, yet the proposal of calling a Security Council meeting was carefully avoided. In his predictable response, U Thant made it clear that, having brought the situation to the notice of the members of the Security Council, he had gone as far as he was mandated under the UN Charter. A frustrated Agha Shahi has described this situation as follows:[213]

"On 22 November came the news that India had attacked East Pakistan. Mrs. Gandhi had said that if Indian troops were stopped it will be considered aggression. I thought this was the right time to go to the Security Council.

"I talked to the Turkish ambassador who said that now that India had entered East Pakistan the attitude of the countries was changing. He wondered why Pakistan did not want to go to the Security Council.

"I reported this view, quoting the words of the Turkish ambassador, to the Foreign Office to make the message more effective.

"I was instructed not to do anything by way of going to the Security Council." (Emphasis added.)

At this time, the United States too informally advised the Government of Pakistan to request for a meeting of the Security Council, but the President remained obdurate even after 3rd December, when the formal war

---

[213] *Interview with Agha Shahi* as reported by Hasan Zaheer, *Op cit*, page 320.

commenced.

Several chroniclers of these events, including some who had witnessed these events very closely, have tried in their own ways to proffer a rationale behind Yahya's obvious reluctance to move the Security Council at this time. These have ranged from wild conspiracy theories on one extreme, to the treacherous advice allegedly given by Zulfikar Ali Bhutto to the other. To our mind, all these explanations are entirely devoid of any hard evidence, logic and common sense. The only reasonable and rational explanation of Yahya's behavior in this respect has been offered by Hasan Zaheer and we gratefully acknowledge it.

Yahya was, till then, quite confident of making meaningful territorial gains on the Western Theatre. So obviously, he did not want international pressures to prematurely force him to accept a UN-sponsored ceasefire before achieving this objective. Evidently, he had a specific timeframe in his mind during which to develop his western offensive unhindered by UN interference. The *grund norm* of his strategy was to end the war only after having captured some meaningful chunks of Indian territory to serve as a bargaining chip eventually.[214] Irrespective of what his real rationale was, Pakistan's eventual projection of the Indian invasion in the Security Council was severely compromised by this initial delay and procrastination.

Thus, at that point of time, by default on Pakistan's part, the only active question on the UN agenda was the plight of the Bengali refugees then present in India. Even as the war raged on with full ferocity along the entire border of East Pakistan from 22nd November onwards, the Third Committee of the United Nations was still engaged in debating this and only this issue. The entire Soviet Bloc as well as most of the West European countries were at that time supportive of the primary Indian position that it was necessary to create conducive political conditions within East Pakistan in order to induce the refugees to return voluntarily. This stand was, however, strongly opposed by most Muslim and Afro-Asian countries as well as China, who had indeed all been perturbed by the blatant Indian aggression against East Pakistan. However, even their principal concern at this stage remained confined to the politicization of an essentially humanitarian issue.

Let us now take a penetrative look at the events happening at the United nations in relation to what was taking place on the ground in East Pakistan.

---

[214] Hasan Zaheer, *Ibid*, page 321.

3rd December

After the outbreak of the formal war between India and Pakistan, Pakistan's Foreign Secretary Sultan Mohammad Khan, as a preparatory measure, requested the formal approval for the designation of a leader of the delegation, to represent Pakistan in the anticipated debates at the United Nations fora. However, the President summarily rejected the proposal, saying there was no hurry.

Ironically, it was India which, on 3rd December, lodged a formal complaint with the Secretary General alleging that it had been attacked by Pakistan. Understandably though, India too desisted from taking the matter to the Security Council. That initiative was indeed to be taken by members of the Security Council like Argentina, Belgium, Burundi, Italy, Japan, Nicaragua, Somalia, the UK, and the USA, who collectively called for an emergency session of the Security Council on 4th December. The Americans on their part had already apprised Pakistan that they were going to raise the issue at the Security Council, whether Pakistan liked it or not.

Apparently, this move made by the US Government was reflective of the internecine strife and difference of opinion between President Nixon and his Secretary of State William Roger. Both of them, at this stage, had widely different perceptions on the issue: President Nixon and Henry Kissinger, his National Security Adviser, had, by then, developed an intense dislike for the Indian Prime Minister Indira Gandhi and both were essentially inclined to favour Pakistan; on the other hand, the State Department, headed by William Rogers, was more in sympathy with the Indian position. The prevalent state of affairs can be judged by the fact that several measures later ordered by Nixon to help Pakistan, particularly supply of weapons and ammunition through third countries, had to be kept concealed from his own Secretary of State and were directly handled by Henry Kissinger.

4th December

The 1606th Meeting of the UN Security Council was held on 4th December to discuss the East Pakistan crisis. At the very outset, Jacob Malik, the Soviet representative, raised the stakes by proposing that the Bangladesh representative must also be invited to participate in the proceedings along with those of Pakistan and India in order to have a balanced and wholesome discussion on the subject. This proposal was strongly opposed by Huang Hua, the Chinese representative, who argued that such a step would be tantamount to interference in Pakistan's internal affairs; this position was supported by Argentina as well.

Exercising its right of reply on this occasion, Pakistan's Agha Shahi blamed India for launching a blatant aggression against Pakistan and also stated that if the so-called Bangladesh representative was invited to participate in the meeting or to address the Council, Pakistan would have to seriously review its cooperation with the Security Council and the United Nations. Samar Sen, the Indian representative, stated that the entry of the Indian forces into Pakistan was a retaliatory step in its efforts to help the people of Bangladesh against oppression and if India was to be stopped from doing so by this Council, India would *deliberately and resolutely have to say no*. Thereafter, the question of Bengali representation in the meeting was deferred for the time being.

After these preliminaries were out of the way, George Bush, the US representative, moved draft resolution S/10416 on behalf of his government, the text of which had already been cleared with the Pakistan Delegation. The Resolution chiefly called for:

- Pakistan and India to take all steps for an immediate cessation of hostilities.

- The immediate withdrawal of armed personnel present on the territory of the other to their own sides of the India-Pakistan borders.

- Authorizing the Secretary General at the request of Governments of India and Pakistan to place observers along the border to report on the implementation of the ceasefire and troops withdrawal.

- Authorizing the Secretary General to use the personnel of UNMOGIP (United Nations Military Observers Group in India and Pakistan), already operative in Kashmir, for this purpose, as deemed necessary.

- Calling upon India and Pakistan and others concerned to exert their best efforts towards the creation of a climate conducive to the voluntary return of refugees to East Pakistan.

In the debate that followed, all the members of the Security Council, except for the Soviet Union and Poland, stressed the urgent need for an

323

immediate end to hostilities and subsequent consideration of the underlying causes of the conflict. In addition, China, and two other countries, emphasized the need for withdrawing the respective forces into their own side of the border. China also made a strong statement condemning India for its complicit role in this crisis and, on its part, pledged full support to Pakistan. The Chinese rhetoric was fully matched by the Soviet representative, who condemned Pakistan roundly and praised India for its restraint thus far.

In the final vote on this resolution, eleven out of fifteen members of the Security Council voted in favour of the resolution; two members abstained (UK and France); and, two members opposed (Soviet Union and Poland). The Resolution thus stood vetoed due to the negative vote cast by the Soviet Union.

As soon as this meeting ended on 4th December, the following Council members also submitted their own draft resolutions:

- Draft resolution (S/10418) submitted by the Soviet Union; its primary objective was mainly to counter the effects of the US resolution. It contemplated a political settlement in East Pakistan as the first action, which in turn would inevitably lead to cessation of hostilities as well. It also called upon the Government of Pakistan to cease all acts of violence by the Pakistan armed forces in East Pakistan, which, in their view, had led to the deterioration of the situation. Significantly, there was no mention of the Indian forces withdrawing to their own side of the border.

- Draft resolution (S/10417) submitted by Belgium, Italy and Japan.

- Draft resolution (S/10419) submitted by Argentina, Burundi, Nicaragua, Sierra Leone and Somalia.

All these draft resolutions were fixed for consideration by the Council in its next meeting, scheduled for 2:30 PM on 5th December.

5th December

On 5th December, before the Council could convene for meeting, the Chinese also submitted a draft resolution (S/10421), apparently in retaliation to the Soviet resolution. This condemned India for having launched large scale attacks on Pakistan and called upon her to withdraw its armed forces from Pakistan territory immediately and unconditionally. It called upon India and Pakistan to cease all hostilities and enjoined upon the members of the United Nations to support the Pakistani people in their just struggle to resist Indian aggression.

By this time, it had become obvious that the super power polarization had fully begun to cast its long shadows on this issue. The submission of these draft resolutions was by itself a stark manifestation of this polarization amongst the comity of the nations. As such, the majority of the Council members had begun to feel somewhat disenchanted with the intensely partisan positions adopted by the USA, the Soviet Union and the Chinese delegations. Hectic discussions took place between the representatives of these countries to identify the essential elements of an ideal resolution, which should not only be effective and balanced, yet be able to avoid a veto by one power or the other. They eventually arrived at the consensus that such a resolution must ideally comprise three basic elements as follows:

- Ceasefire.

- Withdrawal of forces.

- Early political solution in East Pakistan.

Accordingly, the eight non-permanent members of the Security Council (Argentina, Belgium, Italy, Japan, Nicaragua, Sierra Leone, Somalia, and Turkey) began to draft a new resolution on the above lines. The original draft produced by them called for:

- Immediate ceasefire.

- Immediate withdrawal of forces.

- Simultaneous creation of conditions necessary for the return of refugees.

- To make it palatable to the Soviet Union, they had also included a clause about Pakistan ending the state of emergency and ceasing military operations in East Pakistan.

It is a tribute to the prestige and status enjoyed by Agha Shahi that these eight sponsors felt obliged to show the above draft to him before its submission. Predictably, Agha Shahi reacted strongly against the last clause, being an infringement of Pakistan's sovereignty, and it thus had to be deleted.

Agha Shahi also succeeded in getting the word '*simultaneous*' deleted from the third point in the draft by proffering the argument that creation of conditions conducive to the return of refugees cannot be instituted overnight and would necessarily take time. Thus, in the amended draft, the ceasefire and withdrawal of forces were to take effect immediately, whereas the creation of conducive condition was to follow later. The draft (S/10423), that finally emerged after all this effort, was essentially a modification of the original US draft resolution. However, some additional points dealing with political conditions in East Pakistan had been incorporated, mainly to make the draft more palatable to the Soviet Union.

Since many of these very countries had already sponsored the earlier resolutions, and had now also agreed to co-sponsor this new resolution, Draft Resolutions, S/ 10417 and S/10419 were withdrawn to avoid duplication and confusion in the Council. Instead, as mentioned, a new Draft Resolution S/10423 was now jointly moved by these eight members of the Security Council. China too had agreed to support this resolution.

The contents of this balanced and quite reasonable draft were conveyed to the Foreign Secretary Sultan Mohammad Khan on telephone by Agha Shahi personally. Surprisingly, the Foreign Secretary asked him to prolong discussions on this resolution for two days at least, during which, presumably, the President would be able to make up his mind about it.

On this day, 5th December, intense fighting was in progress in East Pakistan, where towns like Darsana, Thakugaon, Kamalpur and Akhaura had already been lost. Meanwhile, nothing much was happening on the Western Front too, and the whole purpose of opening the second front was thereby being compromised by this inaction. This situation was hardly unknown to the members of the Security Council and had, thus, instilled a sense of urgency amongst them, in which environment the procrastination by the Pakistan delegation on this resolution was seemingly rather incongruent. Thus, it became impossible for Agha Shahi to persuade the sponsoring delegates to delay their resolution any longer in wait for the President of Pakistan to make up his mind.

The Security Council held its 1607th meeting, as scheduled, on 5th December, with two resolutions on its agenda: Soviet Union's S/10418; and, the Eight Nations' S/10423. After some acrimonious initial debate, mainly among the permanent members, the resolutions were put to the vote with the following results:

- Soviet Resolution S/10418 received two votes in favour, those of the USSR and Poland. China voted against it while all the other twelve abstained; the resolution thus stood vetoed by China.

- Eight Nations' Resolution S/10423 received eleven votes in favour, two against (USSR and Poland) and two abstentions (UK and France). The resolution thus stood vetoed by the Soviet Union.

The Italian Delegate then moved a short resolution (S/10425) which called for an immediate ceasefire, followed by further consideration of the measures to restore peace in the region by the Security Council; this resolution also was co-sponsored by Belgium, Japan, Nicaragua, Sierra Leone, and Tunisia. (Since this resolution did not envisage withdrawal of forces, Pakistan strongly objected to it and hinted that it would have the resolution vetoed by China.)

At this time, China also decided to press forward its draft resolution S/10421 for consideration by the Council. The ensuing debate on this too was marred by mutual recriminations and vituperative speeches by Huang Hua of China and Jacob Malik of the USSR. In this highly-charged environment, the consideration of both the above drafts was pended for further consultations.

6th December

The next (1608th) meeting of the Security Council was held on 6th December, with the Chinese Resolution S/10421 and the Italian Resolution S/10425 on its agenda. At this time, Jacob Malik, the Soviet Delegate, moved an amendment to the Italian Resolution to the effect that the USSR would agree to an immediate ceasefire provided that the Government of Pakistan was also charged *'to simultaneously give effect to the will of the people as expressed in the elections of 1970'*. At this development, the Italian Delegation felt that the Soviet amendment had, in effect, compromised the very purpose of their resolution. Italy, therefore, decided to withdraw this Resolution; obviously, the Soviet amendment to it also lapsed ipso facto.

By this time, the Soviet Union had to some extent become conscious of its isolation in the Security Council, and so it decided to show a measure of flexibility in its position. Accordingly, the Soviet Delegation circulated yet another draft resolution (S/10428), which was a slight improvement on its earlier draft (S/10418). The new draft visualized an immediate ceasefire as a first step and called upon Pakistan *'to give simultaneous effect to the will of the people of East Pakistan as expressed in the elections of December 1970'.* In plain terms, it enjoined that as soon as the ceasefire took effect, the political situation in East Pakistan must be restored to the pre-25th March position.

The debate on this resolution too was eclipsed by the use of acrimonious and almost abusive language by Jacob Malik while replying to the Chinese criticism of this resolution. Pakistan, on its part, also opposed this resolution vehemently. Considering the highly charged and polarized environment then pervading the Council and the certainty of its being vetoed by the Chinese, the Soviet Delegation withdrew their resolution without a formal vote.

In the words of an astute analyst:[215]

"At this point it may be noted that its acceptance would have avoided the surrender in Dhaka, though the withdrawal of the army from East Pakistan required by it would have been just as humiliating within and outside Pakistan. Moreover, it would not have been easy to persuade China and US, which for their own reasons were not prepared for any compromise with the Soviet Union on the issue of Indian aggression. The military situation, however, was deteriorating so rapidly that after forty-eight hours even this offer of a ceasefire was not available."

In view of the serious situation in East Pakistan, which was in fact deteriorating by the hour, and also the feeling of stalemate which seemed to pervade the proceedings of the Security Council, the non-permanent members of the Council were forced to take the initiative once again. Led by Somalia and Argentina, and backed by US and China, they decided to initiate the 'The Uniting for Peace' procedure for referring the matter to the General Assembly.

Consequently, a six-nation Resolution 303 (1971) of 6 December 1971 was moved in the Security Council, which *'considered the letter dated 4 December from the United States of America and nine other countries addressed to the President of the Security Council and decided to refer the question contained in Document S/Agenda/1606 to the General Assembly at its twenty-sixth session'.* This resolution was duly put to vote; eleven Council members (Argentina, Belgium, Burundi, China, Italy, Japan, Nicaragua, Sierra Leone, Somalia, Tunisia, and the United States) voted in its favour while four (France, Poland, UK, and USSR) abstained. The matter thus stood referred to the General Assembly.

---

[215] Hasan Zaheer, *op cit*, page 373.

7th December

On this eventful day, as Jessore fell to the Indians, Henry Kissinger, on the other side of the globe, was to record that:[216]

'on December 7, Yahya informed us that East Pakistan was disintegrating'.

He also states:

"A report reached us from a source whose reliability we had never any reason to doubt…. 'That India would not accept any General Assembly call for a ceasefire', until East Pakistan was liberated. Thereafter, the Indian forces would concentrate on the southern part of Azad Kashmir 'and continue fighting until the Pakistan army and the air force were wiped out'. Mrs. Gandhi also told colleagues that in case China intervened, 'the Soviets had promised to take appropriate counteraction"[217]

Henceforth, both Nixon and Kissinger would become predominantly worried about the existence and security of West Pakistan and the ultimate fate of East Pakistan ceased to be their primary concern.

On this very day too, the General Assembly of the United Nations convened to consider the reference duly received from the Security Council. Imbued with a deep sense of urgency in view of the critical situation in East Pakistan, the General Assembly, in an unprecedented move, decided to impose a time limit on speeches by the country representatives and did not allow any interruptions in its proceedings until the end of two sessions (2002nd) and (2003rd) held the same day. It had the following two draft resolutions on its agenda for consideration:

- Draft Resolution A/L 647 Revision 1 was essentially similar to draft resolution S/10423 submitted to the Security Council by its eight non-permanent members and vetoed by the Soviet Union on 5th December. It was sponsored by the same countries this time too, but by the time of the vote, the number of its sponsoring countries had swelled to thirty-four.

- Draft Resolution A/L 648, submitted by the Soviet Union, was essentially similar to its earlier Security Council draft resolution S/10428 but which it had withdrawn before it was voted upon.

---

[216] Henry Kissinger, *White House Years*, Boston: Little, Brown, 1979 page 901.
[217] *Ibid.*

About sixty delegates, representing their respective countries, participated in the ensuing debate and most of them expressed serious reservations on the failure of the Security Council to bring an end to a major war between two member countries. This debate too essentially conformed to the pattern already established during the Security Council debates on the subject. Thus, it was marked by acrimonious and vitriolic exchanges mainly between the Soviet and the Chinese delegates on one hand and the Indian and Pakistani delegates on the other.

The Indian delegate Samar Sen, in particular, adopted a blatantly defiant attitude stating that India would not accept the provisions of Resolution A/L 647 Revision 1, even if adopted by the General Assembly. He went on to say:

"The representative of Pakistan was moved about the breakup of his country.....But we have to face the fact that it has broken up; nothing on earth can stop it; it has happened.[218]

Eventually, Draft Resolution A/L 647, now numbered as Resolution 2793 (XXXVI) was put to vote and adopted by 104 votes in favour, 11 against, and 10 abstentions. It called upon the Governments of India and Pakistan to take measures forthwith for an immediate ceasefire and withdrawal of forces to their own side of the border. It also urged both the countries to intensify efforts for the voluntary return of refugees and to deal with the issues which had caused the hostilities. The General Assembly also decided not to vote upon the Soviet draft resolution A/L 648.

Under the Charter of the United Nations, the resolutions adopted by the General Assembly only possess a moral pressure and are not binding on the concerned countries. Thus, the adoption of this Resolution even by a heavy majority of the comity of nations made no material or tangible difference to the situation on the ground. The text of the Resolution was conveyed the same evening by telephone to Islamabad via the Swedish capital Stockholm, the only link available due to the war; however, due to time difference and transmission time, it was already the morning of 8th December when the message was received in Islamabad.

8th December

It will be recalled that on this day, Brahmanbaria had been captured by the Indians, the city of Comilla had been encircled and the Indian forces

---

[218] Hasan Zaheer, *op cit*, page 375.

were advancing towards Chandpur. Situation in the Northwestern and Southwestern Sectors was hardly any better.

Full realization of the grim situation facing the country finally dawned on President Yahya Khan. In his rather naïve estimation, the United Nations was now the only place where some deft diplomatic manoeuvring could retrieve the country's flagging fortunes. He was thus eventually forced to take the step which he was all along really loathe to take. He appointed the ageing Bengali politician Nurul Amin as the Prime Minister-designate, and Zulfikar Ali Bhutto as the Vice Premier/Foreign Minister-designate. Even at this critical time, he did not hand over any real powers to them and merely conferred hollow titles on them to assuage their egos. Bhutto was also instructed to rush to the United Nations and assume the position of the Head of the Pakistan delegation there.

At that time, there were no direct flights leaving from any of Pakistan airports for any European or US destinations. He was therefore constrained to take an Afghan Airline flight to Kabul and then managed to reach New York by 10th December via Rome and Bonn; in Rome, he was ostensibly delayed due to an influenza bout as well. This delay in assuming his fresh responsibilities in New York did cause some adverse criticism from certain quarters, who have ascribed it to the usual conspiracy theories. However, if one takes the commercial aviation situation prevalent in 1971 from Rawalpindi to Kabul to New York, the delay may hardly seem very ominous. In any case, it can hardly be averred that, in the presence of a seasoned diplomat like Agha Shahi, Pakistan's case suffered because of this delay.

Bhutto called Agha Shahi from Bonn on telephone and informed him that he would henceforth lead the Pakistan Delegation at the United Nations. There was a background of some acrimony between the two since Bhutto's earlier stint as the Foreign Minister of Pakistan; ever since then Bhutto had looked upon the seasoned diplomat with a measure of distrust. As Agha Shahi sought to apprise him of the latest developments and the prevalent ambiance in the Security Council, he was cut short by the new Foreign Minister rather abruptly and curtly advised that the responsibility was now on the former's (Bhutto's) shoulders and as such he would now handle the situation. Agha Shahi could only mutter, *"Most welcome"*.[219]

9th December

---

[219] Lt Gen Kamal Matinuddin, *op cit*, page 449.

On this date, the thrusts launched by the Indian IV Corps in the Eastern Sector had reached Ashuganj, Daudkundi and Chandpur on River Meghna; and, General Sagat Singh was already planning to contrive a crossing over this major obstacle. Also, on this very day, a thoroughly disgruntled Governor of East Pakistan was to propose to the President to accord approval to the suggestion made by Paul Mark Henry, the local UN representative in Dacca, to declare Dacca an open city. By this time, the international pressure to accept an early ceasefire had also begun to mount on the Indian Government, which added fresh impetus to their efforts to attain their military objectives as early as possible, particularly the capture of Dacca.

The Foreign Secretary of Pakistan, Sultan Muhammad Khan, informed Agha Shahi in New York that Pakistan had accepted the General Assembly Resolution of 7th December but with the following caveats:

- While conveying formal acceptance of the General Assembly Resolution to the UN Secretary General, Agha Shahi must ensure the inclusion of reference to Article 2 of the UN Charter, as well as paragraphs 4, 5, and 6 of the UN Declaration on the strengthening of International Security, in the body of the Resolution. (Article 2 as well as the said Declaration enjoin respect for the territorial integrity of member states).

- He was also asked to request for concrete action by the UN for cessation of hostilities with immediate effect, withdrawal of forces, and posting of UN observers on both sides of the border.

- Agha Shahi was also formally informed that Zulfikar Ali Bhutto was on his way to New York and the conveyance of this formal acceptance to the Secretary General might be held up till his arrival. However, he was also authorized to convey it immediately in case he considered the delay to be inadvisable.

Agha Shahi was viewing the rapidly changing situation with increasing concern. As a seasoned diplomat, he could hardly have failed to note the anxiety implicit in the Foreign Secretary's instructions on immediate ceasefire and withdrawal of forces; to him it clearly indicated that there could hardly be any realistic possibility now of making territorial gains in the Western Theatre to serve as bargaining chips against losses in East Pakistan. Consequently, Agha Shahi took the decision to immediately convey Pakistan's formal acceptance of the General Assembly Resolution rather than waiting for Bhutto's arrival. This further deepened the mistrust between the two; later on, Bhutto was to register his protest to President Yahya for taking this step without consulting him.

In the wake of the recent news of the fall of Jessore and the rapid advance of Indian forces towards Dacca, the ambiance in the corridors of the UN changed perceptibly and the members of the Security Council began to tacitly accept the ground realities. Consequently, their primary emphasis began shifting essentially towards putting an immediate ceasefire on ground, mainly to stop fighting in the Western Theatre rather than the withdrawal of Indian forces from East Pakistan. Seasoned diplomats like Henry Kissinger were already conscious of the lurking peril for West Pakistan inherent in the emerging scenario.

There was yet another important development on the diplomatic front on this date. Earlier, on 6th December, President Nixon had sent a message to the Soviet leader Leonid Brezhnev, in which he had emphasized restraint and the territorial integrity of the sub-continent. Now, on 9th December, a message had been received in reply from Brezhnev which proposed a ceasefire and resumption of negotiations with Sheikh Mujibur Rahman at the point they were broken off on 25th March 1971. Despite the certainty that it would inevitably lead to independence of East Pakistan, Kissinger viewed it as a good, face-saving formula to ensure the integrity of **West Pakistan**. He, however, refrained from any further consideration of this formula because of his concern that India might attempt to over-run West Pakistan while the modalities of these negotiations were being discussed. He could hardly fail to observe that though the Indian ambassador had, on an earlier occasion assured the US about the territorial integrity of West Pakistan, yet he did not commit anything in respect of Azad Kashmir. [220]

10th December

In East Pakistan, fierce fighting was still in progress in the Hilli area of the Northwestern Sector while on the Eastern Sector, the troops of 57 Mountain Division had begun to cross the Meghna in a bold and imaginative heli-borne operation. The battle had thus further closed in towards Dacca.

It will also be recalled that on this day, a message, signed by General Farman, had been handed over to the UN Representative in Dacca conveying an offer of a ceasefire in the Eastern Theatre.

Because of the time difference, it was still 5:30 AM in New York when

---

[220] Henry Kissinger, *op cit*, pages 903-904.

Agha Shahi was woken up by Brian Urquhart of the UN Secretariat and informed of this message, presumably 'signed by Major General Farman Ali Khan, Military Advisor to the Governor of East Pakistan'. At 8 AM, he was also conveyed the Secretary General's intention to inform the President of the Security Council about *'the collapse of the Pakistan Army in East Pakistan and their request for an immediate ceasefire'.*

Agha Shahi asked the UN staffer to convey his personal request to the Secretary General to hold off further action on the message till such time as he could verify its authenticity from the Government of Pakistan. He also pointed out that General Farman had no authority to ask for a ceasefire. At about 10:30 AM, Agha Shahi received a garbled message from Foreign Secretary Sultan via Stockholm advising him that it (Farman's) was an unauthorized proposal. Agha Shahi immediately informed the Secretary General accordingly.

U Thant, nonetheless, felt obligated to circulate Farman's message for the information of the permanent members of the Council. Farman's message has been considered one of the most controversial events of East Pakistan of that period; it effectively negated even the remotest chance of obtaining some sort of face-saving resolution from the Security Council.

Bhutto reached New York at about 3 PM on 10th December. Agha Shahi describes his arrival as follows:

"I went into the plane as it landed and in the general bustle of getting down told him about Farman's message. When we were in the car along with an army officer of the ISI, Bhutto said, 'Shahi what were you saying about Farman's message in the plane? You were not very coherent.' When I repeated the contents, addressing the army officer he said, 'Look Colonel, we have been betrayed.' [221]

The same evening Bhutto asked Yahya to rescind the authority given to Governor Malik to approach the UN, and also informed him that he had already asked Agha Shahi to inform the Secretary General to disregard the Farman message. Bhutto also threatened that unless his advice was accepted he would return to Pakistan immediately.

Meanwhile, back in Rawalpindi, another important development was taking place, which in fact was a potent indicator of the real overall operational situation, even in the Western Theatre. Henry Kissinger rang up President Yahya and apprised him of the proposals earlier made by

---

[221] Hasan Zaheer, *op cit*, page 389.

President Brezhnev of the USSR. After some discussion, President Yahya agreed with him that the proposals made by Brezhnev should be made the basis of a new UN resolution. In plain terms, it meant a ceasefire in situ, without any withdrawal of forces, and resumption of negotiations with the Awami League leadership at the point they were interrupted in March 1971. Kissinger notes on this occasion:

"In short, Pakistan, in return for an end to Indian military operations **in the West***, was prepared to settle for* **the military status quo in the East**........*and to enter negotiations.......whose only possible outcome could be the emergence of an independent Bangladesh."[222]* (Emphasis added.)

As the news about General Farman's message regarding a ceasefire in East Pakistan began to reverberate in the corridors of the US Government, the person perhaps to be upset the most was Kissinger himself, who immediately called General N A M Raza, Pakistan's Ambassador to the US, to his office and:

"urged him to make the ceasefire proposal consistent with what had been agreed to with Yahya, otherwise the danger to the West would mount as operations in Bengal concluded".[223]

Kissinger, thus, was making it clear to General Raza that unless the ceasefire proposal covered both East and the West, the danger against West Pakistan would appreciably increase. In his astute appreciation, after the Indian army and air formations were shifted from the Eastern Theatre, Pakistan would not be able to offer resistance for more than two to three weeks.

It was also in this meeting that Kissinger informed Raza that the Carrier Group USS *Enterprise* was already on its way to the Bay of Bengal from its homeport Singapore, but that its presence would begin to be felt only after some 48 hours. It was based on this information that, as already mentioned, the President of Pakistan cancelled his earlier message (G-0002) regarding ceasefire and, early on 11th December, sent the following fresh instructions to the Governor of East Pakistan:

"Do not take any action on my last message to you(.) Important diplomatic and military moves are taking place by our friends(.) It is essential that we hold for another 36 hours at all costs(.)Please also pass this message to Gen Niazi and Gen Farman(.)

---

[222] Henry Kissinger, *op cit*, page 905.
[223] *Ibid, page 906.*

The emerging situation was causing great anxiety to President Nixon as well. The same evening, 10th December, Kissinger undertook a secret visit to New York to hold an unannounced meeting with Huang Hua, the Chinese Representative to the UN, in a CIA safe house. The only other persons present on this occasion were General Alexander Haig and George Bush. During this meeting, Kissinger candidly outlined the US policy on South Asia and the details of the Brezhnev Plan, as well as the background of the contemplated UN resolution based on it. However, his main intention was to coax the Chinese to make some offensive move against India in order to ease Pakistan's woes. He said:

"the President wants you to know that if the People's Republic were to consider the situation on the Indian subcontinent a threat to its security, and if it took measures to protect its security, the US would oppose efforts of others to interfere with the People's Republic." [224]

This was as clear an invitation as Kissinger could make to the Chinese to militarily interfere in this crisis and not to worry too much about the Soviet reaction. Huang Hua was however totally non-committal on this subject. He merely confined his remarks to the issues before the Security Council and insisted that withdrawal of forces must take place before the start of negotiations with the Awami League leadership as a matter of principle. Kissinger, however, warned him that insistence on such a position would play into the hands of the Indian and Soviet strategy to dismember Pakistan.[225]

Eventually, on 10th December, President Nixon wrote an urgent letter to President Brezhnev conveying to him the proposal for an immediate ceasefire on both fronts but without any withdrawal of forces.

11th December

A breakfast meeting between Bhutto and Kissinger was held this morning at Waldorf Towers, New York, in the suite of George Bush, then the US Ambassador to the UN. Kissinger opened the meeting with some words of advice to Bhutto, which could hardly prove to be comforting for him at this critical time. He went on to say:[226]

---

[224] Gary J Bass, Op Cit, page 302-303.
[225] Henry Kissinger, Op Cit, page 906.
[226] Henry Kissinger, Op cit, pages, 907-908.

*"Pakistan would not be saved by mock-tough rhetoric. It is not that we do not want to help you; **it is that we want to preserve you**. It is all very well to proclaim principles but finally we have to assure your survival.....**The next forty-eight hours would be decisive**. We should not waste them in posturing for the history books."*

He goes on to record Bhutto's reaction to his advice:

"Bhutto was composed and understanding. He knew the facts as I; he was a man without illusions, prepared to do what was necessary, however painful, to save what was left of his country."

This is how Agha Shahi has recorded this meeting:

"1. Ambassador Raza, George Bush and a State Department official were present in the breakfast meeting. Kissinger gave an analysis of the situation: he was very fond of giving such analyses. He told Bhutto, 'We have received information that after overrunning East Pakistan Indian troops will be transferred to West Pakistan. We should get a ceasefire before that. You are going for withdrawal of forces which is being vetoed by the Russians. But I am going for a ceasefire from the Security Council. However, you should not seem desperate. The best thing would be to go to the Security Council with the Resolution of the General Assembly, which will be vetoed. Then you should go for a ceasefire. The timeframe for this strategy would be determined by you, which would depend on Pakistan forces' ability to hold on.' Kissinger then turned round to Raza who said, *'we will fight to the last.'* " [227]

His main advice to Bhutto was to work out a common position with the Chinese; he said that if the Chinese continued to insist on withdrawal of forces as an essential component of a UN resolution, the United States would lose the ability to be effective despite 'formalistic UN resolutions' and in this respect the next forty-eight hours would be decisive.

Kissinger and Bhutto eventually came to a firm understanding on the future course of action to be adopted at the UN. It was decided that should no reply to President Nixon's letter be received from Moscow about the US proposals on immediate ceasefire in both the theatres by 12th December, the issue would then be taken up in the Security Council. In such an eventuality, the strategy would be to initially demand a ceasefire as well as withdrawal of forces, but in case of a Soviet veto:

---

[227] Hasan Zaheer, *op cit*, pages 395-396.

'we would settle for a simple ceasefire in place, in effect accepting the Indian fait accompli in Bengal. I had to count on Bhutto to make sure the Chinese understood our position'.[228]

By 12th December, Bhutto had finally managed to bring the Chinese round to the above-mentioned US-Pakistan understanding. He made them understand the inherent danger to West Pakistan and its desperation for an early ceasefire. Huang Hua, the Chinese representative finally agreed to support the US strategy of initially demanding a ceasefire as well as withdrawal, but ultimately accepting a ceasefire in situ.

Based on his meetings with Kissinger and Huang Hua, Bhutto sent two detailed messages to the President in the evening of 11th December. In the first one, he roundly blamed the President for putting him in an embarrassing position by delegating blanket authority to Governor Malik for accepting ceasefire in East Pakistan, which eventually precipitated General Farman's letter to the UN representative. The salient points of the second message were as follows:

- He sought to establish his relevance by asserting that his total stay in New York hardly exceeded twenty-four hours and his main concern during this limited period was to re-establish Pakistan's credibility, which stood completely eroded in the aftermath of General Farman's message.
- He underscored the differences in the US and the Chinese perceptions, and his own success in ensuring that the duo adopt a cohesive strategy in the Security Council.

- He strongly recommended that a strong counter-offensive in the Western Theatre and the resultant territorial gains there would increase the pressure on Indians to accept an early ceasefire; it would also inculcate some sense of urgency in the Security Council.

- His main plea before the President was that if the ground situation could be held for a week, the diplomatic position in the UN could take a turn for the better. On the same rationale, he also recommended waiting seventy-two hours before approaching the Security Council.[229]

---

[228] Henry Kissinger, *op cit*, pages 907-908.
[229] Hasan Zaheer, *op cit*, page 397.

338

The same evening, Bhutto rose to address the Security Council for the first time and delivered a long and defiant speech; but it was to fall on deaf ears. The super powers had their own priorities and interests to watch for.

12th December

The deteriorating ground situation in East Pakistan as well as the lack luster performance in the Western Theatre had by now fully forced Yahya to pin all hopes on a UN enforced ceasefire. His anxiety was duly reflected in the messages he sent to Bhutto in response to his messages of the previous day. The first message contained the following instructions:

"Your thinking about delaying reference to Security Council and hold out militarily for at least one week will be fatal to our position and multiply difficulties. The fall of East Pakistan will permit [India]......to switch over to West Pakistan and this will weaken our negotiating position. The situation demands fastest action especially now when Chinese Russian and American thinking alike on question of ceasefire and withdrawal [in that order].

"You have stressed need for a big push in West. This consideration is actively borne in mind but it is a military situation and has to be left to military commanders. We cannot blunder into a situation to our........

"Please consult with all interested parties urgent for moving a resolution in Security Council immediately."[230]

In the second message, the President sought to explain his position viz a viz General Farman's message but the most telling phrase in the message was: *There is no question of surrender but the situation in East Pakistan is such that operations cannot be continued for long.......'.*

Meanwhile, Kissinger conveyed to Vorontsov, the Soviet Ambassador in Washington, that if no reply to Nixon's letter of 10th December was received from Moscow by noon on 12th December, *"we will move unilaterally"*. With vague menace, he also added that, *"we may take other steps".*[231] He was in turn informed by the ambassador that the Soviet Deputy Foreign Minister had been sent to New Delhi to urge restraint. Kissinger, however, was not sure of true Soviet and Indian intentions at this stage. His main worry was that:

---

[230] *Ibid*, page 398.
[231] Telephone conversation between Kissinger and Vorontsov dated 11th December as reported by Gary J Bass, Op Cit, page 300.

'they deliberately kept open the possibility of the kind of annexation [of Azad Kashmir] achievable only by the total destruction of the Pakistan army and the consequent disintegration of Pakistan'. [232]

At this stage, President Nixon sent yet another message on the hot line to Moscow at about midday on 12th December, conveying that *'the Indian assurances still lack any concreteness.'* The message contained a veiled warning as well with Nixon saying, *'time is of essence to avoid consequences neither of us want'.* Along with that, Nixon also ordered to hold up the movement of the Seventh Fleet for twenty-four hours to wait for the Soviet response. In reply, the Soviets vaguely informed him that they were discussing the matter with India and would inform the US of the results as soon as possible.[233]

In the event, the Security Council next reconvened in the evening of 12th December (1611th meeting) at the request of the United States. George Bush, the US permanent representative to the UN, read out a long opening statement blaming India for the war and then moved a draft resolution (S/10446. Rev. 1), which demanded an immediate ceasefire and withdrawal of forces. This was, in essence, the same draft as had been passed by the General Assembly earlier on and entirely in conformity with the strategy earlier worked out by Kissinger and Bhutto just the day before.

Meanwhile, Sardar Swaran Singh, the Indian Foreign Minister, had been sent posthaste to New York as a counter to Bhutto's famed rhetoric. He addressed the Security Council at this stage and again stressed upon their contention that the presence of the Bangladesh representatives was essential for the success of any ceasefire proposal. He also blamed Pakistan for creating conditions leading to the conflict and for mounting a full-scale war on India. In stating this, Sardar Swaran Singh was essentially reiterating the same stance as had just been conveyed by his Prime Minister to U Thant formally. Earlier the same day, a letter written by Mrs. Gandhi, the Indian Prime Minister, had been received by Secretary General U Thant, which had clearly stated that:

"There can be withdrawal of India's forces to its own territory if the rulers of West Pakistan would withdraw their own forces from Bangladesh and arrange a peaceful settlement with those who were recently their fellow citizens but now owe allegiance to the government of Bangladesh".

---

[232] Henry Kissinger, *op cit*, page 908.
[233] *Ibid*, pages 909-911.

340

Sardar Swaran Singh was followed by Bhutto who spoke for over two hours in his classic fiery rhetoric. He reminded the members of the Council that India, with the help of the Soviet Union, was seeking to dismember Pakistan. Bhutto thundered:

"Should the UN allow a member state to be dismembered by force of arms?........We will fight for a thousand years!........A sovereign state cannot be dismembered limb by limb. Today it is Pakistan, tomorrow it will be someone else. The Pandora's Box has been opened. There will be Bangladeshes all over the world including Britain and the Soviet Union."

His words were to fall on deaf ears as the members continued to listen passively.[234]

After the speeches, the US representative pressed for an immediate vote on the resolution. He was vehemently opposed by the Soviet representative, who, apparently in a blatant attempt to gain maximum time for India in which to accomplish its mission, accused the US of forcing the Soviet Union to veto the resolution by pressing for an immediate vote. The meeting was then adjourned till the next day.

13th December

The Security Council met for its 1613th meeting as scheduled in the afternoon. At that time, all the daily newspapers in New York were showing banner headlines announcing that the war in East Pakistan had entered its final and terminal phase. By that time, the Security Council members had also become cognizant of the stark reality that the Soviet Union would regardless continue to veto every resolution till such time as the imminent Indian occupation of East Pakistan materialized. At this stage, the Indians too were hardly interested in the adoption of any resolution at all; they only needed just another twenty-four hours or so to bring their military operation in the east to a successful end. By the time Security Council meeting resumed, it had also become clear that the rapid deterioration of the military situation in East Pakistan had overtaken the US proposals as contained in their under- consideration resolution.

The meeting opened with the Soviet delegation resorting to a long-winded diatribe, condemning Pakistan even more strongly than ever before. He was followed by Sardar Swaran Singh, who too made a very acrimonious speech against Pakistan. The resolution was then put to the

---

[234] Lt Gen Kamal Matinuddin, *op cit,* pages 451-452.

vote: it received 11 votes in favour, two against (USSR and Poland) and two abstentions (Britain and France). The resolution thus stood vetoed.

At this stage, the British and the French delegates, for the first time, sought to make an effort to come up with a compromise resolution acceptable to all. Meanwhile, yet another resolution (S/10451) was moved by Italy and Japan, essentially as a means to keep the issue alive in the Council. Eventually, it too failed to garner any support and was not even put to the vote.

14th December

Pakistan leadership apparently had pinned high hopes in the outcome of the Security Council meeting scheduled for 13th December. Accordingly, General Hamid, the COS Army, had sent the following message of encouragement to General Niazi at midnight 13th /14th December:

"Reference G-1286 UN Security Council in session. Most likely will order ceasefire. Matter of hours. Hold out till UN resolution passed. Fully realize most critical situation Eastern Command"

However, all their hopes came to a naught with the third Soviet veto, as described above. It will be recalled that at about 1:30 PM on 14th December, President Yahya had already sent his fateful message G-0013 to Commander Eastern Command advising him to *'take all necessary measures to stop the fighting........'*. This has been described at length in the previous Chapter.

The morning of 14th December was rather a busy one for the members of the Security Council in New York as they continued to hold hectic discussions and negotiations on the situation in East Pakistan. The daily newspapers were painting a dismal picture of the war situation. The leading story was about the call of the Indian Army Chief to the Pakistan Army to surrender and the Indian official sources had announced that Dacca will be surrounded in the next 24 to 48 hours. Pakistan's negotiating position at the UN had, thus, become tangibly weak, particularly after the receipt of news about General Niazi's offer for ceasefire.

The British and the French delegates handed over the copy of their much-awaited draft resolution (S/10455) to the Pakistan delegation just a few hours before the Council meeting. Its salient points were as follows:
- An immediate ceasefire on the <u>West Pakistan border</u> and on the ceasefire line in Kashmir.

342

- Negotiations between the military commanders of both sides in East Pakistan for an immediate ceasefire.

- Ceasefire to remain in effect until the withdrawal of all forces in both theatres.

- The urgent conclusion of a comprehensive political settlement with the elected representatives of East Pakistan.

- Both governments to accept the offer of good offices of the Secretary General.

There was hardly anything of solace for Pakistan in this resolution, which did not even call for withdrawal of forces and not even an immediate ceasefire in East Pakistan but mere negotiations for it. Yet, at this time, it was the only serious proposal before the Security Council. Pakistan could have had this resolution vetoed by China but then there would have been no resolution at all before the Council; this eminently suited India but at this time the UN was the only hope for survival as far as Pakistan was concerned.

It was in these dismal conditions that the Pakistan delegation attended the Security Council meeting (1614th) in the afternoon of 14th December. There was hardly any discussion on the Anglo-French resolution and the British representative proposed an adjournment for further consultations.

The Polish Delegation had circulated its draft resolution (S/1453) among the Council members but it was formally tabled before the Council meeting on the next day (15th December) in a slightly revised form (S/1453. Rev. 1).

In yet another desperate bid to salvage its integrity, Pakistan requested an immediate meeting of the Council the same evening, which was duly convened (1614th Adl.1.) at less than an hour's notice. However, it could hardly achieve anything in the face of Soviet rigidity.

15th December

The next meeting of the Security Council (1615th) was held at 7 PM (when the dawn of 16th December was already breaking in East Pakistan). The following resolutions were on the agenda for discussion in this meeting:

- The Anglo-French resolution (S/10455), carried over from the previous day.

- The Soviet Union resolution (S/1457).

- The Polish resolution (S/1453 Rev. 1.).

All these resolutions essentially called for a political settlement in East Pakistan one way or another.

- In the Anglo-French resolution, the ceasefire was to take place first, followed by the political settlement in accordance with the principles of the UN charter, thus, ensuring the territorial integrity of Pakistan. It left the withdrawal open-ended and in the context of the Indian presence in East Pakistan, it was in effect the same as the Soviet Draft S/10457 and its earlier version S/10428.

- In the Soviet draft, the ceasefire and the political settlement were to take place simultaneously but there was no mention of the UN charter in it; moreover, the Soviet draft did not call for a withdrawal of forces.

- We shall discuss the Polish Resolution at length shortly.

With the news of Pakistan's imminent surrender filtering in, Bhutto addressed the Security Council for the last time. Faced with grim the prospect that he as a politician would forever be burdened with the responsibility for accepting the surrender, he had by then lost his cool. In a fiery rhetoric for which he was well known, he accused the Security Council of dilatory tactics; he labeled the UN a *"fraud and a farce"* and strongly denounced the neutral attitude shown by Britain and France thus far. In a final, defiant gesture, he dramatically stood up, tore up his notes, and walked out of the Security Council, saying:

"Perhaps this will be my last speech in the Security Council. I have not come here to accept abject surrender. If the Security Council wants me to be a party to the legalizing of abject surrender, then I say that under no circumstances shall I be. I will not take back a document of surrender from the Security Council. I will not be a party to the legalizing of aggression.

"For four days, the Security Council has procrastinated. Why? Because the object was for Dacca to fall....... Why should I waste my time here in the Security Council? I

344

will not be a party to the ignominious surrender of a part of my country. You can take your Security Council. Here you are, I am going."[235]

Since then Bhutto has been constantly accused of deliberately tearing up the Polish Resolution and thus ensuring the surrender of the armed forces in East Pakistan. However, Iftikhar Ali Malik, the APP representative in New York, who was not only present on this occasion but also picked up the torn papers after Bhutto had left, confirms that these were merely Bhutto's own notes and not the Resolution.[236]

As the news of the imminent likelihood of a ceasefire in East Pakistan began to circulate in the corridors of the UN, the British Delegation felt that in view of these developments, it was highly unlikely that their draft resolution would be acceptable to India and the Soviet Union; they therefore decided not to press their resolution any further. The Pakistan mission thereupon sent a telex message to the Foreign Office informing them of this development. It was also intimated that henceforth their efforts would be directed towards obtaining a simple ceasefire resolution with a call for adherence to the Geneva Conventions. The telex also contained Bhutto's considered opinion that *'after the Indian occupation of East Pakistan, inclusion of a political settlement in any resolution would mean juridical sanction of it.'*[237]

Islamabad was also informed that the Soviet representative had been given instructions, at this time, to veto even a simple ceasefire resolution. The most that the Indians would agree to was a loose formulation calling upon the parties to take steps to bring about a cessation of hostilities, leading to lasting peace. (The obvious implication was that the Indians would determine the timing and terms for cessation of hostilities.)

After this, Bhutto did not stay in New York; he flew to Key Biscayne, Florida on 17th December to meet with Kissinger and Nixon on Bebe Rebozo's yatch, where Nixon assured him of ample US military and financial support. He left for Rome by Pan Am Flight 108 on the next day and bided his time there watching the post-surrender developments in Pakistan. His time would come soon!

The Polish Imbroglio

---

235 Maj Gen Fazal Muqim Khan, op cit, page 188.
236 Lt Gen Kamal Matinuddin, *op cit,* page 453.
237 Hasan Zaheer, *op cit*, pages 413-414.

The Polish Resolution has led to a huge controversy in Pakistan where some, mostly Bhutto's opponents, have maintained that it was the best deal under the circumstances to save the honour of the armed forces from an ignominious surrender and so should have been accepted by him; the most vociferous criticism comes from those who have perhaps never read the Resolution fully.

It is however a matter of record that of all the resolutions tabled before the Council on 15th December, the Foreign Office had given its instructions in respect of the Anglo-French Resolution only. Apparently, no notice was even taken of the Polish Resolution nor was it ever considered seriously by the Government of Pakistan. As such, there was hardly any question of Bhutto or, in his absence, Agha Shahi accepting it in defiance of the Government policy.

In view of this persistent controversy, it is important first to examine the Polish Resolution in detail before commenting on the related issues. The operative clauses of the Resolution were:[238]

- Immediate release of Mujibur Rahman (deleted from the revised version).

- Transfer of power to the elected representatives in East Pakistan.

- An interim ceasefire in all areas of Pakistan for a period of 72 hours *after* the beginning of the process of power transfer.

- Regrouping of Pakistani armed forces in East Pakistan to pre-set locations for evacuation from there.

- All West Pakistani civilian personnel and other persons willing to return to West Pakistan, and East Pakistani civilian personnel and other persons in West Pakistan willing to return to East Pakistan to be given an opportunity to do so under the supervision of the United Nations.

- The ceasefire to become permanent *after* the withdrawal of Pakistani troops and the start of their concentration for that purpose during the period of 72 hours.

---

[238] *Ibid.*

- Withdrawal of Indian armed forces from East Pakistan to start *after* the evacuation of nationals from both the wings and the Pakistan armed forces had started.

- The withdrawal of Indian troops to actually start in consultation with the newly- established authority in East Pakistan.

The Polish draft resolution was a fairly deceptive document; innocent looking and innocuous at a cursory glance. However, the conditions prescribed in it for Pakistan to fulfil before a ceasefire came on the ground were the most stringent and specific of all the draft resolutions considered so far by the Council. These conditions would have placed Pakistan forces in considerable jeopardy and entirely at the whims of the Indian Army and the Mukti Bahini. For instance:

- Pakistan had to transfer power in East Pakistan *before* even the interim ceasefire.

- Pakistan had to evacuate all its troops from East Pakistan *before* even the inception of a permanent ceasefire.
- All this while, the Indian forces would have retained full liberty of action in East Pakistan.

The main argument advanced in favour of the Resolution is that the Pakistan troops would have been spared the ignominy and indignity of surrender. However, some very pertinent and significant facts in this respect are usually never taken into account:

- It will be recalled that the Polish Resolution was due to be considered in New York at about 7 PM on 15th December, when it was already the morning of 16th December in Dacca. By 15th December, the Indian forces had already reached the suburbs of Dacca and well poised to walk in the next day. By then, General Niazi's offer of ceasefire had already been made and accepted by General Manekshaw, albeit as a surrender. The Pakistan High Command had also permitted General Niazi to accept the Indian conditions. Thus, Pakistan's acceptance of the Polish Resolution, per se, could hardly have ensured its adoption by the Security Council in time to prevent the Indians from entering Dacca.

- Even if Pakistan had accepted the Polish Resolution, it still may not have, *ipso facto,* evaded the surrender. Even after acceptance by

Pakistan, there would still have been no guarantee of Indian acceptance, who were by then scenting total victory. The Indian delegation would have been very naïve to accept the resolution with alacrity and thus deprive their forces of a historic victory. They could simply have employed the pretext of referring it back to their government for decision and thus gained the requisite time for a *fait accompli*. In fact, Sardar Swaran Singh and Samar Sen would have used every trick in the book to confront the UN with a *fait accompli*.

- Furthermore, the Resolution would still have required Soviet concurrence and they too could certainly have delayed the proceedings for one day at least, on some procedural pretext, to provide the ultimate opportunity to the Indians.

- *One must never neglect the basic dictum of power politics enunciated by the famous French diplomat Talleyrand that what was lost on the ground could not be retrieved on the table.*

According to General Kamal Matinuddin:

"The much talked of Polish Resolution which was circulated on 14 December and which was purported to have been torn up by Bhutto on 15 December could not have had any impact on the results of the conflict. Negotiations for a ceasefire between the victor and the vanquished had already commenced.................. With such a military situation in East Pakistan, no resolution, however supportive it may have been of Pakistan's position, would have achieved anything different to what it turned out to be.......... The Indian delegation in any case could have prolonged the meeting at the Security Council by asking time to consult its government. By the time the reply would have been received, Dacca would have been in their hands."[239]

16th December

The instrument of surrender was signed at the Race Course ground of Dacca precisely ay 4:31 PM on 16th December. It was then early in the morning in New York and at about that time a telex (No. 9648) was being received by the Pakistan Mission from the President of Pakistan. This contained detailed instructions to Bhutto to accept the Anglo-French draft resolution. It went on to blame the US for landing Pakistan in such dire

---

[239] Lt Gen Kamal Matinuddin, *op cit,* page 455.

straits due to their misrepresentations and false promises. Pointedly, there was still not even a mention of the Polish Resolution!

The next meeting of the Security Council (1616th) was held at about noon on 16th December, which the Pakistan delegation did not attend. The Government instructions regarding accepting the Anglo-French resolution could not be carried out as the two sponsoring countries themselves did not wish to pursue their own draft resolution after the news of the surrender. The Indian delegation was however present and read out a statement by the Indian Prime Minister declaring a unilateral ceasefire in West Pakistan as well.

The war was finally over!

Yahya's Mea Culpa

To a Committee comprising some of the senior most civil servants of Pakistan like Ghulam Ishaq Khan and Roedad Khan, President Yahya, in an anguished *mea culpa*, had bared his soul and outlined his basic dilemma:

"There was always the possibility that events in East Pakistan might take the course that they have taken but I had no alternative. People would not have excused me if I had allowed East Pakistan to secede, as the Awami League was determined on doing, without a fight."[240]

---

[240] Hasan Zaheer, *op cit,* page 409.

11

THE GAME OF THRONES

Strike Corps Frozen

The orders for launching the Pakistan's much-awaited counter-offensive by the elite 4 Corps, commanded by Lt General Tikka Khan, were finally given by the Army COS General Hamid at 9 AM on 13th December. The attack was to commence on 16th December but was later delayed by another 24 hours. By that time, it will be recalled, the game in East Pakistan was almost approaching its finale. On 14th December, General Niazi had already offered terms for a ceasefire to General Manekshaw.

As the strike force comprising field formations of Tikka Khan's 4 (Pak) Corps began moving to their forward concentration areas during the night of 14th/15th December, fierce fighting was then in progress in the Shakargarh area of 1 (Pak) Corps. I Corps, the elite Indian strike corps, commanded by Lt General K K Singh (the former DGMO), had launched a determined attack to capture Shakargarh town, putting heavy pressure on the defences of 8 (Pak) Division, commanded by Major General Abdul Ali Malik. General Malik, however, had managed to hold the attack, but at a very heavy cost. All eyes in Pakistan were then riveted on the outcome of the offensive soon to be launched by Pakistan's elite strike corps.

Thus, it fell like a heavy blow when, during the routine briefing at the GHQ Operations Room in the evening of 16th December, General Hamid abruptly said, **"Freeze Tikka."** Till that time, no one then present there had any inkling about the ceasefire/surrender in East Pakistan; as such the orders of the COS were received in pin drop silence, almost in disbelief. Instead of telling them of the surrender at Dacca, General Hamid went on to give two reasons for his orders: first, that the war in Shakargarh area was not going well; and, second, his lack of faith in the capabilities of the PAF to support the offensive adequately.

350

On the insistence of some senior officers present there, a telephone call was immediately made to Lt General Irshad Ahmed Khan, commander 1 Corps. His measured response was that the operation was going according to his plan and that he was quite happy with the situation in his area. Hearing this, Air Marshal Rahim Khan, C-in-C PAF, suggested that if that be so, why not let Tikka go on with his offensive. Nevertheless, General Hamid persisted in his orders and the message was conveyed to General Tikka Khan on phone. On receiving these unexpected orders, Tikka's initial impression was that this was perhaps a fake call and rang back himself to confirm its authenticity. And that was that.[241]

Anxious to avoid the word 'surrender', the mandarins of the Ministry of Information, Radio Pakistan, and the Inter Services Public Relations huddled together and came up with an ingenious formulation. Thus, the press release describing the cataclysmic situation simply read:

"Latest Reports indicate that following an arrangement between the local commanders of India and Pakistan in the Eastern Theatre, fighting has ceased in East Pakistan, and Indian troops have entered Dacca."

President Yahya addressed the nation at 8:30 PM on 16th December and declared his firm resolve to continue with the war in West Pakistan. He went on to say, *"A temporary setback in one theatre of war does not by any means signify the end of the struggle."* The same evening however, apparently unfazed by Yahya's resolve, Indira Gandhi announced a unilateral ceasefire on the Western Front, beginning at 5 PM on 17th December. Thus, by 18th December, it was all over in the west as well.

Reaction in West Pakistan

The country immediately boiled into a great turmoil and for the first time since March 1969, General Yahya's position as the fountainhead of all power had been utterly shaken. After an initial reaction of shocked disbelief, the Nation went into mourning. Similar reaction was discernable throughout the Army too. The rank and file just could not comprehend how and why the ceasefire had been accepted when the bulk of the Army in the Western Theatre was still uncommitted and untested.

The Eastern Garrison had held out for over three weeks against extremely heavy odds in the vain hope that the Army would be able to justify their

[241] Maj Gen Fazal Muqim Khan, *op cit,* page 217.

dictum that the defence of East Pakistan lay in the west. Just the comparison of casualties suffered by the Army in the two wings respectively was sufficient to indicate that 'something was rotten in the state of Denmark.' During this war, the Army in East Pakistan lost 115 officers, 40 JCOs, and 1182 other ranks; while in West Pakistan the corresponding figures were 70 officers, 59 JCOs, and 1482 other ranks.[242] It was apparent that proportionate to the quantum of the two garrisons, the number of casualties in East Pakistan were much higher. (These figures do not include the casualties suffered by the Army from 25th March till the commencement of the war.)

Oblivious to all this, Yahya was still determined to promulgate a new constitution for the country, drafted by a Constitution Commission headed by Justice A R Cornelius, formed by the President a few months ago. Yahya was still harbouring the delusion that he could yet continue to be the President under the new dispensation, with a civilian prime minister. Accordingly, on 14th December the President formed a high-powered Committee comprising M M Ahmed, General Peerzada, Ghulam Ishaq Khan, and Roedad Khan to prepare the draft of a speech to be delivered by him to the nation regarding the new constitution. The final draft of the speech produced by this Committee was then translated into Urdu and both the versions were delivered to the President House in the early hours of 16th December. The Presidential announcement regarding the salient features of the new constitution was originally scheduled for 17th December but was postponed for a day in view of the ominous developments in East Pakistan. However, it was postponed yet again on the intercession of General Gul Hasan Khan, who had rendered the sane and timely advice that this untimely announcement would exacerbate an already sticky situation.

On the night of 18th December, a spontaneous mass reaction, directed against Yahya and his coterie, erupted on the streets of several cities and towns in West Pakistan. The entire populace exploded in a huge, extempore protest everywhere in the country and there were large public gatherings in almost all the cities and towns. A huge crowd had gathered in Rawalpindi and begun to march towards the President House; they were diverted with great difficulty by a heavy contingent of police, personally commanded by the DIG of Rawalpindi, Abbas Mirza. Yahya's personal house in Peshawar was burnt down by a huge crowd there.

Meanwhile, the discontent and reaction in the officer corps had also begun to erupt gradually. Its first tangible manifestation occurred in the elite

[242] Hasan Zaheer, *op cit*, page 419.

formations of Army Reserve North, then under the ad hoc command of Major General Muhammad Bashir Khan. It then comprised: 6 Armoured Division commanded by Major General M I Karim, a loyal Bengali officer; and, 17 Infantry Division commanded by Major General R D Shamim.

At that time, these formations were located around Gujranwala and had not taken any part in the war so far. Whatever the strategic considerations for this inaction, it was inexplicable to their rank and file. Even the common man failed to understand why these formations were never launched despite Pakistan losing a sizeable chunk of land in the nearby Shakargarh area. After the ceasefire, some humiliating anti-Army slogans were raised by the people and at places, the army vehicles were even stoned. At one point, it was under consideration to use the Army to quell these riots but the move was generally resented by the officers, and mercifully never resorted to.

On 18th December, a conference of senior officers of 6 Armoured Division had been called by Major General M I Karim in his HQ, attended by his brigade commanders and his colonel staff Colonel Agha Javed Iqbal. Also, attending on special invitation were Major General Bashir Khan, Commander Army Reserve North, Major General R D Shamim, GOC 17 Division, and Colonel Aleem Afridi, Colonel Staff of Army Reserve North. During this conference, Brig Farrukh Bakht Ali, Commander Artillery 6 Armoured Division (commonly known in the Army as FB Ali), and Brig Iqbal Mehdi Shah, Commander 7 Armoured Brigade, took the stand that the Yahya regime was entirely responsible for the present situation and had thus lost its right to rule over the country. Their main demand was that the Yahya regime must quit and hand over power to the elected representatives of the people. They also demanded that the Army be purged of incompetent and corrupt commanders who were equally responsible for this defeat. In practical terms this demand meant handing over power to Zulfikar Ali Bhutto and his Party. According to Brig F B Ali:

"Even though I was by no means a fan of Mr. Bhutto, I believed that their elected status gave them the right to govern, and obtain the allegiance of the armed forces".[243]

The other participants of the conference generally supported these officers but the views of the three general officers somewhat differed. General Bashir played it safe and so was opposed to taking any formal stand as it would be tantamount to mutiny. General Karim was sympathetic and offered to convey the officers' feelings informally to the GHQ and CMLA Secretariat informally. Later, however, after seeing the strong feelings of his

---

[243] Brig F B Ali, *Email to the author.*

353

senior officers, he consented to take up the issue formally by writing a letter to the GHQ. General Shamim fully committed himself and his Division to the support of the officers of 6 Armoured Division.

Under extreme pressure from his formation commanders, General Karim was forced to send the following top secret message to the GHQ the same day, 18th December:

"From Maj Gen M I Karim, GOC 6 Armoured Division personal for Lt Gen Gul Hassan Khan. All my formation commanders categorically state that their officers and men have lost complete faith in the present government and army leadership. They state that they and their troops will not take up arms against the people to protect the present regime. In case of resumption of hostilities will not fight under present military directive. To preserve integrity and cohesion of country and army absolutely essential immediate change be effected in regime and military leadership. Government must be handed over to leaders acceptable to the people. Events causing acute dissatisfaction among officers and men and situation fast deteriorating." [244]

Brig F B Ali claims that he also took over the effective command of 6 Armoured Division on the next day. According to him:

"Finally, on December 19, I could wait no longer and took over effective command of the Division from General Karim. He tacitly accepted this, and gave me valuable support throughout the succeeding events".

However, General M I Karim has described this event somewhat differently. In his detailed letter on this incident to Gen Gul Hassan dated 2nd February 1972, he states,

"I was in complete control, except for a few minutes on the morning of 19th December when (Brigadier) F B Ali, in his misguided judgment, wanted to spare me the embarrassment (because I was an East Pakistani) of having to send the signal to GHQ." [245]

The same afternoon, 19th December, Colonel Aleem Afridi rang up General Gul Hasan in GHQ and informed him of the situation brewing up in Gujranwala. He conveyed to Gul Hasan that the troops of the two formations were intensely agitated over the loss of East Pakistan and that their demand was that General Gul should personally fly over to Gujranwala and pacify the situation. General Gul Hasan replied that he

[244] Brig A R Siddiqui, *op cit*, Appendix 5.
[245] *Ibid*, Appendix 7.

354

could not absent himself from the GHQ under the present situation and asked Colonel Aleem to come over to the GHQ to discuss the situation. [246]

Colonel Aleem Afridi and Colonel Agha Javed Iqbal arrived in Rawalpindi by an L-19 aircraft and met the CGS in his office at about 4 PM. They had brought with them two letters from Generals Karim and Shamim expressing the outraged feelings of the officers of their respective formations and demanding that Yahya Khan must hand over power to the elected representatives of the people.

In order to ascertain the correct situation, Gul Hasan tried talking to the general officers in Gujranwala but the only one he could contact was General Karim, who confirmed that there was unrest among the troops over the loss of East Pakistan. In desperation, General Gul Hasan called over Air Marshal Rahim Khan to help him handling the situation; both of them then tried their best to pacify the two officers. However, the duo remained adamant and at one stage even threatened to bring a unit to Rawalpindi to remove Yahya and his junta from office. At this point, Air Marshal Rahim and General Gul Hasan felt that the issue was very serious and so must be brought to the notice of the President. Asking the two colonels to wait in the outer office, General Gul and Air Marshal Rahim went over to the COS House and apprised him of the situation. General Hamid advised them to wait for his call for meeting with the President. [247]

Apparently, immediately after this meeting, General Hamid tasked the DG ISI Major General Ghulam Jilani Khan and the DMI Brig Muhammad Iqbal Khan to visit Gujranwala personally to assess the brewing situation. He also apprised General Mitha, the QMG, of this potentially explosive situation and his apprehension that the rebellious troops might march on to Rawalpindi to force their demands. Mitha's advice was to place a company of SSG commandoes at Tarakki Hills, near Jhelum, where the terrain was such that they could even hold a division at bay for an appreciable time. According to Mitha, General Hamid had agreed to this suggestion. General Mitha then talked to General Karim on phone who told him that *'there was bad trouble brewing and he was not allowed to leave the caravan'.*[248]

General Gul Hasan Khan and Air Marshal Rahim Khan eventually met the President in the evening where General Hamid was also present. Gul Hasan narrated all that had happened thus far that afternoon. Yahya tried to talk to

[246] Lt Gen Gul Hasan Khan, *op cit*, page 341.
[247] Ibid; Hasan Zaheer, *op cit*, page 429.
[248] Maj Gen A O Mitha, *op cit*, page 369.

355

General Bashir in Gujranwala but the latter did not want to take the call. After waiting for some time, Yahya went off the line. [249]

The final outcome of this meeting was that a disheartened President agreed to resign and hand over power to the elected representatives. An announcement to that effect was eventually made on Radio Pakistan in the 8 PM news bulletin. After this development, the two officers from Gujranwala were sent back somewhat unceremoniously by General Gul Hasan.

Later the same night, Brig Ghulam Muhammad, Group Commander of SSG, called on the CGS at his house in a somewhat agitated manner and apprised him that he had been ordered by General Mitha to immediately move a company of SSG to Rawalpindi for the protection of the President, the COS, and the GHQ. Since the SSG command was vested in the CGS, Gul Hasan countermanded this order as being unnecessary and uncalled for. In his own heart, Gul Hasan had apprehended that perhaps the real reason for moving this Company to Rawalpindi was related to Bhutto. In his words,

I do not know what role was contemplated for the SSG in Rawalpindi but I can state categorically that the one purpose it was not intended for was to furnish a guard of honour to Bhutto at the airport'.[250]

Meanwhile, Major General Ghulam Jilani Khan, DG ISI, and Brig Muhammad Iqbal, DMI, reached Gujranwala at about 10 PM the same night and headed straight to HQ 6 Armoured Division. There they had a meeting with the three general officers of the recalcitrant formations, Bashir, Karim and Shamim, in the presence of Brig Iqbal Mehdi Shah, and Brig F B Ali. They tried very hard to convince the recalcitrant officers to maintain the unity of the Army, but to no avail. In desperation, they contacted Lt Col Qadir Saeed, CO 9 FF Battalion (17 Division), and asked him if he would agree to surround HQ 6 Armoured Division and arrest the rebellious officers. Colonel Qadir Saeed flatly refused this request and the disappointed visitors had no alternative but to return to Rawalpindi.[251]

On 20th December, President Yahya asked General Hamid to address the GHQ officers in order to assess their feelings as well as assuage their bruised emotions by explaining the rationale behind the acceptance of the

[249] Hasan Zaheer, *op cit*, page 436.
[250] Maj Gen Gul Hasan Khan, *op cit*, page 344.
[251] Hasan Zaheer, *op cit*, page 430.

356

ceasefire. Moreover, the President wanted to accurately gauge the feelings of the officer corps before he actually handed over power to the civilian leadership. Originally, the event was to have been attended by Lt Colonels and above of the GHQ but later it was thrown open to all available officers of the Rawalpindi garrison as well.

The GHQ auditorium was packed to capacity with the officers including four PSOs: Lt General Gul Hasan, Lt General Khawaja Wasiuddin, Major General Khuda Dad, and Major General Abu Bakr Osman Mitha. General Hamid walked in promptly at 12 PM, the appointed time. He stood behind the lectern, surveyed the audience, cleared his throat and began to address the officers. A shakier speech could not have been expected from a man of such a high rank. It was a long and rambling apology for the top planners in the Army and in the administration. His basic message was that *'the country was passing through a grave and most serious crisis, but let us be men enough to face it'*.

The initial reaction was some muffled angry murmurs from the young officers (Lt Colonel and below) seated in the hall and public galleries in the rear. No one seated on the front seats could really make out what was being said but the ugly mood itself was eloquent enough to obviate the need for any words. The ambient atmosphere in the hall was explosive like a volcano ready to erupt. The top brass in the front rows looked isolated and cut off from the junior officers. Initially, the bonds of traditional discipline managed to contain any vocal reaction but soon the dam burst. It was unwittingly triggered by General Hamid himself when he, perhaps out of habit, committed the folly of asking if they had any questions.

A young officer Major Mian Abdus Sami (later Major General), then serving in the Military Operations Directorate, got up and asked why General Tikka's offensive had not been allowed to be launched. General Hamid tried to parry the question by saying that he should ask this from the Military Operations Directorate. Major Sami shouted back, 'I am from that very Directorate'. The angry backbenchers then burst into deafening chants of 'shame', 'shame', mixed with choice expletives. At this point, General Hamid broke down and withdrew from the auditorium and left rather unceremoniously.

The general impression formed by the officers was that much of Hamid's show of grief and shame was simply a fake. His actual mission was to gauge the tempers of the young officers. Had the reaction been found mild and favourable, Yahya would have stayed on even in the new dispensation and, in the worst scenario, been replaced by Hamid. The message from the officer corps, however, was loud and clear.

Fortune Smiles on Bhutto

Meanwhile, Bhutto had since reached Rome, from where he called his close confidante Mustafa Khar and asked whether it was safe for him to return to Pakistan at this time. Khar in turn spoke to Air Marshal Rahim, who relayed his query to the President. The President directed Rahim Khan to send a PIA aircraft to Rome to fetch Bhutto as soon as possible.

In retrospect, an intense power struggle was then in progress in the senior echelons of the Army at this time. Powerful elements were still opposed to allow transfer of power to the elected representatives. There were several lobbies active in the corridors of power. Gul Hasan himself appeared to be in the run for the presidency. Then there was a lobby in favour of inducting Air Marshal Asghar Khan as the president; he himself had conveniently moved to Rawalpindi from his house in Abbottabad and was staying with his close relative Colonel Aleem Afridi, of the Gujranwala fame. The struggle however was mainly decided by the middle cadre of the Army in favour of Bhutto, which under the circumstances was the only viable and realistic course of action; this was also the consensus of the senior civil servants. [252]

Bhutto eventually arrived in Rawalpindi on 20th December. He was received on the airport by General Gul Hasan and Air Marshal Rahim Khan and escorted to the President House, where he was sworn in as the President. One of his first actions was to retire General Yahya, General Hamid and eleven other generals. Lt General Gul Hasan Khan was appointed the C-in-C in his present rank!

But the Game of the Thrones continued to be played!

---

[252] *Ibid,* page 431.

Operational Recommendations Of Major General Khadim Husain Raja to Eastern Command

1. Mil ops to finish before monsoon i.e. 15 May. Grace period of another 15 days. Monsoon break 1 June 1971.

2. Priorities

   a. Seal main routes from Indian Border.
   b. Open main routes of comm—own.
   c. Take main towns.
   d. Visit other towns.

3. Assessment of Tasks

Rajshahi Division (16 Div)

   a. Bn – North of Teasta incl L. Hat   )
   b. Bn – Rangpur   )
   c. Bn – Saidpur   )
      One Bde
   d. Bn – Thakurgaon   )
      Rangpur
(One Army Reg, One R & S Bn and one Armed Regt)

   e. Bn – Rajshahi   )
   f. Bn – Ishtardi   )
   g. Bn – Pabna   ) One Bde Natore
   h. Bde HQ Natore
   i. Arty – Fd Reg

359

j.   Bn – Bogra
k.   Bn – Noagaon   ) Div HQ, One Bde &
     Armed Regt
l.   Bde HQ Bogra
m.   Div HQ Bogra

Total Tps

Div HQ, three Bde HQ, 9 Inf Bns, Armed Regt, Two Fd Regts, one R & S Bn (could economize one inf bn)

Dacca and Khulna Division (14 Div Area)

a.   Khulna – Dacca Civ Divisions.
b.   Problem of open border in Jessore.
Deployment:
a.   Bn – Khulna incl Satkhira
b.   Bn – Jessore
c.   R&S Bn – Jessore
d.   Bde HQ – Jessore
e.   Bn – Khushtia and Mor Bty
f.   Bn – Barisal-Patuakhali
        -   (later to be visited through River route)
g.   Bn – Faridpur
h.   Bde HQ – Faridpur

Total Tps

Two Bde HQ, five bns, R&S, one fd regt and one mor bty.

Dacca

a.   One Bde of three Bns – Dacca City and Cantt
b.   Bde HQ – Joydepur
c.   Bn – Joydepur
d.   Bn – Mymensingh
e.   Fd Regt – Dacca

Total Tps

Div HQ, Two Bde HQ, five bns, and one fd regt.

360

Chittagong Division (9 Div Area)

    a.   Sylhet – One bde HQ, three Bns, More bty.

    b.   Comilla – Div HQ, bde HQ, three bns, One Fd Regt.

    c.   Chittagong – bde HQ, four bns, Mor Bty

Div HQ	Bde HQ	Cav Regt	Inf Bn	R&S	Fd Regt	Mor Bty
1 (Bogra)	3	1	9	1	2	1
1 (Dacca)	4	-	10	1	2	1
1 (Comilla)	3	-	10	-	1	2
3	10	1	29	2	5	4
3	9	1	23	2	4	2
-	1	-	6	-	1	2

Percent shortages

Grand Total

    a.   Could possible economize on one Bn.

    b.   Engr units (RSU, Bly, Navy, Port Bn).

    c.   Army Avn (Helicopters, a few fixed wing).

    d.   PAF (Tpt ac).

4. Development of Ops

Rajshahi Division

a. 23 Bde – Capture Dinajpur and develop ops to the North- Thakargaon- Packhararth
b. 57 Bde – Complete present op and develop op to Bogra along road
c. New Bde – To be built up in Rangpur- Ishurdi and op to Bogra and seal Hilly

Jessore

d. Give them one more Bn
e. Capture area Chuadanga – Meherpur- Kushtia and link up with 57 Bde at Paksey
f. Later one bn to visit Barisal-Patua by river route
g. Later one bn to visit Faridpur by road
h. Addl coy to Khulna. Take Satkhira and seal border as pri

Comilla Sec

i. One more bn to Sylhet and drive South on B baria
j. Comilla grn North to B baria
k. Comilla grn South to Feni and Beyond
l. Chittagong grn at present seal Karnafuli and drive North to Feni to link up with c above

Dacca

m. Bhairab
n. Mymensingh- Jamalpur- Netra Kona- Kishore Ganj

DEPLOYMENT OF PAKISTAN TROOPS
AS IN NOVEMBER 1971

Southwestern Sector (Jessore-Khulna)

This Sector was held by 9 Division, commanded by Major General Muhammad Husain Ansari with its Divisional Headquarters located at Jessore, with following ORBAT:

1. 57 Brigade   Brig Manzoor Ahmed   Jhenida

a. 18 Punjab   Lt Col Matloob Husain
b. 29 Baluch   Lt Col Atta Ullah
c. Company 21 Punjab (R & S)
d. Company CAF
e. 50 Punjab   Lt Col Aijaz Ahmed   (Reached on 29 Nov)

2. 107 Brigade   Brig Muhammad Hayat   Jessore

a. 15 FF   Lt Col Yusaf Zai
b. 22 FF   Lt Col Shams uz Zaman
c. 38 FF   Lt Col Saeed Ullah
d. Company 21 Punjab (R & S)
e. Industrial Security Force (ISF)   Lt Col Khattak
f. Mujahid Battalion   Lt Col Ihsan ul Haq

3. 314 (A) Brigade Col Fazal Hameed   Khulna

a. Sector HQ EPCAF   Lt Col M H Bhatti -
b. Mujahid Battalion   Lt Col Sher Zaman

363

5. Divisional Reserve

a. 6 Punjab   Lt Col Sharif Malik
b. 21 Punjab R & S   Lt Col Imtiaz Waraich   (Less two companies)
c. Indep Armoured Squadron   Maj Maqsood Ahmed
d. Section SSG   Capt Asif

5. Naval Base Khulna   Commander Gul Zarin   4 x Gun Boats

Northwestern Sector - Bogra

This Sector was held by 16 Division, commanded by Major General Nazar Husain Shah with its HQ located at Natore. Its formations and units were as under:

1. 23 Brigade   Brig Akhtar Ansari   Saidpur

a.   8 Punjab   Lt Col Saleem Zia
b.   25 Punjab   Lt Col Muhammad Husain Malik
c.   48 Punjab
d.   26 FF   Lt Col Hakeem Arshad Qureshi
e.   Squadron 29 Cav
f.   48 Field Regiment

2. 34 Brigade   Brig Mir Abdul Naeem   Rangpur

a.   32 Punjab   Lt Col Faheem Haider Rizvi
b.   32 Baluch   Lt Col Raja Sultan Mahmud
c.   12 Punjab
d.   Squadron 29 Cav
e.   117 Mortar Battery

3. 205 Brigade   Brig Tajammul Husain Malik   Bogra

a.   8 Baluch
b.   4 FF   Lt Col Akhlaq Ahmed Abbasi
c.   13 FF   Lt Col Amir Nawaz
d.   Squadron 29 Cav
e. 80 Field Regt

Northeastern Sector (Sylhet- Brahmanbaria)

This Sector was held by 14 Division, commanded by Major General Qazi Abdul Majid, with its headquarters located at Bahrab Bazar. It had the following troops under its command:

4. 27 Brigade   Brigadier Saad Ullah Khan   Brahmanbaria

    a.   12 FF   Lt Col Khilji
    b.   33 Baluch   Lt Col Aftab Qureshi
    c.   Platoon R & S ex 34 Punjab.
    d.   4 x Chaffe and PT 76 Tanks
    e.

5. 202 (A) Brigade   Brigadier Saleemullah   Sylhet

    a.   31 Punjab   Lt Col Abdul Razzaq
    b.   91 Mujahid Battalion
    c.   2 x companies EPCAF
    d.   ½ Wing Frontier Corps
    e.   500 Razakars

6. 313 Brigade   Brigadier Iftikhar Rana   Maulvi Bazar

    a.   22 Baluch   Lt Col Yasin
    b.   30 FF   Lt Col Amir Mukhtar
    c.   Wing Frontier Corps
    d.   210 Mortar Battery

Southeastern Sector (Comilla-Feni)

This Sector was held by 39 (A) Division, a formation hastily raised on 18th October. It was commanded by Maj Gen M Rahim Khan, with its headquarters located at Chandpur, and had the following troops under its command:

1. 117 Brigade   Brig M H Atif   Comilla

    30 Punjab
    25 FF
    23 Punjab

b. 53 Brigade   Brig Aslam Niazi   Feni

    15 Baluch

39 Baluch   Lt Col Naeem
Company 21 AK (This unit landed at Dacca in the middle of November. Its battalion headquarters was detached and tasked to act as a headquarters for 91 (A) Brigade at Karerhat. Two companies were attached with 117 Brigade and one company placed at Chandpur to act as Divisional Reserve. Only one company became available for 53 Brigade.)

3. **91 (A) Brigade   Brig Taskeen-ud-Din   Karerhat**

2 x companies 24 FF
Wing EPCAF
Rangers Battalion
Mujahid Battalion
171 Mortar Battery less troop.

4. **97 (A) Brigade   Brig Atta Malik   Chittagong**

48 Baluch
24 FF less two companies.
2 Commando Battalion less company
Wing EPCAF
Marine Battalion
Troop ex 171 Mortar Battery

Central Sector (Dacca)

This Sector was entrusted to the newly raised 36 (A) Division, commanded by Maj Gen Muhammad Jamshed who was entrusted this task in addition to his primary job as DG EPCAF. Its headquarters was located at Dacca and had the following troops under its command:

1. **93 (A) Brigade   Brig Abdul Qadir   Mymensingh**
    a.   33 Punjab
    b.   31 Baluch   Lt Col Sultan

2. **314 (A) Brigade.**

A loose formation comprising EPCAF wings only, nominally commanded by Brig Bashir Ahmed, Deputy DG, EPCAF.

Deployment- EPCAF

1. HQ EPCAF	DACCA
2. DACCA SECTOR	DACCA
13 Wing	Dacca
16 Wing	Dacca
3. JESSORE SECTOR	JESSORE
4 Wing	Chuadanga
5 Wing	Khulna-Barisal
15 Wing	Chuagacha
4. RAJSHAHI SECTOR	RAJSHAHI
6 Wing	Nawabganj
7 Wing	Naogaon-Patnitola
5. RANGPUR SECTOR	RANGPUR
8 Wing	Dinajpur
9 Wing	Thakurgaon-Pachagarh
10 Wing	Rangpur-Lalmunirhat
6. COMILLA SECTOR	COMILLA
1 Wing	Comilla
3 Wing	Brahmanbaria
12 Wing	Comilla
7. CHITTAGONG SECTOR	CHITTAGONG
2 Wing	Feni
11 Wing	Chittagong-Cox's Bazar
14 Wing	Chittagong- Chittagong Hill Tracts

Annexure C

TROOPS PRESENT IN DACCA AT THE TIME OF SURRENDER

1. Headquarters

    a HQ Eastern Command
    b Rear HQ 14 Division
    c HQ EPCAF (re-designated as HQ 36 (A) Division)
    d HQ East Pakistan Logistics Area
    e Station HQ Dacca
    f HQ Flag Officer Commanding East Pakistan Navy
    g HQ Air Officer Commanding East Pakistan Air Force
    h West Pakistan Police HQ
    i HQ DG Razakars

2. Regular and Para-Military Troops

    a Armoured Corps (Ad hoc Tank Troop) 50
    b Artillery (6 LAA Regiment, HQ Artillery, reinforcements) 700
    c Engineers (Rear Parties of units, HQ Engineers) 500
    d Signals (three battalions, HQ Signals, various static units) 2000
    e Infantry (Remnants of 93 (A) Brigade, who reached Dacca on 13th Dec, and reinforcements)   4500
f Services (Ordnance and Supply Depots and Workshops)   1000
g Navy   500
h PAF   500
I EPCAF (formerly EPR)   4000
J Mujahids   1500

K	West Pakistan Police	2500
L	Industrial Security Force	1500
TOTAL		26250

Note: The above figures exclude sick and wounded as well as hospital staff.

(BASED ON FIGURES QUOTED BY MAJ GEN FAZAL MUQIM KHAN IN HIS BOOK
"PAKISTAN'S CRISIS IN LEADERSHIP", Appendix III)